Reelpolitik II

Communication, Media, and Politics
Series Editor: Robert E. Denton, Jr., Virginia Tech

This series features a broad range of work dealing with the role and function of communication in the realm of politics, broadly defined. Including general academic books, monographs, and texts for use in graduate and advanced undergraduate courses, the series will encompass humanistic, critical, historical, and empirical studies in political communication in the United States. Primary subject areas include campaigns and elections, media, and political institutions. *Communication, Media, and Politics* books will be of interest to students, teachers, and scholars of political communication from the disciplines of communication, rhetorical studies, political science, journalism, and political sociology.

Titles in the Series
The Millennium Election: Communication in the 2000 Campaign, edited by Lynda Lee Kaid, John C. Tedesco, Dianne G. Bystrom, and Mitchell McKinney

Strategic Political Communication: Rethinking Social Influence, Persuasion, and Propaganda, by Karen S. Johnson-Cartee and Gary A. Copeland

Campaign 2000: A Functional Analysis of Presidential Campaign Discourse, by William L. Benoit, John P. McHale, Glenn J. Hansen, P. M. Pier, and John P. McGuire

Inventing a Voice: The Rhetoric of First Ladies of the Twentieth Century, edited by Molly Meijer Wertheimer

Communicating for Change, John P. McHale

Political Campaign Communication: Principles and Practices, Fifth Edition, by Judith S. Trent and Robert V. Friedenberg

The Rhetoric of Redemption, by David A. Bobbitt

Reelpolitik II: Political Ideologies in '50s and '60s Films, by Beverly Merrill Kelley

Forthcoming
New Frontiers in International Communication Theory, edited by Mehdi Semati

Entertaining Politics: New Political Television and Civic Culture, by Jeffrey P. Jones

Women's Political Discourse, by Molly A. Mayhead and Brenda DeVore Marshall

The 2004 Presidential Campaign: A Communication Perspective, edited by Robert E. Denton, Jr.

Politeness and Political Debate, by Edward A. Hinck, Shelly S. Hinck, and William O. Dailey

Media and the Staging of American Politics, by Gary C. Woodward

Reelpolitik II

Political Ideologies in '50s and '60s Films

Beverly Merrill Kelley

ROWMAN & LITTLEFIELD PUBLISHERS, INC.
Lanham • Boulder • New York • Toronto • Oxford

ROWMAN & LITTLEFIELD PUBLISHERS, INC.

Published in the United States of America
by Rowman & Littlefield Publishers, Inc.
A wholly owned subsidiary of The Rowman & Littlefield Publishing Group, Inc.
4501 Forbes Boulevard, Suite 200, Lanham, MD 20706
www.rowmanlittlefield.com

P.O. Box 317, Oxford OX2 9RU, UK

British Library Cataloguing in Publication Information Available

Library of Congress Cataloging-in-Publication Data

Kelley, Beverly Merrill.
  Reelpolitik II : political ideologies in '50s and '60s films / Beverly
Merrill Kelley.
       p. cm — (Communication, media, and politics)
Sequel to: Reelpolitik : political ideologies in '30s and '40s films.
Includes filmography.
Includes bibliographical references and index.
  ISBN 0-7425-3040-X (alk. paper) — ISBN 0-7425-3041-8 (pbk. : alk.
paper)
  1. Motion pictures—Political aspects—United States. I. Title. II.
Series.
  PN1995.9.P6K43 2004
  791.43'658'0973—dc22

                                                    2003026860

Printed in the United States of America

∞™ The paper used in this publication meets the minimum requirements of
American National Standard for Information Sciences—Permanence of Paper
for Printed Library Materials, ANSI/NISO Z39.48-1992.

To Jonathan Sharkey—
a demanding critic, a much prayed-for life partner, a never-boring
buddy, and without a doubt, my favorite husband.

Contents

1   Introduction: A Tale of Two Cities, Parameters,
    the Language of Politics   1

2   Populism in *The Last Hurrah*   9

3   Elitism in *Advise and Consent*   41

4   Fascism in *A Face in the Crowd*   79

5   Antifascism in *Seven Days in May*   111

6   Interventionism in *The Green Berets*   143

7   Isolationism in *The Steel Helmet*   177

8   Cold War Hawkism in *The Manchurian Candidate*   205

9   Cold War Dovism in *Dr. Strangelove, or: How I Learned to
    Stop Worrying and Love the Bomb*   241

10 Conclusion: Myth, Megaphone, Metaphor, Mirror,
    Microscope, and Magic Carpet   283

Ideological Filmography   299

Selected Bibliography   303

Index   311

About the Author   331

Hollywood goes to Washington, D.C., in Advise and Consent. *Courtesy of the Academy of Motion Picture Arts and Sciences.*

1

☆

Introduction: A Tale of Two Cities, Parameters, the Language of Politics

A TALE OF TWO CITIES

Washington, D.C., and Hollywood, California, are company towns in which the show is business and the business is show. Each seems to have sprouted up via a critical mass of power and performers. Both got their start, interestingly enough, as quiet backwater burgs.

Hardly a shining city on a hill, our nation's capital was built on reclaimed swampland. Part-time politicos rumbled down its muddy cow paths from all across this fruited plain. A cadre of Jewish immigrants established the film capital, ironically, on the same site as a failed Christian utopia founded by Horace Henderson Wilcox. Corn-fed Midwestern starlets-in-waiting tooled down its dusty roads to flicker factories where the American Dream was churned out reel after reel.

As Hollywood's power grew, so did its political involvement. The too-close-for-comfort ties between Hollywood and Washington, D.C., are probably rooted in the kindred-spirit ideological and financial relationship between Herbert Hoover and Louis B. Mayer. William J. Clinton (or George W. Bush, for that matter) has nothing on our thirty-first president. It was no coincidence that Mayer, the second M in MGM, was Hoover's first overnight White House guest.

Republicans in both cities were looking forward to smashing smartly through seas of endless prosperity. Then came the Great Depression and, with it, a change of command at the White House. The only prospering Republicans were toiling away in Tinseltown, serving up glitzy and glamorous escapism for two bits, while a determined Democrat held a bulldog grip on the Oval Office for the next dozen years.

The fact that studio heads were not exactly enchanted with FDR is an understatement. Studio artists (writers, directors, and actors), however, carried on a torrid love affair with the liberal, whose creativity and daring matched their own. Not only did FDR find a receptive crowd, politically, among film folk, but he also instinctively understood the potential power of the motion picture. Among his papers, he preserved four boxes of correspondence dealing with both the production and viewing of film in America.[1]

Left-leaning Hollywood woke up to ideological politics in 1934, when Upton Sinclair ran for governor of California. As part of his EPIC (End Poverty in California) crusade, Sinclair announced his intent to tax the movie industry. That campaign promise propelled the moguls to mobilize. They hired the first political consultants, Clem Whitaker and wife Leona Baxter, to launch a nasty smear campaign against Sinclair. Conservative executives produced phony newsreels in support of the Republican incumbent, Frank Merriam, and collected $500,000 in "voluntary" contributions from studio employees. Repercussions from these acts reverberated for twenty-five years: Democratic Party rolls swelled, unionization efforts went into warp drive, and the portal to disgruntled liberal thinkers was supposedly breached by Communists targeting the glamour capital of the world.

Today, both industries employ people doing basically the same jobs—the title may differ but the job description is the same. It's all about image and spin.

Hollywood, even those without reserved parking spaces, really liked Ike. "He appealed to the showmen because of the dramatics of the war itself," claimed Herbert Brownell, Dwight D. Eisenhower's key adviser.[2] In addition, Eisenhower became the first presidential candidate to be animated by Disney. Madison Avenue maven Rosser Reeves produced a series of thirty-second seductions to sell the World War II hero during prime time. The general was said to have cheerlessly moaned, "that an old soldier should come to this!"

After 1972's *The Candidate,* the film that supposedly inspired Dan Quayle to enter politics, commentator Howard K. Smith lamented that politicos were presently being peddled like underarm deodorant, a practice that he claimed cheapened the candidate and voter alike. But politics has never come cheap. Hollywood became the first stop on the money train for national candidates of either political stripe. Paul Newman beat the drum and the bushes for presidential wannabe Senator Eugene McCarthy. Warren Beatty sang out to the rock and roll community to fund Senator George McGovern's bid for the White House. "Chairman of the Board" Frank Sinatra backed the very first "Comeback Kid," Richard Nixon—Sinatra switched parties when he had a falling out with John F. Kennedy over JFK's mingling with the mob.

Despite the fact that most of Hollywood viewed Jimmy Carter with unspecified suspicion, Warren Beatty arranged for a fund-raising gala at which Carroll O'Connor pinned Carter point-blank, asking just exactly what he was going to do for the assembled. An unabashed Carter shot back "absolutely nothing" and won over the room. It was a moment that would have made the title character in 1998's *Bulworth* (written, directed, and starred in by Warren Beatty) proud.

Bill Clinton was not only the "Man from Hope," he was, with or without his sax, the consummate player to the crowd. His smartest move financially, however, was giving plenty of face time to the Democratic machine in Hollywood.[3] Although John F. Kennedy may have been closer to the muscle in moviemaking (perhaps in an even more sinister way than Clinton), JFK wisely opted to play his Tinseltown connection cards extremely close to the vest. Still, who can forget Marilyn Monroe's seductive serenade to the birthday boy?

As both actor and officeholder, Ronald Reagan embodied the schizophrenia of the squabbling siblings who are Washington and Hollywood. Left-leaning Tinseltown ditched the Hollywood insider—not just because he was a Republican, but also because they suspected him of being both traitor and trickster. Ironically, the nation's masters of illusion had decided that the fortieth president did not reside in reality.

Both Babylonian offspring, Washington and Hollywood, have always been mutually suspicious. Each makes an especially easy target and each takes turns accusing the other of threatening the end of civilization as currently known. However, in striving for coexistence, the cities seem to have worked out a modern-day codependency, with Hollywood passively taking the heat for destroying family values, while Washington allows the film capital to aggressively portray politicos as reprobate rogues and praetorian philanderers.

The truth of the matter is both politicians and purveyors of popular culture just want to be loved. Unfortunately, in this tale of two cities, the American public is left with the broken heart.

PARAMETERS, PARAMETERS, PARAMETERS

The precursor to this book (*Reelpolitik: Political Ideologies in '30s and '40s Films*) had three things going for it: (1) the ideologies were organized into opposing pairs, affording a built-in impetus for discussion, (2) '30s and '40s American culture, book-ended by two world wars and punctuated by the Great Depression, proved particularly engrossing to folks "who don't know much about history," and (3) early films, at least those directed by big names, currently enjoy a newfound popularity—witness their wide availability on videotape as well as the popularity of cable channels such as American Movie Classics, the Fox Movie Channel, and Turner Classic Movies. Even the History Channel, ESPN, and the Speech Channel show old movies. It was not much of a faith leap to predict that a second volume, dealing with the world-shaking events of the '50s and '60s such as McCarthyism, Korea, civil rights, Vietnam, TV, assassination, and the Cold War, might find a spellbound audience.

Student reaction to the compulsory viewing of color-challenged (black-and-white) movies as a requirement for a course in film and politics could only be characterized, in the most polite language available, as resistance. Once these undergraduates realized, however, that these films could be an engaging documentation of social, political, and economic history, the fledgling film scholars were able, albeit reluctantly, to open their hearts and their minds to the experience.

Since many of the political movies shot during the '30s and '40s dealt with populism, fascism, communism, and interventionism, the first book compared and contrasted these ideologies with their opposites, namely, elitism, antifascism, anticommunism, and isolationism. The plan for *Reelpolitik II* was to trace these same pairings, if possible, through the '50s and '60s. Just as the House Un-American Activities Committee was able to unearth only Russia-as-ally (as opposed to pro-Communist) films, a review of '50s and '60s movies yielded only Cold War flicks (which neatly divided themselves into hawk and dove categories). Likewise, although there were no films as pro-fascist as *Gabriel over the White House* during the '50s and '60s, *A Face in the Crowd* proved to be a psychological study of a fascist personality, a phenomenon certainly egregiously evident during the McCarthy era.

In the first book, Frank Capra's *Mr. Smith Goes to Washington* was an obvious choice to illustrate the ideology of populism. John Ford's *The Last Hurrah* (1958) likewise exemplifies the fictional conflict between populist Frank Skeffington and patricians led by newspaper editor Amos Force. Skeffington is, for all intents and purposes, James Michael Curley, the head of Boston's Irish-dominated political machine. His loss to a television-savvy candidate anticipates John F. Kennedy's stunning upset over the more experienced Richard Nixon.

Most Great Depression films gave us a "rear-window" view of the rich and famous while remaining somewhat critical of the economically privileged. *The Magnificent Ambersons,* however, treated an upper-crust family facing the shift from agricultural to industrial society with considerable compassion. In the '50s and '60s, however, money and privilege all but defined the political elite in Otto Preminger's *Advise and Consent* (1962). Additionally, Preminger blasted the blacklist just prior to making this film and his point of view seems to resonate in this drama about the elitist American Senate.

Since the fascists had been defeated in World War II, moviegoers weren't likely to shell out money to see a film glorifying any possible Hitler or Mussolini successors. However, Elia Kazan's *A Face in the Crowd* points out just how easily a corny-yet-charismatic fellow can pick up a fanatic following when assisted by television. Lonesome Rhodes further trades on his own popularity to put a fascist into the Oval Office.

While *Citizen Kane* ably illustrated the dark side of fascism for the first book, John Frankenheimer's *Seven Days in May* (1964) provides a prism (labeled "military–industrial complex" by Eisenhower) with which to view fascism in the '50s and '60s in the second book. Scripted by television writer Rod Serling from the successful novel by Fletcher Knebel and Charles W. Bailey, the film chillingly lays out a highly plausible scheme in which the Joint Chiefs plot to overthrow the government. The hawkish General Scott, enraged by the president's plan to end the Cold War (via nuclear disarmament) is the force behind the totalitarian plot. Fortunately, Colonel Martin "Jiggs" Casey, the general's right-hand man, alerts the Oval Office and thwarts the power play by his superior.

In the first book, internationalism (which translated into interventionism after Pearl Harbor) was examined in Michael Curtiz's *Casablanca*. Post–World War II America, while in no mood for another war, was almost immediately embroiled in the Korean conflict (in the '50s), followed by Vietnam (in the '60s). Infuriated by anti-Vietnam protests, John Wayne, in *The Green Berets*, attempted to acknowledge and affirm our troops who were fighting and dying. The film critic Eric Bentley, who labeled the Duke "the most dangerous man in America," contends it was really Wayne who got us into Vietnam. While that may be hyperbole worthy of P. T. Barnum, the movie remains a gung ho piece of propaganda that promotes a pro-interventionist perspective.

After World War I, the United States swung back to isolationism, in no small part because of *All Quiet on the Western Front*, analyzed in the first *Reelpolitik*. After World War II, however, when the United States began to figure prominently as a global player, various factors shattered the delusion that the nation could remain aloof from the sort of foreign entanglements George Washington warned against in his "Farewell Address." Released only six months after the start of the Korean War, *Steel Helmet* was able to mirror the doubts held by a war-weary public, unsure why Americans were fighting in Korea in the first place. The problem with interventionism, at least according to writer–director–producer Sam Fuller, is summarized in the last line of his 1951 film: "There is no end to this story."

Fingering a movie that actually promoted communism in the '50s and '60s proved just as impossible as it did during the '30s and '40s. Although singled out by HUAC, *Mission to Moscow* and *Song of Russia* (vigorously promoted by FDR to celebrate America's spanking-new alliance with the

USSR), when all the evidence was in, were never proven to advance communism. The largely unsuccessful *Our Daily Bread,* a film detailing life on an American agricultural collective during the depths of the depression, was the closest this author could come to a procommunist '30s and '40s film. *Dr. Strangelove,* or: *How I Learned to Stop Worrying and Love the Bomb* turned out to be one of the few '50s and '60s flicks marginally sympathetic to folks living on the wrong side of the Iron Curtain. Stanley Kubrick, Terry Southern, and Peter George illustrated the classic Cold War dove position, namely, no-arms-race-worth-an-accidental-thermonuclear-holocaust, by satirically skewering well-known hawks such as Curtis LeMay, Wernher Von Braun, and Nikita Khrushchev.

Fervent American anti-Communists fought the good fight for more than seventy years before the Berlin Wall came down. In the previous book, King Vidor's *The Fountainhead* provided characters that cinematically illustrated various positions on the anti-Communist continuum. *The Manchurian Candidate* played to America's Cold War paranoia by offering up North Koreans surreptitiously brainwashing an American prisoner of war and programming him to become a political assassin. John Frankenheimer's thriller came out at precisely the time that President John F. Kennedy, bolstered by the Russian response to the Cuban Missile Crisis, was speeding up American defense expenditures as well as directing more military aid to South Vietnam. When JFK was assassinated, Frank Sinatra withheld distribution of the film for nearly a quarter of a century.

FILM SPEAKS THE LANGUAGE OF POLITICS

"Film is one of the products, one of the languages, through which the world communicates itself to itself," contends critic Stuart Samuels.[4] Political films still go unrecognized as a genre, at least as delineated by the majority of critics. The sticking point seems to be that, although the subject matter might be political ideas, movie genres ranging from psychological study to satire are employed to deliver the message—despite Sam Goldwin's admonition against same. While each of the films selected for this work was either threatened or boycotted by groups opposed to the political ideology exemplified, no studio could or should claim (as Hollywood is wont to do) that "it's only a movie."

The waters of political film, in the broadest sense, are too muddy to separate into distinguishable streams. To avoid being sucked into the endless quagmire that results when one links "political" as a descriptive adjective to cinema, the focus of this book became "political ideology," which is defined here as "integrated assertions, theories, and aims that constitute a governmental policy." If one were to include films that promote the myriad of social issues parading as political, 90 percent of films produced during the '50s and '60s would qualify—that's where the author's parameters had to come in.

Additionally, it was important to select critically successful projects in order to appeal to sophisticated twenty-first-century motion picture viewers. While the eight films analyzed in this volume, as well as those discussed in the previous book, were evaluated for factors such as illustration of ideology, prestige of the director, historical accuracy, and production values, the most important consideration was whether or not the film worked as an engrossing story.

Even if a movie deals only peripherally with politics, it socializes the moviegoer to political ideas, values, and behavior. In 1964, Marshall McLuhan, in *Understanding Media*, pointed out that the medium is the message. While his theories may have fallen out of favor today, his claim evidences film's persuasive superiority to other media. The movie industry has plenty of time (the average film runs 120 minutes) to package novel-length political messages into larger-than-life metaphor, a sure-fire way to bypass reason and travel directly to emotions, while television restricts itself to narrating thirty- or sixty-minute episodes. Further, TV, financed primarily by advertising, requires huge homogeneous audiences. Multiplexes, by contrast, enable the moviegoer (who might find himself alone in the dark) the opportunity to self-select that which other media might rule out as a "narrow interest" offering.

Further, the use of stars allows the movie to "borrow" the charisma of the actor/actress and augment the persuasiveness of the communication. Film legends score far higher on the credibility meter than do other media celebrities. While many of the stars in these eight political films may prove largely unfamiliar to students, that is not to say that the considerable talents of John Wayne, Henry Fonda, Andy Griffith, Frank Sinatra, Burt Lancaster, Kirk Douglas, Peter Sellers, and Spencer Tracy would fail to impress.

The major value of film study is the provision of an unconventional venue for analysis. Summarily dismissed by highbrow culture as well as the academy until the '60s, cinematic studies now earn a modicum of respect, yet the potential for academic analysis in general, and political investigation in particular, has remained underutilized. Yet, it is precisely because movies indirectly reflect reality that their employment as a primary source for studying American politics has become so valuable.

In his foreword to the first volume, Steve Allen wrote, "throw away your texts strictly proposing ideological isms, we sometimes are tempted to say. American political ideologies appear to have flourished in darkened theaters. . . . As history cycles Santayana-like toward the millennium, we might profitably look back to see forward. Education, after all, can be entertaining."[5]

As usual, the thoughtful man who gave us the award-winning PBS series *Meeting of Minds* got it right.

NOTES

1. Franklin Delano Roosevelt Papers, Official File 73, Franklin Delano Roosevelt Presidential Library, Hyde Park, New York.

2. Quoted in Ronald Brownstein, *The Power and the Glitter: The Hollywood–Washington Connection* (New York: Vintage, 1990), 122.

3. Ian Scott, *American Politics in Hollywood Film* (Chicago: Fitzroy Dearborn, 2000), 154.

4. Quoted in Steven Mintz and Randy Roberts, *Hollywood's America: United States History through Its Films* (St. James, N.Y.: Brandywine, 1993), 221.

5. Beverly Merrill Kelley, *Reelpolitik: Political Ideologies in '30s and '40s Films* (Westport, Conn.: Praeger, 1998), xvii.

2

☆

Populism in *The Last Hurrah*

The divide between elitism and populism can be large or largely inconsequential. During the '50s, peace seemed to prevail. The decade of the '60s, however, with its horrifying parade of assassinations, race riots, and campus unrest, was a time of teeth-rattling upheaval and dispiriting division. Not since the depression had "the great unwashed" bumped up against the white-knuckle grip of the powers that be with so much vigor and venom. From the constant strife over the meaning of equality to the values crisis arising out of the protracted war in Southeast Asia, the schism between populism and elitism became philosophically deeper, demographically wider, and more enduring than ever before.

HISTORY OF POPULISM

Populism has always been with us to one degree or another and has been a recurring political impetus from the days of the American Revolution. Thomas Jefferson wrote Henry Lee on August 10, 1824, "Men are naturally divided into two parties: (1) those who fear and distrust the people . . . [and] (2) those who identify themselves with the people, have confidence in them, cherish and consider them as the most honest and safe."[1]

Colonial America feared the unrestrained power of all institutions, especially the church, the crown, and the corporation. Take a gander at the Preamble to the Constitution—populism is the "We" in "We, the people." If you believe, as humorist and poet E. B. White does, that "democracy is the recurrent suspicion that more than half of the people are right, more than half of the time," you may well be a populist.[2] The basic idea behind

Spencer Tracy tots up the vote in The Last Hurrah. © *1958, renewed 1986 Columbia Pictures Industries, Inc. Courtesy of Columbia Pictures and the Academy of Motion Picture Arts and Sciences.*

this ideology is that the common people, the just plain folks, have an essential wisdom that not only guides them but also presses them to resist the control imposed by the powerful.

If you were to divide the political world into populists and elitists, populists could best be described, on balance, as trusting popular wisdom over elite expertise. Populism further stresses the role of government in defending the poor and the powerless and, if not rooted in, is certainly inspired by the values of Thomas Jefferson, Andrew Jackson, and Abraham Lincoln.

Populism emphasizes a hierarchical view of the world. Of course, pecking order has always been more obvious to those at the bottom than the top, yet America during the '50s and '60s was much more a "land of opportunity" than it had ever been. Hard work could take anyone (including, as in *The Last Hurrah,* the offspring of an Irish-Catholic immigrant) to the top in business, the church, or politics, despite the absence of a pedigree.

Populism, at least the formal protest movement emerging during the 1890s, seems to be ambiguous. Perhaps this is why biographers of populist film directors such as Frank Capra, King Vidor, and John Ford had such a tough time shoehorning the "convoluted" politics of their subjects into the right (or left) ideological box.

In his revisionist biography, *Frank Capra: The Catastrophe of Success,* Joseph McBride asserts that Capra espoused communism, fascism,

Marxism, populism, conservatism, McCarthyism, New Dealism, jingoism, socialism, and capitalism at various points in his film career.[3] Attributing this tangle of ideologies to a clash between Capra's rigid conservatism and his liberal screenwriters, as McBride does, just isn't credible. Capra, just as a majority of Americans, may have momentarily entertained all sorts of notions after the psychic upheaval of the depression, but both he and they generally returned to a "land of the free" consciousness that Jefferson Smith attempts to articulate in *Mr. Smith Goes to Washington.*

Raymond Durgnat and Scott Simmon, who scrutinized Vidor's life nuance by nuance, found the democratic socialism of *Our Daily Bread* juxtaposed against the libertarian dogma in *The Fountainhead* more than a little jarring.[4] They couldn't understand how both the far right and the far left could claim Vidor for their own.

In an excerpt[5] from his forthcoming Ford biography, McBride wonders how the same guy who led the Hollywood unionization movement in the 1930s and directed *The Grapes of Wrath* in 1940 could end his days supporting Barry Goldwater and Richard M. Nixon. He attributes this seeming paradox to the Irish tradition of secrecy toward one's "inner life." Nonsense.

In his 1981 biography of Ford, Lindsay Anderson chose to minimize Ford's socialist claims, offering up the lame lament that the House Un-American Activities Committee and blacklisting "hardly touched Ford directly,"[6] while trying to pile up evidence of Ford's essential conservatism, namely, his flag-waving sense of patriotism, his choice of right-winger friends (John Wayne and Ward Bond), and his disproportionate pride in his record of military service. In the 1995 *John Ford: Hollywood's Old Master,* Ronald Davis doesn't even bother to reconcile Ford's disparate voting record over the years; he simply asserts Ford "held no consistent political philosophy."[7]

All three are wrong. The explanation is quite simple. Ford, like Capra and Vidor, was a populist. While economic populism leans to the left (viewing wealth and power as unequally distributed), cultural populism positions itself decidedly in the opposite direction, with its core support coming from the religious right.

Populists identify with conservatives because they crave order and tradition. To them, the hierarchical power structure not only is the most logical way to organize the world, but it also reflects the design of the Creator and for the past ten millennia has proven the most efficient means of governing. It should come as no surprise that religious conservatives gravitate toward populism—name an organized religion that hasn't embraced some version of the military model.

Populists also identify with liberals because they see a need for reform. In what is touted as "the land of opportunity," they chafe at the burden of serving as the understructure for those residing on Easy Street. They are willing to start at the bottom, but they also want to be assured of the chance to end up at the top.[8]

Populist politicians have a devil of a time bringing together such seemingly irreconcilable extremes. It might be helpful to revisit the radical definition of leadership offered by Jesus. He proposed that his apostles flip the traditional pyramid on its head, taking the role of servant while elevating the rank and file to the pinnacle position. Franklin D. Roosevelt, in a speech given in Hollywood (of all places) on February 27, 1941, reiterated this advice: "In our democracy, officers of the government are the servants, and never the masters of the people."[9]

Populists have had to dig themselves out of dug-in hierarchical ways of thinking. For example, populism neither commends the liberal solution of handing out welfare nor the compassion-challenged view that says, "I've got mine—now fend for yourself." The idea behind populism is to place self-help in everyone's grasp so that prosperity percolates up from the bottom, as opposed to trickling down from the top, an important distinction that became readily apparent during the explosion of unfettered American capitalism after the Civil War.

Rampant materialism, bottom-line morality, government corruption, and a total void in environmental responsibility marked the "Gilded Age" of Mark Twain. Some 5 million Americans showed up to hear William Jennings Bryan batter big business and the gold standard—an unparalleled glut of partisan enthusiasm.[10] This "Equal Rights to All; Special Privileges to None" candidate would mark the end of his career by prosecuting a young evolution instructor during the so-called Scope's "monkey trial," depicted in Stanley Kramer's *Inherit the Wind* (1960), largely because Bryan believed "teachers in public schools must teach what taxpayers desire taught."[11] More important, however, Bryan opposed the economic and social Darwinism preached by ivory tower dwellers and subsequently employed by industry captains to justify "the survival of the [economic] fittest."

Much as in the post-Enron culture of today, corporations had lost sight of ethics and commercial citizenship. They had forgotten that, at the time of the Constitutional Convention, they had been granted charters only if they promoted the public welfare. It didn't take long for avaricious businessmen to strike mutually beneficial deals with needy/greedy individual states. Promoters no longer had to prove their ventures advanced public welfare. The only obligation assumed by these corporations was to themselves, the only responsibility was to turn money into money. The rich ended up getting richer and the promise of a better life for all remained mostly unfulfilled.

Predominantly agrarian, decidedly democratic, and located at the low end of the economic continuum, discontented populists flocked to the

People's Party of America. This alternative to the two major parties promoted both grassroots democracy and the notion that overstuffed shirts were to blame for impoverishing the plow-and-overalls crowd. Populists demanded answers to public questions involving the role of minorities, the unprecedented wave of foreign immigration, women's rights, and the government's role in shaping social development, monetary policy, and tariff protection.

While some members of the academy view populism as a legitimate ideology, fewer claim its potential as a far-reaching movement.[12] Many consider populism a reactionary response to the times that was eventually consumed with such petty and shallow grievances that, with the return of prosperity after 1896, its justification quietly evaporated. When the 1890 populists faded away, many historians simply relegated what appeared a petered-out political viewpoint as a subset of conservatism.

Populism may only be a cyclical political mood that expresses free-floating resentment of power, dug-in distrust of major institutions, and an impotent sense of personal alienation, but it definitely found a home on the silver screen. Populist directors, like the populists in the seats, seem to burn for simple fairness, for a Sodom-and-Gomorra-like cleansing of the country's morals and a return to the innate wisdom of, *by, and for the people.*

This was also true for Ford's heroes—characters such as Judge Priest in *The Sun Shines Bright,* Ethan Edwards in *The Searchers,* and Wyatt Earp in *My Darling Clementine,* who envisioned themselves as agents of the land, the law, and the Lord. Their job, as they saw it, was to right wrongs, restore honor, and bolster justice. Nevertheless, they also plunked down a steep price for upholding their ideals, often suffering loneliness, isolation, and exclusion. No wonder so few of the folks at the local Bijou, although they identified with Ford's cinematic populists, opted to officially join the People's Party.

Whatever their ineffectiveness as a political force, populists did pave the way, albeit unintentionally, for economic reforms within both major parties—while Republican Theodore Roosevelt championed "the little man," Democrat Woodrow Wilson promised Americans freedom from corporate tyranny.

The defunct People's Party also provided a seedbed for political action extending some five decades into the future. Populists offered an alternative vision for America—a counterculture both democratic and localistic in thrust. Central to this counterculture's popularity was the seeming failure of government, once the Great Depression hit, to make good on the American Dream of shared prosperity. Legislation such as the Social Security Act and the minimum wage sprang out of that unfulfilled promise. The 1929 crash prompted an energetic rhetorical assault on the moneyed and privileged, which Franklin Delano Roosevelt handily harnessed in pushing through his New Deal.

'50s AND '60s POPULISM

With FDR's heavy-handed hold on American government finally over, the five '50s and '60s presidents (who spread themselves all across the populist/elitist continuum) had to figure out how to finesse the populist vote. This was not their father's populism.

First, traditional resistance to big government evaporated when John Q. Public witnessed firsthand Roosevelt's depression-busting New Deal. Fred Harris remembers, "We were for Franklin Roosevelt because he was for us. And he was against those who were against us."[13]

Second, populism, which hadn't gained much of a foothold in urban areas, was being transplanted to big cities by way of the political machine. The only way populists could level the civic playing field against entrenched elites was to organize.[14]

While the downside to the political machine was, not to put too fine a point on it, corruption and graft, any boss who failed to respond to the squeaky wheel or the long-suffering supplicant simply couldn't count on being returned to office. Favoritism was the oil that lubricated the rattle-trap political machine. While it might seem that populists, who supposedly hungered for fairness, would be repulsed by dependence-inducing special treatment, they were not—once political bosses redefined favoritism in egalitarian terms. Case in point: former Speaker of the House Tip O'Neill claimed that Mayor James Michael Curley, the real-life model for *The Last Hurrah*'s Frank Skeffington, delivered some political instruction that turned around O'Neill's career. Curley cautioned, "but always remember, for the person who comes to you, that favor is the most important thing in the world. If he could take care of it himself, he wouldn't to be coming to see you."[15]

Third, television, at least initially, not only invited unprecedented numbers to the polls but also essentially changed the way people voted[16]. Image became more important than issues, and any candidate with a stuffed-to-the-seams war chest and the right political consultant could pass himself off as just about anything he wanted on TV.

Not all presidents during the '50s and '60s were populists, but none would've gotten to the White House without the populist vote. Just as FDR had been able to pull together old Southern Democrats and the machine-organized working class in the North, each subsequent leader of the free world had to marshal a winning coalition.

A "man of the people" in just about anybody's estimation, Harry S. Truman spelled out his populist political philosophy in his 1955 *Memoirs* by insisting, "party platforms are [actual] contracts with the people."[17] "Give 'em Hell" Harry got his first political leg up running for a county commission post on the ever-popular "pothole" platform. He was linked with at least two political machines: Kansas City's Thomas J. Pendergast and Boston's James Michael Curley (whom he granted a 1950 presidential pardon).

Truman took over the family farm at a time when rural populism was still in vogue. He carted those same attitudes, values, and beliefs to the White House, where his critics contended he stunk up the Oval Office with poker-playing roughnecks from Missouri. The plain-speaking Truman, who claimed only three things could ruin a man—power, money, and women[18]—eschewed "big-brass fancy hats," State Department "striped pants boys," and "fuddy-duddies." He lived modestly, and as the chief executive whose desk sported a sign reading "the buck stops here," he definitely knew the value of the dollar. He was the last American president who had not attended college, yet he was one of the best read—his knowledge of history often flabbergasted Ivy Leaguer White House aides.

Dwight D. Eisenhower's life was a play in two acts: the first could arguably be characterized as populist; the second was unquestionably elitist. His deeply religious mother sought to instill a respect for hard work, self-sufficiency, discipline, and education. Abilene, Kansas, was a typical cow town, simple and isolated. In fact, the town lacked paved streets until Eisenhower was twenty years old. Ike relished his modest upbringing, arguing that any child reared in such an environment had been favored by fortune.

When compared to his hyperintellectual opponent, Adlai Ewing Stevenson (who punished the public with puns), Eisenhower could have passed for a People's Party member. The general was much beloved by returning GIs ready, willing, and able to get behind "The Man from Abilene." In 1952, the swing voter (who usually identifies himself or herself as some sort of populist) was king. Eisenhower was swept into office by a margin of more than 6 million votes.

John F. Kennedy may have been a descendant of nineteenth-century Irish–Catholic immigrants, but this Harvard grad was no populist. His father, Joseph P. Kennedy, a multimillionaire businessman, former head of the Securities and Exchange Commission, and ambassador to Great Britain, played no small part in assembling his son's abundantly financed run for the White House.

TV allowed Kennedy to be perceived as a "man of the people," despite the fact that he was anything but an anti-intellectual, antimaterialistic, and antimedia populist. Still, in the Pulitzer Prize–winning *Profiles in Courage,* Kennedy may have summed up the keystone of his populist appeal when he wrote "the true democracy, living and growing and inspiring, puts its faith in the people."[19]

Can a guy who proudly displays his surgeon's stitchery and pulls his puppy dog's ears be anything but a man of the people? Lyndon Baines Johnson claimed that, unlike those who craved power simply to "strut around the world and to hear the tune of 'Hail to the Chief,'" or others who needed it simply to "build prestige, to collect antiques, and to buy pretty things," he desired power "to give things to people—all sorts of things to all sorts of people, especially the poor and the blacks."[20]

Johnson was the eldest son of Sam Ealy Johnson Jr., a struggling Texas hill-country farmer and cattle speculator who provided what can be described charitably as an erratic income for his family. No fancy prep school or Harvard University for LBJ, he attended public school in Johnson City and received his sheepskin from Southwest Texas State Teachers College.

When German chancellor Ludwig Erhard asked LBJ whether he had been born in the requisite-for-populists log cabin, Johnson retorted "no, no, no, you're confusing me with Abe Lincoln. I was born in a manger."[21] Hyperbole was to Johnson what oxygen is to the rest of us.

It was his policy in Vietnam, however, that proved to be Johnson's undoing. Deflecting attention from domestic needs, Johnson's acceleration of American involvement resulted in sharp inflation and fierce faultfinding—especially among draft-age youth. The prolonged struggle that seemed to be leading nowhere made Johnson even more secretive, dogmatic, and hypersensitive to criticism. His usually cocksure political instincts left him, and eroding political support forced him to bow out of the 1968 campaign.

Richard M. Nixon's wife did not wear mink, he pointed out in a televised defense against allegations of slush-fund improprieties. Instead, she adorned herself in "a respectable Republican cloth coat." Even though Nixon claimed to speak for the "great silent majority, " he was never perceived as a man of the people, even though his beginnings in Yorba Linda, California, were remarkably humble. In fact, Nixon spent his life tilting at the establishment. He had always been the outsider: snubbed by the intellectuals at Whittier College, rejected by John Foster Dulles's Wall Street law firm, ignored by Eisenhower as vice president, aced out of the presidency by a Harvard kid, and cold-shouldered by Nelson Rockefeller after losing in California.

Despite the handicap of growing up in a chaotic and hardscrabble household of five boys, Nixon excelled in school, graduating second in his class from Whittier College and third in his class from Duke University Law School. As a card-carrying conservative Republican, however, he wasn't about to whine about inequitable distribution of wealth in this country—he would figure out his own version of the American Dream. He knew it would have something to do with politics. Seeing he could make hay while the "Communist Menace" sun shone, Nixon resolved to red-bait his way into the House and then the Senate. In 1960, Nixon lost the presidency to a bona fide elitist (by only 119,057 out of 68.3 million votes cast). It is interesting to note that student polls at the six Ivy League campuses went overwhelmingly for Nixon.[22]

In 1968, Democrats were bitterly divided over the Vietnam War. Many joined Republicans and anti-Hippie populists to get behind the man who promised "victory with honor" in Southeast Asia and a return to law and order on Main Street. Nixon *was* "the One," as he nabbed the Oval Office, but only by a breathtakingly slim 1 percent margin over Hubert H. Humphrey. This hardly impressive showing did little to convince Nixon he was now a genuine member of the Washington elite and, in fact, led to the paranoid ends–means justification now shorthanded as "Watergate." Nixon's presidency carried populist opposition into the White House, where it shaped national policy in a way that fulfilled both populist dreams and populist nightmares.[23]

As the White House tapes testify, instead of trading ideas with the smart set, Nixon spent his time talking trash with political operatives. His so-called "Enemies List" expanded in direct proportion to mounting disapproval of his administration. Everybody was pleased when Nixon began withdrawing American military forces from Southeast Asia. No one was pleased, however, when Nixon stared at a camera during a 1973 press conference and insisted that he was not a crook.

One reason the populist impulse continues to persist (with Energizer Bunny indefatigability) is because it can always draw attention to the considerable gap between American ideals on one hand and betrayal by those in power on the other. As President William J. Clinton (of all people) once maintained, "the central tenet of every democracy in the end is trust."[24]

SUMMARY OF THE PLOT

One of John Ford's most sentimental send-offs to better days, *The Last Hurrah* examines the end of a political era. Frank Skeffington (Spencer Tracy), who bears more than a fleeting resemblance to James Michael Curley, is gearing up for a fifth and final term as mayor. Knowing it will be the last chance for his nephew, Adam Caulfield (Jeffrey Hunter), to "catch the act," Skeffington invites him to observe, and hopefully to record for posterity, the crafty politico at his best. The venerable Skeffington once again calls on the time-honored torchlight street marches, crackling radio speeches, and assorted glad-handing/baby-kissing that had previously served him well.

He doesn't anticipate that Kevin McCluskey (Charles Fitzsimmons)— a not-too-bright opponent backed by the deep-pocketed, revenge-seeking Norman Cass (Basil Rathbone)—will use television to trounce his well-oiled political machine. Skeffington bids a fond farewell to steadfast cronies (Pat O'Brien, James Gleason, Edward Brophy, and Frank McHugh) as well as childhood friends cum enemies Roger Sugrue (Willis Bouchey) and Cardinal Martin Burke (Donald Crisp) in one of the most protracted death scenes in cinematic history.

POPULISM IN *THE LAST HURRAH*

Populists are known, not so much by what they are for, but by what they are against.

Antimaterialism

In the Scripture according to the populist, not only is the love of money the root of all evil, but also any man who turns his back on principle and tradition risks spiritual bankruptcy. He might gain fame and filthy lucre here on earth but he will be deprived of what is really important—for all eternity.

Skeffington is about as old-fashioned about political campaigning as Ford was about making movies—they both knew the future would render their way of doing business obsolete, but they couldn't seem to help themselves, not even when old-fashioned thinking cost them cash and a position in the pantheon.

Apparently, scalawags can make it through the Pearly Gates if their hearts are in the right place. Novelist Edwin O'Connor based the character of Frank Skeffington on the best-known and most colorful of the big city Democratic bosses, James Michael Curley.[25] Like Skeffington, Curley was a gifted orator and resourceful campaigner who never forgot his Irish tenement roots. Curley/Skeffington distributed well-paying public works jobs, budget-draining pork projects, and innumerable political favors in order to nail down his working-class electoral base. It worked for Skeffington for four terms. The book and movie stop short of sending Skeffington to the slammer, as Curley was in real life in 1947.[26] Instead, Skeffington succumbs to a heart attack (or a broken heart, if Ford had been allowed to write up the death certificate).

Skeffington was the oldest character the sixty-three-year-old Ford had ever chosen for a hero. It would seem likely that a director now in the throes of the contemplative time of life would more readily identify with such a protagonist, but Ford was clueless. In an about-face on the running gag between Skeffington and Ditto, "We certainly are look-alikes, Ditto. Be careful, somebody might shoot you someday," Ford didn't seem to recognize his own literal carbon copy resemblance to Skeffington.

While Skeffington is the consummate image manipulator, Ford was not above a little spin-meistering of his own. He was not born Sean Aloysius O'Feeney, as often reported. The name appearing on his Cape Elizabeth, Maine, birth record and Palm Desert death certificate was John Feeney. He started using the Gaelic version of his real name, presumably, to cement his Irish–Catholic immigrant credentials. Ford would spend his cinematic career exploring populist–elitist clashes, either in the old country or here in multiethnic America. Like Skeffington, Ford used his humble heritage as an excuse to pick at personal psychic scars: "Sure I'm descended from a king of Ireland, with shitty underwear, who slept under a bush."[27]

Skeffington endures his own share of psychic scars—it is, in fact, the humiliating dismissal of his mother as maid that fuels the feud between Amos Force and himself. In the Skeffington version of the story, Force's father simply overreacted when he caught Mrs. Skeffington pocketing two overripe bananas and an apple. While most employers made a practice of looking the other way when the help helped themselves to leftovers, Caleb Force considered Mrs. Skeffington a thief and viciously castigated the hapless maid in front of the whole staff.

Yet it isn't just a lack of generosity that plagues the Force family; they can't seem to forgive, and according to Skeffington they can't forget, especially when the pilfering maid's son ends up as mayor and then governor of the state. An even better illustration of the rectitude vs. riches balancing act promoted by populists can be found in Edwin O'Connor's novel. It seems there is a second and more compelling reason for Amos Force to resent Frank Skeffington. Force has to pay Skeffington an enormous amount of money after losing a libel suit to the mayor.

Skeffington's nephew can likewise attest to the materialism running rampant among the blue bloods—his skinflint editor calls the journalist on the carpet for the trespass of leaving on an electric light. Even though Force subsequently learns that Adam Caulfield is the nephew of his avowed enemy, he continues to keep him in his employ because, bottom line, he realizes "a tidy profit" in syndicating Caulfield's popular column.

When the barbarian Skeffington storms the gate of the ultra-elitist Plymouth Club, he encounters the same sense of "entrenched money" entitlement that Ford would have experienced with Maine Puritans residing in his hometown. The moneyed Brahmins are so rigid, care so little about the people, Skeffington believes that they have to be defeated on every front, including breaching their off-limits citadel.

Why are the elitists so opposed to Skeffington? For Edwin O'Connor, it isn't just that Skeffington is a Democrat while they are Republicans. It isn't even, as Skeffington believes, because he is Irish Catholic while they are Yankee Protestant. The real reason that Skeffington is despised so venomously is because *he's cost them money. For that he must be made to pay with his blood, or at least with a good stiff term in the pokey.*"[28] James Michael Curley, in real life, was made to serve five months in prison for mail fraud in 1947. Skeffington thinks he has this all figured out when he claims, "You have this musty shrine to your blue-nosed ancestors, but my people have the City Hall."

With the exception of his 110-foot ketch *Araner,* John Ford considered himself too populist to plunge into the kind of conspicuous consumption expected by Hollywood. The boat, named for his mother's birthplace, did boast two fireplaces, two bathrooms, red carpets, and a four-poster bed—but it was primarily used as a floating "between-pictures" watering hole for his "stock company," the approximately one hundred actors and technicians routinely recycled among Ford projects.

Ford would maintain that he continued to crank out movies, long past his prime, simply to support the lifestyle to which his wife had become accustomed. Despite the fact that the boarding-school-educated Mary (once a roommate of Dorothy Parker) would have preferred a fashionable Bel Air address, Ford hung on to the unpretentious Odin Street house (purchase price—$14,000)[29] for thirty-four years. Forced out by a Hollywood Bowl parking lot expansion, he reluctantly vacated his modest digs in 1954.

Ford stubbornly refused to travel the Hollywood social circuit (he even turned down a weekend at William Randolph Heart's castle on the California coast) despite Mary's wishes to the contrary. The daughter of a member of the New York Stock Exchange, Mrs. Ford was accustomed to high society. She even rationalized Ford's infidelities with the adage, "if a man didn't have a mistress, it was because he couldn't afford it."[30]

Even though Ford could have afforded two mistresses, he couldn't be persuaded to blow bread on clothes. In fact, except for spiffy but infrequently donned navy uniforms, his wardrobe lacked any sort of sartorial splendor. The classy stage actress Geraldine Page simply wasn't prepared for Ford's disgusting habit of "having a very used handkerchief in his pocket, which he takes out and twists, and puts in the corner of his mouth and sucks on while he's talking. It gets wet with saliva about four inches deep. . . . The visual image of him is so revolting that you have to remember the wonderful things he's done."[31] For a populist, that was the point.

Anti-intellectualism

It's not that populists can't be smart—it's just that if they have brains, they should realize (with appropriate humility) that God-given gifts don't come with bragging rights. Populists can, however, develop their brains, especially if it's a do-it-yourself effort (Abe Lincoln). Modesty dictates, however, that pearls of wisdom are couched in humor and folksy simplicity.

Populists at all costs avoid institutions of higher education, which to their minds are brimful of intellectual show-offs and purported experts who do little more than complicate and obfuscate. Common sense is the well-kept secret behind the sagacity of the common man. The ivory tower dweller probably keeps coming up with so many meaningless "isms" or unworkable Big Ideas simply because he is so isolated from the custodians of conventional wisdom.

Skeffington, like Ford, is a well-read intellectual who knows his history. "My signature will never be as rare as Button Gwinnett's," he quips. It is a good thing that the prep-school educated Winston is there to explain the seemingly opaque punch line to the assembled hangers-on. A roomful of historians, not to mention the folks in the movie theater, might not have recognized the name as a signatory of the Declaration of Independence.

When Ditto gives the mayor a thumbnail sketch of his political opponent, he reports that McCluskey went to the "regular college," not "that place across the river" (otherwise known as Harvard University). The shelves of the mayor's residence are not just crowded with decorator volumes—he is a bona fide autodidact. When his playboy son returns in the wee hours, after a night of cool jazz and hot mamas, he finds his father, as usual, devouring the daily newspaper.

Skeffington also keeps up with current events. He wagers that the lush and lavish coffin that holds the remains of Knocko Minihan could withstand "the hydrogen bomb." Skeffington takes great pains to keep up with news bulletins coming out of Ireland as well. One of Skeffington's opponents is Willard Chase, the local head of Planned Parenthood. Skeffington's campaign manager gives odds that Chase has the same chance of becoming mayor of their predominantly Catholic city as an Arab has of coming to power in Tel Aviv. Skeffington cautions, "don't discount the possibility. Remember the recent Lord Mayor of Dublin!" Filmgoers would have read that Robert Briscoe, who actually held the office of Lord Mayor twice (1956–57, 1961–62), was (believe it or not) a member of the Jewish community.[32]

When he wasn't filming, Ford would plow through several weighty tomes, often history texts, in a single evening. He was considered something of an expert on the Civil War and World War I. Even as a youngster, he kept his nose buried in some Shakespearean play or well-worn edition of poetry. It was the classroom that failed to attract his attention. His grades, from grammar school to high school, were hardly impressive. Today's education experts would have diagnosed him as a classic underachiever.

Although neither man indulges much in self-examination, Skeffington is as conflicted about his life choices as Ford was. That's probably why he invites his nephew to jot it all down, the good and the bad, the triumphs and the mistakes. When Skeffington extracts the loan for his housing project by blackmailing Norman Cass Sr., Norman tells Frank he will live to regret it. Skeffington shoots back "what's one more regret in a lifetime?"

What's one more? This below-the-belt blunder turns out to be the biggest blooper of Skeffington's political career, costing him the election.

The banker ends up giving his opponent a blank check to finance what television commentator Clete Roberts (playing himself) tickets as the "biggest political upset in the history of our city."

The major regret for John Ford was Annapolis. Even more than becoming a filmmaker, Ford dreamed of becoming a naval officer. His plans were thwarted when he flunked the Naval Academy's entrance exam. When the University of Maine at Orono beckoned, rigid course requirements and wealthy undergrads who abused Irish waiters like himself for sport left him disillusioned about higher education. He quit before sitting through a single lecture. Anybody who really knew Ford wasn't fooled by his transparent attempts to belittle intellectuals: "I smell a Phi Beta Kappa. Tell him I no speaka English."[33]

Ford would never submit to intellectual discussion of his own work. To him, all that needed to be said was up there on the screen—not in some pointy-headed professor's psychobabble. In fact, the subject of psychology would lurch him into a state of apoplexy. Unlike the Hollywood glitterati, whose heads were being fashionably shrunk by $100-an-hour "two couches, no waiting" psychoanalysts, Ford had absolutely no respect for Freud. As far as he was concerned, it was little wonder there were no Hamlets around today, with every Tom, Dick, and Harry tickling his id and polishing his libido.

Skeffington, however, might profit from some couch time. Any man who engages in compulsive rituals and public conversations with a dead wife's photograph probably has some serious issues.

Yet for Ford and Skeffington, real men don't talk about feelings, as Skeffington instead adopts, as Ford did also, the persona of the quintessential Irish–American rogue. You don't know whether Lindsay Anderson is talking about John Ford or Frank Skeffington when he notes, "Aggressive and defensive in about equal measure, he was gentle and irascible, bloody-minded and generous, courageous, uncompromising and endlessly evasive."[34]

Skeffington knows he is facing a tough audience when he is introduced to Maeve Caulfield (Dianne Foster), the daughter of his oldest enemy, so he spreads the blarney at least an inch thick: "Your mother was the most beautiful woman in the 3rd ward, except for one—your grandmother Ellen, and you know, you look exactly like her." Nobody took Frank Skeffington. He took them.

Ford was the product of the self-reliant, adventure-seeking Teddy Roosevelt era. He was so terrified of his own sensitivity (and its resultant vulnerability), he kept it permanently just out of reach. Even on his deathbed, the emotionally constipated Skeffington, for his part, won't allow the cardinal to bridge the break between them. It is all about what Ford oxymoronically called being "a man's man." Ford fired the shot heard 'round the feelings-challenged world of men in *She Wore a Yellow Ribbon* when he had John Wayne advise: "Never apologize and never explain. It's a sign of weakness." Women, especially feminists, are still reeling from the insidious effects of Ford's weapon of mass destruction in the battle between the sexes.

Antimedia

Behind the closed door of his office, the managing editor of the *Evening News* scribbles furiously. His boss proves to be, indeed, a Force to be reckoned with as he directs staff to continue to blister the front page with editorial attacks on Skeffington: "On Sunday, the *Evening News* will announce its support for Kevin McCluskey for mayor. We will say we believe he is the best qualified of all the candidates opposing Skeffington. The reasons why we believe this are—reasons will have to be found."

So much for journalistic integrity. Not only is Force unconcerned with truth, justice, and the American way, he doesn't live up to the time-honored ethics of the fourth estate. Instead he cloaks a personal vendetta in the red, white, and blue of the First Amendment by angrily asserting his right to publish what he pleases, while hurriedly backpedaling from even acknowledging, much less being held accountable for, his newspaper's correlative constitutional obligation. While the founding fathers could hardly have conceptualized the World Wide Web (much less radio) as they drafted the Bill of Rights, they realized, for the whole democratic notion to work, an informed electorate was a necessity. The First Amendment, in fact, is the enabling mechanism that allows media to do its job, not just a protection for the press to do as it pleases.

In a democracy, a free press is necessary "to inform the public, to open minds to new viewpoints, and to hold the powerful in check by exposing their sins and criticizing their policies."[35] Providing no forum for civil debate, *The Evening News* gives voice only to the privileged. Failing to connect with the community as a whole, Force's paper ends up cementing divisions and rather than watchdogging the political process as it should, takes a big, bold bite out of its backside.

Force's portrayal exemplifies the reasons for the populist distrust of "the media elite." But it wasn't always so. In its early history, each medium, from printing press to the Internet, brimmed over with populist ideals, but now, with the exception of the World Wide Web, each is ceasing to function as the "free marketplace of ideas," which John Stuart Mill characterized as a continuous process of open dialogue and debate from which truth eventually emerges. Factors such as dependence on advertising, the profit motive (mass media is big business, after all), consolidation of ownership, advancements in technology, and the rickety relationship among power, corruption, and human beings invariably contribute to the pollution of any populist principles that may have initially dominated. In a sense, a "Gilded Age" invariably supplants a medium's "Golden Age."

By the mid-'50s, when *The Last Hurrah* was written, there were four major Boston newspapers. A couple of tabloids, *The Daily Record* and *The Boston American,* were favored by the masses, while the read of choice by the upper crust was *The Boston Herald Traveler and Sunday Advertiser.* The *Boston Globe,* one of the last independent newspapers in the nation, later succumbed to acquisition by the *New York Times.* While Skeffington's beloved city was actually the birthplace of the colonial press, it took only one hundred years for newspapers to be, according to 1890s populists, "largely subsidized or muzzled."[36] So much for the free marketplace of ideas.

Television began its invasion of the American home in 1947. By the mid-'50s, more than half of living rooms featured a black-and-white set. Manufacturers boasted about turning out 5.7 million TVs in 1960. The average household tuned in five to six hours per day.[37] Bostonians had two channel choices when *The Last Hurrah* came out, the NBC affiliate WBZ and WNAC, the flagship of Yankee Network, owned and operated by the Republican *Boston Herald Traveler.*

Since the airwaves basically belong to the people, broadcasters are allowed to operate only if they do so "in the public interest, convenience and necessity." This means sometimes having to provide programming that doesn't attract a slew of advertising dollars. Unlike today, when news divisions are expected to turn a profit, networks formerly poured millions into public affairs. They upended the programming schedule for various jaunts into outer space, allowing Americans to participate directly in mourning their assassinated political leaders, and providing gavel-to-gavel coverage of the Democratic and Republican national conventions.

Admittedly, there was a certain level of coercion exerted by Federal Communications Commission regulation. If the networks didn't do the right thing by the American public, they'd have a tough time hanging on to their licenses to broadcast. The golden age of television, however, was cut short. Rapid advances in cable and satellite technology during the '70s and deregulation fever in the '80s extracted a heavy toll on the marketplace of ideas, rendering it neither free nor the source of much diversity.

Amos Force may be the man you love to hate, but the one-eyed monster proved to be the real villain in *The Last Hurrah.* Skeffington doesn't need tea leaves to predict that television will mutate politics as he knows it. And he isn't adamantly opposed to making an appearance on the boob tube, as long as it is free. He allows news crews to cover an address early in the campaign and then, at the end, he permits an "aw, shucks, sorry you lost" Clete Roberts to talk him into conceding on the air.

Skeffington knows that overcrowding his schedule with speeches, community events (sometimes double-booking breakfast, lunch, and dinner), and assorted baby-kissing are not the most efficient means of collecting votes, but the traditionalist can't help himself. Besides, there is no room in Skeffington's campaign budget for TV spots. He has always been able to count on his shrewd political strategy and *quid pro quo* ward heelers to bring in the ballots.

John F. Kennedy, who had diligently studied at the James Michael Curley–Tip O'Neill school of politics, suspected that the old fashioned grassroots campaign was on its way out.[38] According to Ted Sorensen, "over five hundred speeches, press conferences and statements in 45 states would help, but even the most enormous crowds could total only a tiny fraction of the entire electorate."[39] Kennedy looked to the idiot box for assistance. He had no idea what a smart move that would be.

The Nixon–Kennedy debates proved to be a turning point in American politics. From that moment on, John Q. Public was going to find image more compelling than issues as he weighed his choices for elected office. Like Nixon, Frank Skeffington sells himself as "an experienced leader," while Kevin McCluskey, like Kennedy, provides hope for the future and indirectly disparages ("Would You Buy a Used Car from This Man?") the integrity of his opponent.

Kevin McCluskey may not be the Protestant Bishop's (Basil Ruysdael's) cup of tea—"I prefer an engaging rogue [Skeffington] to a complete fool"—but he is young and handsome (the actor was Maureen O'Hara's brother), and the businessmen of the mummified Plymouth Club backs his television campaign to the hilt.

Senator John F. Kennedy zeroed in on the image-over-issue shift in an article for *TV Guide*. "Honesty, vigor, compassion, intelligence—the presence or lack of these and other qualities make up what is called the candidate's 'image,'" he theorized as he hailed a new breed of candidate whose success depended much more on good looks than guiding principles.[40] According to Kennedy, youth (like McCluskey's) would prove a definite asset in creating a television image that voters like and remember. He acknowledged that intellectuals and politicians might scoff at a perspective that slights factors that should be important to the voter such as political record; views on social, political, and economic questions; and behavior during nontelevised events, yet almost a full year before the Nixon–Kennedy debates, JFK positioned his patrician finger precisely on the nation's political pulse.

Biographers Tag Gallagher and John Baxter postulate that Ford was lampooning Nixon's "Checker's Speech" in McCluskey's paid political spot, because the rented pooch barked during the entire commercial. First, there was no actual dog in Nixon's September 23, 1952, effort to take his case directly to the people (he'd been accused of accepting improper gifts). Second, unlike the halting, cue card–reading Mrs. McCluskey, Pat Nixon never said a word—she merely sat, wax-figure-like, mostly out of frame. Third, the camera didn't visit Nixon's home; he spoke from behind a studio desk, moving toward the camera only to deliver the heart-grabbing close: "the kids, like all kids, loved the dog [Checkers], and I just want to say this, right now, that regardless of what they say about it, we are going to keep it."[41]

The McCluskey thirty-minute infomercial is a cross between *See It Now* (without being hosted by the highly credible Edward R. Murrow) and a Vaughn Meader send-up of Jack and Jackie Kennedy in *First Family*. Ford directed the scene as an over-the-top farce, an understandable decision given his previous comedic work, but jarringly inconsistent with the plot. If Frank Skeffington were such an astute politico, how could a neophyte nincompoop, described by the cardinal as a "mealy-mouthed, maneuverable piece of dough," trounce him by six thousand votes? Right before the TV lights come on, we see the "honest government" candidate inquiring, "What should I call the dog?" There's also the not-so-subtle identification with the Catholics in the audience as the camera lovingly lingers over the mantelpiece where a life-sized portrait of His Eminence smiles down on the freshly scrubbed faces of the Mc-Cluskey brood. The dutiful wife (Helen Westcott), apparently the victim of extreme stage fright, affords the camera an unfortunate close-up of her bent-over bum, which Charles J. Hennessey (Wallace Force) dubs "the posterior for posterity."

By 1960, two years after the release of *The Last Hurrah,* television market penetration had surpassed its tipping point. TV officially dominated all other media. Since the Nixon–Kennedy debates were being broadcast over both radio and television, it was the perfect time to study media effects on politics. Some 79 million adults (nearly two-thirds of the population) viewed or listened to the first debate—clearly the largest campaign audience in recent history. More than four out of five voters tuned in to at least one of the four debates, the average adult saw three, and more than half watched all four. Those who missed the debates on radio or TV soon read about them. The debates, according to Sorensen, were the primary reason for the increased interest in the campaign as well as the record turnout at the polls.[42]

According to various surveys, Nixon won three out of four debates on radio, while Kennedy took the majority on television. It all came down to appearance. Nixon, recently returned from a two-week convalescence from a knee infection, looked gaunt and haggard. Kennedy, who had prepared for the debates aboard his sailboat, appeared tan, vigorous, and confident. The animated Kennedy used short, choppy gestures and a warp-speed delivery—he was clocked at a brisk 210 words per minute.[43] Nixon, in gray suit and ashen-faced after his hospital sojourn, was made up with a beard stick and seemed to fade into the light-colored background. An upper lip dotted with beads of sweat, an uneasy grin at inappropriate moments, and darting eye contact all subtracted from Nixon's credibility with the television audience. On radio, however, his sonorous voice and practiced platitudes made him sound like the elder statesman he thought himself to be.[44]

Television not only changed the way candidates introduced themselves to the voters, but Philo T. Farnsworth's clever little invention wrought other changes in the political process as well. By the end of the '50s, surveys reported twice as many Americans citing television as their primary source of campaign information rather than newspapers or periodicals.[45] The sixty-second sound bite was beginning to replace the information contained in a well-researched newspaper article or thoughtful opinion piece. Pressing the flesh was swapped for paid political spots—more than half the loot in war chests would be spent on television. Campaign managers would rack their brains for new and different ways to stage "media events" (which might draw few voters but many coveted camera crews). In years to come, candidates for the highest office in the land would appear on local talk shows, MTV, and even *Saturday Night Live,* while pseudoelections (called polls) would indicate where the bandwagon was headed.

POPULIST FANTASY THEMES

Land of Opportunity

This fantasy theme finds its roots in the ruggedly independent farmer yeomen who fomented the populism movement of the 1890s. Ford's father, John Feeney, was one of the 4 million who came in search of the American Dream in the long aftermath of the potato famine of 1846. Feeney's Irish sense of community sent him scurrying to the docks, where he greeted newcomers in Gaelic, helped them secure positions, and told them how to cast a ballot.

Political bosses also assisted immigrants in the assimilation process by exchanging whatever the newcomers needed for votes. An equal opportunity employer, Skeffington does not just surround himself with Irish Catholics—he pays attention to the Jewish voice of Sam Weinberg (Ricardo Cortez) and plots strategy with a black ward heeler at the Minihan wake. In fact, in large urban areas such as Boston, real-life political machines balanced their slates of candidates to represent all ethnic groups. Actually, most antigovernment populists categorically opposed New Deal–like redistribution of wealth. For them "the land of opportunity" meant equitable access to (as opposed to "guarantee of") the American Dream. In the novel, Skeffington's nephew, Adam Caulfield, questions why Skeffington lost the election. One friend suggests that FDR-bloated bureaucratic politics, with which Skeffington is assuredly not aligned, might have ended up diluting the favor-granting oil that lubricated Skeffington's political machine.

The downside of the "land of opportunity" fantasy theme occurs when the American Dream is inextricably intertwined with an unremitting work ethic. For John Ford, workaholism led to irreconcilable family problems and Ford disinheriting his only son.[46] New York governor Mario Cuomo likewise touched on physical self-sacrifice in his 1984 Democratic convention keynote address, when he referred to his immigrant father working so hard that his feet often bled. No spring chicken at seventy-two, Skeffington insists on personally seeing every man or woman who takes the time to call at the front door, displaying an ethic that undoubtedly leads to the character's fatal heart attack.

The land of opportunity fantasy theme, which is often coupled by politicians with Horatio Alger mythology, preaches an antivictimization doctrine. One is encouraged to raise one's status, by his or her own bootstraps. Populism's single-minded emphasis on self-help secured a major victory when Clinton signed welfare reform legislation, yet populism without empathy, time and again, has proven a big, fat loser. George W. Bush's answer, at least for the 2000 campaign, was something he called "compassionate conservatism." Democrats consider compassionate conservatism an oxymoron.

No Man Is Poor Who Has Friends

This fantasy theme could be considered a riff on the "money can't buy happiness" refrain. Populists love to pose the query, "he may be rich, but is he happy?" In *The Last Hurrah*, Ford not only spells out life's ultimate achievement, namely, shaking hands with the Grim Reaper while surrounded by loved ones, but also goes one step further. Skeffington's loyal subjects traipse up the grand staircase not only to discuss the upcoming gubernatorial campaign, but also, more important, to pay last respects to their dying Irish king.

It may be one of the most prolonged death scenes in cinematic history, but (as facetiously ascribed to Knocko Minihan) Skeffington "was a lovable man, his friends were legend." In fact, he's so lovable that Skeffington's cronies are joined by Skeffington's perennial opponent, the ebullient Honorable Charles J. Hennessey and his campaign manager, Festus Garvey (Frank McHugh), who hold out hope Skeffington will win the next election: "A man wants to be governor and still wants to be called 'Sonny'—what we can *do* with that!"[47] The cardinal and Roger Sugrue, Skeffington's estranged childhood chums cum enemies, arrive just in time to say "bon voyage." The moral to the story: when your enemies show up at your deathbed, you are rich beyond measure.

Victory in Defeat

This fantasy theme is as ingrained in the Irish character as storytelling. For most of their history, the Irish have been occupied by more powerful neighbors. Even though they keep trying to free themselves from the control of others, they never seem able. Two options are available to losers: (1) give up or (2) translate "survival" into "the ability to fight anther day." While populists will never become a major force in American politics, they keep surviving to fight another day. In fact, they usually make up the swing votes needed for either a Republican or a Democratic victory, so, in that sense, they can claim victory in defeat.

In the end, Skeffington's downfall is inevitable. In *Minority Report,* written in 1956, H. L. Mencken gets it right: "When I hear a man applauded by the mob, I always feel a pang of pity for him. All he has to do to be hissed, is to live long enough."[48] Although Skeffington never loses the support of his Irish constituents, their dwindling numbers have grown insufficient to win, especially when McCluskey is able to mobilize marginal under-forty voters via television. When Skeffington's campaign staff, especially Ditto, begin the "we wuz robbed" act, Skeffington won't let them whine. He suddenly appears unperturbed, if not downright gracious. During previous campaigns, Skeffington has come to the realization that he has gotten by on his own wits, energy, and guts so this particular upset doesn't subtract one IQ point from his genius for politics. Even as he plods home alone from election headquarters, with McCluskey's victory parade moving in the opposite direction, you can sense he's mulling over future prospects, including a run for the governor's mansion. The avid reader might even turn the words of Agnes Sligh Turnbull over in his mind: "defeat in itself was part and parcel of the great gambling game of politics. A man who could not accept it and try again was not of the stuff of which leaders are made."[49]

Ford's Irish melancholy manifested itself best in loss. When the director showed the audience Ma Joad burning her letters before the California trip, Abe Lincoln grieving at the grave of Anne Rutledge, or Ethan Edwards voluntarily exiling himself from his family, loss wasn't the end of the story; it was the beginning. The deceased, such as Skeffington's Kate, are in fact tangible influences in Ford's films, since the desires of their dearly departed hearts are willingly shouldered by the living. Skeffington, according to Lee Lordeaux, acknowledges Kate's "continuing significance in his life" by slipping Gert Minihan a thousand dollars, white-lying that he was just Kate's messenger.[50]

Ironically, Ford won his first Oscar for direction in 1935 with *The Informer,* but deliberately stayed away from the Academy Awards ceremony, fearing (in the opposite of this fantasy theme) defeat in victory. François Truffaut noted in 1974 that Ford "gave the impression that he never sought out this celebrity and, indeed, that he never accepted it."[51] Actually, he was terrified, according to Scott Eyman, of seeming to need the awards he would then conspicuously display.[52]

POPULISTS IN POWER: FORD AND SKEFFINGTON

Despite populist leanings, Skeffington with his political machine (like Ford with his film company) heads up an elitist organization that can be thought of as both anachronistic and patriarchal.

As a political boss, Skeffington cuts ethical corners, puts his city in financial jeopardy, and exposes new citizens to the dark side of democracy, but he does accomplish some good. In fact, the urban infrastructure in Skeffington's hometown would not exist had not his political machine cut through red tape, filled administrative positions, awarded contracts, dispensed favors, and rewarded supporters. Unfortunately for those like Skeffington, midcentury reforms such as the direct primary, the merit system for public employment, public welfare programs, and competitive bidding for government contracts were already hastening the decline of the political machine.

With studio system moguls dying off, the movie industry at the time of *The Last Hurrah* was moving away from the director as auteur. The motion picture "as product" would propel a new paradigm in which the producer would wield most of the clout, yet Ford remained a collaboration-free tyrant.

Frank Nugent, screenwriter for *The Last Hurrah*, admits that while Ford could "be rude and frequently insulting . . . [he could] also be affable, charming, genial and generous in his praise. (I prefer not to tell you what the percentage is.)"[53] Ford expected every individual in his employ to work eighteen-hour days. He went to great lengths to guarantee realism, sometimes endangering actors in the process. He would ferret out psychological chinks and poke around psyches until he got a response. He demeaned, degraded, and disgraced members of his cast and crew. He regularly reduced both males and females to tears. Those who took the abuse stuck around largely because Ford created an enveloping, addictive feeling of family. Further, Ford could be counted on to be ferociously loyal to actors who passed his muster. His casting process was simple; when word got out that Ford was about to start a new film, members of his "stock company" camped out at his office until signed to the picture.

Ford forced himself to put up with writers. His creative mind saw film in pictures, not words. Neither writers nor producers were permitted on the set once shooting started. Ford would summon the same stable of scribes,[54] first, because they understood and tolerated his quirks and, second, because they knew to leave plenty of blank space for him to conjure up the visual imagery. In fact, when Ford actually did spend time with his family, son Patrick recalls that he would often sit and sketch faces and scenes with charcoal.[55]

Ford intended to make *The Last Hurrah* as controversial as the book had been, but when Columbia honcho Harry Cohn died a few days into shooting, a fresh executive team clamped down, ordering massive script revisions. How much wholesale butchering went on is impossible to say, but with Curley's libel lawsuit against Edwin O'Connor still up in the air, the studio was taking no chances. Cuts probably involved details that would identify Skeffington as Curley. In the book, Skeffington is always addressed as "Governor," but except for a single reference that must have escaped detection ("he can't get over the fact that her son became mayor of the city and governor of the state") the movie identifies Skeffington as a four-term mayor of some unspecified municipality in New England. Ford was understandably distressed, but allowed, "there's still lots of good stuff left in. I think it makes you gulp in a couple of places."[56]

James Cagney had been Ford's first choice for Skeffington, but Cagney wasn't eager to work with Ford again after *Mister Roberts*. Ford next called on the Hepburn–Tracy connection. Ford's six-month affair with Katherine Hepburn in 1936 had him considering leaving his wife, but his Catholic faith, Kate's ferocious independence, and his masculine ego kept him in check. Since they remained friends, Ford harbored no qualms about asking Hepburn to use her influence with Tracy to overcome an unresolved tiff between the two men dating back to the early '30s. In fact, when Ford was slotted to direct Tracy in *Old Man and the Sea* (1958), Tracy begged off with the admonition, "the only worry is that he'll shoot picture, you, me, and the boy."[57] Tracy, who received $200,000 to star in *The Last Hurrah*, *was* Skeffington.[58] He also shared a great deal in common with the director—both were brooding Irishmen, periodic alcoholics, classic introverts, psychologically conflicted, and publicly dismissive about their work.

The psychological distance between Skeffington's contemporaries and their offspring anticipates the so-called generation gap, which became a buzzword during the early '60s, when President Kennedy singled out and summoned American youth to "ask not what your country can do for you; ask what you can do for your country."[59] His death in 1963 not only stunned and overwhelmed Americans of all ages, but also liquefied the links Kennedy had carefully forged between teens and "the establishment." Student radicals, dropouts, and hippies revolted, scorning traditional standards, venerating self-indulgence, and sneering at discipline.

Skeffington's generation was able to escape the immigrant tenements by becoming policemen, priests, or politicians, but they grieved the total assimilation of their own children into the American culture. Look at Skeffington's self-absorbed son. He's a parasite, heedlessly indulging his own desires and causing his disappointed father to shrug a heavy shoulder at the confession that Junior's "too busy" to catch a televised speech, to register to vote, or to hold his father's hand as Skeffington slips into the next world.

While Junior Cass isn't responsible for his lack of intellectual prowess, it would seem that anyone who can master sailing could probably find a meaningful way to contribute to society. Instead of allowing his son to suffer the consequences of his actions, the senior Cass continues to whip out his checkbook whenever Junior screws up. It's not surprising that both fathers, mired in tradition, addicted to heavy-handed control, and lacking a moral compass of their own, turn out young men who, in turn, spurn tradition, attach themselves to superficial pursuits, and lack the discipline to function as independent adults. In fact, Ford essentially tells a one-sided story in *The Last Hurrah*. Scott Eyman comments, "Nobody outside of Skeffington's own generation has any dignity at all, and that lack of respect undermines the picture."[60]

Instead of only offering Skeffington's point of view, why didn't Ford get Caulfield to pose the hard questions? He is a journalist, after all. Instead of getting bogged down with whether or not a funeral is the proper place to troll for votes, why not cut to the crux of the matter—"Uncle, why are you such a control freak?" The nitty-gritty of populism is empowering the governed, but that's patently impossible as long as the leader fails to liberate those in his charge. The self-sacrificing Greatest Generation may have wanted to protect their offspring from the deprivation they experienced during the depression, but they didn't do the boomers any favors by keeping them dependent and narcissistic. Perhaps that constitutes the *real* generation gap.

Ford seemed to plumb his own life for some of the comedic material used in *The Last Hurrah*. "The Marching Chowder and Total Abstinence Society" is a play on "The Young Men's Purity, Total Abstinence, and Yachting Association," the nickname adopted by frequently invited guests aboard Ford's yacht, the *Araner*. When Norman Cass Jr. (O. Z. Whitehead), privately known around the Plymouth Club as "the Commodore," affects a yachting cap, Ford could have been peering into a mirror. Although usually bedraggled, Ford possessed a full selection of beautifully tailored and immaculately maintained naval uniforms that he pulled from the closet at any opportunity. In fact, when he was shooting at West Point, he showed up at a somewhat casual event in full navy regalia while the assembled generals were garbed in civies. Ford wasn't content with merely a military wardrobe; he lusted after medals as well. He spent years plotting, entreating, and name-dropping. Although he was never awarded the Silver Star or Commendation Ribbon, the persistent Ford eventually acquired nine decorations, including the Purple Heart.[61]

Ford saw nothing wrong with reaching back to recycle what had worked in previous productions. Unfortunately, by 1958 his gags were tired, his formerly radical imagery seemed hackneyed, and his cinematic shorthand for character types was perceived as distasteful. In *The Last Hurrah,* Skeffington sarcastically observes that the presence of Delia Boylan (Jane Darwell) at funerals "is almost as invariable as the corpse's" and advises her to get a hobby. Ford hands the actress the task of portraying a perpetual mourner, whose thick Irish brogue and widow's cackle hang disconcertingly heavy in the air. Ford perpetuates the stereotype of the disingenuously pious Catholic by having Boylan frequently punctuate the dirt she's dishing on the diseased with "and God be good to him."

Edwin O'Connor described Norman Cass Jr. as a "very old undergraduate." Ford had him speak with a lisp. The speech impediment not only wasn't necessary to the plot, but Ford's movie audiences also found it offensive. While elementary-school-age kids might have trouble with sibilants, most full-grown men are perfectly capable of learning to tuck their tongues behind their two front teeth. Speech therapists, even five decades ago, were able to work wonders with phrases like "sloop race."

Ford learned the hard way that race was no longer considered fodder for fun, and his later films, in fact, were being interpreted as narrow-minded, bigoted, or downright insensitive. Humor has always been a touchy business, even decades before political correctness reared its meddlesome head. Yet Ford, obsessed with injustice linked to race and class, had actually tried to shine a monster klieg light on the intolerance American society had for centuries relegated to cobwebbed corners. He was one of few directors concerned with minorities before it became commercially fashionable to be. He was rightfully furious when critics mistook him for a racist and a reactionary. For Ford, it was always a question of probing the tensions arising out of the relationship between individual origins and status quo situations. Whether Irish or African American, Indian or cavalry, WASP or whore, Ford always played the individual against the stereotype. Ford's detractors only saw the stereotype. Ironically, *All in the Family's* Carroll O'Connor, who suffered similar barbs when he played bigot Archie Bunker, pushed for a TV remake of *The Last Hurrah* in 1977.

Two of Ford's favorite symbols are evident in *The Last Hurrah*: the parade and the floral tribute. The movie begins with a multitude of marchers warbling the Skeffington jingle through the streets of Boston and ends with a silent queue of mourners filing up the elegantly curved staircase. Just so the Brahmins won't miss the point, Skeffington deliberately schedules the completion of his hard-won housing project on St. Patrick's Day. He vows to lead a full-blown "Wearin' of the Green" procession past the heavily curtained windows of the snooty Plymouth Club.

When the audience first meets Frank Skeffington, he is slipping a fresh rose into the waiting vase before his wife's portrait. Ford frequently used flowers to honor the dead—from Anne Rutledge in *Young Mr. Lincoln* to Judge Priest's beloved wife in *The Sun Shines Bright*. When Skeffington's constituents crowd his living room with a veritable bower of bouquets, Ford wants you to know that the dying mayor was not without mourners.

Ford was also a huge fan of populist music. He opens *The Last Hurrah* with a medley of Americana: "Pony Boy," "Hail, Hail, the Gang's All Here," and "Ta-Ra-Ra-Boom-Dee-Ay." In all likelihood, Ford wrote the Skeffington jingle. He pulled together every campaign cliché ("the man with the plan," "true blue," "our favorite son") employed by creators of political ballyhoo during that era. Musical scores for Ford films were often variations on familiar folk themes and, to his mind, played a more important role than dialogue. When Ford began planning a film, he went about quietly doing his research, often requesting the music of the period. Frank Nugent observed that Ford never started shooting unless he was "well-armed with a strange miscellany of fact and fancy to toss casually at writer, wardrobe man, and everybody else who comes under the gleam of his Celtic eye."[62]

Ford's *The Last Hurrah* leaves a nagging and largely unanswered question—What exactly do Cardinal Martin Burke (Donald Crisp) and millionaire Roger Sugrue (Willis Bouchey) have against Frank Skeffington? "We were all born down here together, then drifted our different ways," Skeffington laments to Caulfield.

All three have suffered the "Irish need not apply" prejudice and cruelty doled out to immigrants. All three have clawed their way out of roach-infested poverty, yet Sugrue and Burke recoil whenever reminded of their humble beginnings. The millionaire's inferiority complex is obvious. Having worked his way through Harvard and, in time, becoming the sole proprietor of a chain of women's specialty shops, Sugrue is not, according to O'Connor "a bad man, but he was worse: he was a self-made one."[63] When Skeffington forgives the cardinal without requiring an apology or explanation, he does so knowing that his old pal has never overcome the deep-seated feelings of inadequacy and insecurity that plagued most immigrants.

All three childhood chums share the same deeply held religious convictions, yet Sugrue and Burke have bought into a very narrow view of spirituality. As a so-called professional Catholic, Roger Sugrue has appointed himself arbiter of morals for clergy and congregant alike. He sees Skeffington as an unorthodox practitioner of the faith who failed to defer to any spiritual confessor. It was, after all, the parish priest who traditionally channeled an Irishmen's self-destructive behavior into socially acceptable conduct. Perhaps His Eminence believed he should have played that role in Skeffington's life.

While all three enjoy the materialistic trappings of their high rank, it is Skeffington who remains the populist at heart. He may have pilfered millions from taxpayers, but it flows out of his hands and into the pockets of the needy. In the novel, the cardinal pegs Skeffington as a financially irresponsible keeper of the city's coffers, but adds "but you don't shoot Santa Claus. Isn't that what [Al] Smith said about Roosevelt? It's much truer of

Skeffington. The people come to him with empty stockings and he fills them: with jobs, dentures, eyeglasses, money."[64]

While all three have scaled the heights of elitist institutions, only Skeffington fails to bequeath a legacy of excellence. As the cardinal observes in the novel, Irish Catholics were just beginning to flex their political muscle—what they needed was a spokesperson. Skeffington, a scoundrel from the beginning, was simply the wrong man: "The difference was that in New York, they produced Al Smith, while we produced Frank Skeffington. We have been answering for it ever since."[65] Sugrue summarizes with "He has let down his community, yes, but, first and foremost, he has let down his inheritance, his people, and his religion!"[66]

Skeffington has, according to his two oldest critics, besmirched his God-given gift for politics with an end-justifies-the-means modus operandi. Skeffington, unlike Sugrue and Burke, lives his life in a goldfish bowl that magnifies his every act, and whether you are friend or foe ultimately evidences your case for saint or sinner. At Skeffington's deathbed, Sugrue argues "at least he made his peace with God. If he had it to do over again, he would do it differently." A sly Skeffington, not quite ensconced behind a harp, shoots back, "like hell, I would!"

As the novel eulogizes, "that to have lived a long life, to have left the lot of many of those around you a little bit better than it once was, to have been genuinely loved by a great many people, and to have died in God's good grace, is no small thing to have happened to any man."[67]

THE AUDIENCE RESPONDS

The Last Hurrah was scheduled to shoot in thirty-five days with a budget of $2.5 million.[68] Ford was contracted to receive $125,000 plus 25 percent of the gross.[69] Production began on February 24, 1958, went eight days over schedule, but wound up $200,000 under budget.

Actress Anna Lee (Gert Minihan) insisted that Ford, who had not been permitted to supervise the editing, was disappointed in the picture. So was the audience. The domestic gross for *The Last Hurrah* at the end of the first year was fair, a mere $950,000. The gross receipts as of May 1963 totaled $1.2 million. By the end of August 1971, Columbia carried a loss of $1.8 million on the picture.[70]

The Last Hurrah had all the elements of a Ford classic: a story based on a best-seller, a proven box-office draw in the lead, the greatest collection of scene stealers in the business, and tasteful cinematography captured by the prestigious Charles Lawton Jr. So what went wrong? That's the same question Skeffington's troops posed as McCluskey wiped the mayor's nose by six thousand votes.

Ford didn't hold with sneak previews to test audience reaction. He insisted on making the picture he wanted to make. But the fact that Ford was universally respected as a director did not free him from the vagaries of a fickle public. It had been a good decade since a Ford story had found a significant audience. Ford would soon learn that 1958 moviegoers were in no mood to see an out-of-date politico lose to a boob on the boob tube.

Had the gutless Columbia executives not gutted the crookedness and rascality out of Skeffington, *The Last Hurrah* might have been a different story. Hennessey tells Caulfield "Vote for me and atone for your uncle's sins." What sins? Threatening the manager of the Plymouth Club with building inspectors? Muscling a banker into floating a loan for slum clearance? Liberating prime rib and booze from municipal agencies to cater a wake for an indigent widow? The law eventually saw Curley in jail after a lifetime of crookedness and rascality.

Critic and director Lindsay Anderson lays the failure on Ford's advanced years. "Age accounted for the slackening of grasp, the faltering of poetic thrust, and it arrived, as it so often does, with a change in the climate of culture, with altered expectations from his audience, and different demands from the industry of which he had been a part so long."[71]

To succeed, the movie had to balance sentimentality with laughs, and Ford seriously overestimated his gift for comedy. Screenwriter Nunnally Johnson observed that Ford couldn't handle eccentric characters. He chose, instead, to rely "on a kind of old-fashioned bed-slat comedy idiom."[72] By 1958, humor based on stereotypes was out of vogue.

Further, with *The Last Hurrah* there was none of the unique, eye-popping imagery you had come to expect with Ford. The esteemed director was now in his midsixties, his eyesight practically gone, his brain battered from hard drinking, and his body so fatigued he'd have to sneak naps in a portable dressing room next to the set. Ford seemed paralyzed by a fear of failure, depressed by a faltering faith in America, and distressed by his financial encumbrances (the upkeep on the *Araner* as well as the Bel Air hacienda). Argosy, the production company started with Merian Cooper, was going belly-up. He still grieved over the death of his brother Francis. Martin Jurow, John Wayne's agent, concluded Ford was "no longer physically able to do the pictures he wanted to do, yet he wanted to keep active."[73] Perhaps all he could muster at that stage of his life was merely going through the motions.

Ford biographer Scott Eyman compared *The Last Hurrah* to "a big fat pitch down the middle of the plate that unaccountably gets popped up."[74] In comparison to his runaway hits and Oscar-winning masterpieces, *The Last Hurrah* dims in the afterglow. Ford, like so many other directors, had become a victim of his own success.

NOTES

1. Thomas Jefferson, *Letter to Henry Lee* (August 10, 1824), quoted in Wesley D. Camp, *Word Lover's Book of Unfamiliar Quotations* (Paramus, N.J.: Prentice-Hall, 1990), 252.

2. E. B. White, *The Wild Flag* (1946), quoted in Leonard Roy Frank, ed., *Quotationary* (New York: Random House, 1999), 39.

3. Joseph McBride, *Frank Capra: The Catastrophe of Success* (New York: Simon and Schuster, 1993).

4. Raymond Durgnat and Scott Simmon, *King Vidor, American* (Berkeley: University of California Press, 1988).

5. Joseph McBride, "Fellow Traveler or Redbaiter," *Los Angeles Times Magazine*, June 3, 2001, 18.

6. Lindsay Anderson, *About John Ford* (London: Plexus, 1981), 149.

7. Ronald L. Davis, *John Ford: Hollywood's Old Master* (Norman: University of Oklahoma Press, 1995), 202.

8. Brian Neve, *Film and Politics in America: A Social Tradition* (London: Routledge, 1992), 29.

9. Franklin D. Roosevelt, *Speech in Hollywood, California* (February 27, 1941), quoted in Daniel B. Baker, *Power Quotes* (Detroit: Visible Ink, 1992), 225.

10. Richard Norton Smith, "Introduction," in Lonnie G. Bunch III, Spencer R. Crew, Mark G. Hirsch, and Harry R. Rubenstein, *The American Presidency: A Glorious Burden* (Washington, D.C.: Smithsonian Institution Press, 2000), 14.

11. George McKenna, *American Populism* (New York: Putnam & Sons, 1966), 130.

12. Lawrence Goodwyn, *Democratic Promise: The Populist Movement in America* (New York: Oxford University Press, 1976).

13. Fred Harris, *The New Populism* (Berkeley, Calif.: Thorpe Springs, 1973), 6.

14. Robert Thompson, "American Politics on Film," *Journal of Popular Culture*, 20, no. 1 (1986): 35.

15. Tip O'Neill with Gary Hymel, *All Politics Is Local* (Holbrook, Mass.: Adams, 1994), 169.

16. Voter turnout started to decline in 1964, when baby boomers started to reach the age of majority.

17. Harry S Truman, *Memoirs, Vol. II: Years of Trial and Hope* (1955), chapter 13, quoted in John Bartlett, *Familiar Quotations*, 16th ed. (Boston: Little, Brown, 1992), 655.

18. Quoted in David Halberstam, *The Fifties* (New York: Fawcett Columbine, 1993), 22.

19. John F. Kennedy, *Profiles in Courage* (1956), quoted in Frank, *Quotationary*, 197.

20. Doris Kearns Goodwin, *Lyndon Johnson and the American Dream* (New York: Harper and Row, 1976), 53–54.

21. Quoted in Robert Dallek, *Flawed Giant: Lyndon Johnson and His Times 1961–1973* (Oxford: Oxford University Press, 1998), 4.

22. Jeffrey Bell, *Populism and Elitism: Politics in the Age of Equality* (Washington, D.C.: Regenery, 1992), 6.

23. Leonard Silk and Mark Silk, *The American Establishment* (New York: Basic, 1980), 314.

24. Bill Clinton in Gwen Ifill, "Bill and Al's Traveling Medicine Show, *New York Times,* September 9, 1993, quoted in Frank, *Quotationary,* 197.

25. Mayor of Boston (1914–18, 1922–26, 1930–34, 1947–50), governor of Massachusetts (1935–37), congressman (1911–14, 1943–47). Curley fought release of the film and took author Edwin O'Connor to court. The case was settled privately for $25,000 in damages.

26. This was Curley's second term in jail. In 1904, he was briefly imprisoned for impersonating a friend at a civil service exam.

27. Scott Eyman, *Print the Legend: The Life and Times of John Ford* (New York: Simon and Schuster, 1999), 338.

28. Edwin O'Connor, *The Last Hurrah* (Boston: Little, Brown, 1956), 34.

29. O'Connor, *Last Hurrah,* 69.

30. O'Connor, *Last Hurrah,* 68.

31. Quoted in Davis, *John Ford,* 264.

32. Personal interview with Terry Wogan, Dublin City Archives, June 8, 2001.

33. Eyman, *Print the Legend,* 338.

34. Anderson, *About John Ford,* 9.

35. William Miller, Annis-May Timpson, and Michael Lessnoff, "Freedom from Press," in *Elitism, Populism and European Politics,* edited by Jack Hayward (Oxford: Clarendon, 1996), 67.

36. John D. Hicks, *The Populist Revolt* (Lincoln: University of Nebraska Press, 1961), 436.

37. J. Fred MacDonald, *One Nation under Television: The Rise and Decline of Network TV* (Chicago: Nelson–Hall, 1994), 145.

38. In 1946, Kennedy won retiring James Michael Curley's Congressional seat.

39. Theodore C. Sorensen, *Kennedy* (New York: Bantam, 1966), 220.

40. John F. Kennedy, "Television: A Force in Politics," *TV Guide* (November 14, 1959), 6–7.

41. Richard Nixon, *Checkers Speech* (September 23, 1952), quoted in Bartlett, *Familiar Quotations,* 733.

42. Sorensen, *Kennedy,* 220–37.

43. Paul Irwin Rosenthal, "Ethos in the Presidential Campaign of 1960: A Study of the Basic Persuasive Process of the Kennedy–Nixon Television Debates" (Ph.D. diss., University of California, Los Angeles, 1963), 149.

44. Rosenthal, "Ethos," 141–66.

45. Sorensen, *Kennedy,* 220.

46. Davis, *John Ford,* 288–89.

47. In *The Last Hurrah,* the gubernatorial candidate's name is Rutherford K. Allen, but in real life, Tip O'Neill claimed Jim Curley belittled Patrick "Sonny" McDonough with the line "imagine someone named 'Sonny' wanting to be Mayor." Quoted in O'Neill, *All Politics,* 15.

48. H. L. Mencken, *Minority Report* (1956), quoted in Baker, *Power Quotes,* 226.

49. Agnes Sligh Turnbull, *The Golden Journey* (1955), quoted in Baker, *Power Quotes,* 240.

50. Lee Lordeaux, *Italian and Irish Filmmakers in America: Ford, Capra, Coppola, and Scorsese* (Philadelphia: Temple University Press, 1990), 103.

51. François Truffaut, *The Films in My Life,* translated by Leonard Mayhew (New York: Simon and Schuster, 1975), 63.

52. Eyman, *Print the Legend*, 159.

53. Anderson, *About John Ford*, 244.

54. Frank Nugent, Laurence Stallings, Dudley Nichols, and James Warner Bellah.

55. Eyman, *Print the Legend*, 302.

56. Davis, *John Ford*, 286.

57. Eyman, *Print the Legend*, 461.

58. Tag Gallagher, *John Ford: The Man and His Films* (Berkeley: University of California Press, 1986), 500.

59. John Fitzgerald Kennedy, *Inaugural Address* (January 20, 1961), quoted in Bartlett, *Familiar Quotations*, 741.

60. Eyman, *Print the Legend*, 462.

61. Eyman, *Print the Legend*, 282.

62. Anderson, *About John Ford*, 244.

63. O'Connor, *Last Hurrah*, 137.

64. O'Connor, *Last Hurrah*, 94

65. O'Connor, *Last Hurrah*, 93.

66. O'Connor, *Last Hurrah*, 22.

67. O'Connor, *Last Hurrah*, 408.

68. Eyman, *Print the Legend*, 460.

69. Gallagher, *John Ford*, 500.

70. Eyman, *Print the Legend*, 462.

71. Anderson, *About John Ford*, 208.

72. Anderson, *About John Ford*, 247.

73. Davis, *John Ford*, 287.

74. Eyman, *Print the Legend*, 462.

Charles Laughton and Walter Pidgeon debate on the floor of the Senate in Advise and Consent. *Courtesy of the Academy of Motion Picture Arts and Sciences.*

3

☆

Elitism in *Advise and Consent*

Renowned "historian" Homer Simpson observed, "The whole reason we have elected officials is so we don't have to think all the time." Garry Wills, who's racked up a little more academic wallop than Simpson, put it another way: "Politicians fascinate because they constitute such a paradox; they are an elite that accomplishes mediocrity for the public good."[1]

Presidents from George Washington to George W. Bush have tried to straddle the middle of the teeter-totter between being perceived as "men of the people" by the electorate while being elevated to elitist status by the office itself.[2] Jeffrey Bell, author of *Populism and Elitism: Politics in the Age of Equality*, nails the conflict between elitism and populism as "the most important argument in politics today" and calls for a definitive difference rather than the usual left/right political ideological distinction.[3] Case in point: when Governor Bill Clinton's 1992 polls indicated swing voters were being turned off by his Ivy League education (Georgetown, Oxford, and Yale Law), he provided the media with "a-picture-is-worth-a-thousand-words" photo ops. His "populist" excursions to fast-food joints not only goosed up his poll numbers but also assured his victory over patrician George H. W. Bush, who knew not the price of a loaf of bread.

HISTORY OF ELITISM

Best-selling author Ferdinand Lundberg remarked that elected officials in this country may talk like Thomas Jefferson, but they walk like Alexander Hamilton.[4] A society, by definition, generates elites[5] and elitism has

41

reigned during the past five thousand years. Until 1775, governments around the world had been almost entirely monarchical. No country larger than a city-state had ever been able to sustain an independent democracy or republic. In fact, the notion of political equality hadn't gained a sufficient foothold for arguments between populism and elitism to exist, much less matter.

Elitism is rooted in the work of Plato (who was born into an aristocratic Athenian family) and the writings of Aristotle (whose wealthy father served as physician to the King of Macedon). Both philosophers were highly critical of democracy. Plato took considerable exception to yanking away control from experts in governance and reassigning it to the lowborn. His case wasn't just the typical "mob rule" attack on popular sovereignty; he also rejected an aristocracy of birth or an oligarchy of wealth in favor of "philosopher kings." Aristotle objected to democracy on the grounds that government by the people was, in actuality, domination by the economically disadvantaged. He fully expected motivated rabble-rousers to eventually rectify the situation by unceremoniously dispossessing the rich.

America Not a Democracy

At no time, at no place, and by no individual have the American people officially certified the United States as a democracy. As historians Charles and Mary Beard argue in *America in Midpassage*, "The Constitution did not contain the word [democracy] or any word lending countenance to it, except possibly the mention of 'we, the people,' in the preamble. . . . When the Constitution was framed, no respectable person called himself a democrat."[6]

In popular American folklore, as well as official rhetoric, legitimate power is seated in the people.[7] In his first inaugural (April 30, 1789), George Washington added, "The preservation of the sacred fire of liberty, and the destiny of the republican model of government, are justly considered as deeply, perhaps as finally staked, on the experiment entrusted to the hands of the American people."[8] Yet as a democratic republic, certain fundamental rights—private property, freedom of unpopular speech, and religious eccentricity, to name a few—are permanently sequestered from assault by fanatic or fleeting expressions of popular will. It is interesting to note that our version of popular sovereignty may have actually resulted from a compromise. Delegates in Philadelphia who needed constitutional consensus between, on the one hand, those advocating the concentration of power in the federal government and, on the other, those advocating the dispersal of power among the states brokered the deal.

The United States, you see, was founded on a contradiction. Except for the Civil War, we've lived quasipeacefully with that contradiction for more than two hundred years.

James Madison, a transplant from a plantation at Montpelier (Virginia) by way of Princeton University, mobilized the Constitutional Convention. His dirty little secret was that the Constitution and pure democratic principles were inherently inconsistent. Despite supposedly placing power in the people, the founding fathers feared that the populace might be led astray by the rhetoric of some silver-tongued demagogue who merely mimicked national sentiment. The framers also insisted on an obligatory, if not perpetual, brake on populist participation.

In the Gettysburg Address, Lincoln refers to a nation dedicated to the proposition "that all men are created equal," words penned by Thomas Jefferson in 1776. That's not quite true. America is actually dedicated to arguing about the *meaning* of that proposition. At various times, this nation has cleaved over slavery, immigration restriction, women's suffrage, a progressive income tax, and of course, elitism versus populism.

The debate over what to call our first chief executive furnishes a useful example. John Adams was no monarchist—his American Revolutionary credentials were impeccable. He proposed that the American president be called "His Majesty" or "His Highness." Despite the assumption (inherent in the Declaration of Independence) that royal personages are inherently evil, Washington frequently allowed himself to be publicly crowned with laurel wreathes. This wildly popular chief executive realized he would lead a populace that knew only monarchical rule and would be, in essence, a republican king. "Mr. President" seemed the best appellation at hand.

The quarrel between the Federalists and the Anti-Federalists was essentially a clash between two utopian visions, both supposedly linked to a future explosion of individual happiness and collective prosperity, yet neither of which could/should prevail. To Anti-Federalists such as Thomas Jefferson and James Madison, Thomas Paine's *The Rights of Man* (1791) embodied the gist of their quixotic dream. Paine argued that once the last ashes of feudalism were whisked away, a radical transformation would internalize the essential discipline of government within the citizenry. Federalists such as George Washington, John Adams, and Alexander Hamilton, however, wanted to bind Americans together via a brawny and activist central government, fueled by commerce and industry.

What the Anti-Federalists intuitively grasped, however, even though there had always been power incommensurately exercised by the upper echelon, was that "elite" had become a dirty word for postrevolutionary American culture. Despite the fact that republican government prevailed in America only because the best and the brightest eased it through its initial and most vulnerable phase, anyone who uplifted elitist values violated the working premise of the revolution, namely, seating sovereignty within the people. The only kind of political upper echelon permissible was one that, in fact, rejected its elitist status.

Future politicians would get around this dichotomy by ostensibly speaking "for the many" instead of defending the interests "of the few." Andrew Jackson and his fellow populists contended that political leaders who possessed (largely undefined) "genius" were able to articulate and translate public opinion with the unerring accuracy of an Athenian direct plebiscite. "The great charm," according to *Populism* author Margaret Canovan, "of 'the people,' for a politician—and the fundamental source of exasperation for a political scientist—is the term manages to be both empty of precise meaning and full of rhetorical resonance."[9]

Once in office, elected officials are fully expected to conduct themselves as elitists. They may direct a nod toward populism by refusing the chauffeured limousine, but upon taking the oath of office, they assume the mantle and behave as if essentially large and in charge. Populism really only reasserts itself in the lives of officeholders during the ballot box ritual by which they resubmit themselves to the popular will.

Elitism, strictly speaking, is a belief in the principle that government ought to be confined to individuals (usually power-based in economic, political, military, religious, or academic institutions) who transcend ordinary circumstances by being positioned to make consequential decisions. And while eventually the United States would develop into a nation of laws and institutions capable of surviving corrupt or incompetent public officials, early on America needed an honorable and virtuous elite in order to endure. In his writings on elitism, even Plato expected his "guardians" to transcend selfish interests while furthering community welfare. Fortunately, the founding fathers were such men.[10]

Most of the high-profile American revolutionaries, although they might have rebelled against the previous political elitist doctrine (divine right of kings), remained elitists themselves, moving easily from post to post atop the major institutions. White and male, this aggregation of public figures was hardly representative of the population. Neither, however, had they arrived with the distinguished pedigrees of those movers and shakers who breathed the rarefied political air of either England or France. It is safe to say most of the early patriots—not just the poverty-born Benjamin Franklin and Alexander Hamilton—would have languished in obscurity anywhere else.

Yet, because America never had to endure feudalism, no entrenched, titled, and hereditary aristocracy attempted to block political headway. There were no high church dignitaries, no safely ensconced landlords, and no dug-in army brass to thwart progress in the name of birth and prerogative. The American Revolution sealed any colonial pretensions to nobility—loyalists fled and their estates went up for grabs. The founding fathers had become the propertied, prestigious, and powerful. Laissez-faire[11] capitalism simply did not find natural predators on the seemingly boundless real estate geographically isolated from war-mongering neighbors, teeming with natural resources, and bustling with a ready, willing, and able labor force.

Thomas Jefferson, who usually sounded the popular view that rank, birth, and "tinsel-aristocracy" would finally shrink into insignificance when confronted with the abundant opportunities of the New World, refined the traditional elitist argument in an 1813 exchange with John Adams: "I agree with you that there is a natural aristocracy among men. . . . [T]he grounds of this are virtue and talents. That form of government is best that prevents the ascendancy of artificial aristocrats and provides for the ascendancy of the natural aristocrats, the elite of virtue and talent."[12] In a natural aristocracy, some individuals will rise above others, but their sons and daughters will not enjoy the guarantee inherent in a hereditary aristocracy. If deficient in talent or virtue, American aristocratic progeny would not be immune from economic reorganization, which might thrust a newly emerging elite ahead of them. America enjoys a populist meritocracy, which promises upward mobility through hard work, public education, and the liberal application of common sense.

ARGUMENTS IN FAVOR OF ELITISM

Jean-Jacques Rousseau, who exerted significant sway on the American revolutionaries, wrote in his 1762 *Social Contract*, "In the strict sense of the term, a true democracy has never existed, and never will exist."[13] In *Political Parties*, Robert Michels offers up the ultimate deal maker for elitism with his justification of "The Iron Law of Oligarchy": "society cannot exist without a 'dominant' or 'political' class, and the ruling class, whilst its elements are subject to a frequent partial renewal, nevertheless constitutes the only factor of sufficiently durable efficacy in the history of human development.[14]

If elitism is inevitable, how might the presence of political elites be integrated into a government that purports to establish power in the people? First, democratic elitism must disallow authority to be entrenched by heredity or life-long terms. Constant turnover, "new blood," as it were, tends to minimize the corrupting nature of power. Second, the electorate should be allowed, on a regular basis, to select between competing elites. Arising contenders should not be prevented, at least not in perpetuity, from gaining access to the system. In fact, according to a Florida State University study, there seems to be not only a great deal of upward mobility in this country, but also a robust "circulation of elites."[15] Third, since "dog-eat-dog" elected elites must nibble support from shifting coalitions, they are forestalled, for the most part, from forming permanent monopolistic alliances.[16] Finally, the ordinary man should not be prohibited from playing a pivotal role as well—he can exercise his franchise; pressure the powers that be via petitions, demonstrations, and boycotts; or if really motivated, hoist himself up the success ladder by personally running for office.

The decision to locate the nation's capital in Washington, D.C., permits an apt illustration re the wisdom of fostering a plurality of elites. Philadelphia was the apparent shoo-in for two reasons: geographic centrality and the preponderance of major banking and commercial institutions. Europe, America's role model, traditionally situated centers of government in highly developed urban areas—not in some uninhabited marsh. The property on the Potomac garnered little support until Hamilton's "assumption proposal," a plan to direct the Federal government to undertake the states' post–American Revolution liabilities. The largely debt-free South strenuously resisted until locating the District of Columbia in their neck of the woods was tossed on the table at a Monticello dinner party.

French-born architect Pierre Charles L'Enfant's vision for the nation's capital further evidences the wisdom of fostering a plurality of elites. He included two focal points in his blueprint—the Capitol and the President's Mansion—physically placing the two buildings more than a mile apart to symbolically reinforce the separation of powers between the legislative and executive branches.

Hierarchies are a time-tested, highly efficient method to conduct business, run governments, fight wars, and transfer information. Only by taking "all men are created equal" to the equality of outcome extreme can folks, who supposedly live in the real world, consider some headless amoeba-like organization as a superior alternative to the hierarchical model. While modern management can warble the praises of collaboration over a pecking-order power structure, the buck has to stop somewhere.

Furthermore, all men are *not* created equal—they possess a diversity of abilities, and certainly specific abilities in varying degrees. Further, society does not value abilities equally. Perhaps we should—but migrant farmworkers, musicians, and caregivers do not pull down the same salary, status, and celebrity as software CEOs, rock stars, and campaign consultants. Despite the fact that America aspires to egalitarian ideals, even our representatives in Congress are largely unrepresentative of the average American. Take a careful look at the aphorism "may the best man win." The voter weighs the candidates with respect to "unrepresentative" characteristics such as persuasive power, superior intellect, and good looks. In fact, voters write off office-seekers who parallel their own ordinariness.

In the eighteenth and nineteenth centuries, the threat of tyranny arose from power-hungry and arbitrary elites. Jefferson's support for a constitutional system of checks and balances was launched by his panic over the possibility of an abusive few holding sway over the country. The Bill of Rights was appended to the Constitution to armor majority rule. By the midtwentieth century, however, it was not the elites who presented the threat of tyranny; it was the masses. During the '50s, personality research and a plethora of public opinion surveys documented a surprisingly weak commitment to democratic values, while red-baiter Joseph Mc-Carthy enjoyed widespread support from all strata of society.[17]

Additional arguments supporting elitism fall under, at worst, the belief that the masses are inherently incompetent to govern themselves and, at best, the nature of majority rule as undermining both liberty and culture.

From the ancient Greek philosophers to modern political consultants, proponents of elitism have assumed the public lacks knowledge, rationality, and self-control.[18] Despite a high rate of literacy and mandated public education, empirical studies evidence, year after year, that the average voter is poorly informed, prejudiced, and apathetic.[19] Political scientist Robert Hollinger wrote, "Most people, even with optimum educational opportunities, cannot achieve the sort of rational development that is needed for self government."[20]

Our democratic republic has become synonymous with "majority rule," which, however, can and does undermine liberty. In order to address the resulting tension, the founding fathers attempted to safeguard the minority with the Bill of Rights. In a pluralistic society such as ours, however, unless debate is fostered and furthered (which is unlikely with an apathetic or ignorant populace) minority points of view will, in essence, be silenced.

Further, experts point out that majority rule likewise leads to "lowest common denominator" leveling. The ultimate result is a coarsening of the culture. William Henry pulls out a contemporary example with "a generation of elitist editors and writers who saw journalism, both print and broadcast, as a sacred opportunity to teach and uplift the citizenry [being] supplanted by a mob of shameless panderers who 'edit' by readership survey."[21]

ELITISM DURING THE '50s AND '60s

One only need dust the power grab that is the American presidency today for Franklin Delano Roosevelt's supersized fingerprints.[22] While he may have been justified in wresting considerable chief executive clout during the emergency presented by the depression, his successors never gave it back.

Additionally, after Roosevelt, Americans seemed to carry in their heads an unwritten job description for the president that could not be found under Article II, Section 1, of the Constitution. The leader of the free world must be credentialed not only as a policy advocate, crisis manager, and mediator of foreign affairs, but also as a living symbol of American democracy as well as apparent heir to Washington, Jefferson, Jackson, and Lincoln.

Polling has been keeping elected officials "in touch" with constituents since Franklin Delano Roosevelt signed on Haley Cantril. While haphazardly selected straw polls date back to 1824, when the *Harrisburg Pennsylvanian* and the *Raleigh (North Carolina) Star* first probed political popularity, scientific opinion polls (sampling subjects according to a demographic representation formula) were refined by pioneers George Gallup, Elmo Roper, and Archibald Crossley—just in time for FDR's 1936 race against Alf Landon. The continuous, institutionalized analysis of public opinion is intended to narrow the "credibility gap" between the elitists in office and the populist-favoring electorate. Newly elected U.S. congressmen, senators, and state governors routinely employ polling to inform their decisions. In fact, President Nixon relied on surveys to figure out whether or not he should resign. In 1974, the American public told him, loud and clear, to get out of town.

America was in an elitist mood in 1952. The allure of populism was declining, as economic, political, and military elites were able to wrench authority from decentralized religious, educational, and family institutions. Furthermore, separation among the big three elites was growing mushy. President Dwight D. Eisenhower had come to fear the powerful "merchants of defense" who aided and abetted the arms race with the Soviet Union. In his farewell address (January 17, 1961), he advised the American people to keep an eagle eye on the escalating muscle of the "military–industrial complex." He warned against the potential abuse of power by a massive military coupled with a burgeoning arms industry: "We must never let the weight of this combination endanger our liberties or Democratic processes. We should take nothing for granted."[23]

Who could be more elitist than a general sporting five stars on his epaulets? The mammoth Allied invasion of France on June 6, 1944, served as Dwight D. Eisenhower's foremost military achievement. He turned down all offers to run for the presidency in 1948, claiming the army credo against officers mixing in politics. His party affiliation, too, seemed to be a mystery—Eisenhower hadn't voted once during his quarter century of military service. In fact, he turned a thumbs-down on a $40,000 offer from *McCall's* magazine to reveal his political allegiance. Just before the 1952 campaign, however, Eisenhower allowed a supporter to leak that he had gone Republican in the 1950 New York elections. That November, he effortlessly trounced Democratic candidate Governor Adlai E. Stevenson of Illinois and gathered around him a cabinet of economic elites—facetiously described as "eight millionaires and a plumber"[24]—along with a rigid (military-type) hierarchy headed by a hitherto nonexistent chief of staff.

The other elitist president during this period was John F. Kennedy. After JFK's older brother, Joseph Jr., was killed in World War II, the senior

Kennedy turned to his number-two son to bring the Kennedy name into the political arena. The old Boston Irish political machine,[25] JFK's *PT 109* war record, and oodles of Joe Sr.'s banking, shipbuilding, real estate, liquor importing, and motion picture money netted twenty-nine-year-old Kennedy a seat in the Eightieth Congress. The Eleventh District elected the "A new generation offers a leader" candidate by a margin of seventy-eight thousand votes,[26] but Kennedy knew little about Boston and was, in fact, forced to rent an apartment to establish legal residence. His fellow Representatives regarded the frequently absent JFK as intelligent, indifferent, and something of a playboy.

Kennedy couldn't wait to move on to the Senate—in 1954, he defeated Henry Cabot Lodge Jr. by 70,737 votes. Kennedy, who considered himself wealthier, better educated, and more ambitious than his colleagues, didn't bother to make any more chums in the Senate than he did in the House—a *faux pas* that would come back to haunt him when his pet presidential programs got bogged down on the Hill, unable to escape congressional arithmetic. While candidate Kennedy never had to worry as long as Daddy nourished his campaign coffers, governing Kennedy sorely needed the political capital he failed to bank while serving under the Capitol dome.

After the Eisenhower avalanche in 1956, Kennedy immediately set his sights on the 1960 Democratic presidential nomination. Television, hundreds of speaking engagements, and an extraordinary public relations coup for the '50s—the cover of *Time*—boosted Kennedy into national prominence and, ultimately, the Oval Office.

As first family, the Kennedys seized the public imagination as an American equivalent to royalty. Courtesy of wife Jacqueline, high culture was ushered into a tastefully redecorated White House. The couple hosted recitals, concerts, and poetry readings. JFK peopled the West Wing with luminous intellectuals—especially academics who admired commanding and charismatic political figures, a subject that Kennedy examined at great length in his own books. The man who exhorted the nation to "ask not what your country can do for you; ask what you can do for your country," ironically saw himself as an idealist, sans the usual illusions.

After Kennedy's death, Jackie intimated that the brief, shining moments of his presidency were reminiscent of the legend of Camelot. Journalists, historians, and the American public helped polish the image of JFK as a noble knight—until revelations of sexual indiscretions decades later tarnished the armor.

Prior to Watergate, the voters seemed to share the myth that, upon inauguration, each occupant of the Oval Office would eventually become infused with competence, morality, and benevolence. They really believed that a president's interests would become subservient to the interests of the country, and media journalists weren't about to disabuse them of that faith, holding back every scrap of scandal about Eisenhower and Kennedy that might denigrate the presidency.

Harry Truman observed that a good politician once had to be 75 percent ability and 25 percent actor, but he could see the day when the reverse would be true.[27] By the mid-'50s image *was* everything. In fact, Joe Kennedy employed his own public relations apparatus as well as his media friendships to suppress the future president's medical problems, daughter Rosemary's retardation, daughter Kathleen's affair, son Teddy's driving record, and various other family shortcomings, real and imagined.

That great image maker, television, gave elitist candidates the power to pass themselves off as "gee-whiz" populists or don any special interest hat that might help them succeed at the ballot box.[28] Dwight D. Eisenhower was the first presidential hopeful to discover he could exploit his popular appeal through the emerging medium. Rosser Reeves, who brought us TV commercials promising "fast, fast, fast" Anacin relief, produced the highly successful "I Like Ike" and "Man on the Street" political spots that introduced the general's pleasing personality into millions of living rooms. Most historians credit Kennedy's vigorous and energetic showing during the televised debates as the deciding factor in his presidential election. In fact, Richard Nixon, in summarizing his performance on September 26, 1960, remembers, "at the conclusion of our postmortem, I recognized the basic mistake I had made. I had concentrated too much on substance and not enough on appearance."[29]

SUMMARY OF THE PLOT

When the Republicans took over the House in 1995, Newt Gingrich handed out a reading list to incoming conservative freshmen. Allen Drury's *Advise and Consent* was listed as number 1. At a time when young people weren't even voting, the novel sparked an interest in public service and garnered significant admiration for the grand yet grubby world of politics. The movie went on to detonate the dome right off the Capitol, as the story exposed the high-level machinations going on right under the nose of Lady Liberty.

Otto Preminger's 1962 portrait of the Senate is nothing like Frank Capra's idealized *Mr. Smith Goes to Washington*. Based on the Pulitzer Prize–winning best-seller, the film pivots on the confirmation of a controversial secretary of state nominee, Robert Leffingwell (Henry Fonda). The president (Franchot Tone) marshals his forces in the Senate, led by majority leader Robert Munson (Walter Pidgeon) and majority whip Stanley Danta (Paul Ford). They face off against populist Seabright Cooley (Charles Laughton) and minority leader Senator Warren Strickland (Will Geer).

Brigham Anderson (Don Murray), who chairs the Foreign Policy sub-committee conducting the confirmation hearings, refuses to line up be-hind Leffingwell. He's morally repulsed by the fact that the nominee com-mitted perjury, with the seeming knowledge and approval of the president, by failing to mention his youthful involvement in a Communist cell. Anderson is unwilling to acquiesce to the situational ethics currently steering Washington in what he considers the wrong direction. His foot-dragging provides the opportunity for ruthlessly ambitious Senator Fred Van Ackerman (George Grizzard) to attempt to blackmail Anderson with proof of a homosexual encounter Anderson experienced while stationed in Honolulu. Cornered, Anderson commits suicide.

Advise and Consent is a tale of two secrets. Otto Preminger, unlike Charles Dickens, leaves his audience to decide whether Leffingwell or Anderson has done the far, far better thing.

THE SENATE AS AN ENDURING HIERARCHY

Allen Drury claimed the greatest publicity his book ever received was a photo of John F. Kennedy and Richard M. Nixon poring over a dog-eared copy of *Advise and Consent*. The two senators had bumped into each other at the airport, and an alert newspaper photographer documented the event for publication; Doubleday bought the photo to run over advertis-ing copy reading "nearly everybody's reading *Advise and Consent*."

When Dolly Harrison (Gene Tierney) hosts Lady Kitty Maudulayne (Hillary Eaves) and Madame Celestine Barre (Michele Monteau) on a con-gressional tour, the two (as spouses of the British and French ambassa-dors, respectively) are probably too sophisticated for the American civics lesson presented in the film by their socialite tour guide. Harrison is re-ally speaking to the folks at the Bijou, who hadn't been subjected to this much information about the inner workings of the Senate since Clarissa Saunders spelled out the progress of a bill or the fine art of filibustering to Jefferson Smith in *Mr. Smith Goes to Washington.*

In the *Advise and Consent* civics lesson, Otto Preminger, "the only ab-solute dictator ever to make a film about democracy," was aiming "to show that the power of the executive branch, of the President, is very much checked and balanced by the power of the Senate which represents the people."[30] Preminger, with all the fervor of a naturalized citizen, suc-cessfully conveys a democratic republic in which no single individual holds enough power to overtake the entire government.

If you pay attention during the film, you will learn that the Senate con-sists of two senators from every state, each serving a six-year term, with a third of the terms expiring every two years. The Connecticut Compromise (July 16, 1787) provided equal representation from each state in the upper house (as opposed to the representation based on population in the House of Representatives) and somewhat leveled the playing field between large and small states. Originally, the Constitution mandated that senators be chosen by state legislators instead of by popular election, but that provision never sat well with the voters, especially populists. As early as 1892, the People's Party included the direct election of U.S. senators as a platform plank, but it took twenty-one years for the Seventeenth Amendment to become a reality.

The Constitution gives the Senate certain unique powers. In addition to ratifying treaties, the Senate may accept or reject, by majority vote, presidential appointments to federal judgeships (including the Supreme Court), ambassadorships, cabinet posts, and high-level positions in the executive branch of the federal government. While hardly a rubber stamp (given the amount of debate these appointments engender), the Senate usually makes the president happy. Rejection was rare during the '50s and '60s, although during the Eisenhower administration, the Senate turned down Lewis Strauss for secretary of commerce.

The Constitution gives the vice president the task of presiding over the Senate, although these days he rarely attends routine debate, showing up only for important votes or parliamentary decisions. The vice president has no vote unless the members of the Senate are deadlocked. During his eight years in office, John Adams cast thirty-one votes, more than any subsequent vice president, due in no small part to the modest size of the Senate. Additionally, after Adams's initial foray into Senate debate, the membership voted to silence the vice president. "My office is too great a restraint upon such a Son of Liberty," the chagrined Adams was heard to lament.[31]

The president *pro tempore* of the Senate, usually the most senior senator of the majority party, is more likely to officiate day to day. In the final scene of the movie, Seabright Cooley can't help but milk the drama as he assumes his place on the dais. The president's death, which elevates Harley Hudson to the Oval Office, doesn't present Cooley with his first opportunity to preside—the job would have been old hat to the grizzled old-timer, who would often substitute for an otherwise occupied vice president.

If the Senate, as Washington correspondents have been claiming for decades, "is the most exclusive club in town," then the majority leader and his whip (Bob Munson and Paul Danta) are the inner circle. Elected by members of the party in control, the majority leader directs Senate floor activity and helps coordinate the timing of legislative debate. The primary political resources of the leader are parliamentary knowledge and persuasion, although some individuals holding the office have been known to strong-arm or overtly threaten resistant colleagues. Normally, quid pro quo trades are made—assistance with proposed legislation, prize committee assignments, or the promise of home state pork customarily grease the passage of key votes.

Similar leadership exists on the other side of the aisle. Minority leader Warren Strickland, in constant touch with his troops, has already counted noses before breakfast and is able to inform Munson that eighteen to twenty members of his party will oppose the nomination of Leffingwell.

The bulk of Senate business is conducted through a highly structured committee system. There are more than a dozen standing committees considering and reporting on all legislation, one special committee on aging, three investigative select committees, and one hundred subcommittees. A Foreign Relations subcommittee, with the power to hold hearings and conduct investigations, poked into Leffingwell's nomination. Individual senators, on average, serve on three committees and eight subcommittees.

The majority party selects chairs, who wield considerable prestige and influence. In practice, the deciding factor is seniority—the chair usually goes to the majority party senator with the longest continuous service on a particular committee. That's why when Munson passes over Fred Van Ackerman in favor of junior Brig Anderson, Ackerman considers it a slap in the face.

The Senate determines its own rules. Perhaps the most distinctive feature of Senate procedure is the tradition of extended open debate—that is, any senator can mouth off about a bill or an issue indefinitely, unless two-thirds of the senators present and voting adopt a motion to close debate. Jefferson Smith's twenty-three-hour and thirty-minute filibuster in *Mr. Smith Goes to Washington* was an unforgettable illustration of this obstructionist strategy. During the 1950s and 1960s, southern Democratic senators frequently employed filibusters to delay or quash civil rights measures. In 1975, the Senate altered its standing Rule XXII to permit sixty senators to end debate, which, while an easier means of curtailing the filibuster, hardly eliminated the practice.

Leaders of the two major parties, who always sit near the front of the chamber, are the only members who have preassigned seats. The other senators may choose their desks at the start of each session. Years ago, seniority carried a front-row position but post-1985, when gavel-to-gavel television coverage became available on C-SPAN, many senior senators opted for the more camera-friendly locations in the rear.

Although there is no mention of political parties in the Constitution, the Senate since the beginning has been organized along party lines. The center aisle divides Democrats from Republicans—the party with the greatest number sits to the right of the presiding officer, and the minority party takes their places to the left. Desks can be literally moved from one side to the other to reflect electoral victories. The Democrats were large and in charge from 1955 to 1981.

Senators have also been carving their names in the antique wooden writing tables ever since Daniel Webster. You may remember a quaking Jimmy Stewart grabbing hold of the desk supposedly used by the Senate's greatest orator as he lurches to his feet to deliver his maiden address.

However, Capra exercised more than a little poetic license in *Mr. Smith Goes to Washington*—the Webster desk is always assigned to the senior senator from New Hampshire.

Senators take great pains to maintain ties (business associations, club memberships, and religious affiliations) back home. Even after building seniority and/or when coming from a safe district, senators cannot completely shed their parochialism. Any claim to national leadership must be hedged by personal attention to local constituents. While Old Glory is prominently displayed in Brig Anderson's office, the state seal, flanked by two dramatic Utah landscapes, leaves no doubt with visiting constituents where their senator has left his heart.

Gracie Allen, in her lightweight tome, *How to Become President*, joked "the Senate is the only show in the world where the cash customers have to sit in the balcony."[32] The essential ingredient to Senate success, the amount of time senators must spend cultivating wealthy donors, was conspicuously absent in the movie. While Vice President Hudson does reminisce about the days when he was the "Happy Governor from Delaware counting revenue from corporate set-ups, having tea with the duPonts," there is no other mention of what California Lieutenant Governor Jesse Unruh called "the mother's milk of politics."

Campaign financing irrevocably yokes corporate or personal wealth with the political system. According to *Fortune* magazine, as of May 1968 half the nation's sixty-six known centimillionaires were also top political donors.[33] Will Rogers contended that politics had gotten so expensive "that it takes lots of money to even get beat with."[34] In fact, journalists rolled their eyes in disbelief when the 2002 gubernatorial contest in California topped $140 million.

When Munson rebukes the president with the admonition "the U.S. Senate is no trifle," the senator from Michigan isn't just honing his proficiency for understatement. Because of the Senate's unique "advise and consent" authority over presidential cabinet appointments and the fact that longer terms and smaller membership concentrate political clout, the Senate is commonly regarded as the more prestigious and influential of the two houses of Congress. It is likewise interesting to note that the Senate's 9,126 square feet are slightly greater than half the size of the House, which quarters more than four times as many members.

When Herbert H. Lehman was asked why he was running for a second Senate term after serving as governor of New York, he kidded, "After you have once ridden behind a motorcycle escort, you are never the same again."[35] Lehman was being ironic—senators clearly brandish more brawn than state governors, despite the latter being able to call out the state police. More significant, there's something so beguiling about working among "monuments to monumental men"[36] in Washington that it trumps the view from any governor's manse.

Senators, who are required by law to be at least thirty years old, U.S. citizens for nine years, and bona fide residents of their home state, are clearly unrepresentative representatives. When C. Wright Mills wrote *The Power Elite* in 1956, a senator was usually male (there was a single exception), native born, Protestant, solidly upper or middle class, college educated, and around fifty-seven years of age. Most had previously held local or state office. It should come as no surprise, despite Shakespeare's directive, that 65 percent listed "attorney" as their nonpolitical occupation, at a time when only 0.1 percent of Americans practiced law.[37]

As VIPs in the nation's capital, senators expected to have flights held for them, to waltz into government offices and walk out with confidential records, to get the news before it hit the *Washington Post*, and to live where everybody, from paperboys to flight attendants to doormen, knew their names. The downside, however, was that after a while some senators came to believe themselves inherently worthy of the perks, privileges, and prestige that accompanied the office. H. L. Mencken may have been right when he observed, "the typical politician is not only a rascal but also a jackass, so he greatly values the puerile notoriety and adulation that sensible men try to avoid."[38] Yet, critic Mark Shivas offers a more charitable, albeit idealistic, point of view: "They are ordinary human beings who rise to tasks of giant stature, and it is the relation between their ordinary humanity, and the size of their tasks, which makes them people of stature once more."[39]

CODE OF CONDUCT

Political commentator Charles Krauthammer once pointed out, "If we insist that public life be reserved for those whose personal history is pristine, we are not going to get paragons of virtue running our affairs. We will get the very rich, who contract out the messy things of life; the very dull, who have nothing to hide and nothing to show; and the very devious, expert at covering their tracks and ambitious enough to risk their discovery."[40] And Krauthammer didn't even know Fred Van Ackerman. Allen Drury positioned his McCarthyesque character on the left with the rationale that "every once in a while, the electoral process [without regard to liberal or conservative] tosses to the top someone smart and glib and evil."[41] What Van Ackerman and McCarthy shared was a plan to demagogue their way to the top via a rising fear of communism. They likewise caused their colleagues to become a cohesive, common-goaled institution—united against them.

Members of a top social stratum such as the Senate know each other, see each other socially and, in making decisions, take each another into account. This power elite by and large forms an impenetrable social and psychological entity, defined by what separates them from everybody else. Harvard historian and descendant of two presidents, Henry Brooks Adams, reminds us that "Although the Senate is much given to admiring, in its members, a superiority less obvious or quite invisible to outsiders, one Senator seldom proclaims his own inferiority to another, and still more, seldom likes to be told of it."[42]

What has kept the Senate from devolving into a snarl of scrapping siblings is a code of behavior based on the traditional elitist values of self-discipline, self-denial, civility, and honor. Lord Chesterfield, chiefly remembered for his *Letters to His Son* (1774), could have been outlining the Senate's unwritten but rigidly enforced stipulations when he wrote about "an absolute command of your temper; . . . dexterity enough to conceal a truth without telling a lie; sagacity enough to read other people's countenances; and serenity enough not to let them discover anything by yours."[43]

Political scientist Ralph K. Huitt, who observed the Senate during the early '60s, found that successful senators are not only circumspect, courteous, and collegial, but are also expected to serve a lengthy apprenticeship, to specialize in few policy areas, to put in interminable work hours, to deposit political capital for future use, and to master the art of accommodation—simply stated, "you have to go along to get along." More than anything else, Huitt found a senator must be "proud of the institution and ready to defend its traditions and perquisites against all outsiders."[44]

Van Ackerman may lack self-discipline, self-denial, and civility, but what really scuttles his career is his dishonor, precisely defined by the dull razor blade Brig Anderson uses to end his life. Even the irascible Seab Cooley manages to scrounge up a little integrity when the majority leader not so diplomatically nails him with his culpability in the Anderson tragedy—his ingrained sense of honor guilt trips the old curmudgeon into eating crow.

Van Ackerman justifies surrounding himself with an entourage of sycophants by referring to them as his "brain trust." "You can't hold down a senator's job just by kissing babies and shaking hands these days," he lectures the majority leader. His arrogance seems to know no bounds. He expects his fledgling peace organization to morph into a nationwide movement. By his calculation, he's well on his way to becoming a household name.

If only Van Ackerman could meet his colleagues halfway. He doesn't even seem able to respond to a little good-natured kidding. When a snickering Danta, who sits on the Indian Affairs investigative select subcommittee, inquires if Van Ackerman intends to make peace with the Kickapoo Indians, Van Ackerman walks off in a huff. Apparently the junior senator from Wyoming, who rages, "Do you think it's funny?" at every opportunity, doesn't believe anything is.

To be perfectly fair, no Dutch uncle ever sits Van Ackerman down and reveals the facts of life, Senate-wise. When Van Ackerman clumsily lobbies for subcommittee chair, the president's adviser and the majority leader seem to indulge his boorishness. When he disrupts Dolly Harrison's party with a rude rant, she forgives his juvenile breach of courtesy. When he presumes to speak for Leffingwell, who is scurrying off to discredit a damaging witness, the controversial nominee merely grants Van Ackerman his First Amendment rights. Apparently having earned permanent outsider status, the senator from Wyoming isn't even considered worth mentoring.

Van Ackerman just can't understand why Anderson is "in the club" and he's not. "You force me to offend you," confesses Munson and still Van Ackerman doesn't get the hint—he later volunteers to bully Anderson into "cooperating." Van Ackerman seems to be a pariah in training: Seab Cooley rushes by without making eye contact, Lafe Smith (Peter Lawford) belittles his sexist attack on Senator Bessie Adams (Betty White) with "oh, Fred, come off it," and the president refuses to return his phone messages.[45]

What is really disturbing is Van Ackerman's palpable if not psychopathic envy of Brig "he knows how to be a senator" Anderson. At the televised hearing, the limelight-seeking Ackerman can hardly resist the opportunity to grandstand. He escalates his aside snipes at Anderson—feigning outrage at his incompetence, either from the sidelines or by occasionally slithering down to a microphone. Outside the caucus room, he relentlessly rides Anderson, culminating in a not-so-thinly veiled threat on the floor of the Senate that is so over the top it raises the ire of the normally complacent vice president himself.

The majority leader and whip have realized from day one that they have a problem with Van Ackerman. "He doesn't belong here," Danta warns. "Someday, you'll have to cut him off the vine." Without missing a beat, Munson murmurs, "he'll fall off." That day finally comes with the knowledge of Van Ackerman's role in Anderson's death. "We tolerate just about anything here, Fred," admits Munson. "But you've dishonored us."

In the book, Van Ackerman is censured. In the film, he's allowed to stay on because Munson and Danta don't want Anderson's "tired old sin" trotted out in a Senate investigation. "You can stay," he is told, but first Munson, then Danta adds the ominous proviso "if you want to," implying that being shunned by one's colleagues is a far more stinging penalty than being expelled outright.

While both book and movie remind us "that any similarity to individuals living or dead is purely coincidental," Andrew Sarris believes *Advise and Consent* fits into an entirely new film genre called "political science fiction, in which fact and fantasy are peculiarly interdependent."[46] Drury doesn't provide much information about Van Ackerman as a child, but if he was anything like McCarthy, he was probably withdrawn, shy around strangers, and attached to his mother at the hip. However, just like McCarthy, Van Ackerman has grown into a loud and aggressive adult, swamping childhood insecurities with frequent and highly agitated displays of temper. Just like McCarthy, Van Ackerman is gifted at abuse, self-dramatization, brazenness, and duplicity; he also physically resembles the youngest member of the Eightieth Congress. Folks may consider bullying a crude political tactic, but it proved stunningly effective for the real-life McCarthy, as well for the fictional Van Ackerman.

Drury, who attended the races with McCarthy in the early '50s, remembers the freshman senator as "a harmless politician who was just looking to make his mark on history." To his admirers, "Tail Gunner Joe" became heroism personified, the lone Marine vet taking on the nation's power elite. Scholars disagree as to whether McCarthy expressed a basic populist appeal. Although he attacked eastern intellectuals and the establishment, there is little evidence that McCarthy gave any thought to the welfare of the masses. His support came mainly from the extreme right.

The Senate survives a diversity of opinion not just because of enforced standards of civility (e.g., senators address all comments to "Mr. President," never to each other), but also because each senator, with maturity and experience, finds that the partisan view with which he arrived softens as he embraces the concept of collegiality.

The majority leader, as the ballot battler for his party, attempts to straddle the ideological middle. Although antagonistic to appeasement and leery about Leffingwell's qualifications for secretary of state, Munson is forced to throw his support behind his president's choice. Even after the movie ends, the audience knows that Munson must gird his loins for the next political battle, namely, getting Hudson's secretary of state candidate confirmed.

Drury admits he modeled his Democratic majority leader after Republican Senator Robert A. Taft.[47] Slender, soft-spoken, and scholarly, Taft seemed the polar opposite of his portly presidential father. Like Munson, this eight-term legislator, known as "Mr. Integrity" to his Senate colleagues, toiled tirelessly behind the scenes, with unruffled modesty and quiet efficiency. Taft is the only senator memorialized by a monument, and his name has become synonymous with strict constitutional constructionism. The Taft–Hartley Act of 1947, especially its mandatory "cooling off" period, has short-circuited countless strikes. Most relevant to *Advise and Consent*, Taft refused to buckle under to McCarthy when the red-baiting senator sought to block Eisenhower's nomination of Charles Bohlen as ambassador to the Soviet Union.

Drury uses Munson as his moral plumb line. In fact, in the book, Munson resigns in the wake of Anderson's demise. In the movie, although disappointed that the vice president doesn't exercise his tie-breaking vote to confirm Leffingwell, the majority leader informs the new president that he can count on his support.

There would be nothing but gridlock if senatorial divisions split along ideological lines on every issue. For two centuries, the American Senate attempted to put the nation's business before partisan politics. Drury, however, noted a significant shift during the '90s: "politicians are more divisive, less civil than before. These people just have to realize that if they want to get anywhere they have to be more accommodating with their opposites in trying deals out."[48]

The nomination of Leffingwell seems to deepen philosophical differences in the fictional Senate as well. Battle lines are drawn along Leffingwell's seemingly innocuous phrase "outworn principles." An incensed Cooley rants, "I'd rather go out of this world standing on my two hind legs and fighting like a man for the things I believe in than to yield and concede and crawl till there was nothing left of our freedoms and our way of life than a handful of lost dreams and a fistful of dried dust." Accommodationists, however, agree with Leffingwell that "this kind of damn the torpedoes, full speed ahead" thinking became anachronistic in the nuclear age.

While a "let's agree to disagree" mindset works with policy issues, it doesn't seem to translate to the personal level. When the vice president muses, "what I don't understand, Brig, is why you are going it alone," he underlines the irrationality of Anderson's final act. Brig may be Munson and Danta's idea of a senator, but he clearly disdains "all for one and one for all" collegiality every time he thwarts overtures of support.

The majority leader, whose chief occupation is to bridge troubled waters, is more than willing to hatch an acceptable compromise. Cooley, out cooling his heels on a park bench, volunteers his help as he slyly confesses, "you have a very powerful, devious friend [in me]." Smith, apprised of the extortion attempts by Anderson's wife, actively seeks out his friend to extend advice and assistance. Even Hudson proffers a sympathetic ear on the plane ride back to Old Foggybottom.

Anderson's no-way-out feelings pivot on the premise that he is right, and anyone who insists on wiggle-room-sized, situational ethics is wrong. His absolutist "there is no room for accommodation in an honorable man" position costs him his life. It would seem that both Van Ackerman and Anderson are plagued by a demon whose name is Pride.

Alger Hiss assumed major political significance during the Cold War, transcending the specific issues and evidence brought out at his trials. Testimony confirmed the existence of a critical internal security breach in the State Department, semilegitimizing the witch hunts conducted by both the House Committee on Un-American Activities and Senator Joseph McCarthy during the early '50s. According to Andrew Sarris, "one might go further and say that the Hiss–Chambers confrontation has cast its shadow over the entire book. Without this historical reference in the mind of the reader, the plot of *Advise and Consent* would collapse under the weight of its melodrama."[49]

Even without Leffingwell's "egghead" soliloquy, moviegoers instantly recognized the arrogant Alger Hiss in the character of Robert A. Leffingwell.

A former State Department official, Hiss was born into a patrician Baltimore family. He was an exceptional student, graduating Phi Beta Kappa from Johns Hopkins. One of the best and brightest at Harvard Law, Hiss developed a relationship with Felix Frankfurter, who subsequently sent Hiss to Washington to clerk for Supreme Court justice Oliver Wendell Holmes.[50]

Hiss's friendship with Frankfurter and his marriage to a socialist sent his politics careening to the left. Being tapped to represent the United States at the Dumbarton Oaks, Yalta, and San Francisco conferences positioned Hiss on the fast track. The future looked rosy until Whittaker Chambers, an admitted ex-Communist and senior editor at *Time*, identified Hiss as a member of a Communist cell operating in Washington, D.C., during the mid-'30s.[51]

Hiss, unlike Leffingwell, who was able to use Herbert Gelman's mental illness to invalidate claims made against him, was eventually convicted on two counts of perjury. Hiss's conviction, however, rode on two pieces of circumstantial evidence—typewritten facsimiles of original State Department documents and summaries in Hiss's own handwriting. Hiss went to his grave claiming he was framed. His misfortune, however, vaulted Richard Nixon into the vice presidency and Whittaker Chambers onto the bestseller list.

Even though Gelman's testimony is riddled with inaccuracies, he basically tells the truth ("if I did [remember for sure], would anyone believe me?") about Robert Leffingwell, Hardiman Fletcher (AKA James Morton), and Max Bukowski. Leffingwell, whom the Russian ambassador Vasily Tashikov calls "our friend," avoids being exposed as a Communist, since Brig Anderson, in the hopes that the president will voluntarily withdraw his nomination, withholds Fletcher's confession.

THE LOYAL POPULIST OPPOSITION

Seabright Cooley came to Washington the same year Woodrow Wilson, "that professor from Princeton," moved into the White House. The senator from South Carolina considers himself a populist, so populist, in fact, that he rides the city bus rather than taking a taxi as other senators do.

His language and his manner arise out of the Deep South. He doesn't just sit, he "settles himself like an old bull frog on a lily pad." When he spots a despondent Anderson, he observes, "you look like you've got the burden, son. You've got 'em treed [like a possum]. Look out they don't shinny down on top of you." When Lafe Smith accuses Cooley of acting out of an "aged crust of prejudice," Cooley laments that Leffingwell has caused "able, sensitive young senators, taught courtesy at their mothers' knees, to turn upon their elders."

His opponents aren't just folks with differing points of view, they are evil. Not only are they evil, they will lead the country "straight to perdition." In answer to the majority leader's question, "Have you had your fire and brimstone this morning?" Cooley drawls out the "yes" for three beats and then adds "laced with hot bourbon and branch water. 'Spect you can see the flames comin' out of my ears." At the end of the film, when both Cooley and Munson release their votes, the roll call reveals one surprise after another. Cooley chortles "I haven't had so much fun since the cayenne pepper hit the fan."

Cooley feels compelled to flee his Senate office confines for a few hours each day, winter and summer. His faith in the healing power of nature leads him to an elm-lined park across from the Capitol where he ponders the powerful and devious elite. When the contemptuous Leffingwell labels his principles as "outworn," Cooley can scarcely contain his consternation. Yet, when Munson gets Cooley to realize that his personal attempt at blackmail has contributed to a colleague's death (Cooley had threatened to tell the press that Anderson was withholding vital information about Leffingwell's Communist ties if Anderson did not publicly oppose Leffingwell), Cooley is ashamed. He realizes he has been motivated by his own oversized ego and petty vindictiveness. He shocks the Senate by doing the right thing and asking forgiveness. In fact, his apology is the first discourse he delivers without hubris or hyperbole.

There would be none of these new-fangled television politics for Cooley—he is committed to the personal touch. Drury writes: "There followed a short, intensive campaign in which he had only token opposition but during which he visited every town and hamlet in the district and personally shook the hands of all but a scattered few of its residents."[52] Despite the fact that America has welcomed the age of high-powered media campaigns, folks, especially southern folks, never forget the man who knocks on the front door.

Political commentator Chris Matthews unequivocally identifies Seabright Cooley as Richard Russell, "the quiet, backroom power-broker who ruled the U.S. Senate single-handedly in the late 40s and early 50s."[53] The Georgian's authority in the Senate was unquestioned. He, like Cooley, was considered a one-man check on presidential authority and a master in the art of the parliamentary maneuver.

Both factual and fictional characters came from big southern families and were raised in small Southern towns. Russell was born in Winder (Georgia), the fourth of thirteen children. Like Cooley, he was a lifelong bachelor and student of American history. Further, Russell, like Cooley, never retired at night without reading the *Congressional Record* from cover to cover.

Russell entered politics during the early '30s. While, as a populist, he felt that a crisis of depression-era magnitude had justified FDR's massive government intervention, he opposed any future Democratic presidential plans to build on the New Deal. He also objected to loosening immigration laws. At the heart of Russell's populism was his unwavering belief in personal freedom. He tried to keep the family farm as the centerpiece of American life. He favored distributing surplus commodities to the poor, liberal farm loans, and increased agricultural research spending. His biggest frustration came with the seemingly relentless midcentury urbanization of America.

Charles Laughton, who played Seabright Cooley in the film, journeyed to Washington several weeks before rehearsals started. He and Allen Drury became fast friends during the filming. Laughton honed his portrayal of Drury's favorite character by observing John C. Stennis, Senate leader of the southern conservative wing of the Democratic Party and expert on national defense, for several weeks. Laughton was able to corner the busy senator and coax him into reading Cooley's lines into a tape recorder. After weeks of practice, Laughton finally mastered the Mississippian's syrupy drawl.[54] Laughton also met Senator Hubert Humphrey at a party Preminger threw for Congress and the *Advise and Consent* cast and crew. The gregarious gentleman from Minnesota, who seemed to know everyone in the room, astounded Laughton. "How is your niece, Mary Jane, getting along?" "Is your mother-in-law, Mrs. Compton, feeling better?" "Did your brother Sam get that New York job?" "My God," exclaimed Laughton, realizing both politics and acting are high-maintenance careers, "those guys are on all the time."[55]

ELITISM FANTASY THEMES

If, as British classicist Enoch Powell contends, "a populist politician is a politician who say things because he believes them to be popular,"[56] then what does an elitist politician say? Well, the last thing he will admit is that he is an elitist. Yet, since voters seem to lust after the same things that elitists do, namely, knowledge, sex, money, and success, they, like populists, may not be immune to the allure of the well-placed fantasy theme.

Knowledge Is Power

This fantasy theme is derived from the wisdom of Francis Bacon. When the British statesman and philosopher wrote *"Nam et ipsa scientia potestas est,"* he wasn't kidding.[57]

In *Advise and Consent*, the president denies Harley M. Hudson (Lew Ayres) information to keep him weak and ineffective. Vice President Truman was almost totally ignorant of Roosevelt's chronic illness, possessed only a broad overview of Roosevelt's plans, and like FDR's other vice presidents was left completely out of the loop when the president made important policy decisions. In the film, Hudson is forced to ask the unaskable ("How is the president's health"), since he hasn't been called into the Oval Office in six weeks. Having heard rumors that all was not well, he is forced to pump the majority leader for information. Next in line to an ailing executive, Hudson wants and needs to be prepared.

According to the Constitution, the vice president has only two jobs—to preside over the Senate and to remain available, 24/7, to take the oath of office should the president die, fall ill, or be removed from office. Truman began to sit behind his "the buck stops here" sign only eighty-three days after being sworn in as vice president. In fact, the thirty-third president had to hit the ground running—he spent his first year bringing a world war to an end, rebuilding Europe, and stopping Soviet expansion.

John Adams came up with the first vice president joke by describing his job as "the most insignificant office that ever the Invention of Man contrived or his Imagination conceived."[58] He was the first to experience the paradox of languishing purposelessly on the outside while being a proverbial heartbeat away from the inside. Subsequent occupants of the office have simply lengthened the list of complaints. In his book *The Vice President,* Finley Peter Dunne speaks in terms of inhabiting a prestigious political prison.[59] The observation "The vice-presidency ain't worth a pitcher of warm piss" is generally attributed to John Nance Garner, the Texan serving under FDR as the thirty-second vice president of the United States.[60] His paucity of passion for the New Deal earned him the silent treatment, a modus operandi Roosevelt perfected by the time Truman moved into Blair House in 1945.

In 1944, the Democrats tapped Truman as Roosevelt's running mate after weeks of Machiavellian maneuvering over retaining the controversial, ultraliberal Henry A. Wallace on the ticket. Truman, like "housewives' delight" Harley Hudson, emerged as a happy compromise and was nominated on the third ballot.

Neither Hudson nor Truman hungered for the White House. When Truman received word that FDR had passed away, he confessed, in all humility, that there must have been a million men better qualified to assume the office. The fictional vice president likewise fears he lacks guts to govern. "The country can go to hell," says Hudson, "before I can grow big enough to see over the desk."

Hudson naming his own secretary of state starts out as a spur-of-the-moment decision, but something happens to the vice president after he learns of the president's demise. He commits, and with that commitment he seems to acquire the stature and self-assurance befitting the presidency. In fact, Hudson's demeanor is more than faintly reminiscent of the decisiveness that characterized Truman once he stepped out of the shadow of FDR. Within ninety days of becoming president, Truman would decide to drop the atomic bomb.[61]

Hudson and Truman were the same, in public or private—ethical, empathetic, and easygoing. Each was customarily addressed by his first name, until that twinkling of an instant in which a man's death elevated each to "Mr. President." Brig Anderson, after briefly chatting with the vice president on the plane, has already arrived at the conclusion that Hudson is "probably the most underestimated man in Washington." Equally underestimated, Truman was probably the last president with whom ordinary people could identify. The blunt, salty, and unpretentious populist was living testimony that, indeed, in America, anyone could become president.

Power Is the Greatest Aphrodisiac

The title of this fantasy theme originated with Henry Kissinger, the influential and prestigious secretary of state under Richard Nixon and Gerald Ford.[62] Also a foreign policy consultant to John Kennedy and Lyndon Johnson, Kissinger restored U.S. relations with the People's Republic of China, negotiated a truce in Vietnam, and arranged, via "shuttle diplomacy, " a cease-fire in the Arab–Israeli War of 1973. He shaped the foreign policy of four presidents. With a Nobel Prize on the mantelpiece, Kissinger found he could date pretty much whomever he pleased.

From Benjamin Franklin to William Clinton, women have found political powerhouses particularly irresistible. Franklin was nicknamed "Papa Ben" as the result of exercising his sexual proclivities during an ambassadorship to France. Grover Cleveland couldn't start a stump speech without getting heckled by "Ma, Ma, where's my Pa?" James Garfield and Franklin Roosevelt both took mistresses, but not to the White House. Clinton was caught lying about his Oval Office trysts with Monica Lewinsky and when John F. Kennedy's extramarital dalliances became common knowledge, they wiped the shine off of Camelot.

The sexually compulsive Lafe Smith was not, according to Drury, modeled after the thirty-fifth president but was, in fact, a composite of several randy senators.[63] Kennedy was so miffed that Drury hadn't intentionally immortalized him, that he never invited the *Advise and Consent* novelist to the White House. You can understand why Kennedy, as well as many viewers, might have thought Lafe was really JFK. Not only is Smith played by Kennedy's real-life brother-in-law, Peter Lawford, but also his character is a real lady-killer. Invited to lunch by the French ambassador's wife within days of her arrival and caught hustling a "5'8" blonde, little cleft in the chin, black dress, mink stole" out of his hotel room before breakfast, Smith with his philandering causes the majority leader to deliver a stern lecture about the need to marry and "stabilize." Of course, Munson, it might be argued, should practice what he preaches—during the film, he carries on a "backstairs" (make that, "back elevator") affaire d'amour with Dolly Harrison. And while Kennedy did make Jacqueline Bouvier his wife during his first year in the Senate, a wedding band didn't seem to ring him in.

When Gene Tierney (who played Dolly Harrison in the film) sat right next to the real-life president at a White House luncheon in 1962, it was not the first time they had met. Sixteen years earlier, on the set of *Dragonwyck*, Kennedy and Tierney were clearly smitten with each other. Tierney noted in her autobiography that Kennedy "had the kind of bantering, unforced Irish charm that women so often find fatal" and found they shared so much: both were Irish, both loved movies, and Tierney's daughter Daria, like Kennedy's sister Rosemary, was severely retarded.[64] It was their religious and political differences[65] that raised noisy objections by respective family members. In fact, Gene's brother, enrolled at Harvard at the same time as Kennedy, was not shy about lambasting rich Democrats with liberal notions. The Kennedy clan couldn't have been too happy with Tierney's impending divorce either. One day, seemingly out of the blue, Kennedy observed, "you know Gene, I can never marry you." That ended the relationship, and Tierney reconciled with Oleg Cassini. Postscript: In 1960 Tierney sent president-elect Kennedy a telegram that read, "Congratulations, I knew you would make it," even though she had voted for Richard Nixon.[66]

Unless an elected official's excessive behavior becomes public, Washington customarily winks at the indiscretions of its citizens. When Representative Wilbur Mills, chair of the House Ways and Means Committee, was collared by the cops in 1974 for cavorting in the Tidal Basin with "Argentine Firecracker" Fanne Foxe, he clearly went too far. Putting his paramour on the payroll also violated the unwritten "don't ask, don't tell" policy,[67] as Representative Wayne Hays, who hired the typing-challenged Elizabeth Ray as a "confidential" secretary, learned the hard way—he ended up resigning in disgrace in 1976. Finally, it's not a good idea to bait the press into sussing out a scandal. Democratic presidential contender Gary Hart doubled-dared journalists (intrigued by adultery allegations) to follow him around. They obliged, presenting him with photographic documentation of his extramarital "monkey business" with Donna Rice.[68] He bowed out of the race on March 11, 1988.

Money *Can* Buy Happiness

Generous political contributors have always been rewarded with top governmental appointments. David Packard (of Hewlett–Packard) got Nixon's nod as deputy secretary of defense and FOPs (friends of the president) from Joseph P. Kennedy to Perle Mesta were named ambassadors.

Where the elites meet has changed over the years. Prior to World War II, embassies served as the centers of activity in Washington society. At present, charities such as the Symphony Ball or the canine show bring the privileged together.

In the late 1940s, Gwendolyn Cafritz, the widow of a wealthy real estate entrepreneur, vied with socialite Mesta (immortalized in the Broadway musical *Call Me Madame*) for the "A" list in Washington. Their competition titillated society writers—in 1957, when Cafritz was photographed shaking hands with her rival, the event was reported with all the pomp reserved for East–West arms accords. Although it was generally believed that Mesta held the advantage, her ambassadorship to Luxembourg removed her from the Washington social scene, allowing Cafritz to assume the mantle as the capital's "hostess with the mostess."

The line from *Advise in Consent*, "any bitch with a million dollars, a big house and a good caterer can be a social success in Washington," could have been said about either Mesta or Cafritz. The latter later stirred wealth, effervescence, and numerous business and government contacts into a powerful concoction of the sort of lavish events that, in Washington, are as much a part of political life as sessions of Congress. She never discouraged media coverage and over the years achieved a celebrity status equal to most of her glittering guests.

Preminger restaged a Cafritz-style fete for *Advise and Consent* at the Tregaron estate of former Russian ambassador Joseph E. Davies. Celebrated socialites fell all over themselves to be included—along with stage-struck politicians and their stage-struck spouses.[69] The filming, however, didn't turn out to be all that glamorous for the unpaid VIP extras. Drinks were strictly nonalcoholic, theatrical lights brought the temperature up to "sweltering," and control freak Preminger, with his omnipresent megaphone, barked orders until the wee hours of the morning.

Preminger opting for Gene Tierney in the role of Dolly Harrison was inspired. Not only an Oscar-nominated actress, she had also become a titled lady by marriage to Count Oleg Cassini. While serving as hostess to Aly Khan, she was mentored by cafe society mistress Elsa Maxwell. Her southern California chums included the hoi polloi of Hollywood. While filming *Advise and Consent* in Washington, she and husband Houston oilman Howard Lee made the rounds, including dinner with Bobby and Ethel Kennedy, a sail on the presidential yacht, and a gala at the French embassy.[70]

Winning Isn't Everything, It's the Only Thing

This fantasy theme, inspired by Green Bay Packers coach Vince Lombardi, explores what Drury called "the rough game underneath the backslaps and the handshakes and the big noble speeches."[71] The blunt application of political power can best be seen in the Franchot Tone character, loosely based on FDR. The unnamed chief executive conceals a bad ticker, just as

Roosevelt masked his own medical problems. Like Roosevelt, Drury's president dies without being able to attend the peace conference he initiated. He makes bombshell decisions without consulting either cabinet or congressional leadership and fears his seemingly ineffectual vice president (Hudson, who in this respect is a counterpart to Truman) will allow his legacies (liberal foreign policy, versus FDR's New Deal) to be undermined by congressional conservatives.

The Franchot Tone character snaps "I haven't any time to run a school for presidents" after Munson suggests that Hudson should be brought into the loop. In fact, Drury's book paints the president as a somewhat Machiavellian leader who grants tacit permission for Van Ackerman to do his dirty work. Preminger's version leaves it to the viewer to draw any conclusions as to what the president knew and when he knew it.

FDR, whose enemies saw him as devious, deceitful, and dictatorial, was simultaneously the most loved and most hated of all presidents. When the chief executive in *Advise and Consent* confesses that history won't have much good to say about him, he could be parroting the thirty-second president.

When Anderson drags his feet on the subcommittee vote, the president takes his case to the American people via a Washington correspondents' banquet (an annual event at which the press is "honor bound not to be reporters"). In one fell "grab your pencils" swoop, the president dictates a story to the tuxedo-clad scribes, liberally spun from the children's classic *The Three Little Pigs*. Seab Cooley and Brig Anderson are together cast in the role of the Big, Bad Wolf. "The president is standing by his nominee, despite Cooley's wind storms and Anderson's tunneling . . . no matter what." The left-leaning press, greatly enamored of the intellectual Leffingwell and sympathetic to appeasement politics, doesn't need much convincing. Still, Washington correspondents don't get to vote on presidential appointments—that's up to the Senate. In the book, Leffingwell returns to his manual typewriter while Orrin Knox is elevated to secretary of state by Hudson.

General George Patton once mused, "A slave stood behind the [Roman] conqueror . . . whispering in his ear [the] warning that all glory is fleeting."[72] In *Advise and Consent*, whatever power the chief executive may wield while alive is reduced to a four-word note: "the President is dead." Even while campaigning for a fourth term over Thomas E. Dewey in 1944, Roosevelt knew he was fatally ill. The hubris that nudged the fictional president likewise propelled Roosevelt to hog the reins beyond his own physical capacity.

Like Roosevelt, the film's president attempts to end his presidency with actions that promote peace. Leffingwell's appointment to head up the State Department is such a move. With respect to Roosevelt, critics who hotly contested Roosevelt's wisdom in handing Eastern Europe over to the Soviets have opined that his deteriorating physical condition nudged him toward appeasement rather than aggression. Even though Churchill expressed serious reservations about Stalin's credibility, Roosevelt refused to listen, seemingly caving in to Stalin's demands.

Roosevelt's abrupt death from a massive cerebral hemorrhage on April 12, 1945, catapulted a woefully unprepared Truman into the White House. Like the president in *Advise and Consent*, Roosevelt left oodles of unfinished business, especially in the area of foreign affairs, for his successor to clean up. Perhaps when winning is the only thing, it's the people who lose.

THE POPULIST VS. THE ELITIST

Allen Drury was a populist trying to pass himself off as an elitist. Even though Drury reminded folks that he could trace his ancestry back to Tristram Coffin, his political preference gave him away.[73] The president he most admired was LBJ and he yearned to see Colin Powell assume the Oval Office.[74] He claimed Harry Truman was the most instantly likable person he ever met, with Ronald Reagan coming in a close second. Although he found Richard Nixon "very weird, very odd,"[75] he choked back his reservations and accepted a commission to write *Courage and Hesitation: Inside the Nixon Administration* in 1972. He also admitted he voted for Bill Clinton the first time around, but eventually thought that Clinton's "fanatic and rather pathetic search for historical meaning" was akin to McCarthy's megalomania.[76]

Otto Preminger, by contrast, was an elitist trying to pass himself off as a populist. According to son Erik Lee Preminger (whose mother was Gypsy Rose Lee), "The key to my father's personality goes back to his upbringing in Vienna [where he was] brought up in a rarefied, upper-class environment. He even had his own private reading room at the Vienna Library. In short, Otto had everything he ever wanted, including his own way."[77]

A volatile mixture of temperament, talent, tantrums, and tenacity branded Preminger "Otto the Terrible," "Premier Preminger," and "The Most Hated Man in Hollywood." His uninterrupted outbursts of ego-wilting rage quickly turned admirers into adversaries. As Andrew Sarris once quipped, Preminger was "a director with the personality of a producer."[78] The darling of the elitist Cahiers du Cinema kept an inelastic hold on subject, script, selection of equipment, and supervision of publicity. He even signed all payroll checks, a practice that caused Sam Goldwyn to fume, "he tried to take over my job."[79] Preminger liked to boast "when the producer and the director of my pictures have an argument, the winner is always me."[80] In fact, of the twenty-seven films he directed, he produced more than half.[81]

Preminger also liked to think of himself as an antielitist reformer. He maintained that the black list was never about communism. On the contrary, it was an "obvious way for the studio bosses to deny talented writers and directors their due and force them to write under pseudonyms for 10 cents on the dollar."[82]

Preminger is also credited with breaking the production code. Starting with *The Moon Is Blue,* he simply snubbed the Legion of Decency, causing priests to sermonize about the film and actually stand outside theaters taking names. The morality watchdogs at the Hays Office likewise withheld their approval of the movie because of subject (adultery) and language ("virgin" and "pregnant"). When the film proved to be a hit, the cudgel formerly used to beat down producers (people won't buy tickets) finally lost its wallop. With movie audiences dwindling daily, being denied the production code seal generated talk and ticket buyers. Preminger further tested censorship limits on taboo subjects and objectionable language with such films as *The Man with the Golden Arm* (drug addiction), *The Court Martial of Billy Mitchell* (criticism of government), *Anatomy of a Murder* (rape), and *Advise and Consent* (homosexuality).

Preminger did manage to overstep in *Advise and Consent,* however, with his selection of Martin Luther King Jr. to play a senator from Georgia, in the sort of promotional scheme that had worked in *Anatomy of a Murder,* in which he cast Joseph Welch as the judge.[83] King was initially intrigued ($4,500 for his appearance would have gone to charity)[84] until acrimonious protest generated by white southerners (Georgia state senator John Greer and Georgia governor Ernest Vandiver) proved counterproductive to the cause. It would take five more years in the real world before a black would be elected to the Senate, the first since Reconstruction.[85]

Preminger, whether consciously or not, did what he could to eliminate what he considered Drury's antielitist bias. The blackmail trail doesn't lead into the Oval Office, as it did in the book. Preminger downplayed Leffingwell's intellectual arrogance with Henry Fonda, who played the Great Emancipator in *Mr. Lincoln* and populist Tom Joad in *Grapes of Wrath.* Wendell Mayes created sympathy for Leffingwell with a light and breezy "egghead" monologue that never appeared in the book. He also softened Leffingwell by fabricating a warm and fuzzy relationship with a son. By stacking the final Senate vote, prematurely killing off the chief executive, and avoiding the question of whether or not an ex-Communist and "bald-faced liar" should/could be secretary of state, Preminger effectively ripped the populist intestines out of Drury's book.[86]

WHEN YOU CAN'T LIVE WITH YOUR MISTAKES:
THE ELITISM OF PERFECTIONISM

Preminger's *Advise and Consent* leaves a nagging and largely unanswered question—why did Brig Anderson commit suicide? All men miss the mark. While contemporary society no longer speaks in terms of sin, we do manage an occasional glance backward, with added wisdom outweighing regret at our "mistakes." Why was Leffingwell able to live with his experimentation with communism while Anderson wasn't able to live with his experimentation with homosexuality?

First, a little book background on Anderson to fill in what Preminger left out of the film: Anderson's father held a high position in the Mormon hierarchy, and while he may have tolerated, even expected, Brig to do a little premarital sexual research in college, the senior Anderson would have been horrified by what happened in Honolulu. Anderson may have been JFK-caliber striking, yet he was hardly as assertive with the ladies. Although Anderson racked up dozens of sexual encounters with women, he was decidedly not the Don Juan type—he rarely initiated affairs but rather allowed himself to be seduced by whomever found him attractive, including Ray Schaff. When it came time to settle down and get married, he chose a classy and connected wife who could prop up his political career without demanding high maintenance in return—in or out of the bedroom. In an interview with Preminger, Peter Bogdonovich theorized that the "I know we haven't had a very exciting marriage" line merely underscores Anderson's latent homosexuality. Preminger responds "No, I disagree with you there. I think this happens in many marriages. If you read statistics, you can find that nearly 50 percent of all women are not particularly fond of continuous sexual relations."[87]

Preminger may have highlighted the homosexual element to pay off at the box office, but he also really believed that seeing Schaff again forced Anderson to confront unresolved guilt.[88] Having a movie character mouth the word "homosexual" was still verboten in a 1962 Hollywood. So Preminger invented the character of Manuel the pimp and the gays-only Club 602 so that through wardrobe and affectations he could hint at what Drury could spell out directly. In the novel, Schaff telephones Anderson to confess that Van Ackerman offered him a great deal of money to disclose and evidence their dalliance in Hawaii. A letter and a photograph make their way, through a series of implausible coincidences, from Brig Anderson's old Army trunk to the hand of the president. Drury provides no dramatic confrontation in which Anderson shoves his old lover into the gutter, but then Preminger likewise omits Schaff's suicide—in the book, Schaff jumps off a bridge when he discovers his betrayal has cost Anderson his life.

Woodrow Wilson admonished the Princeton University class of 1879, "most of the errors of public life . . . come, not because men are morally bad, but because they are afraid of somebody."[89] While Preminger shows Anderson both attracted and repelled by homosexuality, Drury attributes Anderson's final encounter with a dull razor blade to battle fatigue, a numbing that envelops his heart and mind.[90]

Anderson's sense of honor must have reminded moviegoers of Frank Capra's Jefferson Smith. Leffingwell may be responsible for the rejection of Anderson's power bill, but Anderson doesn't carry, à la Seab Cooley, a grudge—he's open to hearing what Leffingwell has to say before he casts his vote. He doesn't seek the subcommittee chair but doesn't shirk it either. He continues to protect the president, even though Van Ackerman's bullying and the blackmailer's badgering (he doesn't realize they are one and the same) grind him down.

Brig Anderson is not only intelligent, articulate, and matinee-idol handsome, he is the poster boy for traditional family values. His life seems perfect. His daughter Pidge means so much to him that he shoehorns time in his crowded schedule to help her feed her fish and tuck her in—even if Mr. Sandman beats him to the punch.

Drury looked for an equally odious secret to balance Leffingwell's foray into communism. He recalls borrowing from a real-life incident involving the outing of a politician's gay son by political opponents.[91] "That story showed me how cruel politics could be," said Drury, contending that even in the late '90s, a senator closeting a homosexual past could still cause a scandal.[92]

Production Code administrator Geoffrey Shurlock told Preminger that all homosexual references in the movie would have to go. Preminger, who had already released two popular films without the production seal, wasn't about to knuckle under to Shurlock. A few months later, the Motion Picture Association of America (MPAA) announced homosexual references if "treated with care, discretion and restraint" might be approved. In *Celluloid Closet*, Vito Russo writes that Preminger seized the moment.[93] Shurlock hovered over the project, however, insisting that homosexual characters not be weak-wristed or flamingly flamboyant. Preminger, who was directed to characterize homosexuality as an alternative lifestyle, chose Greenwich Village beatniks. This translated to the screen as a walkup crowded with "cats" and a dimly lit saloon illuminated by a tacky colored light wheel.

In case you didn't pick up on the total absence of females in Club 602, said to be fashioned after a popular New York haunt of the early '60s,[94] the voice of Frank Sinatra (famous for gay anthem "Strangers in the Night") in the background croons the lyrics, "let me hear a voice, a secret voice that will say 'come to me' and be what I need you to be." By failing to cast homosexuality in a negative light, *Advise and Consent* appeared to condone perversion—at least that's the way it looked to conservatives in the audience. Preminger never felt the need to point out the unintended consequence to Shurlock and the other bluenoses at MPAA.

If you simply view *Advise and Consent* as a conflict pitting the private sin of being a closeted homosexual against the political sin of being a closeted Communist, you only get entry-level meaning. Sexual indiscretions have been overlooked in politics since Benjamin Franklin carried on in eighteenth-century France.[95] Drury, however, can't resist picking at populist–elitist battle scabs. At one point in the book, Brig Anderson and

Lafe Smith, waxing philosophical, attempt to answer the question, "Who am I to judge?" Anderson counters, "But somebody's got to."[96] That position costs him his life.

THE AUDIENCE RESPONDS

Since buzz for the novel jump-started interest in the movie, Columbia had to pay a bonus to Drury for each and every week *Advise and Consent* basked on the best-seller list. At ninety-three weeks, the book holds the record for longest run on the *New York Times* fiction list. Critic Andrew Sarris, who had a tough time plowing through Drury's paragraphs, which tumbled nonstop down each of the novel's 750 pages, delivered a backhanded compliment to Preminger, "it is one of the paradoxes of the cinema that good movies are more likely to be derived from bad novels, than from good novels."[97]

Voyeurism accounts for a large part of *Advise and Consent*'s appeal. Preminger promised viewers a behind-the-scenes glimpse into Washington wheeling and dealing, including a little sexual perversion, political conspiracy, and obstruction of justice thrown in for good measure. *Newsweek* wasn't impressed, calling the film "one of the most reprehensibly sensational movies in years."[98]

Tom Kelly, who covered Congress for the *Washington Daily News* when *Advise and Consent* came out, recalls its enormous impact on the nation's consciousness. While there was still "very little interest . . . in the legislative process, . . . I doubt that there was one American in 1,000 then who understood how the committee system in Congress really operated. . . . [*Advise and Consent*] showed how this huge machine that affects your life really works."[99] Preminger concurs: "I think the politics in the film are really a background. People told me before I made the film—and I haven't disproved it yet—that it will not be understood easily in other countries. I don't know why people shouldn't understand. After all, the Americans don't know much about the intricacies of American politics either."[100]

History buffs who fail to heed the "any resemblance to individuals, living or dead, is purely coincidental" warning have amused themselves by playing "Who's Who" among Drury's characters—from the vice president who gets no respect to the divisive senator who heads up a nationwide peace movement. Just when they think they have nailed the identify of Drury's real-life role models, a critical detail rings wrong, for example, the McCarthyesque character turns out to be a Commie-loving peacenik or the Truman-like vice president confesses to hobnobbing with elitists like the duPonts.

When *Mr. Smith Goes to Washington* premiered on October 16, 1939, a third of the politicians in attendance walked out and Ambassador Joseph P. Kennedy shot off a cablegram demanding that the film, which he saw as pro-Axis propaganda, be withdrawn from distribution in Europe. Otto Preminger shouldn't have been surprised at the furor *Advise and Consent* created in Washington. Like Capra, Preminger held a private showing for Congress. As the movie ended, Senator Clinton P. Anderson sputtered, "The film creates a wholly incorrect impression of the Senate."[101] Senator Stephen Young rose from the audience to announce he would introduce a bill preventing Columbia from distributing the picture outside the United States.[102] U.S. Information Agency chief Edward R. Murrow raised strenuous objections, largely arguing that instead of giving our enemy ammunition, Hollywood should create a "favorable image" of Americans to show foreign nations. The American Legion protested in full force, decrying *Advise and Consent* as an "irresponsible defacement of the image of the U.S." and picketing theaters.[103]

At the same time, the *New Yorker*'s Brendan Gill wrote "Mr. Preminger has provided an altogether harmless entertainment, . . . thus our enemies will be obliged, as usual, to draw as much comfort as possible from the fact that everyone in the picture is notably well-fed, well-housed, well-heeled, and well-clothed."[104] The news from abroad was good. *Le Monde,* one of the largest newspapers in heavily government-censored France, ran a front page story marveling at America's freedom of expression. Preminger added: "This country's tolerance of free expression is its greatest asset."[105]

The film seemed to be a political Rorschach test. While some conservatives could live with the homosexual subject matter, they couldn't abide the way Preminger ruined Drury's book. To their thinking, Preminger and Wendell Mayes did more than just "tamper" with the novel; by writing out Orrin Knox, slighting the villainous Supreme Court justice, and smudging presidential involvement in Anderson's suicide, Preminger and Mayes turned Drury's political message on its ear. To those who opposed appeasement, there was no starch in Drury's cautionary tale.

For liberals, especially appeasement advocates, Preminger's version of the Drury novel remained nothing more than a right-wing political morality play and they unceremoniously dismissed both book and film as such. Drury still felt the sting of their criticism nearly four decades later, when he commented: "The hostile liberal press has . . . branded me a reactionary. They [couldn't] forgive me for being anti-Soviet, but I think history has proven me right."[106]

Advise and Consent was not as faultfinding with the American political system as it was of a man who might abuse his office. Just remember, the film came out a decade before Watergate. Perhaps Preminger had his own crystal ball tucked away somewhere.

NOTES

1. Quoted in *Time* (April 23, 1979): 229.
2. See Thomas R. Dye and L. Harmon Zeigler, *The Irony of Democracy: An Uncommon Introduction to American Politics,* 5th ed. (Monterey, Calif.: Duxbury, 1981).

3. Jeffrey Bell, *Populism and Elitism: Politics in the Age of Equality* (Washington, D.C.: Regnery Gateway, 1992), 3.

4. Ferdinand Lundberg, *The Rich and the Super-Rich* (Secaucus, N.J.: Carol, 1968).

5. See G. William Domhoff, *The Power Elite and the State: How Policy Is Made in America* (New York: de Gruyter, 1990); Harold Lasswell and Daniel Lerner, *The Comparative Study of Elites* (Palo Alto, Calif.: Stanford University Press, 1952); Robert Lynd, "Power in American Society," in *Problems of Power in American Society,* edited by Arthur Kornhauser (Detroit: Wayne State University Press, 1957.

6. Charles A. Beard and Mary R. Beard, *America in Midpassage,* vol. 2, (New York: Macmillan, 1939), 922–23.

7. In Greece, the birthplace of democracy, *idiote* means "private citizen."

8. George Washington, *First Inaugural Address* (April 30, 1789), quoted in John Bartlett, *Familiar Quotations,* 16th ed. (Boston: Little, Brown, 1992), 337.

9. Margaret Canovan, *Populism* (London: Junction, 1981), 285–86.

10. A Scripps Howard News Service poll reports Americans are overwhelmingly convinced that members of the Second Continental Congress were motivated by selflessness rather than dreams of personal gain when they signed the Declaration of Independence.

11. French for "minimal governmental interference in market transactions."

12. Jefferson to Adams, October 28, 1813, in Thomas Jefferson, *Writings,* edited by Merrill D. Peterson (New York: Library of America, 1984), 1305–1306.

13. Jean Jacques Rousseau, *The Social Contract and Discourse,* book III, chapter 4 (1762; reprint, London: Dent, 1973), 217.

14. Robert Michels, *Political Parties: A Sociological Study of the Oligarchical Tendencies of Modern Democracy,* translated by Eden Paul and Cedar Paul (Glencoe, Ill: Free Press, 1958), 406.

15. Michael Curtis, ed., *The Great Political Theories,* vol. 2 (New York: Avon, 1981), 343.

16. Thomas R. Dye, *Who's Running America? Institutional Leadership in the United States* (Englewood Cliffs, N.J.: Prentice–Hall, 1976), 212.

17. Dye, *Who's Running America?* 212; Suzanne Keller, *Beyond the Ruling Class* (New York: Ayer, 1963), 273–74.

18. Peter Bachrach, *The Theory of Democratic Elitism: A Critique* (Boston: Little, Brown, 1967), 31.

19. William Miller, Annis–May Timpson, and Michael Lessnoff, "Freedom from Press," in *Elitism, Populism and European Politics,* edited by Jack Hayward (Oxford: Clarendon, 1996), 84.

20. Robert Hollinger, *The Dark Side of Liberalism: Elitism vs. Democracy* (Westport, Conn.: Praeger, 1996), xvii.

21. William A. Henry III, *In Defense of Elitism* (New York: Doubleday, 1994), 6.

22. Actually, you could mark the beginning of the gradual expansion of the presidency at Teddy Roosevelt and Woodrow Wilson.

23. Dwight David Eisenhower, *Farewell Address to the American People* (January 17, 1961), quoted in Bartlett, *Familiar Quotations,* 678.

24. His pick for secretary of labor, Martin P. Durkin, once headed up a plumber's union.

25. Ward heelers took the Harvard grad to neighborhood bars, where he passed out cigars to working-class voters.

26. Gene Tierney with Mickey Herskowitz, *Self-Portrait* (New York: Berkley, 1980), 132.

27. Harry S Truman in Francis X. Clines, "Images: Roosevelt to Reagan," *New York Times,* October 14, 1984, quoted in Leonard Roy Frank, *Quotationary* (New York: Random House, 1999), 614.

28. Henry, *Defense of Elitism,* 198.

29. Richard Nixon, *Six Crises* (1962), quoted in Frank, *Quotationary,* 81.

30. Andrew Sarris, "Otto Preminger," *American Film* (June 1989): 71. Mark Shivas, "Why Preminger?" *Movie* 2 (September 1962): 26.

31. Quoted in Joseph Ellis, *Founding Fathers: The Revolutionary Generation* (New York: Knopf, 2001), 166.

32. Gracie Allen, *How to Become President* (1940), quoted in Rosalie Maggio, *Quotations by Women* (Boston: Beacon, 1992), 63.

33. Dye, *Who's Running America?* 79.

34. Will Rogers, *The Autobiography of Will Rogers* (1949), quoted in Frank, *Quotationary,* 82.

35. Herbert H. Lehman, in Barbara Tuchman, "An Inquiry into the Persistence of Unwisdom in Government," *Esquire* (1980), quoted in Frank, *Quotationary,* 612.

36. From *Ronald Reagan's First Inaugural,* January 1981.

37. Donald R. Matthews, *The Social Background of Political Decision-Makers* (New York: Doubleday, 1954) 248–49.

38. H. L. Mencken, "The Constitution," *Baltimore Evening Sun,* August 19, 1935, quoted in Frank, *Quotationary,* 613.

39. Shivas, "Why Preminger?" 28.

40. Charles Krauthammer, "Pitygate: School for Scandal," *Time* (September 10, 1984): 76.

41. Allen Drury, *Advise and Consent* (Garden City, N.J.: Doubleday, 1959), 452.

42. Henry Brooks Adams, *The Education of Henry Adams* (1907), chapter 7, quoted in Bartlett, *Familiar Quotations,* 535.

43. Lord Chesterfield, letter to his son (January 15, 1748), quoted in Frank, *Quotationary,* 611.

44. Ralph K. Huitt, "The Outsider in the U.S. Senate: An Alternative Role," *American Political Science Review* 65 (June 1961): 568.

45. Margaret Chase Smith, the first woman to serve both in the U.S. House of Representatives (1940–49) and in the Senate (1949–73), was Drury's model for Bessie Adams.

46. Andrew Sarris, "Film Fantasies, Left and Right," *Film Culture* 34 (Fall 1964): 28.

47. Margo Hammond, "The Insider Outsider of Washington," *St. Petersburg Times* (September 6, 1998), 1D.

48. Hammond, "Insider Outsider," 1D.

49. Sarris, "Film Fantasies," 28.

50. Joseph P. Lash, *From the Diaries of Felix Frankfurter* (New York: Norton, 1975), 35.

51. Whittaker Chambers, *Witness* (New York: Random House, 1952), 550.

52. Drury, *Advise and Consent,* 154.

53. Chris Matthews, "Is There Any Question about Who's Boss in US Senate?" *San Diego Union Tribune,* March 15, 1989, B11.

54. Otto Preminger, *Preminger: An Autobiography* (Garden City, N.Y.: Doubleday, 1977), 150.

55. Richard L. Coe, "The People's Representatives," *Washington Post*, November 20, 1977, F3.

56. Enoch Powell, *The Listener*, May 28, 1981, quoted in Daniel B. Baker, *Power Quotes* (Detroit: Visible Ink), 229.

57. "Knowledge is power." Francis Bacon, *Meditationes Sacrae* (1597), quoted in Bartlett, *Familiar Quotations*, 158.

58. John Adams, letter to Abigail Adams (December 19, 1793), quoted in Bartlett, *Familiar Quotations*, 338.

59. Finley Peter Dunne, *Dissertations by Mr. Dooley*, "The Vice-President" (1906) quoted in Bartlett, *Familiar Quotations*, 603.

60. Attributed to John Nance Garner, quoted in Bartlett, *Familiar Quotations*, 605.

61. Hiroshima on August 6, 1945, Nagasaki on August 9, 1945.

62. Henry Kissinger, *New York Times*, January 19, 1971, quoted in Baker, *Power Quotes*, 249.

63. Hammond, "Insider Outsider," 1D.

64. Tierney, *Self-Portrait*, 129. Kennedy's father invested in films and, by then, his liaisons with Marion Davies and Gloria Swanson were widely known.

65. The Tierneys were Episcopalian Republicans, while the Kennedys were Catholic Democrats.

66. Tierney, *Self-Portrait*, 141.

67. Where do you think the military got the idea?

68. *Monkey Business* was the name of the sailboat on which photographers found Hart "relaxing" with Rice.

69. It is interesting to note that for the movie *Exodus*, which required a vast mob scene, the audacious Preminger enticed thirty thousand people to pay for the privilege of being in the movie by buying lottery tickets.

70. Howard Lee was formerly married to Hedy Lamarr.

71. Drury, *Advise and Consent*, 104.

72. General George Patton, *Time* (March 18, 1991), quoted in Baker, *Power Quotes*, 250.

73. Coffin was one of the founders of Nantucket settlement in New England.

74. Hammond, "Insider Outsider," 1D.

75. Hammond, "Insider Outsider," 1D.

76. Hammond, "Insider Outsider," 1D.

77. Quoted in John Stanley, "Two Week Tribute: Otto the Terrible's Hollywood Reign," *San Francisco Chronicle*, September 19, 1993, 23.

78. Quoted in Tim Pulleine, "The Hard Man Who Made Good," *Guardian*, April 24, 1986.

79. Quoted in Stanley, "Two Week Tribute," 23.

80. Desson Howe, "Appreciation: Perfectly Preminger," *Washington Post*, April 24, 1986, D1.

81. Howe, "Appreciation," D1.

82. Stanley, "Two Week Tribute," 23.

83. It was Welch who inquired of Senator McCarthy, "Have you no decency, sir?" during the televised Army–McCarthy hearings.

84. Preminger, *Preminger,* 158.

85. In 1967, Edward W. Brooke of Massachusetts became the first black member of the U.S. Senate since Reconstruction (when two African Americans served).

86. Drury considered Preminger's film such a gross defilement of his intent that he pulled the film rights to *A Shade of Difference.*

87. Peter Bogdanovich, *Who the Devil Made It* (New York: Knopf, 1997), 634.

88. Shivas, "Why Preminger?" 26–27.

89. Woodrow Wilson, *Speech to the Princeton University Class of 1879,* June 13, 1914, quoted in Baker, *Power Quotes,* 223.

90. Drury, *Advise and Consent,* 440–41.

91. David Bratman reports when Senator Lester Hunt (D-WY), was black-mailed over his son's arrest for homosexual solicitation, the senator shot himself in his office. See "The Fictional Senate of Allen Drury's *Advise and Consent,*" home.earthlink.net/~dbratman/drury.html.

92. Hammond, "Insider Outsider," 1D.

93. Vito Russo, *The Celluloid Closet: Homosexuality in the Movies* (New York: Harper & Row, 1987), 121–22.

94. Russo, *Celluloid Closet,* 141.

95. Drury, *Advise and Consent,* 445.

96. Drury, *Advise and Consent,* 346.

97. Sarris, "Film Fantasies," 28.

98. *Newsweek,* June 11, 1962, 99.

99. Quoted in Ken Ringle, "Allen Drury, Father of the DC Drama," *Washington Post,* September 4, 1998, D1.

100. "Interview with Otto Preminger," *Movie* 4 (November 1962): 18.

101. "A Patriotic Movie," *Life* (July 1962): 74–75.

102. In fact, Preminger slipped a negative of the film out of the country to prevent confiscation in case Young's bill was successful.

103. *Variety,* January 7, 1962, 1.

104. Brendan Gill, *New Yorker* (June 9, 1962).

105. Preminger, *Preminger,* 159.

106. Hammond, "Insider Outsider," 1D.

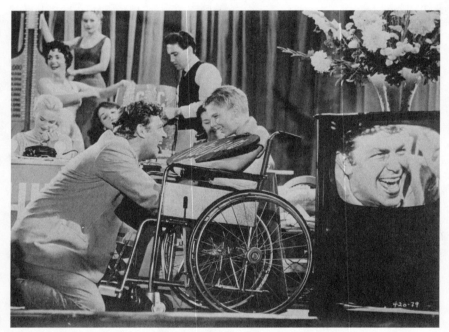

Andy Griffith demonstrates the political power of television in A Face in the Crowd. *Courtesy of Castle Hill Productions, Inc., and the Academy of Motion Picture Arts and Sciences.*

4

☆

Fascism in *A Face in the Crowd*

In 1946, Alfred Rosenberg, the Nazi condemned to death at Nuremberg, declared, "Within fifteen years, we will begin to be talked about again, and within twenty, Nazism will again be a force."[1] From the vantage of the twenty-first century, it doesn't appear that Rosenberg's optimism was as ill founded as Americans would like to believe.

September 11, 2001, did not just jar the smug self-confidence of the American people; it also invited the same sort of fascist thinking that swirled around the edges of the American psyche during the depths of the depression.

The USA Patriot Act alarmed not just knee-jerk liberals but also right-wing libertarians. At first, a righteous indignation at terrorists who plied their nasty trade right in our own backyard elbowed out troubled feelings, but when the Electronic Privacy Information Center, the Gun Owners of America, the American Civil Liberties Union, the American Bar Association, and conservative members of Congress realized what was happening, they audibly gagged at the unprecedented police powers (to wiretap, detain noncitizens, and conduct search-and-seizure raids) being invoked.

Since the United States was purportedly "at war," critics, at least for the moment, held their noses and their tongues, but when President Bush instituted secret Third World dictator–type military tribunals to try suspected terrorists on the heels of an antiterrorism law so broadly drafted that it could disrupt the lives of ordinary Americans, critics barked "enough is enough."

The panels would have approached kangaroo courts, holding the power to execute without the conventional safeguards of the judicial system. Because of the stink raised by opinion writers, talking heads, and elected officials, civil liberties were not sacrificed for the mere promise of national security.[2] It would seem that Americans, except in times of exceptional strain, simply will not accept the fascist notion that a leader's actions or decisions cannot be questioned or challenged.[3] They contend that the First Amendment includes finding fault with the president himself.

Peeled down to essentials, fascism has been characterized as the totalitarian organization of government and society by a single-party dictatorship, fiercely nationalistic, categorically anti-Semitic, rampantly militant, and emphatically imperialistic.[4] This definition, however, should also pay homage to the industrial sector, which every fascist dictator found indispensable to the success of his regime.[5]

Italy under Benito Mussolini in 1922 was the first to embrace fascism. Nazi Germany followed suit in 1933. Spain was introduced to fascism by Francisco Franco after a civil war beginning in 1936. Japan evolved fascist institutions out of its industrial state and traditional imperial background during the '30s. Argentina turned to fascism under the leadership of Juan Domingo Perón in 1946.

PRECONDITIONS FOR FASCISM

Throughout the '30s, most of the globe was attempting to stomach a stinging economic crisis. Massive unemployment persisted even among the historically immune skilled labor force, opportunities for professionals were scarce or nonexistent, middle-class savings were wiped out, and bankruptcy became widespread. Fascist assurances of currency control, strike elimination, increased efficiency, decreased waste, enhanced productivity, and the cultivation of worldwide markets seemed to provide ample justification for intervention in the economy. Hitler's ability to put more than 6 million unemployed Germans to work on his vast rearmament and building program guaranteed his popularity and eventual dictatorship.[6]

Fascist despots took advantage of a widespread lack of confidence in the reigning political systems. While communism, much to the surprise of doctrinaire Marxists, took root in preindustrialized, predemocratic countries, fascism didn't seem to catch on unless the nation had experienced democratic rule and technological advancement. Argentines found themselves losing faith with party politics and democratic government, not only because former President Ramon Castillo corrupted the provincial election system, but also because the depression-battered economy still continued to favor the wealthy.

People in spiritual despair are particularly vulnerable to the promises of fascism. Germany, Italy, and Japan entered World War I with the expectation of gaining territory and status; however, post-1918 reality fell considerably short. Despite counting itself among the victors, Italy's relative political, social, and economic backwardness put an immense strain on all aspects of social life. Disorientation, isolation, and alienation trailed rapid urbanization and industrialization. Feelings of uselessness arose out of the inability to secure a job. Traditional values were sacked, with nothing to fill the void. Folks found themselves deeply mired in moral anguish and confusion. When Hitler and Mussolini came along, calling for self-sacrifice, discipline, and comradeship, the desperate and despondent were more than happy to oblige.

Fascism could not have prevailed had it not been for paramilitary organizations composed of disillusioned ex-servicemen who attached themselves to fascist politics. Seduced by elaborate uniforms that evoked the camaraderie of the trenches, Hitler's goose-stepping marchers, puffed up with pride, participated in torchlight parades and swelled the numbers attending mass meetings.[7] Mussolini's "black shirts" were essentially right-wing gangsters who specialized in brutalizing socialist politicians, breaking up strikes, and trashing leftist-controlled newspapers. Their weapon of choice—clubs and, oddly enough, castor oil, whose powers as a laxative not only shamed the victim but, on occasion, proved fatal via dehydration.[8] Fed up with political fraud, loss of prestige, and the incessant arm-twisting by the Axis powers to fight during World War II, Perón's secret military lodge masterminded a coup that catapulted him to the top of the military heap.

At times of economic dislocation, folks can't help being sucked in by a dreamer, especially one who dreams the impossible dream. It didn't hurt that the fascist mass propagandists wove their symbolism and pageantry into a glittering cosmic struggle between good and evil. A new world order called the "Greater East Asia Co-Prosperity Sphere" sent Japan hellbent on a quest to extend its grip over five continents. Hitler commissioned a painting of himself as a Wagnerian knight on a white horse, emancipating his people from suffering and shame. Francisco Franco of Spain exalted peasant life in his oratory, embarking on a string of rhetorical quests for the "new man"—however, the "new man" cruised the countryside in a black Rolls Royce with an entourage of red-bereted bodyguards.[9] Mussolini visualized himself as the next Caesar, who would recreate the glory that had once been Rome.

THE FASCIST MODUS OPERANDI

Any fascist at the top of his game squanders no time in exploiting crisis conditions. Hitler persuaded the aging German president to invest him with emergency powers. Cautioning that Italy must expand or decay,

Mussolini invaded the militarily weak Ethiopia, armed with a policy of extermination and poison gas. Juan Domingo Perón took advantage of the January 1, 1944, earthquake that leveled San Juan and left ten thousand dead. Spain's *El Caudillo,* Francisco Franco, cannily anticipating the World War II tide shifting to the Allies, dragged his feet every time Italy and Germany sniveled for support.

To gain control, fascists merge with the existing machinery of power, but after a while this loose coalition evolves into a state in which despots abolish freedoms to consolidate their clout. Mussolini suppressed civil liberties, annihilated the opposition, and imposed an open dictatorship. Hitler appropriated the racist Nuremberg Laws to abridge the rights of Germany's Jews. Franco wielded bureaucratic red tape to harass Spaniards into loyalty. Peron thwarted his enemies by gagging critical newspapers, gerrymandering districts to reduce oppositional congressional representation, and tossing those resisting his leadership in jail. From 1937 on, Japan trended toward totalitarian thought control and total censorship.[10]

Fascists realize that they must redirect repressed hatred and hostility away from their dictatorial excesses and toward real or imaginary opponents. Hitler's "enemy list" included the Bolsheviks, the Jews, and the vindictive victors of World War I. While Mussolini decried the same adversaries as *der Führer,* he found little or no support for anti-Semitism by the Italians. Franco went to war against the Republicans. Perón made rhetorical hay by constantly haranguing his audiences about American imperialism and the treachery of international finance. Japan blamed the United States for a thwarted effort to set up a protectorate over China.

The prevailing noninterventionist mood also lubricated the advancing fascist machine. When Japan snatched Manchuria, the West looked the other way. As Mussolini stole Ethiopia, the League of Nations may have cleared its collective throat, but it remained noticeably silent. Horrifying memories of World War I turned off any European hankering to save the Spanish Republic. By March 1937, a Gallup poll reported 94 percent of Americans were opposed to going to war, *any war.*[11] Even when Hitler showed his hand with Austria and the Rhineland, the democracies sat by, largely twiddling their thumbs.

CHARISMATIC LEADERSHIP

In *Fascism in Europe,* S. J. Woolf concluded, "There can be no doubt about the crucial importance of the leader to a fascist movement; no movement without a leader succeeded in establishing itself as a regime."[12] Not only does fascism need a leader, but a charismatic leader, thank you very much.

To Hitler, *Führerprinzip* dictates that the leader represents the collective spirit of the Volk—thus, fascist leaders were thought to possess a special supernatural insight and considered, if not virtually infallible, certainly above criticism. Hitler saw himself as *Führer*,[13] a Father to the Fatherland, graciously extending security to his followers but, unbeknownst to them, exacting a debt of dependence in return.

Charisma is one of those seemingly undefinable characteristics—like obscenity—that you know when you see. The relationship of charisma to credibility is obvious. If credibility operates in persuasion as the degree of probability assigned to a message, then the degree of probability with a charismatic communicator is close to 100 percent.[14] That is not to say that a fascist can fool all of the people all of the time, but a fascist can certainly fool enough of the people enough of the time, if Hitler, Mussolini, Franco, and Perón are any indication.

With respect to physical appearance, Hitler seemed the most unlikely of charismatic candidates. He was short and dark—as far, in fact, from the typical tall, fair Aryan as possible.[15] His unintentionally comic brush of a moustache provided fodder for ridicule, from Charlie Chaplin's *The Great Dictator* to Jack Benny's *To Be or Not to Be*. His real attractiveness lay in his incredible energy, resonant voice, and piercing eyes.[16] Despite his small stature and rigid manner, Hitler was said to possess an "electrifying personality" that could bring both men and women under his hypnotic spell.[17]

Hitler also understood the power of language. He skillfully crafted speeches to achieve maximum emotional effect. For example, when the subject was Nazism, his script was filled with positive words such as "strength" and "youth." When the topic was the Jews, he sprinkled his speech with epithets such as "vermin," "lice," and "maggots."[18]

It was during Hitler's aimless existence among the displaced of Vienna that he first became captivated by the promulgation of propaganda and the large-scale organizational accomplishments of Mayor Karl Lueger's political machine.[19] Hitler observed that giant demonstrations such as torchlight parades or mass meetings seemed to burn conviction into an individual, no matter how inconsequential he or she might initially feel. And he learned that when he seemed to be meeting resistance, he could lengthen his harangues and use the resulting audience fatigue to press his point home. Finally, he became skilled at telling people exactly what they wanted to hear, whether that meant allaying the fears of the *Mittelstand*, who feared slipping back into the proletariat, or conciliating European nations who grew suspicious of his intentions. Hitler spelled out his "big lie" theory in *Mein Kampf*.[20]

Mussolini, for his part, simply exuded animal magnetism. The media, as well as Mussolini himself, considered *Il Duce* a sublime sex symbol.[21] Well-built and athletic, he frequently appeared on horseback or emerging from the cockpit of a plane—always making sure a photographer was present. When he was going for "the ferocious look," he would scowl and purse his lips into a pretty pout. His broad, pale face and enormous dark eyes rolled back into his head could be disarmingly dramatic. Further, as the vain Italian began to age, he shaved his head and employed a corset to nip and tuck a thickened middle.

Ironically, for someone who was to become one of Europe's greatest orators, the baby Benito had great difficulty learning to speak. The mature Mussolini used few gestures and, once finished, would return to an immobile, rock-solid stance, thus setting himself apart from the customarily highly animated Italian. When he spoke, his words, so forceful they seemed to be etched in stone, virtually rang with sincerity, decisiveness, and finality. He tried to give the impression his arguments were simply irrefutable. A picture of *Il Duce* captioned "Mussolini is always right" hung in every Italian classroom from 1922 to 1945.[22]

Franco cut quite a stirring figure in his narrow-belted jacket, highly polished boots, and skin-tight jodhpurs. As a small-for-his-age youngster, "Franquito" was the object of cruel bullying, but he continued to ride, swim, and play football. Eventually, he developed into a fit, if not adventurous adult and a highly decorated soldier who, although seriously wounded on more than one occasion, was blessed with a dead-on instinct for survival. Not only was Franco known as a stalwart general, he was a man's man, whose arduous hunting excursions persevered until the dictator was well into his sixties.

No one could believe that Perón, not a particularly handsome man, could attract an actress/radio personality such as Eva Duarte, much less make her his mistress, then wife. Although fascism is profoundly antifeminist, Evita became, in effect, Perón's copresident.[23] Her death from cancer was a serious blow to the Perón regime. She continues to be revered, and for a few years after her demise it even looked as though efforts to get her canonized would succeed.

Japanese fascism hasn't played a noteworthy role in the discussion so far. Unlike other fascist countries, Japan envisioned the embodiment of its national ideal, not in some charismatic leader, but in the god-like emperor. General Hideki Tojo, the general who served as premier during World War II, was anything but charismatic. He failed to exercise control over the emperor, his senior statesmen, and the navy (the major contributors to Japan's ultimate defeat). He couldn't even commit *hara-kiri*. Realizing occupation forces were on the way, he shot himself—but missed his heart. He was subsequently hanged as a war criminal in 1948.

AMERICAN FASCISM DURING THE '50s

Although few American films during the '30s and '40s actually promoted fascism, the culture that produced the Hollywood Anti-Nazi League and the Motion Picture Democratic Committee also harbored folks who flirted with fascism both off screen and on.[24] Harry Cohn of Columbia Pictures was tickled pink to release his documentary on Mussolini. According to Neal Gabler, a visit to the dictator in Rome inspired Cohn to redecorate his own office to resemble the digs of *Il Duce*.[25] In 1934, MGM proudly publicized Italy's National Fascist Association of Motion Pictures and Theatrical Industries Gold Medal, bestowed on Wallace Beery for his film portrayal of Pancho Villa. Who would have imagined three silver screen luminaries would establish right-wing, paramilitary troops in Hollywood? George Brent, who in his youth was forced to flee Dublin because of his subversive activities during the Irish rebellion, sponsored the California Esquadrille.[26] Victor McLaglen founded the California Light Horse Regiment to fight against anyone "opposed to the American ideal, whether it's an enemy outside or inside these borders."[27] Gary Cooper and Arthur Guy Empey launched the Hollywood Hussars in the spring of 1935. *The Motion Picture Herald* reported that the regiment was "armed to the teeth and ready to gallop on horseback within an hour."[28]

By 1950, fascism abroad, with the exception of Spain and Argentina, was decidedly dead. Yet, a sort of "friendly fascism" seemed to be gaining ground right here in America. In his book by the same name, Bertram Gross reminds us of the Sinclair Lewis novel in which a racist, anti-Semitic, flag-waving, army-backed demagogue wins the 1936 presidential election and establishes an Americanized version of Nazi Germany. Gross was more than convinced that *It Could Happen Here* could happen now, and those looking only for black shirts, mass meetings, and men on horseback could very well miss it. As he predicted: "In America [fascism will] be super-modern and multi-ethnic—as American as Madison Avenue, executive luncheons, credit cards, and apple pie. It would be fascism with a smile."[29]

While on camera, the members of the House Committee on Un-American Activities (commonly known as HUAC) *were always smiling.* The 1947 and 1951 hearings were less about investigating Hollywood communism than about a wholesale attack on the personal freedoms of industry employees, specifically those rights guaranteed by the First and Fifth Amendments to the Constitution.

Martin Dies, 1937 HUAC chair, set the tone for all future anti-Communist investigations with a modus operandi that included vague and sweeping accusations, the assumption of guilt by association, and outright intimidation, especially effective in pushing witnesses into fingering former associates. Critics of HUAC contended that the committee disregarded the civil liberties of its witnesses and that it consistently failed to fulfill its primary purpose, which interestingly enough was only to *recommend legislation.*

The most significant problem with HUAC, however, was the committee's failure to ever evidence real Red propaganda flickering across the country's silver screens. HUAC never proved that members of the Communist Party or Communist front organizations had actually produced subversive movies. As for fingering leftist images and seditious dialogue in American movie fare, the hearings failed miserably.

J. Parnell Thomas (R-New Jersey), who engaged in the same sort of media posturing honed to a fine art by McCarthy, subpoenaed forty-one prominent writers, actors, and directors.[30] The twenty-two so-called friendly witnesses (including writer Ayn Rand, studio heads Jack Warner, Walt Disney, and Louis B. Mayer, and actors Gary Cooper, Robert Taylor, Robert Montgomery, George Murphy, Richard Arlen, Adolphe Menjou, and Ronald Reagan) were treated with respect and allowed to read prepared statements. While acknowledging the presence of Communists in Hollywood, each and every one categorically denied that a Communist had ever injected his or her ideology into a film. Of the nineteen so-called unfriendly witnesses, only eleven were directly questioned about their membership in the Communist Party. Bertolt Brecht hightailed it back to East Germany after giving evidence, so that left HUAC with the "Hollywood Ten."[31]

Keep in mind that it is perfectly legal in the United States to join the Communist Party. The Hollywood Ten had only three options: (1) they could perjure themselves by denying Communist Party membership; (2) they could admit the truth, lose their jobs, and be forced to name others who were members; or (3) they could plead the Fifth Amendment.

Two directors (Edward Dmytryk and Herbert Biberman)[32] and eight screenwriters (John Howard Lawson, Dalton Trumbo, Albert Maltz, Alvah Bessie, Samuel Ornitz, Adrian Scott, Ring Lardner Jr., and Lester Cole)[33] chose option number three. As a result, they were held in contempt of Congress, despite the fact that the right against self-incrimination is guaranteed by the Fifth Amendment. The Hollywood Ten were likewise denied their First Amendment right to read an opening statement or respond with comments critical of the committee. If they tried, they were abruptly dismissed from the witness table, often in the midst of a response, while the committee investigator subsequently read his version of the truth into the *Congressional Record.*

The contempt citations led to six- to twelve-month prison terms after the Supreme Court refused to reverse the convictions.[34] The "blacklist," an old tactic successfully used against union organizers, was not wielded by HUAC, but by studio executives who met shortly after the hearings. The Hollywood Ten either did not work in this country or used pseudonyms during the rest of the decade.[35]

To counter the reckless and illegal attacks by HUAC, a group of Hollywood liberals led by actor Humphrey Bogart, his wife Lauren Bacall, John Huston, William Wyler, Danny Kaye, and Gene Kelly established the Committee for the First Amendment (CFA). The organization dispatched a contingent of famous actors and actresses to testify in Washington, sponsored two national radio broadcasts critical of HUAC, and took out negative ads in *The Hollywood Reporter* and *Daily Variety.*

However, studio heads, waving fat contracts in the faces of CFA members, held the power to order their employees to cease and desist. Protest gave way to self-interest and the CFA eventually collapsed.[36] In fact, Bogie was pressured to pen a piece for *Photoplay* in which he admitted his trip to Washington had been ill advised and that he had in fact been duped into testifying by Larry Parks, Irving Pichel, and the Hollywood Ten.[37]

Totally ignored in the hysteria generated by HUAC was reality. The Hollywood studio system was based on hands-on control by the moguls, who had en masse adopted Sam Goldwyn's "If you want to send a message, use Western Union" as a mantra.[38] Studio bosses didn't make ideological films because ideological films didn't sell tickets. The moguls repeatedly testified that even if a "pro-Communist" passage turned up in an early draft, no such material ever made it past the razor-sharp hatchet of the studio editor.

In 1951, HUAC returned for a second round, with John S. Wood (1949–52) and Harold Velde (1953–54) in charge. This time, however, the committee opted to slam individual motion picture employees, not the motion picture industry itself. The committee compiled a list of 324, including Lillian Hellman, Dashiell Hammett, Sidney Buchman, Abe Burrows, Jeff Corey, Will Geer, Karen Morley, Dorothy Parker, Clifford Odets, Larry Parks, Arthur Miller, Pete Seeger, John Garfield, and Howard Da Silva. Innumerable others found themselves guilty by association. By the time the hearings were over, the Bill of Rights was left in tatters. Coercing witnesses to "name names" became the unofficial preoccupation of the committee. Witnesses were expected to admit regret and could only "prove" their sincerity by giving up those in attendance at Communist functions.

The fear of losing a career or ending up in the slammer swelled the ranks of Tinsel Town stool pigeons with names such as Edward Dmytryk, Lloyd Bridges, Sterling Haydn, Frank Tuttle, Larry Parks, Leo Townsend, Isobel Lennart, Roy Huggins, Richard Collins, and Lee J. Cobb. Ex-Communists such as *A Face in the Crowd*'s Budd Schulberg and Elia Kazan held if there was, indeed, a Communist conspiracy, that it was appropriate, if not patriotic, to blow the whistle.[39] Kazan had stated publicly that he never regretted his testimony. "If I had my life to live over," he told *U.S. News and World Report*, " I wouldn't do anything differently," yet in his autobiography, *A Life* (1988), he endeavored to defend his role as a friendly witness even as he recounted the traumatic toll his testimony exacted on others.[40]

Otto Preminger and Kirk Douglas finally cracked the blacklist by crediting former "Hollywood Ten" member Dalton Trumbo for scripting, respectively, *Exodus* and *Spartacus* in 1960. It also became common knowledge that

Trumbo's sometime collaborator and fellow blacklistee, Michael Wilson, had written the blockbuster *The Bridge on the River Kwai* (1957) and was completing the script for *Lawrence of Arabia* (1962). After that, some blacklisted writers, actors, and directors went back to work. John Frankenheimer helped Martin Balsam, Kim Hunter, and Eli Wallach off the list.[41] Sam Jaffe, who had nabbed an Academy Award nomination for *The Asphalt Jungle* in 1950, had been reduced to teaching high school math, but he eventually bounced back as the popular Dr. Zorba on the *Ben Casey* television series. Lee Grant, who refused to testify against her first husband, screenwriter Arnold Manoff, was out of work for twelve years. Resurfacing in the '60s, she eventually walked away with two Oscars, one for acting (*Shampoo*, 1975) and the other for directing (*Down and Out in America*, 1986).

For most blacklisted performers, however, the future remained grim. Some stayed abroad.[42] Dozens forfeited their marriages. Even more endured permanent financial ruin. Mental and physical suffering seemed to hound the blacklistees as lives and livelihoods continued to elude their control. The esteemed Clifford Odets found himself finished as a writer. To friends and family, the deaths of John Garfield, J. Edward Bromberg, and Canada Lee were linked to their committee appearances. According to Otto Preminger, the blacklist contained more than four hundred names.[43] Less than 10 percent resumed their Hollywood careers once it was over.[44]

William L. Shirer, author of *The Rise and Fall of the Third Reich*, told the *Los Angeles Times* that America might be the first country in which fascism comes to power through democratic elections.[45] That came too close to being true on February 9, 1950, when a first-term senator from Wisconsin decided to deliver a little talk to the Women's Republican Club of Wheeling, West Virginia.

Herblock drew a famous cartoon depicting McCarthy emerging from a Washington, D.C., sewer, carrying a bucket of tar and a broad brush. Like most fascists, McCarthy knew how to exploit crisis conditions. After World War II, the United States' alliance with the Soviet Union ended, the Cold War began, and the Red Scare tilted into full force. The USSR's quick turnaround from trusted friend to deeply feared enemy created strong anti-Soviet, anti-Communist suspicions in America. In addition, the Soviet Communists had the atomic bomb. The United States responded by adopting a national security mentality, and the possibility of Communist infiltration could no longer be denied. McCarthy's addle-brained accusations hit the Senate agenda at exactly the same time Julius and Ethel Rosenberg were arrested for treason and Alger Hiss, a State Department official and former adviser to President Franklin Roosevelt, was convicted of providing classified documents to admitted Communist Whittaker Chambers.[46]

To his admirers, the senator from Wisconsin was heroism personified— "Tail Gunner Joe," taking on the nation's power elite in a doughty crusade against godless Communists. The American religious right, celebrating God's existence and human spiritual redemption, stood as a natural enemy to communism. From the time of Lenin through the Gorbachev era, conservative Americans vigorously defended religious freedom and church sovereignty. Distrust of the Soviet Union was most vociferously voiced from behind American Catholic pulpits.

McCarthy further played on the crisis of confidence plaguing the Truman administration. During his 1946 campaign for the Senate, the opportunistic McCarthy echoed the GOP attack on Truman (whose administration supposedly harbored Communists) and began his practice of smearing opponents as "pinko." As a Senate freshman, he dug in with other ardent anti-Communists and took the Communist threat to the airwaves.

Just prior to 1952 election, the cocky, darkly handsome senator built a coalition including the dispossessed military, who supported General MacArthur's desire to take the Korean War into Red China; Joseph P. Kennedy and other World War II isolationists; the China lobby, who endorsed Chiang Kai-shek's dream of overthrowing Mao Zedong; and returning Chinese missionaries, who had witnessed Communist abuse firsthand.[47]

Abolishing freedoms in order to consolidate their clout, McCarthyites were able to pass the 1950 Subversive Activities Control Act, which called for government employee loyalty tests and resulted in a spate of spurious investigations. In addition, the act appointed a Subversive Activities Control Board and required Communist action or front groups as well as individuals to register with the U.S. attorney general. A constitutional concern, however, was that the control board was given absolute power to determine which organizations/individuals would be labeled "Communist." In 1952, The McCarran–Walter Immigration Act, passed over Truman's vociferous veto, invested the State Department with authority to prohibit foreigners with alien political beliefs or affiliations from entering the country, a throwback to the Alien and Sedition Act of 1798. Under the law, current and former Communists, as well as homosexuals, anarchists, and those whom the State Department deemed "prejudicial to the public interest," could be turned away. The legislation was finally amended in 1987 to disallow denial of entry on the basis of alien attitudes or affiliations. Finally, McCarthyites roused twenty-six states to enact laws barring Communists from running for public office, twenty-eight states to pass laws denying state or local civil service jobs to Communists, and thirty-two states to require teacher loyalty oaths.[48]

Like other fascists, McCarthy was adept at manipulating the press and playing fast and loose with the truth. Rarely off page one for four years, he launched allegations an hour before deadline so that writers would run out of time before fact checking. Commentators such as Walter Winchell, Westbrook Pegler, and H. V. Kaltenborn lent McCarthy credibility as they transmuted his hyperbole into headlines. When reporters had the cheek to write anything critical about McCarthy, they found themselves under investigation.[49] David Halberstam summed up the senator's powers of manipulation with, "McCarthy [just] understood the theater of it all."[50]

Richard Powers, in his 1996 book, *Not Without Honor,* maintained that the 1950 Wheeling, West Virginia, speech, "was, in retrospect, the greatest disaster in the disastrous history of American anticommunism."[51] At the very least, the address gave a foretaste of McCarthy excesses to come, with its allegation of 205 Communists securely entrenched in the State Department. In actuality, the list was McCarthy's laundry slip.[52] Further-more, McCarthy's red-baiting rhetoric was actually contrived by *Washington Times-Herald* reporters Ed Nellow and George Waters along with *Chicago Tribune* writer Willard Edwards, who derived it from HUAC communications, a Nixon speech on Alger Hiss, and FBI reports to the Senate Judiciary Committee.[53] The Wheeling speech launched McCarthy's furious yet futile hamster-wheel course, forcing first McCarthy, then his defenders, to escalate audacious claims and counterclaims. Truman summed up McCarthy's true impact on communism when he quipped that McCarthy was the "Kremlin's greatest asset in America."[54]

McCarthy ramped up the reckless attempts of his role model (HUAC chairman Dies) at character assassination as he endeavored to turn individuals, whether card-carrying members of the Communist Party or not, into faceless symbols he could berate, humiliate and, eventually, eliminate. Since he was immune to prosecution for slander on the floor of the Senate, McCarthy flailed at all manner of targets, including fellow senators Ralph Flanders, J. William Fulbright, Guy Gillette, and Robert C. Henrickson, as well as Secretary of State Dean Acheson, Ambassador-at-Large Philip C. Jessup, Owen Lattimore (a noted specialist on Asian affairs in the State Department), and even President Harry Truman, who McCarthy once described as "an SOB . . . who would let red waters lap at all our shores"[55] and, on the occasion of Truman's dismissal of MacArthur, as some sort of drunken decision maker.

Even the highly esteemed George C. Marshall was not beyond McCarthy's reach. On June 14, 1951, McCarthy rose to his feet and informed the Senate that the World War II supreme commander/defense secretary had been a life-long minion of the Soviet Union. Powers described McCarthy's claim as "the red web thesis raised to the grandiose levels of cosmic madness."[56] During the course of his eleven-year Senate career, McCarthy was able to disrupt both the Truman and Eisenhower administrations, shrivel morale throughout every branch of the federal government, and obstruct, for months at a time, serious congressional business. He never uncovered a single Communist.

The boob tube provided the nation with a window into McCarthy's world and would prove the camera-keen demagogue's undoing. Edward

R. Murrow, considered the moral leader of the television industry, took on McCarthy and his shoddy tactics with his CBS show *See It Now* on March 9, 1954. Offered free time to reply, McCarthy, true to form, called Murrow names, tried to besmirch his character, and behaved as boorishly as Murrow predicted he would. After McCarthy's April 6 appearance, it was clear that Murrow had splintered McCarthy's brash veneer. His reign of terror was now on life support.

Twenty million viewers watched the Senate's Army–McCarthy hearings from April to June 1954. All four networks (ABC, NBC, CBS, and DuMont) broadcast the proceedings for thirty-six days at the specific request of President Dwight Eisenhower.[57] McCarthy's volatile temper, incessant "point of order, point of order" interruptions, cruel badgering of witnesses, irresponsible smear tactics, and utter lack of grace disgusted the viewers. When McCarthy attacked a member of the army defense staff for having belonged to a pro-Communist organization while in law school, army counsel Joseph N. Welch's "Have you no sense of decency, sir?" hung accusingly in the air.

On June 11, Senator Ralph Flanders, a Vermont Republican once labeled as senile by McCarthy, introduced a resolution calling for censure. Majority leader Lyndon B. Johnson named a special committee, chaired by Republican Arthur V. Watkins of Utah, to investigate the accusation. He carefully handpicked members so that McCarthy couldn't later claim he had been railroaded. On December 2, the Senate voted 67–22 to condemn McCarthy for contemptuous, contumacious, and denunciatory behavior.

HUAC continued until 1975, but ironically the reputation of the committee became victimized by its association with McCarthyism.

SUMMARY OF THE PLOT

A Face in the Crowd is a contemptuous look at America's fickle relationship with media-created celebrities. Marcia Jeffries (Patricia Neal), a radio reporter in dogged pursuit of local human-interest stories, discovers Lonesome Rhodes, played by a pre-Mayberry Andy Griffith, in a Tommyhawk County drunk tank. Rhodes, who has survived by his wits and on the kindness of gullible strangers, sees a meal ticket in Marcia's microphone. The guitar-toting hillbilly becomes KGRK's[58] voice of the common man, as he speaks the God's honest truth, flavored with an Arkansas drawl. The radio audience, especially pie-baking housewives, adores him because he seems to perceive their private yearnings and public humiliations. Rhodes boards the American Dream express to Memphis, where he becomes a $1,000-a-week television star. He then leapfrogs to the network, where he becomes a media adviser to a deep-pocketed fascist with an eye on the Oval Office. The hero with the folksy fables and cracker-barrel philosophy,

however, has feet of clay. After Marcia flips the "on air" switch at an op-
portune moment and lets the television audience in on the "real" Rhodes,
his career descends faster than the penthouse elevator that has transported
him to the top of the world. His TV show writer, Mel Miller (Walter
Matthau) reduces Lonesome's life story to an unsympathetic but best-
selling biography entitled *Demagogue in Denim.*

ONE NATION UNDER TELEVISION

That the McCarthy denouement occurred on television rather than radio
demonstrated the TV's emergence as the dominant medium in America.
By the late '40s, viewers in urban centers such as Los Angeles, Chicago,
New York, Philadelphia, and Baltimore were replacing their living room
radio consoles with the one-eyed monster. By 1950, a tipping point had
been reached and television walked away with the bigger audience.[59]

Subsequently, radio witnessed a mass exodus of national sponsors such
as Lever Brothers, General Foods, Ford Motors, R. J. Reynolds,
Colgate–Palmolive, and Procter and Gamble. *Variety* characterized the
abrupt advertising shift to television as the "greatest exhibition of mass
hysteria in show biz annals."[60] During the last six months of 1951, expenditures for TV advertising rose more than 195 percent. Radio claimed advertising dropped only 5 percent initially, but the industry would soon be
trapped in a nasty and seemingly never-ending downward spiral.

Television took its toll on a variety of recreational activities. As early as
1949, government statistics cited a falling off in movie attendance, book
purchases, admissions to professional sporting events, attendance at the
theater, and patronage of restaurants and bars. Soon, the decline in the
study habits of schoolchildren would be blamed on the TV.[61] When radio
megastar Fred Allen learned about television, he could scarcely contain
his enmity: "it's a device that permits people who haven't anything to do
to watch people who can't do anything."[62]

When McCarthy launched his attack on communism in 1950, there
were 3.8 million television sets. By the time *A Face in the Crowd* was released in 1957, that number had risen to 38.9 million (or 78.6 percent penetration).[63]

Talent agent extraordinaire William Morris chose an explosive
metaphor when he wrote in June 1949, "Television has the impact of an
atomic bomb. It is increasing the people's intellect in proportion to a
bomb's destructive power for blowing them to pieces. And it's a foregone
conclusion that national advertisers will go into TV or go out of business."[64] His prediction was supported by a U.S. Department of Commerce
report concluding that television would become the nation's leading sales
tool due to its effectiveness as "a combination of moving pictures, sound,

and immediacy."[65] It took only six years for advertisers to step up their television spending to $1 billion. In 1955, the total profits for NBC, CBS, and ABC swelled 116 percent.[66] On the *Public Broadcasting Laboratory* show in 1969, Edward P. Morgan observed, "once upon a time, television was supposed to operate in the public interest, but lo and behold, it has captured the public and made it a product—a packaged audience, so to speak, which it sells to advertisers."[67]

As far as Mr. and Mrs. John Q Public were concerned, television equaled entertainment. They didn't expect to be enlightened, instructed, or even spiritually uplifted. The idiot box was a medium of escape, a relaxing way to pass the time. Those who desired cultural refinement, program diversity, or a free education were at liberty to turn off the set and pursue those goals elsewhere.

Television, as film director Elia Kazan gleelessly admitted in the preface to the *Face in the Crowd* screenplay, "had won first place in the entertainment field."[68] Mesmerized millions were perfectly willing to put up with fellows who "come out and tell you with horrifying cheerfulness about soup or soap or cigarettes."[69]

In 1940, when political observers began to suspect that the new medium of radio was shaping voting behavior, researchers led by Paul Lazarsfeld examined the impact of mass media on American presidential politics. The findings led to the development of Lazarsfeld's "two-step flow theory of communication," which holds that voters aren't directly swayed by media but rely on knowledgeable opinion leaders for election information.[70] Subsequent studies of the 1952 and 1956 presidential elections substantiated Lazarsfeld's theory.[71]

Yet, as television emerged as the dominant medium, political observers would again raise fears about the impact of media on the American political process. Conclusions, brought by various researchers, were mixed. Early television coverage of the United Nations Assembly proceedings was credited with lending a hand in popularizing the international body and consequently helping to reverse traditional American isolationist policy.[72] TV was also lauded for playing a substantial role in diluting the power of political parties, boosting the influence of paid and free media, and even before the 1960 Nixon–Kennedy debates, facilitating the ability of a candidate to emphasize image over issues.

With respect to *A Face in the Crowd*, Elia Kazan disclosed: "The thing that drove us was our belief in the theme, our anticipation of the power TV would have in the political life of the nation. 'Listen to what the candidate says,' we urged, 'don't be taken in by his charm or his trust-inspiring personality. Don't buy the advertisement; buy what's in the package.'"[73]

Since 1960, hundreds of studies measuring the influence of television on politics have been conducted. The results boil down to the following: when it comes to choosing a candidate, the mass media function *in addition to* a variety of social and psychological factors. A vote for the opposition party, for example, is unlikely to result from media exposure. Even before election season begins, roughly two out of three who usually cast a ballot have already committed to a candidate. Far more commonly, the media play a role in reinforcing existing attitudes or crystallizing ambiguous attitudes. That is not to say that television doesn't persuade. National candidates wouldn't waste millions of dollars on a medium that doesn't work hard for them. For politicians, television has become the easiest and most economical way to keep the party faithful on board as well as pull in those voters seesawing on the margins.

Fearing in 1952 that General Dwight D. Eisenhower was going to dump him because of a secret slush-fund scandal, Richard Nixon gave TV the nod. Rather than allow his side of the story to be sifted through the press, the vice-presidential candidate went directly to the American people. The "Checkers" speech ended up saving Nixon's spot on the Republican ticket.

Although television cameras had been rolling into the Democratic and Republican conventions since 1949, it wasn't until Eisenhower engaged Anacin ad man Rosser Reeves that the medium was used to promote a presidential candidate. Ike's series of forty twenty-second political spots prompted George Ball, a Stevenson staffer, to observe "they have invented a new kind of campaign—conceived not by men who want us to face the crucial issues of this crucial day, but by the high powered hucksters of Madison Avenue."[74] Perennial candidate Adlai Stevenson himself weighed in with an indignant "the idea that you can merchandise candidates for high office like breakfast cereal—that you can gather votes like box tops—is, I think, the ultimate indignity to the democratic process."[75] Ironically, he delivered this remark at the national convention, which was orchestrated by an ad agency in the employ of the Democratic Party.

A Face in the Crowd arose out of a series of conversations between Bud Schulberg and Elia Kazan about television's inherent dangers, as well as its extensive potential for good. They wondered how much more compelling Huey Long would have been with the telly at his disposal, they commended Richard Nixon for the efficacy of his "Checkers" speech, and they held Senator McCarthy responsible for the harm he did to his own cause. Their discussions touched on the media coaching of public figures,[76] network execs view of the average watcher as "a retarded twelve-year-old," and the way the boob tube could seemingly make or break a performer or a politician—overnight.[77] They should have also discussed the inherent bias that colored their observations—wasn't it television that was luring former moviegoers away from the medium that paid their bills?

As Schulberg and Kazan began to immerse themselves in marathon television viewing in the interest of research, they discovered that "every once in awhile, something brilliant comes out of the box."[78] But for the most part, Schulberg and Kazan agreed, the news wasn't good. Their qualms about the influence of mass culture on American society in general, and the potential of television to aid right-wing movements in particular, were not groundless.

In the preface to the screenplay, Kazan wrote, "we took cognizance of the new synthetic folksiness that saturated certain programs, and the excursion into political waters by these 'I-don't-know-anything-but-I-know-what-I-think' guys."[79] The filmmakers were just as enraged as Adlai Stevenson at the prospect of television peddling artificial, made-to-order personalities with the same success with which it sold soap and soup. With that notion in mind, they set off for Madison Avenue, where according to Kazan they chatted up the big shots, lunched with the medium-sized shots, and hoisted a few with the little shots.[80] They got an inside look at advertising and much of what they saw showed up in *A Face in the Crowd*. Kazan confided: "We watched many sessions on the selling of Lipton's tea, the discussion of the word 'brisk' and how to picturize it. The discussions were really ludicrous; you could hardly keep a straight face at them. But as well as the ridiculous side, you could feel the intense, neurotic pressure they all worked under."[81]

But Kazan and Schulberg didn't stop there. They then hit the nation's capital to interview Stuart Symington and Lyndon Johnson about the role of television in politics. According to Kazan, they listened, made notes, compared notes, and discussed what they had seen. "Out of these conversations and the mutual desire to say something about [television], this giant of our times, came the shape of the picture."[82]

In a piece for the *New York Times*, Kazan summed up *A Face in the Crowd* in nine words: "There is power in television. It can be perverted."[83]

But isn't that begging the question?

THE FOLKSY FRAUD

By the early '50s, the United States had just emerged from two decades of disruption, bookended by the Great Depression and World War II. Americans welcomed television into their homes because it not only brought the glamour of movies with the convenience of radio, but also provided material proof that a time of trouble had finally ended. A brand new TV signified success as well as compensation for years of sacrifice. For an investment of a couple of hundred dollars, Americans could reap hours of entertainment, ensure family togetherness, and participate in a national cultural community.

At times of dislocation, folks can't seem to help being sucked in by any sort of dreamer. Just as Hitler, Mussolini, Franco, and Perón before him, Lonesome Rhodes just wants folks to believe he is the common man speaking to the common man. Kazan and Schulberg make no bones about using the "f" word, but they blend their brand of fascism with a hayseed populism that allows Rhodes to summon "everybody who's got to jump when somebody else blows the whistle" into his clutches.

There's no doubt that Lonesome Rhodes is a composite of several real-life figures. Filmmakers Schulberg and Kazan readily admit to the relationship between Lonesome Rhodes and fascist southern demagogue Hugh Pierce Long. It may seem odd that Long, known as "America's own Fascist," would urge redistribution of wealth and oppose big business, but don't forget that populists seem to straddle the usual left/right political expectations. As Kazan points out, "Huey Long did a lot of good in Louisiana."[84] Between 1928 and 1935, he put Louisiana residents to work on state-supported projects, including a massive, up-to-date highway and bridge system and an improved port and airport for New Orleans; he decreased utility and transportation rates; he provided free textbooks, free school lunches, free night-school courses for adult illiterates; he modernized state hospitals; and he pulled together enough appropriations to enable Louisiana State University to become a nationally recognized educational institution. Rhodes's scorn for his audience, according to Kazan "is what fascism really is."[85] Kazan and Schulberg were especially cognizant of what they called "a phenomenon that was happening in America at the time. We were always talking about and looking out for native grass-roots fascism. Folks overlook the fact that fascism contains attractive elements of populism."[86]

Symbolic of all his accomplishments, Long erected a skyscraping state capitol to symbolize the state's upward mobility. The parallel in *A Face in the Crowd* shows Rhodes receiving the gold key to the top two floors of New York's finest hotel, the Sherry Towers, and the private elevator that transports him down as well as up.

But like Rhodes in *A Face in the Crowd*, Long was a gifted image manipulator who used nicknames as a kind of shorthand to encapsulate identity. Even though Long was a shrewd lawyer, he tried to appear ignorant, pretending to humble hillbilly origins while in reality his family was college educated and decidedly middle class. As Larry Rhodes becomes "Lonesome," Long adopted the moniker "Kingfish" from the popular *Amos and Andy* show. For radio fans, Long's logic was obvious—those who sneered at the Kingfish's buffoonery often underestimated the man to their own peril.

Long, like Rhodes, was a salesman, songwriter, and star. Like the Vitajex-hawking Rhodes, Long peddled Cottolene, a cottonseed cooking-oil substitute. Rhodes's free-falling, half-story, half-song rendition of the old Jelly Roll Morton ballad "Free Man in the Morning" wins him a stint on WGRK's *Early Bird Show*, while Long penned "Every Man a King" as well as two rousing fight songs for Louisiana State University.[87] The Lonesome-as-institution montage in *A Face in the Crowd* alludes to a country-wide network of fan clubs. Long's Share Our Wealth societies mushroomed all over America, providing what could have been the political base for his long-intended presidential bid.

To Joey De Palma (Anthony Franciosa), Lonesome Rhodes is going to be the next Arthur Godfrey and, in fact, De Palma sells Rhodes as such during a frenetic bidding war among Madison Avenue advertising agencies. Ben Gross could have been describing Lonesome Rhodes when he penned: "The women tell me [Godfrey] has sex appeal; his voice, resonant and tinted with warm tones, conveys an inherent magnetism."[88] By the time he hit television, Godfrey was well on his way to becoming an entertainment icon.[89] Godfrey reached his peak in the early '50s, when 82 million Americans watched him during his nearly ten hours of programming a week.[90] His shows generated more than 10 percent of CBS's total revenues.[91] *Arthur Godfrey's Talent Scouts* (broadcast simultaneously on radio and television) as well as *Arthur Godfrey and His Friends* ended up in the top ten.[92] After hip surgery, Godfrey received forty thousand "get well" letters and cards a week.[93] Churchgoers lit candles and petitioned heaven for his recovery. CBS, at great expense, erected a transmission tower on his farm so Godfrey could broadcast from home.

Like that of Rhodes, Godfrey's success resulted from a homespun humility. Godfrey observed that radio announcers seemed to harbor a superiority complex, showed off to their mass audiences instead of speaking to a single individual, and failed to really listen to their guests. He translated these conclusions into a relaxed, conversational style that became his well-compensated trademark.

Delivering commercials live during the course of the show allows Rhodes, as it did Godfrey, to skewer the advertiser. In Memphis, Rhodes refuses to kowtow to Mr. Luffler and ends up being dumped by the mattress company advertiser. Even though Godfrey couldn't help himself from poking fun at Lipton Chicken Noodle Soup, the company wasn't about to destroy their golden egg–laying goose, so they grinned and bore it when he would swirl his spoon through a bowl of hot soup and cluck, "Mmmmm. Noodles, noodles, noodles. Where's the chicken?"

Like Rhodes, when Godfrey allowed his ego to do his thinking for him, he eventually lost the audience. In 1950, Godfrey uttered "damn" and "hell" on one of his live broadcasts and had a rough time weathering the disdain of the viewers, the affiliates, and CBS officials.[94] Godfrey's most costly mistake, however, was firing singer Julius La Rosa on the air.[95] Viewers equated this high-handed tactic with throwing a surrogate son out of the house for no good reason. In fact, Godfrey's downward spiraling career inspired Mel Miller's "Whatever happened to what's-his-name?" speech, which he delivers after Marcia allows the audience to hear Rhodes's assessment of his fan base.)

Unlike Joey De Palma, Marcia Jeffries sees Will Rogers in Lonesome Rhodes. According to Kazan, this compelling secondary story in *A Face in the Crowd* focuses on Jeffries' belief that "she's found a personality with great potential for good."[96]

To Marcia, Rhodes is an old-fashioned mixture of honesty, independence, and shirt-off-the-back sentimentality. The first thing Lonesome does in Memphis, in an inside-the-art-and-the-artifice gesture, is to actually show the viewers the monitor, the red light on the camera, and the cigar he got from Hymie, the grip.

Abe Steiner (Henry Sharp), a theatrical agent from Memphis who claims to have "discovered" Grand Old Opry's Hank Williams and Eddy Arnold, agrees with Marcia and tells Lonesome, "Mr. Rhodes, you put me in mind of Will Rogers when he first came to Memphis. I can make you a star, boy, if you'll put yourself in my hands."

When the Vitajex sponsor, General Haynesworth (Percy Waram), first meets Rhodes, he remarks that Will Rogers may have been "just a gum-chewing, rope-twirling cowboy, but he got to where he was by telling off Presidents and kings." Haynesworth envisioned Lonesome Rhodes as a Rogers-like "influence, a wielder of opinion, an institution positively sacred to his country, like the Washington Monument." And sure enough, "under [Haynesworth's] wing," Rhodes finds himself flying to Formosa to "do an interview with the head man over there." He's invited to meet with the top brass at a Pentagon psychological warfare conference. Like a good little fascist, Lonesome joins with the machinery of power.

Will Rogers's "voice of the common man" had a pronounced Oklahoma drawl, occasionally muted by a mouthful of chewing gum. Born of mixed Cherokee descent, Rogers liked to boast that his ancestors may not have come over on the Mayflower, but they did meet the boat. Like Rhodes's "well, chop me up an' sell me for dog food" persona, Rogers affected a pose of ignorance. He accentuated his rural background and lack of formal education with colloquial expressions ("hokum"), intentional misspellings ("natchel self") and homespun grammatical errors ("well, got all my feet through but one"). In reality, he was a voracious reader ("All I know is just what I read in the papers"), a thoughtful commentator, and skilled in the use of the pun, metaphor, and hyperbole. Common sense underlined every jest. By assuming the stance of a good-natured, naïve country boy, Rogers was able to lampoon politicians, business tycoons, and foreign dignitaries without seemingly causing offense. The cowboy philosopher also resonated with the American public—an estimated 20 million readers looked forward to his columns, syndicated in 350 newspapers, over the years. Without the assistance of a single joke writer, Rogers penned more than 2 million words.[97]

Rogers may have nominally belonged to the Democratic Party ("because it's funnier to be a Democrat") but he was largely a populist. In fact, the easygoing guy who "never met a man he didn't like" at one time pub-licly supported the Fascist regime of Benito Mussolini. Although fre-quently asked to run for public office, he invariably refused. *Life* magazine talked him into accepting the facetious Anti-Bunk Party's presidential nomination in 1924. The party platform was "Whatever the other fellow don't do, we will." Despite the fact that Rogers distrusted the motives and methods of those in power, his success brought him face time with as-sorted fat cats and business tycoons. You could say he ended up joining the establishment he mocked for a living, since he counted Calvin Coolidge, Herbert Hoover, and Alfred E. Smith as close personal friends.

With publicity stunts such as buying a house for Mrs. Cooley and start-ing up charities such as Brother's Keepers and the Summer Camp for Crippled Children, Rhodes merely plays at being a philanthropist, but Rogers was the real deal, an easy touch for a worthy cause who donated both his earnings and his talent. In addition, in stark contrast to Rhodes, there has never been a media idol as honest, upright, and squeaky clean as Will Rogers. He wed his childhood sweetheart and never again felt the need to ogle another woman. Further, Rogers maintained a strong sense of honor and public decency, even when it cost him personally.[98]

WHAT WENT WRONG

As Rhodes's fan base increases, his public candor, modesty, and benefi-cence fall sway to his private mendacity, arrogance, and treachery. Power not only corrupts, but it also tends to magnify emotional immaturity and any extant psychological insecurities.[99]

Rhodes's psychological problems are rooted in his obsessive need for love from the audience. Rhodes doesn't marry the smart woman who might propel him toward his better self; he elopes with a seventeen-year-old baton twirler who represents the American public "all wrapped up with a yellow ribbon into one cute little package." Unfortunately, Betty Lou (Lee Remick), the physical culmination of his love affair with the mass audience, ends up in bed with Joey De Palma—the *real* Lonesome Rhodes (since De Palma owns 51 percent of the voting stock in L. R. En-terprises). Further, knowing how fickle the American public can be, the savvy agent signs up "the next Lonesome Rhodes" (Barry Mills) and has the younger, easier to handle replacement waiting in the wings.

In the end, when Beanie (Rod Brasfield) can't pacify Rhodes with the cheers, guffaws, and applause from the mechanical response machine that Rhodes invented "for home use," Rhodes goes into "desperation mode." The audience can't help but feel contempt for the falling star who tries, quite pathetically, to frighten a black waiter, employed to serve at his "vic-tory" banquet, into giving him the love, love, love he craves.[100]

RHODES AS A COMMUNICATION CONSULTANT

In *The Phantom President* (1935), the first film to poke fun at the "selling of a president," a group of fascist-minded senators believe Theodore Blair (George M. Cohan) is the sort of "great man" who can get the nation out of the depression, but he just lacks the charisma. Peter Varney (also George M. Cohan) is a snake oil salesman with charm and confidence to spare, so they enlist Varney to get Blair elected.

Charisma can come from a telegenic appearance, a sense of self-possession, animal magnetism, or a "he really knows what he's talking about" expertise. Kazan believed that cult figures such as Rhodes have "this magical thing, confidence, or beauty, or talent that people are attracted to."[101] Yet, it's one thing to exploit your own charisma; it's quite another to try and transplant that attribute into someone else.

While the friends of General Haynesworth have the money, they don't have an electable candidate. "We've got to face it. Politics have entered a new stage. The television stage. . . . We've got to find thirty-five million buyers for the product we call Worthington Fuller." The charisma-challenged senator isn't so sure. He rationalizes, "I know that's not what the American people want to hear, but I think I know what they need." Nevertheless, after Beanie (who represents the average voter) assesses Fuller's performance as "flatter than last night's beer," Fuller relents.

Rhodes nicknames the bald politico "Curly," informs him that pressing his lips together makes him look like a sissy, invites him to loosen up by making fun of himself, and suggests Fuller come on camera with a pet.

The second stage in the "Fuller for President" campaign requires Rhodes to star in a new television show featuring "a bunch of colorful country characters a'sittin' around a'listenin' to Lonesome Rhodes soundin' off on everything from the price of popcorn to the hydrogen bomb." The *Lonesome Rhodes Cracker Barrel* introduces a voter-friendly Fuller, who waxes philosophical about the Daniel Boone spirit and reckons "we need big men, not big government." As a result, Fuller's Gallup poll numbers blast from 3 to 11 percent.

Schulberg and Kazan are so busy playing Curly for laughs that they fail to realize a Worthington Fuller type getting into the Oval Office, even with Lonesome's help, is neither menacing nor believable. If Fuller were a threat, wouldn't he more closely resemble the sneaky senator from Wisconsin than the likable Ike? Kazan admitted, "Our senator, you feel, is such an ass, that you never think he might win. I think we made fools of the side we didn't like."[102] Critics agreed. Fuller and his fascist political group never really present a clear and present danger. Furthermore, the liberal values of Kazan and Schulberg were "personified by a remarkably weak and indecisive character, the television writer, able to express his disgust only through some improbable high-flown dialogue."[103]

WHAT MAKES MEL RUN?

Kazan remembers his first lunch in the Twentieth Century–Fox commissary. He was told that the legendary Darryl F. Zanuck, flanked by a phalanx of producers, supped behind the closed doors of the executive dining room. The studio's famous directors were assembled along the best wall, gazing out over the oversized dining room, each at his reserved table, being served by his favorite waitress, also reserved. The center tables were occupied by a veritable constellation of stars. But it took Kazan several weeks to become aware of "a sorry group at a remote table. Their isolation was so evident that it seemed planned. They laughed in an hysterical way, giddy or bitter." He didn't have to ask. This is where the writers ate lunch.[104]

Mel Miller, AKA "Vanderbilt '44" or "The Frontal Lobe," couldn't be anyone but Budd Schulberg, even though Phi Beta Kappa Schulberg actually attended Dartmouth College. An off-the-cuff performer like Rhodes really doesn't need a writer, but the network insisted. Miller ends up composing copy for Lonesome Rhodes comic books, that is, when he's not lusting after Marcia, cracking wise about his megalomaniacal employer, or bellyaching about what little respect the writing profession commands.

Mel can usually be found either in a bar or in the "Writing Department," where he and a couple of other hacks while away the hours throwing darts—at a photograph of Rhodes's face. Posters reading "Classics Adapted While You Wait—We Also Take in Laundry" and "Please Remove the Straw from Your Hair Before Leaving This Room" decorate the walls. "Here you see the lepers of the great television industry," offers Mel as he gives Marcia the twenty-five-cent tour.

Kazan, also a Phi Beta Kappan, really didn't care for the Miller character: Mel "hasn't much gumption or strength," he allowed, but someone had to be an antifascist mouthpiece and Schulberg tapped the mealy-mouthed Mel for the honor.[105]

CREATION OF A GOLEM

Mary Shelley based her Frankenstein monster on the golem character from sixteenth-century Jewish folklore. In 1920, the medieval legend was translated into a German film classic that so impressed Boris Karloff, he painstakingly mimicked actor Paul Wegner's awkward statue shuffle eleven years later in the movie *Frankenstein*. According to legend, real-life Rabbi Judah Lowe (1520–1609), later given the name "the Maharal," feared for his community's safety when anti-Semites in Czechoslovakia circulated vicious rumors about Jews mixing the blood of Christian children into matzo. The rabbi slapped together a humanoid figure made of clay and wielded a little cabalistic hocus-pocus naming the creation, and the golem drew his first breath.

For a while, the golem diligently toiled at Prague's Alt Neu Synagogue—when he wasn't protecting the Jews—and the Maharal loved him. However, the golem began to change—he seemed taller than before and the rabbi could barely perceive the mark of Truth on his forehead. Most of all, the superpowered giant had become so infused with ego that he would no longer do what was right. He suddenly went completely off the reservation, spilling the blood of those he was meant to defend. Eventually, the rabbi was forced to trick him into allowing the life force to drain from his body. The moral of the story, of course, is that every golem is imperfectly made and only God can safely bring life into being. When man turns to creation, he might manage the broad strokes, but he invariably misses the subtle, but oh-so-necessary, nuances.[106]

Marcia called on the magic that is electromagnetic waves to create Lonesome Rhodes. Yet, it's only after she names him that her superpowered golem begins to live. According to François Truffaut, "As she develops the program [A Face in the Crowd], she unearths a bearded brute in a prison in a scene that is the most important moment of the film. It is the trigger that will catapult this man, Rhodes, out from the under-belly of society. She asks his name, and he answers, 'Rhodes.' 'Rhodes what?' 'I see, just Rhodes.' She takes the microphone and says, 'His name is Rhodes but his last name is Lonesome.' The spirit of the film is contained in that sentence. A small journalistic trick starts the whole machinery."[107] Obviously, in Truffaut's version something got lost in the translation from English. The actual exchange in the film begins with Marcia inquiring, "What's your first name?" To which Rhodes replies "Jack, Mack, what's the difference?" Then Marcia informs the listening audience, "He calls himself 'Lonesome' Rhodes."

What does Marcia love about her creation? According to Kazan, "He saw the truth and said it right away. And there was the real source of his power."[108] Rhodes is a truth-teller in a hypocritical world. He has a knack for seeing into the spirit, putting his finger on unexpressed feelings, and blurting out loud what everybody realizes but doesn't dare articulate. A veteran engineer tells Marcia, "That's the first time I ever heard the real truth go out over this mike. Rings like a silver dollar."

If you are going create a man, you had better start with unadulterated clay. Rhodes was a hard-drinking, two-timing phony when Marcia first spied him in jail. He was, to somewhat understate the case, a man of varied and excessive appetites. When Marcia theorizes "you put your whole self into that laugh, don't you?" He counters, "Marshy, I put my whole self into everything I do."

His father, a spieler with a two-bit carnival, ran off when Rhodes was "knee high to a beer barrel." His mother carried on with a series of so-called uncles. As Rhodes confesses, "seemed like there wasn't a town in Arkansas or Missouri I didn't have an uncle in. Yes, Ma'am, my old lady sure was generous about taking in relatives." The first Mrs. Rhodes (Kay Medford) tries to set Marcia straight about Lonesome: "Larry thinks he has to take a bite out of every broad he sees. And as soon as he does, he calls 'em tramps and drops 'em. It's all part of his psycho-something or other." But Marcia refuses to believe her.

Marcia catches her first undeniable glimpse of Rhodes's clay feet after catching him shacking up with the buxom waitress from the juke joint. He responds by trying to turn the tables on her: "you cold fish respectable girls, . . . inside you crave the same things as the rest of em."

Marcia sees the power even before Rhodes does. "How does it feel?" she inquires, "saying anything that comes into your head and being able to sway people like this?" Power, however, changes Marcia's golem. Rhodes seems to grow larger than life and Marcia has trouble perceiving the mark of Truth on his forehead—especially as the train heads for the big time and Marcia hears Rhodes mutter under his breath "Boy am I glad to shake that dump." When he sees a look of horror cross her face, he quickly shifts gears, "Aw, honey, I was only kidding."

Marcia conceals her suspicions and, in Kazan's words, "keeps the ambivalence going," especially after Rhodes makes pretty "I need you" speeches. According to critic Douglas Brode, however, what Marcia fails to grasp is that the creation is often cleverer than the creator.[109] Not only does this golem relish the taste of raw power, but also his craving starts to grow. Rhodes becomes so infused with ego that he will no longer do what is right.

Marcia continues to fool herself into thinking that if she just loves Rhodes enough, he will become the man she sees when she gazes into his big brown eyes. She tells Mel, "I found him—he's—well, he's mine for better or worse—and I keep doing my small best to make him better." Yet Mel is not fooled and eventually forces Marcia to face the fact that Rhodes has gone off the reservation, spilling the blood of those he was meant to defend.

Marcia ultimately accepts her responsibility as creator. She tricks Rhodes into revealing himself. The disenchanted audience drains the life force out of him.

There's a revealing postscript to this little tale. According to Kazan, "the realest story" in *A Face in the Crowd* had little to do with American politics or even life behind the scenes of the television industry. It concerned what he calls "women as conscience." The director, who had launched the film careers of Marlon Brando, Julie Harris, James Dean, Carroll Baker, Warren Beatty, and Lee Remick, used to counsel his actors, "The only way to understand any character is through yourself."[110]

Kazan confessed that both he and Schulberg had chosen Marcia-type women as wives. Kazan speculates that Schulberg is the kind of guy who is attracted to a woman who represents the "right" way or the "best" life.[111] But if the intimate drama of the film has an emotional reference to Schulberg, it has an equal, if not greater, reference to Kazan, who in his autobiography details in uninhibited kiss-and-tell-all specificity how, despite the occasional dalliance, he clung to wife Molly Day Thatcher because she represented the "very heart of America, which my family had come here to find.[112]

THE AUDIENCE RESPONDS

Since 1957, reception of *A Face in the Crowd* has ranged from absolute acclaim to nasty negatives. On the plus side: Kazan "can tease humor out of a situation or wring the last gasps of emotion from a scene without becoming maudlin. Such is his talent," or Kazan and Schulberg's "treatment of TV was not exaggerated," or "this film will help educate the film audience into an understanding of how public opinion is manipulated."[113] The disenchanted carped that Kazan "hacks and haws with such ill-considered fury that the patient soon becomes a mere victim and the satire falls to pieces," or "all that effort—to beat a straw man into the dust."[114]

Although on the whole film reviews were kind and the German film critics evidenced their approval with an award in 1957 for the screenplay, the movie-going public just wasn't ready for such intense introspection. This was a time when Communists were trying to destroy America. In Kazan's estimation, " I think a picture that tries to do something as difficult as this picture, has to be perfect and I don't think we were, not quite."[115]

The film fell short of perfection in at least three areas. First, an overarching political bias caused Kazan and Schulberg to caricature critical characters such as Rhodes and Fuller.[116] Second, both critics and the folks at the Bijou require a pigeonhole to categorize a film. Just exactly what is *A Face in the Crowd*? Even Kazan was hard-pressed to pick a genre. Third, the ending in which Rhodes exposes his true revulsion for his audience—once he believes he is off the air—is hackneyed, to say the least. The *Variety* headline "Lonesome's All-Time Blooper Tops Uncle Don's" may allow the filmmakers to claim they are merely paying "homage" to the radio kiddie host who reportedly added, "that should hold the little bastards" at the end of his show, but moviegoers had just seen the same ending the year before in Jose Ferrer's tour de force, *The Great Man*. Released in 1956, Ferrer's film also used a sincere, uncorrupted human being to momentarily seize advantage of the "live" nature of programming (the influential medium's real vulnerability) to let the public in on a behind-the-scenes truth about the star.[117]

Kazan sums it up best: "I think I let the audience off too easily, in a position where they could patronize [Rhodes], where they could look down on him, and say, 'Oh, those jackasses! How could they be taken in by that man!' But they shouldn't feel that. They should say: '*I* could be taken in.'"[118]

NOTES

1. S. J. Woolf, Editor, *Fascism in Europe* (London: Methuen, 1981), 353.

2. Military tribunals must now be public and the verdict unanimous.

3. Lincoln suspended the writ of habeas corpus during the Civil War, while Presidents Johnson and Nixon plotted to mute the loyal opposition during Vietnam. The 1940 Smith Act, which made the advocacy of revolution a criminal offense, was upheld by the Supreme Court during the height of the Korean War, yet restrictions on the constitutionality of revolutionary propaganda and organizations were progressively eliminated a decade later.

4. William Ebenstein and Edwin Fogelman, *Today's Isms,* 9th ed. (Englewood Cliffs, N.J.: Prentice-Hall, 1985), 99.

5. Bertram Gross, *Friendly Fascism: The New Face of Power in America* (New York: Evans and Company, 1980), 3.

6. See Ian Kershaw, *The Hitler Myth: Image and Reality in the Third Reich* (Oxford: Oxford University Press, 1987); John Toland, *Adolf Hitler* (New York: Doubleday, 1976); and Alan Bullock, *Hitler: A Study in Tyranny* (New York: HarperCollins, 1964).

7. Hermann Rauschning, one of Hitler's early colleagues, believed that marching not only kills thought but also ends individuality.

8. See Ivone Kirkpatrick, *Mussolini: Study of a Demagogue* (London: Oldhams, 1964); Denis Mack Smith, *Mussolini* (New York: Vintage, 1982); MacGregor Knox, *Mussolini Unleashed, 1939–41: Politics and Strategy in Fascist Italy's Last War* (Cambridge: Cambridge University Press, 1982).

9. See S. F. A. Coles, *Franco of Spain* (London: Neville Spearman, 1955); Brian Crozier, *Franco: A Biographical History* (London: Eyre and Spottiswoode, 1967); and Stanley G. Payne, *The 1936–1975 Franco Regime* (Madison: University of Wisconsin Press, 1987).

10. Arnold C. Brackman, *The Other Nuremberg: The Untold Story of the Tokyo War Crime Trials* (New York: Morrow, 1987); Courtney Browne, *Tojo: The Last Banzai* (New York: Holt, 1967); and Robert J. C. Butow, *Tojo and the Coming of the War* (Princeton, N.J.: Princeton University Press, 1961).

11. Quoted in Gross, *Friendly Fascism,* 20.

12. Woolf, *Fascism,* 12.

13. Primarily used in a religious context and culturally understood as "God the Father."

14. Beverly Merrill Kelley, "The Impact of John Dean's Credibility before the Senate Select Committee on Presidential Campaign Practices" (Ph.D. diss., University of California at Los Angeles, 1977), 48.

15. George L. Mosse, *Masses and Man: Nationalist and Fascist Perceptions of Reality* (New York: Fertig, 1980), 185–86.

16. See Adolf Hitler, *Mein Kampf,* translated by Ralph Manheim (Boston: Houghton Mifflin, 1971). His energy level was probably due to injections of methamphetamine.

17. Max J. Skidmore, *Ideologies: Politics in Action* (San Diego: Harcourt Brace Jovanovich, 1989), 173.

18. Skidmore, *Ideologies*, 181.

19. Ironically, Hitler survived in Vienna by residing in homeless housing operated by charitable Jews.

20. Hitler, *Mein Kampf*, 231.

21. Laura Fermi, *Mussolini* (Chicago: University of Chicago Press, 1961), 147–49.

22. Ebenstein and Fogelman, *Today's Isms*, 107.

23. The biology of women according to the Nazis (characterized by the phrase *Kinder, Küche, und Kirche*, or children, kitchen, and church) renders them inferior to males in the classroom, on the battlefield, and in politics.

24. The ultimate profascist film would have to be Leni Riefenstahl's *Triumph of the Will* (1934), a stunning documentation of upturned faces worshipping Hitler and the Sixth Nazi Party Congress in 1934 Nuremberg, Germany. Riefenstal, who had a tough time negotiating the American release of her film, ironically provided the defeat behind the triumph—Frank Capra was able to use her *Triumph of the Will* for anti-Nazi propaganda in the "Why We Fight" series.

25. Neal Gabler, *An Empire of Their Own: How the Jews Invented Hollywood* (New York: Doubleday/Anchor, 1989), 152.

26. Carey McWilliams, "Hollywood Plays with Fascism," *Nation* 140 (May 29, 1935), 623–24.

27. Quoted in Anthony Slide, "Hollywood's Fascist Follies," *Film Comment* 127, no. 4 (July–August 1991), 63.

28. Slide, "Fascist Follies," 63.

29. Gross, *Friendly Fascism*, 3.

30. Thomas would later be jailed himself for accepting kickbacks.

31. Most of the Hollywood Ten's films dealt with antifascist themes. These included *Hotel Berlin* (1945), *The Master Race* (1941), *Crossfire* (1947), *Sahara* (1943), *Pride of the Marines* (1945), *Destination Tokyo* (1944), and *Thirty Seconds over Tokyo* (1944).

32. Dmytryk directed *The Caine Mutiny* (1954), *Raintree Country* (1957), *The Young Lions* (1958), and *Walk on the Wild Side* (1962); Biberman was also a screenwriter, and his *Salt of the Earth* (1954), released in the United States in 1965, was voted the year's best picture by the French Motion Picture Academy.

33. Lawson was the first president of the Screen Writers Guild; Trumbo, prior to the blacklisting, was one of the highest-paid Hollywood writers and won the best screenplay Oscar for *The Brave One* (1956) under the pseudonym Robert Rich; Maltz collaborated on such patriotic fare as *Destination Tokyo* (1944) and the Oscar-nominated *Pride of the Marines* (1945); Bessie was nominated for an Academy Award for the original story of the patriotic action film *Objective Burma* (1945) and served as a member of the Abraham Lincoln Brigade in the Spanish Civil War; Ornitz was recruited by Hollywood in the early days of talkies and shared credit for the screenplay *Three Faces West* (1940); Scott was identified in 1951 as a Communist by Edward Dmytryk, the director of most of his films; Lardner scripted the Academy Award–winning *Woman of the Year* in 1942 and went on to write *M*A*S*H* in 1970; and Cole was credited with *The Invisible Man Returns* (1940).

34. Dmytryk, who later agreed to cooperate, ended up serving an abbreviated sentence.

35. See Patrick McGilligan and Paul Buhle, *Tender Comrades: A Backstory of the Hollywood Blacklist* (New York: St. Martin's, 1997).

36. Steven Mintz and Randy Roberts, *Hollywood's America: United States History through Its Films* (St. James, N.Y.: Brandywine, 1993), 195–96.

37. Humphrey Bogart, "I'm No Communist," *Photoplay* (March 1948).

38. The tight-fisted control of the studios goes back to the Motion Picture Patents Company, which refused to identify actors and actresses. They were afraid that if performers became popular, they might demand more money.

39. Kazan was denied the American Film Institute's Life Achievement Award, but he did receive an honorary Oscar.

40. *Contemporary Authors Online* (Gale Group, 2000). Reproduced in *Biography Resource Center* (Farmington Hills, Mich.: Gale, 2001), www.galenet.com/servlet/BioRC. Elia Kazan, *A Life* (New York: Doubleday, 1989).

41. Louis B. Parks, "Veteran Director Returns to Form," *Houston Chronicle,* March 5, 2000, 10.

42. Donald Ogden Stewart, Carl Foreman, Paul Jarrico, and Sidney Buchman went to Europe, while Albert Maltz and Dalton Trumbo lived in Mexico.

43. Otto Preminger, *Preminger: An Autobiography* (Garden City, N.Y.: Doubleday, 1977), 117.

44. Dan Georgakas, "Hollywood Blacklist," in *Encyclopedia of the American Left,* edited by Mari Jo Buhle, Paul Buhle, and Dan Georgakas (New York: Oxford University Press, 1998).

45. Quoted in Gross, *Friendly Fascism,* 6.

46. During the 1948 Hiss hearings, a new Republican House member, Richard M. Nixon, leveraged his national exposure into a Senate seat in 1950 and the vice presidency in 1952.

47. Craig R. Smith, *Silencing the Opposition: Government Strategies of Suppression of Freedom of Expression* (Albany, N.Y.: State University of New York Press, 1996), 159–60.

48. Smith, *Silencing the Opposition,* 164–65.

49. Smith, *Silencing the Opposition,* 160.

50. David Halberstam, *The Fifties* (New York: Fawcett Columbine, 1993), 54.

51. Richard Gid Powers, *Not without Honor: The History of American Anticommunism* (New York: Free Press, 1995), 235.

52. Smith, *Silencing the Opposition,* 159.

53. Powers, *Not without Honor,* 242.

54. Powers, *Not without Honor,* 242.

55. Smith, *Silencing the Opposition,* 163.

56. Powers, *Not without Honor,* 244.

57. Stanley J. Baran, *Introduction to Mass Communication: Media Literacy and Culture* (Mountain View, Calif.: Mayfield, 2001), 220.

58. K-Jerk, get it?

59. J. Fred MacDonald, *One Nation under Television: The Rise and Decline of Network TV* (Chicago: Nelson–Hall, 1994), 50.

60. *Variety,* October 18, 1950, 23.

61. MacDonald, *One Nation,* 67.

62. Quoted in Halberstam, *Fifties,* 180.

63. MacDonald, *One Nation,* 59.

64. *Television* (June 1949): 31.

65. Reported in *Variety,* August 17, 1949, 32.

66. MacDonald, *One Nation,* 60.

67. MacDonald, *One Nation,* 53.

68. Budd Schulberg, *A Face in the Crowd: A Play for the Screen* (New York: Bantam, 1957), 16.

69. Schulberg, *Face in the Crowd,* 16.

70. See Paul Lazarsfeld, Bernard Berelson, and Hazel Gudet, *The People's Choice* (New York: Columbia University Press, 1968).

71. See Angus Campbell, Phillip E. Converge, Warren E. Miller, and Donald E. Stokes, *The American Voter* (New York: Wiley, 1960).

72. MacDonald, *One Nation,* 69.

73. Kazan, *A Life,* 568.

74. Quoted in Stephen Fox, *The Mirror Makers: A History of American Advertising and Its Creators* (New York: Morrow, 1984), 307.

75. Fox, *Mirror Makers,* 310.

76. *A Face in the Crowd* anticipates the quiz show scandals of the late '50s.

77. Kazan and Schulberg used the elevator as a metaphor for upward (and downward) mobility.

78. Schulberg, *Face in the Crowd,* 16.

79. Schulberg, *Face in the Crowd,* 16.

80. Schulberg, *Face in the Crowd,* 16.

81. Michel Ciment, *Kazan on Kazan* (New York: Viking, 1974), 113.

82. Schulberg, *Face in the Crowd,* 17.

83. Elia Kazan, "Paean of Praise for a Face in the Crowd," *New York Times,* May 26, 1957, II, 5.

84. Ciment, *Kazan on Kazan,* 118.

85. Jeff Young, *Kazan: The Master Director Discusses His Films* (New York: New Market, 1999), 251.

86. Young, *Kazan,* 235.

87. "Every Man a King" was his perennial campaign slogan and the title of his 1933 autobiography.

88. Quoted in Steven D. Stark, *Glued to the Set: The 60 Television Shows and Events That Made Us Who We Are Today* (New York: Free Press, 1997), 224.

89. Godfrey was so popular that *Broadcasting–Telecasting Magazine* speculated that it was only a matter of time before the second syllable of "Godfrey" would be dropped.

90. *The Scribner Encyclopedia of American Lives, vol. 1: 1981–85* (New York: Scribner's Sons, 1998). Reproduced in *Biography Resource Center* (Farmington Hills, Mich.: Gale, 2001), www.galenet.com/servlet/BioRC.

91. *Scribner Encyclopedia.*

92. MacDonald, *One Nation,* 65.

93. *Scribner Encyclopedia.*

94. MacDonald, *One Nation,* 101

95. *Scribner Encyclopedia.*

96. Kazan, *A Life,* 568.

97. *Dictionary of American Biography, Supplements 1–2: To 1940* (New York: American Council of Learned Societies, 1944–1958). Reproduced in *Biography Resource Center* (Farmington Hills, Mich.: Gale, 2001, www.galenet.com/servlet/BioRC.

98. *Dictionary of American Biography.*

99. Thomas H. Pauly, *An American Odyssey: Elia Kazan and American Culture* (Philadelphia: Temple University Press, 1983), 219–20.

100. Kazan felt compelled to employ booze ("the Jack Daniels School of Acting") to get someone as affable as Andy Griffith to play such an unapologetic monster.

101. Ciment, *Kazan on Kazan*, 118.

102. Ciment, *Kazan on Kazan*, 115.

103. *BMI/Monthly Film Bulletin* 24 (December 1957), 147.

104. Schulberg, *Face in the Crowd*, 8.

105. Schulberg, *Face in the Crowd*, 21. Schulberg joined a study session that later became a Communist Party Youth League Group, but he quit in 1940 when the group criticized his stories as too individualistic and decadent.

106. Beverly Kelley, "Man a Poor Substitute for God in Creation Department," *Ventura County Star*, July 16, 2001, B5.

107. François Truffaut, *The Films in My Life*, translated by Leonard Mayhew (New York: Simon and Schuster, 1975), 113–14.

108. Ciment, *Kazan on Kazan*, 114.

109. Young, *Kazan*, 236; Douglas Brode, *The Films of the Fifties: Sunset Boulevard to On the Beach* (Secaucus, N.J.: Citadel, 1980), 225–27.

110. *International Dictionary of Theatre*, vol. 3, *Actors, Directors, and Designers* (New York: St. James, 1996) Reproduced in *Biography Resource Center* (Farmington Hills, Mich.: Gale, 2001, www.galenet.com/servlet/BioRC.

111. Kazan, *A Life*, 569.

112. Kazan, *A Life*, 569. His parents, the Kazanjoglous, immigrated to New York City in 1913.

113. Mandel Herbstman, *"A Face in the Crowd—A Review," Film Daily*, May 28, 1957, 6. Connie McFeeley, *"A Face in the Crowd," Magill's Survey of Cinema*, II, edited by Frank N. Magill (Englewood Cliffs, N.J.: 1981), 738–40. Quoted in Kazan, *A Life*, 566.

114. *Time*, December 24, 1956, 61. Quoted in Kazan, *A Life*, 567.

115. Ciment, *Kazan on Kazan*, 119

116. Pauly, *American Odyssey*, 219–20.

117. Brode, *Films of the Fifties*, 227.

118. Ciment, *Kazan on Kazan*, 115.

John Frankenheimer and Burt Lancaster defuse a fascist coup in Seven Days in May. *Courtesy of the Academy of Motion Picture Arts and Sciences.*

5

☆

Antifascism in
Seven Days in May

After Joseph McCarthy's censure by the Senate in 1954, the press began to neglect him, despite having considered him "page one" news during the previous four years. McCarthy was crushed. "Why," he questioned Don Henderson, an Associated Press writer from Milwaukee. "Why was a statement that had been news in 1950, not news in 1954?" McCarthy, still hungry for headlines, hatched a scheme in which he would deliver a pro–civil liberties speech. Wouldn't that pique journalistic interest? How about if he explained that, upon reflecting on the writings of, say, Thomas Jefferson, he had seen the error of his ways and was now willing to repent? McCarthy, however, had little faith in his brainstorm. In fact, he bet Henderson that the *Milwaukee Journal*, which had never printed a positive word about him, wouldn't publish the story. He was right. The idea of a fascist like McCarthy aligning himself with a civil libertarian like Jefferson was too difficult for any journalist to swallow.[1]

In the same vein, nobody was going to buy nazism and its natural enemy, communism, climbing into bed together. The world had a tough time trying to wrap its collective mind around the Nazi–Soviet Pact of August 23, 1939. The notion of a fervently anti-Communist Germany coming to terms with an equally antifascist USSR was, in a word, mind-boggling. From Hitler's point of view, however, linking up with the Soviets was an indispensable preliminary to his imminent attack on Poland. From Stalin's point of view, having been rebuffed by Britain and France, he saw no alternative but to work out matters with Nazi Germany. Besides, Hitler had tossed in entrée to the Baltic States as part of the bargain. The deal, inked in Moscow, included a nonaggression pact, a trade agreement, and a secret protocol that provided for a German–Soviet partition of Poland.

World War II started within two weeks. The pact remained in force until Hitler's invasion of the Soviet Union in 1941.

THE COST OF FIGHTING FASCISM

While no official casualty count exists, World War II was clearly the deadliest war in history. Of the 100 million soldiers involved, 27 million perished. In addition, some 25 million civilians breathed their last and 3 million simply disappeared off the face of the earth.[2] On the Allied side, the Russians gave up the most—some 26 million fell in "the "Great Patriotic War against Hitlerite Fascism,"[3] while China lost 10 million, Poland 5.8 million, France 600,000, and Great Britain 400,000.[4] American combat casualties were estimated at 300,000 dead and nearly 700,000 wounded.

The Nazis glommed on to the assassination of Ernst von Rath, a German legation secretary, as an excuse for Kristallnacht, "the night of broken glass." Over November 9–10, 1938, storm troopers massacred 100, set 267 synagogues ablaze, and detained 20,000 in prison. Germany's Jews were forced to pay a $400 million atonement fine for damages to their own property.

By January 30, 1939, Hitler had publicly trumpeted his intent to exterminate "the Jewish race in Europe." By the following year, in a *blitzpogrom,* Hitler herded the entire Jewish population of Poland into walled ghettoes patrolled by armed guards. There, rape, brutality, murder, and atrocities became commonplace.[5] The scenario was replayed later in Denmark, Norway, Holland, Belgium, Luxembourg, and France.

Even though 700,000 perished due to disease and starvation, the Reich deemed Jewish prisoners economically burdensome, so they shipped them to concentration camps, where they were either worked to death or eradicated via the gas chamber. In March 1942, 80 percent of all who would eventually become Holocaust victims were still alive. Eleven months later, 80 percent were dead.[6]

When Germany assaulted the USSR in June 1941, four special *einsatzgruppen,* or mobile killing units, were deployed against Soviet civilians. The worst act of violence occurred at the Babi Yar ravine in Kiev, where nearly thirty-four thousand were mowed down by machine gun.[7] But firing squads proved too slow, too inefficient, and too destructive to German morale (soldiers were reluctant to shoot women and children). Gas chambers at Auschwitz–Berkenau, said to accommodate four thousand at a time, provided a new and improved means of murder. After twenty minutes of exposure to Zyklon-B, still bodies could be stripped of valuables and incinerated. According to the Nuremberg Tribunal, the Jewish death toll came in at 5,721,800.[8]

ENEMIES OF FASCISM

Antifascism has always been an essentially reactive force. Even though those who stood against Hitler, Mussolini, and Franco vastly outnumbered those in support, millions were slaughtered before most twentieth-century antifascists were jolted awake. The entire world was slow to comprehend that those espousing the ideology were close to critical mass. In 1924, Italy's Giacomo Matteotti exposed hundreds of armed violence and election fraud cases, and for his trouble Mussolini's men sent him to sleep with the fishes. Europe, which should have been shocked that a civilized country such as Italy had resorted to stomping out dissent by assassination, merely dozed. At the same time, Hitler, imprisoned for staging a national revolution a tad prematurely, was busy working on his autobiography. The slender tome detailed Hitler's plan for world domination, marshaled his arguments for *lebensraum,* and delineated his need to obliterate Bolshevism.[9] Yet, nobody seemed to be paying attention. In fact, Hitler had a hard time getting his own countrymen to read his book.

Internal Resistance

You would have thought, first and foremost, Germans would have suspected Hitler's methods and motives. On May 18, 1937, Cardinal George Mundelein of Chicago mused, "Perhaps you will ask how it is that a nation of 60 million intelligent people will submit in fear and servitude to an alien, an Austrian paperhanger, and a poor one at that." It seems, added Mundelein, that the brains of 60 million people had been removed, without a single individual seeming to notice.[10]

Barely three months after Hitler collected the title "Chancellor of the Reich," his minister of the interior, Hermann Göring, declared war on "filth" and launched the first concentration camp at Dachau, where German homeless (not necessarily Jews) were involuntarily housed. By the first day of 1934, the Law for the Prevention of Genetically Diseased Children went into effect. An estimated 100,000 to 350,000 Germans were sterilized.[11]

On the same day that German troops overran Poland, Hitler halted his sterilization schedule and inaugurated a secret program of euthanasia. Initially, the business in Poland seemed to distract the populace from Hitler's scheme, illegal under the laws of the Third Reich. In fact, his program roused few suspicions, except among the victims' close relatives. Once the German people woke up, however, they did not sit still for the murder of Germans, despite the fact that the Reich considered these individuals unproductive, incurably insane, or merely politically bothersome.

Heinrich Himmler, the head of Hitler's SS, lusted to "cleanse the nation's body." He systematically purged 70,273 so-called feeble-minded along with German vagrants, alcoholics, work dodgers, welfare recipients and, of course, Communists, pacifists, and democrats.[12] The idea was to exterminate those "unworthy of living" in order to free up scarce public funds for the healthy, productive members of society. The first documented case of "Operation Mercy Killing" occurred in 1939, and the practice ended abruptly in 1941. By then, public awareness had been aroused and Hitler could no longer distance himself from his own culpability. Clemons von Galen, a German Catholic priest, fronted two successful protests against Hitler's euthanasia program. A third antieuthanasia demonstration against Hitler actually stopped his special Munich-to-Berlin train and threatened Hitler's personal safety.[13]

Almost from the outset, the Spanish Civil War (1936–39) symbolized what would become a worldwide struggle between fascism and democracy. Franco began a reign of terror aimed at the physical liquidation of all his potential enemies. Concentration camps were instituted, tens of thousands were shot, and mass executions continued until 1944. Madrid radio called men and women from all lands to come to the aid of Spain's legitimate government. The cry resonated with depression-era Americans fretting over the appeasement policies of the democracies, FDR's refusal to grant Spain aid (America' official position was neutral and isolationist), and the men/munitions pouring in from fascists to assist Franco. Mussolini sent fifty thousand men and Hitler grabbed the opportunity to battle test his weapons before taking on the rest of Europe. Largely recruited by the American Communist Party, nearly three thousand idealistic college students, professors, trade unionists, artists, actors, and writers (and even three acrobats) made up the Abraham Lincoln Brigade. Almost half of them ended up pushing up daisies in Spanish soil.

But perhaps the most poignant decision to volunteer in Spain was made by German antifascists, many escapees from Nazi concentration camps. A "transplanted" resistance movement, these brave souls took up arms against those they were unable to fight at home. In the Fatherland itself, no rooted resistance was allowed to arise, although an odd assortment of military and civilian Germans did initiate a modest underground. In fact, this crowd attempted to assassinate Hitler by exploding a bomb at his military headquarters in East Prussia on July 20, 1944.

In France, Italy, and Belgium, secret resistance forces assembled and evolved, gradually gathering strength and emerging in early June 1944 to drive Germans and pro-German collaborators from their respective countries.

Communists

Communists, along with socialists, labor leaders, moderate leftists, and idealistic liberals, are intrinsically antifascist. It is no wonder that Hitler scapegoated Marxists, as well as Jews, for the troubles Germany had seen. In fact, Hitler was able to sweep into power by blaming, without evidence, the burning of the Reichstag on Communists. During the first year of Nazi occupation in the Soviet Union, 500,000 Communists were summarily executed, including Soviet government administrators and Communist Party officials. By 1944, Ukraine had given up 1 million souls.

Communists liked to distinguish themselves from fascists by claiming that the requisite proletarian dictatorship and one-party state were only temporary political mechanisms. They further contended that, unlike in the fascist countries, their leaders weren't glorified; their culture wasn't racist, imperialistic, or violent; and rather than promoting nationalism, Communists battled class on a worldwide stage. Every one of their claims were voided by the regimes of Mao Zedong and Joseph Stalin, who during the twentieth century sounded the death knell for more than 90 million, including 65 million in China and 20 million in the former Soviet Union. Hitler's Germany ranked a distant second or possibly even third in total victims.[14]

In the mid-1930s, the Soviet Comintern adopted a new tactic in regard to fascism. Communist Party members were urged to join in coalitions with radical socialists and other leftist groups called "popular fronts." A particularly dicey situation developed in 1934 France when a political scandal involving the floating of worthless bonds prompted a demand for the end of the Republic, instead of merely turning the incumbents out of office. The French Popular Front, grasping the jeopardy to the Communist cause if fascists triumphed, got busy and in a surge of patriotic fervor shepherded labor reforms (wage increases, the forty-hour week, paid vacations, and collective bargaining) through the legislature.

Labor

With fascist regimes large and in charge, labor leaders had a great deal to squawk about. Benito Mussolini employed his black shirts to suppress strikes and attack leftist trade unions. In 1924, Mussolini himself "organized" the economy in order to dodge industrial disputes and step up productivity. All producers, which included virtually every Italian, were funneled into fascist-controlled corporations that determined working conditions, wages, prices, and industrial policies.

Following the same script, Juan Domingo Perón essentially forced all Argentine workers, entrepreneurs, professionals, and students into government-dominated organizations.

Hitler replaced labor unions with the strike-forbidding National Labor Front and, under *Führerprinzip*,[15] factory employers were set up as sub-führers and given total control, subject of course to government supervision. Hitler employed all Germans (except for vagrants, alcoholics, work dodgers, and welfare recipients, who were subject to "Operation Mercy Killing") in an extensive public works program, which included super-highways, housing, reforestation, and swamp drainage, with his vast rearmament program absorbing the remainder of the unemployed.

In Japan, the Munitions Mobilization Law of 1937 handed over the economy to the military, while the General Mobilization Law of 1938 delivered total control over Japan's workforce. In 1940, all unions were abolished and workers were funneled into a single massive government labor association doling out minimal benefits.

Religious Resistance

Could opposition by the Catholic Church have successfully curbed the Nazis? Hitler realized the power of public protest—that's why he quickly distanced himself from domestic euthanasia when German demonstrators appeared on the scene.

In *Mein Kampf,* Hitler wrote that a direct confrontation with the Catholic Church would prove disastrous to his cause.[16] In *The Catholic Church and Nazi Germany,* Guenter Lewy makes the rather prickly point that both "German public opinion and the Church were a force to be reckoned with *in principle*" (italics mine).[17]

Hitler, who attempted to keep his more odious policies under wraps, managed to quash vocal opposition via the unbridled power of the Gestapo. His most effective weapon, however, in staving off resistance to his plans was essentially muzzling 23 million German Catholics via a Papal agreement. According to the terms of the Concordat (similar to the Lateran Treaty struck between Pius XI and Mussolini) the Church agreed to keep religion out of politics (essentially forbidding clergy-led protests against the Führer's policies) if Hitler would grant "complete freedom" to confessional schools.

Hitler kept his part of the bargain for about as long as it took for the ink to dry. In honoring his obligation, Pope Pius XI ordered German bishops to swear allegiance to the National Socialist regime: "In the performance of my spiritual office and in my solicitude for the welfare and interest of the German Reich, I will endeavor to avoid all detrimental acts which might endanger it."[18] It was essentially a gag order that His Holiness extended not only to his clergy, but to himself as well. In June 1943, when Pius XII, successor of Pius XI, addressed the Sacred College of Cardinals on the extermination of the Jews, the pontiff refused to speak against Hitler: "Every word We address to the competent authority on this subject, and all our public utterances, have to be carefully weighed and measured by Us, in the interests of the victims themselves, lest, contrary to Our intentions, We make their situation worse and harder to bear."[19]

Facing a choice between totalitarianism on the right and totalitarianism on the left, the head of the Roman Catholic Church opted for fascism as the lesser of two evils. With godless Bolshevism, His Holiness reasoned, the goal was to wipe out all religion, while with Hitler and Mussolini, the pontiff allowed himself to be seduced by the fairy tale that the Church would become an equal partner. Most important, it would seem that Pius XI's personal experience in the Polish–Soviet War intensified his emotional horror of communism and left fascism as the lesser evil.

What Pius XI failed to realize when he signed the Concordat is that (1) no leader of a totalitarian scheme is ever wedded to the truth, (2) the Catholic Center Party in Germany and the Catholic Popular Party in Italy, which the pontiff opposed, were pushing more for workers' rights than some sort of Communist state, and (3) Hitler's insistence that a German can't be both a Nazi and a Christian, along with his ghastly racist beliefs and deification of self, made him a here-and-now enemy of both Christ and His Church. There may well have been, as some scholars have suggested, some anti-Semitism brewing at the Vatican, but it is more plausible that the pontiff was as irked with his clergy getting mixed up in politics as Hitler was.

Only the pontiff really knows what guided his hand as he affixed his signature to the Concordat, yet he had to realize that any role Church leadership might play in a concerted Catholic protest of Hitler's policies would be seriously undermined by Papal agreement. Still, according to John Toland, "The Church, under the Pope's guidance had already saved the lives of more Jews than all the churches, religious institutions and rescue organizations combined and was presently hiding thousand of Jews in monasteries, convents and Vatican City itself."[20]

Passive resistance by clergy in Germany was documented only sporadically. For example, Monsignor Bernard Lichtenberg of Berlin closed each evening service with a prayer for prisoners in concentration camps and fought against the deportation of Jews. Father Rupert Mayer battled for workers' rights in Munich. Cardinal Faulhaber became a martyr to the antifascist cause. Dietrich Bonhoeffer, a young Lutheran pastor who made an attempt on Hitler's life, once told his students that only those who cry out for the Jews may also croon Gregorian chant.

Outside of three clergy-led protests against Hitler's euthanasia program, only a few religious demonstrations have been officially recorded. Two massive rallies were prompted by the removal of crucifixes in schools— a so-called Mother's Revolt in Bavaria and another protest in Oldenburg. In addition, the SS was forced to back down at a 1943 Rosenstrasse protest when women married to Jews demanded the return of their husbands. Other major protests may have been stricken from the record or remain largely unchronicled. Even though compliance increasingly became the price tag for survival, Jews, without weapons, weakened by disease and starvation, and abandoned by the apathetic Allies, did manage to resist throughout the war. They joined partisan units operating from North

Africa to Belorussia and initiated uprisings in the Krakow, Bialystok, Vilna, Kaunas, Minsk, Slutsk, and Warsaw ghettoes. In fact, not only did rebellions occur in many concentration camps, but inmates also actually managed to destroy both Sobibor and Treblinka.

The Democracies

The global depression seemed to blanket Europe in dictatorships. By 1939, only Great Britain, France, Holland, Belgium, Switzerland, Czechoslovakia, Norway, Sweden, Denmark, and Finland, out of twenty-seven European countries, remained democratic enough to encourage elections in which political parties competed and citizens were permitted to vote as they pleased. Britain, like the United States, remained firmly attached to representative institutions and democratic principles. Not a single seat in Parliament went to either a Communist or a Fascist in 1931, and even four years later the Communists snatched only a single spot.

Hitler had no use for democracy. He lumped it together with communism and labeled the mishmash "Jewish." Mussolini, who alleged that democracy accentuated class struggle and splintered politics into countless minority parties, dismissed the ideology as passé. What can you expect from folks who eschew civil liberties? Mussolini reduced the Italian parliament to a nonentity, curtailed universal male suffrage, and set up special tribunals to try opponents of the regime. Under Hitler and the Nuremberg laws of 1935, Jews were forced to forfeit all citizenship rights, forbidden to intermarry, driven from public office, and ruined in private business (not to mention beaten, tortured, and killed). Since Franco wielded bureaucratic control over employment and food, he could harass any resistant Spaniards into compliance. Perón thwarted his opponents by gagging critical newspapers, gerrymandering congressional districts, and tossing political enemies into the pokey.

The Western powers' response to fascism, namely, the Munich Pact of September 30, 1938, was appeasement. The French were understandably reluctant to brawl with the fascists. They had lost 1.4 million during World War I, including virtually half of all French males between the ages of twenty and thirty-three. England, still recuperating from the Great Depression, suffered considerable loss of life during the Great War. Less concrete but just as influential on British leadership was a collective free-floating anxiety involving bombs and bloodshed that continued to saturate Great Britain's nightmares. In fact, in 1933, students at Oxford signed a pledge to never take up arms, under any circumstances.

Neville Chamberlin, a principal architect of appeasement, took the position that Hitler should be allowed to annex the Sudentenland, an area of Czechoslovakia with a largely German-speaking population. He was convinced that the Munich Pact would not only satisfy Germany's need for expansion but would secure "peace in our time." His successor, Winston Churchill, already wise to Hitler's strategy of gradual encroachment, swore that the Munich Pact, which cast a death sentence on Czechoslovakia, was nothing more than outright surrender to the Nazis. Churchill further observed that Britain and France, now faced with a choice between war and dishonor, had opted for dishonor and next they would have war. He was right—the demand for the Sudentenland was only a prelude to more ambitious land grabs, and appeasement ended when a disillusioned Britain and France declared war on Germany on September 3, 1939.

Human rights is a relatively modern concept, but the roots go back to ancient Greek and Roman thought, specifically, the notion of a "natural law" to which one might appeal when faced with injustice by one's own government. While international law typically recognizes national sovereignty, the doctrine of humanitarian interventionism, developed during the nineteenth century, anticipates the potential for dictators to commit "crimes against humanity." The systematic terror and abuse of national sovereignty waged by fascist regimes made the need for humanitarian intervention excruciatingly clear to most antifascists, but the Western Powers, in an isolationist mode, chose not to act.

The "free world" was clued in to German atrocities early on. Even after World War II began and Hitler kept a lid on news, intelligence reports as well as firsthand testimony afforded the West reliable accounts of the Holocaust. In June 1942, headlines on both sides of the Atlantic detailed the massacre of more than 700,000 Polish Jews and reported the Nazi boast that it would wipe out all trace of the Jewish race on the European continent.

The British and the Americans, despite mouthing soaring sentiments, actually granted sanctuary to very few Jews.[21] The Danes, however, defied Germany during the occupation and transported every one of their 6,500 Jews to safety in Sweden. Finland rescued four thousand of their Jews. Even Japan, which fought against the Allies, provided refuge for five thousand European Jews in Manchuria in appreciation for financial aid by a Jewish firm during the Russian–Japanese War.[22] The Jews also found various protectors among the ten thousand farmers, industrialists, factory workers, housewives, salesmen, government officials, nuns, and priests who have been officially honored by Jewish survivors as the "Righteous among Nations."[23] These individuals risked arrest, torture, and death to shelter Jews, to assist in escapes, to provide medical care, and to adopt Jewish orphans.[24]

ANTIFASCISM DURING THE '50s AND '60s

The more aggressively the United States interfered with Soviet expansionism and communism in China, Korea, the Philippines, and Indochina, the more repressive things got at home. Beginning with Executive Order 9835, Truman's security program (March 1947 through December 1952) investigated 6.6 million individuals without detecting a single case of espionage. The hearings, conspicuously missing a judge and a jury, encouraged the use of secret evidence and paid informers.[25] Next, the HUAC double-feature hearings in Hollywood abridged industry employees' First and Fifth Amendment rights while dealing in vague and sweeping accusations, the assumption of guilt by association, and unqualified intimidation. Finally, as a result of the four-year sideshow created by character assassin extraordinaire Joseph McCarthy, his supporters were able to pass the 1950 Subversive Activities Control Act, the 1952 McCarran–Walter Immigration Act, and a variety of state laws barring Communists from running for public office, denying civil service jobs to Communists, and requiring teacher loyalty oaths.

The government didn't have to work too hard to create crises during the Cold War. The rivalry with the Soviet Union was real—post–World War II Russia was rebuilding its industry and regaining military strength. She was making a comeback, despite a smashed economy and the demise of 22 million.

The Red Scare forced Communist antifascists in the United States underground. The American Communist Party stumbled around in complete disarray. Prosecuted under the Smith Act (in *Dennis v. United States*), eleven of the party leadership ended up cooling their heels in jail.[26] Party membership rolls shrank and Communist influence in the trade union movement grew feeble. The American Civil Liberties Union (ACLU), self-avowed advocate of antifascism, dragged its heels at the prospect of defending anyone remotely considered "pink," even one of their own. The ACLU likewise distanced itself from Julius and Ethel Rosenberg as well as the defendants at the first Smith Act trial.

Thanks to a booming postwar economy and income redistribution resulting from union successes as well as the progressive income tax, the middle class grew fat. For the first time, a growing class of Americans enjoyed health insurance, vacations, savings accounts, and liberty from landlords as they flocked to the crabgrass frontier of the suburbs, buying up lavish (compared to Levittown) multihued and multimodeled homes, all within a few blocks of essential (and not so essential) retail businesses and services.

Not everyone, however, agreed that an expanding economy was the best measure of human happiness. A psychological shift was taking place. The job description for a corporate employee included such carved-in-granite requirements as conformity, congeniality, and a closet full of gray flannel suits. White-collar workers were compelled to squelch individual needs in return for security and affluence. Worse still, sociologist C. Wright Mills observed that newly prosperous Americans were becoming disconnected from the spiritual heritage valuing honest workmanship and "doing-the-right-thing" morality.[27] James Baldwin calculated the ultimate psychic price tag when he wrote, "The American equation of success with the big time reveals an *awful* disrespect for human life and human achievement" (italics mine).[28]

David Riesman, in *The Lonely Crowd*, trained his sociological lens on a populace that no longer seemed inner-directed, but opted to take their moral and ethical cues from the larger corporate community to which they desperately yearned to belong.[29] Unlike the highly independent, Protestant work ethic–inspired pioneers, inventors, entrepreneurs, and artists who came before them, '50s-era Americans had grown increasingly more concerned with blending in than standing out. Housewives filled their time, now freed up because of labor-saving devices, with neighborhood coffee klatches, Tupperware parties, and PTA meetings, while their ever-loving spouses, who got home long after the kids were in bed, swapped serenity, freedom, and individuality for whopping paychecks, impressive-sounding titles, and job security for life. According to David Halberstam, "The new threat to the human spirit came not from poverty but from affluence, bigness and corporate indifference [as well as] from bland jobs through which the corporation subtly and often unconsciously subdued and corrupted the human spirit."[30] Thus alienation, frustration, and powerlessness became as evident in comfy middle-class suburbia as in potholed working-class neighborhoods.

America, however, shivered in a culture of fear; the newly well-heeled protected their digs with burglar alarms, the government became obsessed with security, both Republicans and Democrats agreed that the Soviets ("We will bury you") endangered the American way of life, and everybody felt menaced by "the bomb."

The signs that America was uneasy in Eden included escalating expenditures for life insurance, best-selling books capitalizing on a "high price of success" message, and the wild popularity of "the family that prays together stays together" campaigns.[31] In fact, in 1960, more than a billion dollars went into building new churches and synagogues, more than forty times the total in 1945.[32]

In *Friendly Fascism: The New Face of Power in America*, Bertram Gross confesses, "I am worried by those who fail to remember—or have never learned—that Big Business–Big Government partnerships, backed up by other elements, were the central facts behind the power structures of old fascism in the days of Mussolini, Hitler, and the Japanese empire builders."[33] C. Wright Mills, who attributed American domestic and foreign policy to three mutually reinforcing elites (corporate, governmental, and military), was extremely concerned, according to Todd Gitlin, about "hidden authority, authority that was tacit, veiled and therefore not at issue in public life."[34]

Mills, a burly nonconformist fond of sporting khaki, flannel, and combat boots, was known to roar into the parking lot at the elitist Columbia University on a BMW motorcycle. He insisted on becoming a cross-disciplinary scholar (philosophy, history, economics, and journalism) during the era of ivory tower specialization. While serious scholars scrupulously avoided the pull of contemporary events and freelance writing, Mills busied himself tracing parallels between German and American corporate capitalism for popular consumption. According to David Halberstam, Mills seemed to see fascist Germany as the prototype for the modern corporate garrison state. The only thing that might stop it, he wrote, "was the powerful force of organized labor."[35]

Labor in the United States had unionized one-third of the nonagrarian workforce and elevated millions of wage earners into the middle class,[36] but critics complained that the movement was being corrupted by a nasty kind of nationalism. Further, in the mid-'50s, the investment of labor union pension funds became the new growth industry on Wall Street. Traditional adversaries had become strange bedfellows.

But antifascists got their say in 1960 as they ushered in a veritable cultural revolution, not only opposing the nationalism and militarism fueling Vietnam and the Cold War, but also going up against the entrenched racism, and later the sexism, in America.[37] On New Years Day 1960, Reverend Martin Luther King Jr. informed segregationists that the integration movement was unstoppable: "We will wear you down by our capacity to suffer, and in the process, we will win your hearts."[38]

There was, of course, fascist-like repression by "the establishment" on every front, keeping the ACLU constantly engaged in raising funds and dispatching attorneys to protect civil liberties. Southern sheriffs battered civil rights workers. Police officers tear-gassed, water-hosed, and clubbed antiwar protestors. The Ohio National Guard slaughtered four students at Kent State.[39] J. Edgar Hoover prepared and weekly updated a master file of candidates to arrest during "a national emergency." "Operation Chaos," a special operations unit of the Central Intelligence Agency (CIA), spied on demonstrators. Government records, later pried open by the Freedom of Information Act, revealed illegal wiretaps, the planting of evidence, harassment of a First Amendment–protected press, the unauthorized opening of private mail, and out-and-out forgery by local and federal law enforcement.[40]

Students for a Democratic Society president cum University of California, Berkeley professor Todd Gitlin found himself personally battling in the antifascist trenches during the '60s. He helped organize "the first sizable demonstration at the White House against the war in Vietnam, . . . scampered through clouds of tear gas to get away from billy clubs and bayonets at the Democratic Convention, . . . saw a comrade gashed by a chunk of concrete as we integrated an amusement park, . . . saw our organizing office reduced to rubble when police turned it upside down in a raid for planted drugs."[41]

Most Americans counted themselves as members of the "silent majority" to which Nixon appealed.[42] For them, convention had always trumped contention. Largely law-abiding citizens, they were riled by the glut of disruptive and destructive demonstrations. These folks had endured the depression, served and sacrificed during World War II, and toiled arduously for a piece of the pie. They recoiled in horror as their daughters and sons, for whom they had scrimped and saved, were jailed for civil disobedience. They were further sickened when their offspring mocked traditional values—*their* values—by burning flags, bras, and draft cards.

Despite an initial disapproval, the persistent protestors eventually won the hearts and minds of Mom and Dad. At the invitation of bishops, preachers, ministers, and rabbis, parents of belligerent boomers ended up delivering a flurry of petitions and prayers to Washington, which according to Senator Everett Dirksen turned the tide for the passage of the Civil Rights Act.[43] During the late '60s, the antiwar effort managed to pull in thousands of middle-class conservatives, in direct proportion to the enmity the Nixon administration aimed toward their Vietnam-protesting offspring.[44] In 1973, the most powerful nation in the world, despite maximum military effort (in fact, stopping just short of nuclear warfare) had to admit defeat, and the antiwar movement was indispensable in bringing troops homes.

SUMMARY OF THE PLOT

Released a scant nine weeks after John F. Kennedy's assassination, the edge-of-your-seat thriller *Seven Days in May*[45] poses the question, "could a military *coup d'etat* ever take place in the United States?" General James Matoon Scott (Burt Lancaster) is counting on it. President Jordan Lyman (Frederick March) and his political crony, Senator Raymond Clark (Edmond O'Brien) are warned by Colonel Martin "Jiggs" Casey (Kirk Douglas) that Scott is up to no good. While Lyman and Clark mean to stop him, Scott, considered a genuine American hero by the public, has also garnered the support of the Joint Chiefs, possession of a secret air force base, and the unshakable belief he must shield the country from an appeasement-crazed chief executive who would give the country away to the Soviets. The president, who's reluctant to use incriminating letters from Scott's former mistress (Ava Gardner), fights back, armed only with the Constitution and a few close friends. Released two years after the Cuban Missile Crisis, *Seven Days in May* is steeped in Cold War tension. The threat of nuclear war at the time was real, the potential for exploiting the nation's mistrust was obvious, and any president advocating a peace agreement with the Russians would seem to be committing political *hara kiri*.

The original theatrical trailer for *Seven Days in May* begins with the words, "there are some who would say, it can't ever happen here."[46] With that, the countdown (suggested in the film's title) begins.

> The First Day: When a Marine colonel wondered who was inciting screaming mobs in Madison Square Garden.
>
> The Second Day: That uncovered secret meetings in Washington back alleys.
>
> The Third Day: When unknown men prepared to kidnap the president from his private vacation resort.
>
> The Fourth Day: That brought a secret presidential messenger's death in a plane crash in Spain and a senator of the United States is held against his will.
>
> The Fifth Day: When a woman found her past being used for blackmail.
>
> The Sixth Day: The discovery of a desert base for an airborne task force kept secret even from the president of the United States.
>
> The Seventh Day: When the head of the Joint Chiefs of Staff dares the president of the United States to stop the conspiracy that couldn't be proved.

THE MILITARY–INDUSTRIAL COMPLEX

The military, inherently nationalistic and elitist, is a perfect spawning ground for future fascists. In Spain, Argentina, and Japan military men were swept into power before World War II. In Italy and Germany, fascism could not have prevailed had it not been for paramilitary organizations, manned by disillusioned ex-servicemen, providing Mussolini and Hitler with muscle to consolidate their clout. Members of the military class in Germany either openly supported Hitler or remained neutral, despite the dawning realization that Nazi leadership not only harbored criminals but protected possible psychopaths. Fascism in Italy also received big backing from the military brass.

Unfortunately, the rigid hierarchy of the military does manage to shelter those near the top from personal accountability. Nonetheless, under the U.S. Constitution, the highest-ranking general still has to answer to the commander in chief. President Harry Truman made that fact abundantly clear to General Douglas MacArthur during the course of the Korean War. From Truman's point of view, MacArthur had not only spoiled the American effort to engineer a cease-fire in March 1951, but he also made his disagreement with the president public with a letter read in Congress. On April 11, 1951, Truman relieved MacArthur of his command with "If there is one basic element in our Constitution [that is indispensable], it is civilian control of the military."[47]

In fact, not unlike a fascist regime, the armed service subordinates the individual to the state. Every soldier is indoctrinated into self-sacrifice and conformity "for the good of the service." The military not only demands but receives blind obedience, rationalizing that in the heat of battle there is no time to answer questions or submit an order to a democratic show of hands. Further, secrecy becomes the regrettable price tag for security. William Ebenstein and Edwin Fogelman warn about the military's vulnerability to fascist propaganda: "Even in a strong and well-established democracy, professional military personnel tend to overestimate the virtues of discipline and unity; where democracy is weak, this professional bias of the military becomes a political menace."[48]

In *Seven Days in May*, Colonel Jiggs Casey asserts: "As a military officer I steer clears of politics." Mixing politics and the military is a surefire way to ignite a fascist takeover. Fletcher Knebel, who authored the book on which the film was based, wrote in the November 19, 1963, issue of *Look* that the central issue in the novel, written during a time when the United States was compelled to keep a massive military force at the ready, was the Constitution. "American ideals must become a living person," he noted, "and we must fight for her survival."[49]

But that's not to say that there aren't politics in the military. A smart soldier, like a smart fascist, joins with the machinery of power by ingratiating himself to higher-ups and making them look good. He knows advancement is a zero-sum game and while many are called, few are chosen. His goal is to clamber up the ranks as quickly as possible for a payoff that includes more pay, prestige, and privilege. Typical is *Seven Days'* Admiral Barnswell (John Houseman), described in a veritable cascade of clichés in the book, "He always keeps his nose clean, he never sticks his neck out. He likes to know how the wind's blowing before he commits himself."[50]

Further, many of the qualities valued in the military, such as bravery, integrity, and strength of character, are identical to the qualities that constitute charisma in a political leader. George L. Mosse writes about "the new man," an integral aspect of fascist philosophy that finds its basis in "an ideal of male strength and beauty, upon an aggressive virility, an *élan vital*, which we have attributed to the pilot who dominated the skies."[51] In fact, the whole idea of hero worship may well have originated with a military hero such as the Old Testament's David, who waged war on the Philistine enemy with nothing more than a sling and a few stones. For his trouble, the humble shepherd boy was elevated to king.

The problem with fascist hero worship, however, is that, after the hero has saved the people, someone else has to save the people from the hero. Aldous Huxley underscores the problem with his prediction, "Duces and Fuehrers will cease to plague the world only when the majority of its inhabitants regard such adventurers with the same disgust as they now bestow on swindlers and pimps."[52]

Just as a fascist state curtails civil liberties, so does the military. In fact, the military tribunal and the court-martial operate well outside usual constitutional protections enjoyed by the civilian population. Preserving discipline and order are the highest priorities of the armed forces. When a soldier joins the service, he is asked to voluntarily relinquish any rights or freedoms that might interfere with those priorities.

Fortunately for the United States, presidents who had formerly distinguished themselves in the military didn't become fascists. George Washington may have been commander in chief of the Continental Army, but he considered himself, first and foremost, a farmer. Andrew Jackson was able to bottle up most of his fiery fascist potential, although his political enemies dubbed him "King Andrew" for good reason. The Whigs picked William Henry "Tippecanoe" Harrison because he was considered a war hero, but dying after only a month in office left him little time to develop any fascist tendencies. Franklin Pierce, known as "the Fainting General" because of a spooked horse and an unfortunate groin injury, was too devoted to the bottle to make an effective dictator. President Lincoln backed Ulysses Grant during the war because he was such an effective general, but in the presidency he turned out to be everybody's perfect patsy. General James Garfield was assassinated before anyone could tell what kind of leader he might become, fascist or otherwise. Teddy Roosevelt of Rough Rider fame would have made a fine führer—he had charisma, energy, and the burning conviction he was always right—but he insisted on passing himself off as a progressive reformer instead. The worshipful electorate who pressed General Dwight D. Eisenhower into service in the Oval Office was most fortunate. While he could have taken America for a ride, this "soldier of democracy" tried to head her in the right direction.

In his September 17, 1796, "Farewell Address," George Washington warned: "they will avoid the necessity of those overgrown Military establishment which, under any form of government, are inauspicious to liberty, and which are to be regarded as particularly hostile to Republican Liberty."[53] Dwight D. Eisenhower echoed his predecessor's sentiments 171 years later, adding a wrinkle of his own by employing speechwriter Malcolm Moos's phrase "the military–industrial complex." The thirty-fourth president foresaw nothing but galloping inflation and bottomless outlay in the nuptials of a mammoth military with a burgeoning arms industry. According to Howard Zinn, at the start of 1950, the military got its mitts on 30 percent of the federal budget. By 1955, the amount had run up to a staggering 64.5 percent of the total.[54]

"This country," Eisenhower had cautioned, "can choke itself to death piling up [military] expenditures just as surely as it can defeat itself by not spending enough for protection."[55] But the glut of military spending didn't stop with Ike. Once John F. Kennedy was elected, he likewise moved to up the Pentagon's take.[56]

Postwar capitalism had succeeded beyond anyone's wildest dreams. The war had done nothing less than recharge the American economy. Corporate profits rose from $6.4 billion in 1940 to $10.8 billion in 1944. In fact, Charles E. Wilson, then president of General Electric, was so tickled with the rejuvenated economic situation that he suggested a continued alliance between business and military in order to create a "permanent war economy."[57] He got his wish.

The Cold War extended the military–industrial partnership well into peacetime. A Senate report from the '50s showed that the one hundred largest defense contractors held 67.4 percent of the military contracts, and (as difficult as this is to believe) employed more than two thousand former high-ranking officers of the military.[58] It looked unlikely that any man could put this happy marriage asunder.

By 1962, as a result of what turned out to be fabricated scares about a Soviet buildup and missile or bomber gaps, the United States felt pressured to stockpile the equivalent of 1,500 Hiroshima atomic bombs. In fact, America's crushing nuclear superiority over Russia was more than enough to destroy every major city in the world. To deliver this overwhelming firepower, the United States also acquired more than fifty intercontinental ballistic missiles, eighty missiles on nuclear subs, ninety missiles located at overseas stations, seventeen hundred bombers capable of reaching the Soviet Union, three hundred fighter–bombers on aircraft carriers, and one thousand land-based supersonic fighters.[59]

Seven Days in May director John Frankenheimer had his own take on the power of the military–industrial complex. He told Gerald Pratley, "They can either make or break a town, a city. If defense contracts are not renewed, or bases are closed, the whole economy of a city collapses."[60]

WE HAVE MET THE ENEMY AND HE IS US

President Lyman, the ultimate peacenik, truly values every human being and strives to make friends out of foes. Lyman's "enemy's an age" soliloquy, however, outlines the major precondition for a fascist coup d'etat on his watch—namely, circumstances killing "man's faith in his ability to influence what happens to him." In real life, the October 4, 1957, launch of Sputnik left the United States in the space race dust. Hostile crowds in Latin American spitting on Vice President Richard Nixon told America, loud and clear, she had somehow "lost her greatness."

Despite pockets of prosperity, most folks were feeling alienated, frustrated, and powerless. The newspaper article Paul Girard (Martin Balsam) marks up with a grease pen headlines Lyman's dismal 29 percent Gallup approval rating.[61] Senator Raymond Clark explains, "You can't gear a country's economy for war for 20 years, then suddenly slam on the brakes and expect the whole transition to go like grease through a goose."

Furthermore, the general mood in the country is fear. Folks may not know that President Lyman is constantly trailed by a black box filled with secret nuclear war codes, but "the bomb" ticks away in their minds. As Senator Clark continues, "We've been hating the Russians for a quarter of a century. Suddenly we sign a treaty that says in two months they're to dismantle their bombs, we're to dismantle ours, and we all ride to a peaceful glory."

According to Lawrence H. Suid, even when scared spitless by the prospect of world destruction, Americans weren't about to accept the prospect of disarmament.[62] Scott plays to this sentiment when he argues, "now we're asked to believe that a piece of paper will take the place of missile sites and Polaris submarines, and that an enemy who hasn't honored one solemn treaty in the history of its existence will now, for our convenience, do precisely that." Even Colonel Casey tells the president that he believes "we're being played for suckers." However, once the treaty is ratified by two-thirds of the Senate, Casey admits, "I don't see how we in the military [who have taken an oath to uphold the Constitution] can question it. I mean we can question it, but we can't fight it."

True believer Scott, however, believes he can "fight it" and calls on the archconservative Senator Frederick Prentice (Whit Bissel), the goose-stepping Colonel Broderick (John Larkin), the right-wing political TV commentator Harold McPherson (Hugh Marlowe) as well as air force general Parker Hardesty, marine commandant William Riley, and army general Edward Dieffenbach.

The rigid hierarchy of the military plays a significant role in Scott's usurpation of power. He has been able to withdraw substantial funds from the Joint Chiefs contingency fund, construct a secret air force base, surreptitiously shift troops around the country, and rein in Colonel Henderson's (Andrew Duggan's) civil liberties, because of the military expectations of blind obedience, the need for secrecy, and the extraconstitutionality of military law.

Democracy provides an obvious alternative to sneaking around and plotting treason. Lyman reminds Scott, "You ask for a mandate from a ballot box . . . you don't steal it after midnight when the country has its back turned." All Scott has to do is wait one year and nine months for the next presidential election to come around. Before that time has elapsed, Scott argues, all that will remain of the country will be rubble and 100 million dead bodies.

THE SEVEN DAYS IN MAY ENEMIES OF FASCISM

The entire world may have been sluggish to realize the threat of fascism, but in *Seven Days in May*, although Jiggs Casey admires General Scott's candor and lack of pretension, his superior officer's snowballing political aspirations immediately concern him. Although the relationship between Casey and Scott seems pretty superficial (with the lighthearted jesting and ham-handed brownnosing) you realize Casey is no longer a happy camper. In fact, he cringes when Scott disparages "one-worlders" and actually uses the term "Motherland" in a television appearance. Jiggs becomes seriously suspicious when (1) Scott's aide, Colonel Murdock (Richard Anderson), overreacts to some gossip about a Preakness pool,[63] (2) Scott lies about getting to bed early even though Casey sees him meeting with Senator Prentice, (3) General Hardesty's ashtray yields a crumpled peace of paper with the words "ECOMCON" and "Site Y" and Sunday's date, (4) the navy is conspicuously absent at a Joint Chiefs meeting, and (5) Lieutenant Dorsey Grayson (Jack Mullaney) is abruptly transferred to Hawaii.

The lessons of Italy and Germany have not been lost on President Lyman either. He isn't about to lose an election mandate to a military takeover, but he must also consider his poor poll showings and the probability that Scott will lie about getting presidential approval for the secret base and ECOMCON. Lyman needs help in building a case against Scott, but he can't afford to be caught crying "wolf." He is amazed at how few really trustworthy people are in his rolodex.

In the book, the president is relieved to find Casey is no nutcase. In fact, Jiggs's most recent psychiatric exam reads: "This officer is normal in all respects. He exhibits no anxieties, has no phobias and is free from even the minor psychiatric disturbances common to a man of his age. Few men examined by this department could be given such a clean bill of mental health."[64]

Casey, you see, is the critical piece of the puzzle. Even though historically the military has produced many fascists, it has been able to get rid of them as well—for example, Juan Domingo Perón (September 19, 1955). Once the people realize that a dictator is firmly entrenched in the country, they turn to the military to return morality and legal authority. If Casey does not come forward, they hope Commander of NORAD Barney Rutkowski (described as "a hardnosed by-the-booker, with a computer screen right next to his bed") will voice his suspicions to Lyman.

Lyman assembles an investigation team from a short list. Each member is personally tied to him but not to each other. First is friend of twenty-five years and an appointments secretary, Paul Girard. The cigarette case Girard uses to carry Admiral Barnswell's confession is inscribed "To Paul, with all my affection, Jordan Lyman." Lyman selects Arthur Corwin (Bart Burns), the chief of the White House Secret Service detail, as number two because of his loyalty to the office. Even though Corwin dislikes Lyman's predecessor intensely, he has never mouthed a bad word against the former president in Lyman's presence. The third man, Christopher Todd (George Macready) was Wall Street's ranking corporate attorney before Lyman tapped him to be secretary of the treasury. The press paints Todd as sharp, cold, cultivated, and sardonic; and in fact, although he is intrigued with the idea of a conspiracy, he demands courtroom-level evidence.[65] When he gets his definitive proof, however, he swings immediately to the other side, demanding instant justice. He is, as Lyman puts it, "no politician." Fourth, and last, is Ray Clark (Edmond O'Brien), the alcoholic senator from Georgia who finagled the presidential nomination for Lyman on the third ballot. He manages to keep sober during his sojourn at Site Y by flushing the whiskey delivered to his door every hour, vowing, "Jordy boy, you are walking in a parade with both your legs shot off. I'm not going to make matters worse by getting drunk." Critic Elaine McCreigh applauded O'Brien's performance with "he makes the boozing Senator Clark a weary and rumpled man who frequently surprises the audience with his humor and even more with his ultimate efficiency and courage."[66]

A single sentence in Lyman's nomination acceptance speech won him the campaign against incumbent Edgar Frazier: "We will talk till eternity, but we'll never yield another inch of free soil, any place, any time."[67] The Democrats ended up carrying all but seven states in the first real landslide since Eisenhower. Now with the treaty, however, the honeymoon is over, and the voters are starting to consider Lyman a pawn of the Communists.

Lyman may be "a weak sister" but his analysis extends several chess moves beyond Scott's. The president quietly reminds the general that once the country was controlled by a military dictatorship, the Soviets would, without hesitation, violate the treaty, despite the popular Scott holding the helm.

IT *COULD* HAPPEN HERE

Eisenhower was not the first president to concern himself with the unwarranted influence exerted by a partnered business and military. As Hitler, Mussolini, Tojo, and Franco were consolidating power abroad, Franklin Delano Roosevelt personally experienced a brush with a fascist military takeover. Allegedly, banking interests got together to hatch an elaborate plan to destabilize "the Roosevelt Revolution," to place a military dictator in the Oval Office, and to establish an Americanized form of fascist state. The American Legion, filled with peeved Bonus Army veterans, was to impose order and the whole affair was to be financed by the House of Morgan. Two-time Congressional Medal of Honor recipient Major General Smedley Darlington Butler was nominated to lead the coup; however, the schemers hadn't anticipated his opposition, even though this was the same guy whom President Hoover had to threaten with a court-martial for trashing Mussolini in public. In November and December 1934, Butler stunned members of HUAC as he laid out precise particulars about the conspiracy.[68]

In Lyman's "the enemy's an age" speech[69], he first identifies the man on the white horse as Senator McCarthy. Like Scott, McCarthy knew how to exploit crisis conditions, especially the post–World War II turnaround of the Soviet Union from friend to foe and the national security mentality provoked by the threat of nuclear holocaust. McCarthy's popularity as "Tail Gunner Joe" was certainly analogous to Scott's distinguished war record. Finally, just as Scott exploited Lyman's plummeting approval numbers, McCarthy played on the crisis of confidence plaguing the Truman administration, building a coalition of naysayers that included a dispossessed military.

Lyman's second nomination for the man on the white horse is Major General Edwin A. Walker. In November 1961, the commander of the Twenty-Fourth Infantry Division in West Germany was relieved of his command by John F. Kennedy, following an army investigation into the charge that he had been indoctrinating troops with far-right propaganda. Although he claimed he was being persecuted for his zealous anti-Communist views, the subsequent congressional probe established that not only did General Walker plead the military equivalent of the Fifth Amendment to charges he told his men to consult a John Birch Society guide before voting, but also he made derogatory statements about government officials in public, conduct the military considers "unbecoming an officer."[70] According to Lawrence H. Suid, "while General Walker was atypical, the armed services would have been hard-pressed to categorically deny that under the right circumstances, a group of military men might plot to seize power."[71]

There was nothing radical or even new, claimed President Kennedy in defense of his decision to can Walker, about protecting the military from direct political involvement or requiring that educational talks given to the men remain nonpartisan and accurate. Further, Kennedy did not see reprimanding Walker as some sort of new curb placed on the military's freedom of speech[72] as does the cinematic Scott, who takes personal umbrage at the president's criticism he is too political—"is my uniform a disqualification?" Like Lyman, President Kennedy was supported by military leaders who understood "the importance of the proper relationship between the military and the civilian . . . which has existed for so many years."[73]

In fact, Kennedy was Fletcher Knebel's inspiration for the novel. Soon after the Bay of Pigs incident, Knebel happened to overhear Pentagon generals disparaging JFK for weakness and indecision during a national crisis. The incident started Knebel to musing about the nature of the American political system. "There sat a young president who had just suffered a severe reverse, a man currently being ridiculed by generals and admirals of a powerful world-wide military machine. Why did not the military attempt to seize power in America? Coups were common elsewhere in the world."[74] In his autobiography, *Washington Post* editor Ben Bradlee recalls that Kennedy "felt badly used—and that's an understatement—by the Joint Chiefs of Staff, especially General Lyman L. Lemnitzer, their chair, after the

Bay of Pigs invasion. The Joint Chiefs [had] never trusted Kennedy in the first place, and he [had] never trusted them again."[75]

Lyman, however, fails to mention the most obvious candidate for the man on the white horse. Handsome and imposing, Douglas MacArthur was Hollywood's idea of a general. Although screenwriter Rod Serling gave Burt Lancaster the same kind of carefully pressed uniform and spotless shoes MacArthur affected, he wisely stayed away from caricaturing MacArthur's signature gilt-edged cap, corncob pipe, and swagger stick. Moreover, MacArthur's resemblance to Scott is more than superficial. Scott, who has worked his way up to the coveted position of chairman of the Joint Chiefs, the veritable pinnacle of the Pentagon heap, is a military hero whose bravery, integrity, and strength of character are evidenced by the four silver stars on his shoulder boards as well as the Congressional Medal of Honor and two distinguished service crosses on his chest. MacArthur was likewise the quintessential soldier–hero. The five-star general, whose active service spanned thirty-three years, was commander of General John J. Pershing's famous Rainbow Division, army chief of staff, supreme commander of the Allied forces in the Southwest Pacific, commander of the Allied occupation forces in Japan, and commander in chief of the United Nations' forces in Korea. MacArthur could usually be found where the combat was fiercest—he recklessly exposed himself to enemy fire on a number of occasions. Scott was wounded six times in the service of his country.

According to the book, Scott shot down seven ME-109s in one day, served as one of the first jet aces in Korea, and distinguished himself as a dazzling air commander whose pinpoint bombing and tactical air cover almost compensated for scarce ground forces.[76] Casey claims Scott's uniform only sports half the medals or "fruit salad" he deserves. MacArthur, similarly, was the most decorated American brigadier general. In addition, his leadership ability was amply demonstrated in his West Point reforms, bold military campaigns with minimum logistical support, and enlightened administration of the Japanese occupation.

Scott, like MacArthur, is an eloquent orator who indulges in rich imagery and stirring slogans. Scott captivates the Senate select committee when he says, "I think the signing of a nuclear disarmament pact with the Soviet Union is at best an act of naïveté and at worst an unsupportable negligence. We've stayed alive because we've built up an arsenal, and we've kept the peace because we've dealt with an enemy who knew we would use that arsenal." MacArthur's "Farewell Address" to the joint session of Congress on April 19, 1951, defended his actions on the grounds that in war there is no substitute for victory. The general closed his speech on a note that choked up his supporters: "I still remember the refrain of one of the most popular barracks ballads of that day, which proclaimed most proudly that old soldiers never die, they just fade away. And, like the old soldier of that ballad, I now close my military career and just fade away."[77]

Like MacArthur, Scott likes to adorn himself in false modesty, despite an ego the size of a small country. Although he tells the president he doesn't have the slightest interest "in his own glorification," he actually believes only he can save America. MacArthur, likewise, denied any personal agenda other than "God bless America," but even while on active duty, made three bids, all unsuccessful, for the Oval Office.[78] According to Casey, Scott not only has an intuitive sense about politics but, to Casey's knowledge, has never made a major blunder, either military or political. MacArthur, who deliberately provoked career-ending troubles, could have taken a lesson from Scott, who protested Korean War policies preventing the air force from bombing across the Yalu by going through channels and keeping out of the public eye.[79]

Scott demonstrates condescension toward superiors that surpasses insubordination, much as MacArthur did. Scott tells the president, "And then when this nation rejected you, lost faith in you, and began militantly to oppose you, you violated that oath [of office] by not resigning from office and turning the country over to someone [like me] who could represent the people of the United States." Ordered by Truman not to give speeches or interviews, MacArthur manipulated his supporters into releasing letters, highly critical of Truman's foreign policy, to the press. In the end, MacArthur's commander in chief gave him his walking papers, as Lyman does with Scott.

Finally, one has to be struck with the lopsided ends–means justification in the actions of both generals. Scott is so afraid of the Communists breaking the treaty, he is willing to overthrow the government and shred the Constitution he has sworn to protect. During the summer of 1932, MacArthur was so afraid of a supposedly Communist-riddled Bonus Army he disregarded two direct orders from President Hoover. While sporting a full array of battle ribbons, he launched a savage assault on ten thousand ragged and unarmed veterans. He set tanks on them and torched the tents where they lived with wives and children. In the ensuing melee, several youngsters were killed. Franklin D. Roosevelt once confided that MacArthur was one of the two most dangerous men in America, the other being Governor Huey Long of Louisiana.[80]

ONE NATION UNDER TELEVISION

When television began building an audience, which increased some 400 percent between 1948 and 1960, the new medium caused a sizable slump in the bottom line of the motion picture industry. Weekly theater attendance declined 50 percent.[81] The total number of films plunged from 391 in 1951 to 131 in 1961. Hollywood's mass audience was gone by the late '50s.[82]

The film industry attempted to fight back. Studios just said "no" to advertising films on TV, refused to release classic movies to show on the new medium, wrote clauses into contracts forbidding stars to appear on TV, and prayed that Americans would realize that no nine-inch television could compete with the larger-than-life screen at the local Bijou.

But folks kept choosing the convenience of staying home to watch free entertainment over the movie theater. Film attendance continued to slip, as 90 percent of American homes boasted sets by the early '60s. The Hollywood dream factory tried to recapture audiences with such technical wizardry as 100 percent color, improved sound systems, wrap-around Cinerama, 3-D special effects, and "smell-o-vision."[83] Film companies offered youth $300,000 cheapies (*I Was a Teenage Werewolf*, 1953, and *Hercules*, 1956) and offered mature ticket buyers big-budget spectacles with extravagant sets and casts of thousands (such as *The Robe*, 1953, or the $44 million *Cleopatra*, 1962). With the relaxation of content restrictions, moviemakers could exhibit subject matter that was verboten on TV, although excesses in soft porn sex and blood-spurting violence eventually led to the establishment of a voluntary ratings system.

What movie moguls had yet to try was the sincerest form of flattery, namely, imitation. That was something television veterans John Frankenheimer and Rod Serling couldn't help doing with *Seven Days in May*. "To become an old pro," chuckled septuagenarian Frankenheimer years later, "you have to start as a young director."[84] Frankenheimer traced his first stint in TV to "The Harry Howard Ranch Hour," an infomercial before the term was invented, produced by a California cattleman. Howard's instructions to the twenty-one-year-old neophyte were simple and direct—point one camera at the cows and the other at the sponsor.

Better assignments followed, including work with Sidney Lumet for *You Are There*. Frankenheimer recalls, "There was an extraordinary group of actors, writers, and directors who came together in the '50s in this new medium. Nobody knew what the rules were. It allowed us to do good work."[85] This was a time when the emerging medium was small enough to be elitist. Those who forked over hundreds of dollars for television sets expected quality programming. The wunderkind Frankenheimer ran up an imposing string of 152 live television dramas, including the original *Days of Wine and Roses* for *Playhouse 90* in 1958, and earned five Emmy nominations. Then, with three remarkable releases for the silver screen in 1962 (*Birdman of Alcatraz*, *All Fall Down*, and *The Manchurian Candidate*), Frankenheimer became one of Hollywood's top directors. Critics lauded his flair for interior drama and fluid camera work, which directly evolved from his television know-how. In those days, Frankenheimer was as apt to show you the back of an actor's head as his emotion-filled face.

Unique for a writer, Serling himself became a television icon by introducing each episode of his five-season hit, *Twilight Zone*. His movie script for *Seven Days in May* read exactly like a television screenplay—with lots of talking, plenty of heat, rapid pacing, the hint (not the actuality) of passion, and crystal-clear good guy/bad guy characterizations. Also imitative of early television, Serling not only employed few sets and shortened the scenes as the plot thickened, but also used music to provide aural cues. The Jerry Goldsmith score, with stark military drumbeat and jazzy piano/xylophone scales, supplied a constant undercurrent of peril.

Serling could readily identify with the armed service experience. In fact, his World War II stint contributed to his decision to become a writer: "I was bitter about everything and at loose ends when I got out of the service. I think I was writing to get it off my chest."[86]

Frankenheimer shot several scenes as documentary or newsreel footage—in fact, *Seven Days in May* led the way for such fictionalized documentaries as *Z* and *Medium Cool* (1969). *Time* observed, "Director John Frankenheimer uses his camera as though it had been invented by the CIA."[87] *The New York Herald Tribune's* Judith Crist wrote that as you watch the film, "you sweat it out with the top men as frustration and disaster, the iron fist of the military and the frightening deterrent of a public showdown crowd in upon them."[88] During the demonstration in front of the White House, the police officer's back and the protestor's face are noticeably out of focus and other characters move out of frame. The grainy quality of the Pentagon scenes look more like network news footage, and the shaky zoom and the hand-lettered chalkboard in the Blue Lake Secret Service material are amateurish enough to appear authentic. According to *Variety*, "both Serling and Frankenheimer have outstanding credits in television . . . and their experience shows through. . . . [The film] achieves some of its wallop at times via the quiet underplay (it has its explosive moments too) that has been witnessed in the top-quality drama that TV has sporadically yielded."[89]

In *Seven Days in May*, the director introduces one one-eyed monster after another—futuristic video phones, security camera monitors, wall-size film viewing displays, control-room monitors, home TV sets. As Casey watches General Scott's speech to a veterans' group, a television console borders the scene.

When the president asks Scott to resign, Scott decides, Nixon-like, to take his case directly to the people, using ECOMCON (military alphabet soup for Emergency Communications Control, which was responsible for preserving the security of television, telephone, and radio in time of attack or national emergency) to break in and black out President Lyman's televised news conference.[90] Scott is forced to back off, however, when Lyman demands and gets the resignations of Scott's fellow Joint Chiefs conspirators.

The president resorts to television to save the state, while Scott attempts to take over television to destroy the Constitution. In fact, TV's credibility is a secondary theme of the movie. Stanley Kauffmann of the *New Republic* mentions Lyman's "the enemy's an age" speech as "typical of the TV *raisonneur*

anxious to be brave but neat."[91] Americans tend to believe television, especially live television, whether it is reporting the evening news or documenting a moon landing. That's why it was so important for Frankenheimer to
create locales that appeared as realistic as possible. Because John F. Kennedy
so relished the best-seller about military brass taking over the country (he
quipped "I know a couple who might wish they could"),[92] the president
nudged Pierre Salinger into playing tour guide so Frankenheimer could observe and more accurately reproduce the living quarters and Oval Office.
Frankenheimer was also allowed to attend press conferences to observe protocol and format firsthand. The director later received permission to film en-
trance/exit scenes at the White House and to actually stage a riot in front of
the mansion. Frankenheimer remembers Kennedy promising "when we
wanted to shoot at the White House he would conveniently go to Hyannis
Port that weekend."[93] Ironically, the demonstration scene was filmed two
days after Kennedy signed the 1963 Nuclear Test Ban Treaty in Moscow, and
actual picketers had to be relocated to make room for the fictional riot.[94]

Frankenheimer didn't bother to garner military assistance for the
movie. While the director did visit the office of General Maxwell Taylor,
then chair of the Joint Chiefs of Staff, Taylor made his authorization contingent on a script submission. Frankenheimer interpreted this proviso as
a covert form of censorship and never followed up. Without asking permission but prepared to beg forgiveness, Frankenheimer secreted cameras in the cargo hold of a parked station wagon and shot sequences of
Kirk Douglas entering and exiting the Pentagon in his role as a marine officer.[95] Since the actual Pentagon corridors are far longer than the set
Frankenheimer constructed, he had to force perspective by dressing
midgets as officers and placing them as far back as possible in the shot.[96]

Another time, Frankenheimer needed aircraft carrier footage, so he
chatted his way aboard the USS *Kitty Hawk*. The duty officer bought
Frankenheimer's yarn about needing to film a small boat in the San Diego
harbor from the vantage point of the ship. Once the sequence was completed, the cheeky director didn't stop there. In fact, before leaving,
Frankenheimer got three more scenes, in addition to the services of two
sailors and one of the ship's officers as extras, which did not amuse the
Department of Defense.[97]

THE AUDIENCE RESPONDS

Seven Days in May allows the viewer to journey into the political affairs
zone from the very moment the titles roll over a backdrop of the U.S. Constitution. As the countdown from seven concludes with the numeral "1,"
the number morphs—first, into an arrow held by the eagle on the presidential seal, second, into a menacing missile, and third, into a wrought-
iron fence fronting the White House. The movie didn't open until Febru-

ary 1964—it was delayed by a month to avoid the appearance of capitalizing on Kennedy's assassination.

The picture, budgeted at $2.2 million, was a smash at the box office and the
darling of the critics. Edmond O'Brien copped an Oscar nomination as best
supporting actor. *Variety* noted, "O'Brien is a standout as a southern senator
with an addiction to bourbon and an unfailing loyalty to the President."[98]
Cary Odell and Edward G. Boyle were contenders for best art direction.

Bosley Crowther of the *New York Times* gave high praise to the film, calling it a "hymn to democracy" that offered "considerably more than melodrama and sensationalism . . . contained in its not too far-fetched specu-
lations. There is, in its slick dramatic frame, a solid base of respect for . . .
the capacities of freedom-loving men."[99] Arthur Knight of *Saturday Review*
seconds the motion: "what *Seven Days in May* sets forth with great ur-
gency and some eloquence is that the destruction of our democracy is an
act of subversion, no matter how patriotically motivated, and that our
country, shorn of its Constitution, becomes a meaningless symbol."[100]

In fact, most critics commented on the film's plausibility. *Variety* noted
that Frankenheimer's runaway hit was "more genuinely for-real today
than anybody's version of a twilight zone. It is done with such absence of
false melodrama—that there's not a suggestion of far-fetchedness in the
basic premise."[101] Gerald Pratley adds, "The entire plot of the film, a fantasy of disaster, is totally believable in the manner in which it is portrayed,
due to [Frankenheimer's] calm, assured control, and his hypnotic involvement of audiences."[102]

If there was a recognized flaw, it was Serling's depiction of Jordan Lyman. Audiences were turned off by the president's holier-than-thou tone
as he harped away at the inviolability of the Constitution. *Saturday Review*'s Arthur Knight mentions Serling's frequently platitudinous dialogue, and critic Elaine McCreigh contends that even though the viewer
may agree with the ideas in Lyman's speeches that espouse democratic
values, the movie is least significant when it propagandizes.[103]

While *New York Times* critic Bosley Crowther may have pronounced the
dialogue "vivid and trenchant," there was one line of Ava Gardner's that
didn't ring true to Frankenheimer.[104] In fact, the director admitted he cringed
every time he heard "I'll tell you the truth. I'll give you a steak medium rare
and the truth, which is *very rare*," and he added "everything could be better
if I had more time. Maybe Hitchcock saying 'life is a compromise' is right."[105]

Seven Days in May broke new ground for the political thriller genre.
Frankenheimer had previously piqued interest with the *Manchurian Candidate* and Sidney Lumet offered up *Fail-Safe* the same year. BMI described
Seven Days in May as "a wild and ominous fantasy of disaster . . . which
find[s] the power game, as played out in the corridors of White House
and Pentagon, more stimulating than James Bond."[106]

Seven Days in May possessed international appeal. According to *Variety*,
"There's obviously a keen awareness of the United States presidency by

peoples abroad, this awareness having been enhanced by the assassination of President John F. Kennedy, [adding] to the global interest in *Seven Days*."[107] Frankenheimer also weighed in on the discussion by recalling that the French told him "we could never make [*Seven Days in May*] here." Frankenheimer believed that no other nation in the world made films as provocative, self-critical, and socially revealing as those directed by Americans. He further contended that Russian critics might give learned discussions on the "lack of realism" in selected American films, yet Russian directors, as well as those in other countries, were limited in their choice of content "because they lack the political freedom" we enjoy.[108]

And isn't that the point anyway?

NOTES

1. David Halberstam, *The Fifties* (New York: Fawcett Columbine, 1993), 253.
2. Thomas Roder, Volker Kubillus, Anthony Burwell, *Psychiatrists: The Men Behind Hitler* (Los Angeles: Freedom, 1995), 5.
3. Seamus Martin, *Irish Times,* May 10, 2000, 13.
4. Roder et al., *Psychiatrists,* 6.
5. See Robin Williams' film *Jakob the Liar* (1999). The *blitzpogrom* was a Nazi rapid-fire campaign of persecution/extermination directed against the Polish Jews.
6. "Review of Christopher R. Browning's *Ordinary Men,*" *Kirkus Review,* February 1, 1992.
7. "War Crimes," *Grolier Multimedia Encyclopedia,* (CD-Rom, Grolier Electronic Publishing, 1995).
8. Roder et al., *Psychiatrists,* 4.
9. *Lebensraum* refers to the "living space" needed to feed the German population and to allow for expansion that ended up including Eastern Europe and Russia.
10. John Cornwell, *Hitler's Pope: The Secret History of Pius XII* (New York: Penguin, 2000), 183.
11. Roder et al., *Psychiatrists,* 48. On the Law for the Prevention of Genetically Diseased Children, see Edward Dmytryk's *Hitler's Children* (1943).
12. Roder et al., *Psychiatrists,* 58.
13. Roder et al., *Psychiatrists,* 63.
14. Quoted by James P. Pinkerton, "Macro or Micro, Socialism Is a Bad Idea," *Los Angeles Times,* January 15, 1998, B15.
15. The leadership principle.
16. Adolf Hitler, *Mein Kampf,* translated by Ralph Manheim (Boston: Houghton Mifflin, 1971), 105–107.
17. Guenter Lewy, *The Catholic Church and Nazi Germany* (New York: McGraw Hill, 1964), 199.
18. John Toland, *Adolf Hitler* (New York: Anchor, 1976), 316.
19. Toland, *Adolf Hitler,* 760.
20. Toland, *Adolf Hitler,* 760.
21. Toland, *Adolf Hitler,* 760.
22. Toland, *Adolf Hitler,* 760
23. See the film *Schindler's List* (1993).

24. Martin Gilbert, *The Holocaust: A History of Jews of Europe during the Second World War* (New York: Henry Holt, 1985), 188.

25. See Douglas Miller and Marion Nowak, *The Fifties: The Way We Really Were* (New York: Doubleday, 1977).

26. The Smith Act (June 28, 1940) required registration and fingerprinting of all alien residents. The U.S. Supreme Court upheld its constitutionality in 1951.

27. See C. Wright Mills, *The Power Elite* (New York: Oxford University Press, 1956).

28. James Baldwin, *The Price of the Ticket: Collected Nonfiction, 1948–1985* (New York: St. Martin's/Marek, 1985), 230.

29. David Riesman, *The Lonely Crowd: A Study of the Changing American Character* (New Haven: Yale University Press, 1973).

30. Halberstam, *Fifties*, 528–29.

31. Todd Gitlin, *The Sixties: Years of Hope, Days of Rage* (New York: Bantam, 1993), 17–18. During Eisenhower's first term, the phrase "under God" was added to the Pledge of Allegiance and "in God We Trust" was added to the currency.

32. Maurice Isserman and Michael Kazin, *America Divided: The Civil War of the 1960s* (Oxford: Oxford University Press, 2000), 242.

33. Bertram Gross, *Friendly Fascism: The New Face of Power in America* (New York: Evans, 1980), 3.

34. Todd Gitlin, "Critic and Crusader: The Exemplary Passions of C. Wright Mills," *Los Angeles Times*, May 28, 2000, B4.

35. Halberstam, *Fifties*, 531.

36. Isserman and Kazin, *America Divided*, 14.

37. Truman had integrated the military during World War II, but black soldiers came home to find it was white supremacy business as usual, especially in the South. Later, the unanimous decision of the Supreme Court in the 1954 *Brown v. Board of Education* decision held racial segregation in public schools unconstitutional and opened the door for change. At the same time, after World War II, Rosie the Riveter wasn't ready to relinquish her wartime earnings and self-satisfaction to an unemployed ex-serviceman.

38. *Washington Post*, January 2, 1960, A9.

39. See Bill Warren, ed., *The Middle of the Country: The Events of May 4th as Seen by Students and Faculty at Kent State University* (New York: Avon, 1970).

40. See Gitlin, *Sixties*.

41. Gitlin, *Sixties*, 2–3.

42. Nixon liked to boast that the "silent majority" sent fifty thousand letters and thirty thousand telegrams after his speech, but White House staff had actually organized the "spontaneous response."

43. John Morton Blum, *Years of Discord: American Politics and Society, 1961–1974* (New York: Norton, 1991), 147–48.

44. Blum, *Years of Discord*, 355–56.

45. Remade in 1994 as an HBO movie, *The Enemy Within*.

46. See Sinclair Lewis, *It Can't Happen Here* (New York: HarperTrade 1973).

47. Harry Truman, *Memoirs: Years of Trial and Hope* (Garden City, N.Y.: Doubleday, 1955), 17.

48. William Ebenstein and Edwin Fogelman, *Today's Isms*, 9th ed. (Englewood Cliffs, N.J.: Prentice-Hall, 1985), 102.

49. Fletcher Knebel, "The White House Was Pleased, the Pentagon Was Irritated," *Look*, (November 19, 1963): 95.

50. Fletcher Knebel and Charles W. Bailey II, *Seven Days in May* (New York: Bantam, 1963), 138. *Seven Days in May* was Houseman's film debut, not *Paper Chase,* as commonly believed.

51. George L. Mosse, *Masses and Man: Nationalist and Fascist Perceptions of Reality* (New York: Fertig, 1980), 240.

52. Aldous Huxley, "Decentralization and Self-Government," *Ends and Means: An Inquiry into the Nature of Ideals and into the Methods Employed for Their Realization* (1937), quoted in Leonard Roy Frank, *Quotationary* (New York: Random House, 1999), 358.

53. George Washington, *Farewell Address* (September 17, 1796), quoted in Frank, *Quotationary,* 508.

54. Howard Zinn, *A People's History of the United States: 1492–Present,* revised ed. (New York: HarperPerennial, 1995), 428.

55. Quoted in Halberstam, *Fifties,* 616.

56. Zinn, *People's History,* 428–29.

57. Zinn, *People's History,* 416–17.

58. Zinn, *People's History,* 429.

59. Zinn, *People's History,* 429.

60. Gerald Pratley, *The Cinema of John Frankenheimer* (London: Zwemmer, 1969), 113.

61. This fictional number was supposedly the lowest in Gallup's history prior to Watergate.

62. Lawrence H. Suid, *Guts and Glory: Great American War Movies* (Reading, Mass.:, Addison-Wesley, 1978), 201–205.

63. The Preakness Stakes horse race runs on Saturday. By starting the countdown on a Monday, the filmmakers got themselves into a continuity bind.

64. Knebel and Bailey, *Seven Days in May,* 119.

65. Knebel and Bailey, *Seven Days in May,* 100.

66. Elaine McCreigh, "Seven Days in May," in *Magill's Survey of Cinema,* vol. 2, edited by Frank Magill (Englewood Cliffs, N.J.: 1981), 2144–49.

67. Knebel and Bailey, *Seven Days in May,* 51.

68. See L. Woolf, "Franklin Delano Roosevelt vs. the Banks: Morgan's Fascist Plot, and How It Was Defeated" (Part II), *American Almanac* 8, no. 24 (July 4, 1994).

69. "The enemy's an age—a nuclear age. It happens to have killed man's faith in his ability to influence what happens to him. And out of this comes a sickness, and out of sickness a frustration, a feeling of impotence, helplessness, weakness. And from this, this desperation, we look for a champion in red, white, and blue. Every now and then a man on a white horse rides by, and we appoint him to be our personal god for the duration."

70. Walker sought the protection of Article 31 of the Uniform Code of Military Justice. The John Birch Society maintained that former President Eisenhower, John Foster Dulles, Allen Dulles, and other high government officials had been Communist dupes.

71. Suid, *Guts and Glory,* 201–205.

72. Theodore C. Sorensen, *Kennedy* (New York: Bantam, 1966), 321.

73. Sorensen, *Kennedy,* 321.

74. *Contemporary Authors Online* (Gale Group, 2000). Reproduced in *Biography Resource Center* (Farmington Hills, Mich.: Gale Group, 2001), www.galenet.com/servlet/BioRC.

75. Benjamin C. Bradlee, *A Good Life: Newspapers and Other Adventures* (New York: Simon and Schuster, 1995), 219.

76. Knebel and Bailey, *Seven Days in May*, 36.

77. Frederick C. Packard Jr., ed., *Great Americans Speak* (New York: Scribner's Sons, 1951), 104–105.

78. In 1944, 1948, and 1952.

79. Knebel and Bailey, *Seven Days in May*, 35.

80. Benjamin Frankel, ed., *The Cold War, 1945–1991* (Farmington Hills, Mich.: Gale Research, 1992). Reproduced in *Biography Resource Center* (Farmington Hills, Mich.: Gale Group, 2002), www.galenet.com/servlet/BioRC.

81. Stan Le Roy Wilson, *Mass Media/Mass Culture* (New York: McGraw Hill, 1993), 197.

82. Brain Neve, *Film and Politics in America: A Social Tradition* ((London: Routledge, 1992), 211.

83. Odors piped through theater air ducts.

84. Bob Ross, "Games Legend Recaptures Youthful Flair," *Tampa Tribune*, February 26, 2000, 12.

85. Louis B. Parks, "Veteran Director Returns to Form," *Houston Chronicle*, March 5, 2000, 10.

86. *Contemporary Authors Online.*

87. "Seven Days in May," *FilmFacts* 7, no. 9 (April 2, 1964): 41.

88. "Seven Days in May," *FilmFacts*, 41.

89. *Variety*, February 5, 1964, 6.

90. During the Cuban Missile Crisis, ExComm was the abbreviation for the Executive Committee of the National Security Council.

91. "Seven Days in May," *FilmFacts*, 40.

92. Sorensen, *Kennedy*, 684.

93. Charles Higham and Joel Greenfield, eds., "Interview with John Frankenheimer," in *Celluloid Muse* (London: Angus and Robertson, 1969), 82.

94. Pratley, *Cinema*, 220.

95. Pratley, *Cinema*, 114.

96. Susan King, "Director's Insight Spices *Seven Days in May*," *Chicago Sun-Times*, June 9, 2000, 26.

97. Suid, *Guts and Glory*, 204–205.

98. *Variety*, February 5, 1964, 6.

99. Bosley Crowther, "Screen: A Plot to Overthrow the Government," *New York Times*, February 20, 1964, 22.

100. "Seven Days in May," *FilmFacts*, 40.

101. *Variety*, February 5, 1964, 6.

102. Pratley, *Cinema*, 107.

103. McCreigh, "Seven Days in May," 2149. Knight is quoted in "Seven Days in May," *FilmFacts*, 40.

104. Crowther, "Screen," 22.

105. Pratley, *Cinema*, 224–25.

106. *BFI/Monthly Film Bulletin* 31 (March 7, 1964): 323–24.

107. *Variety*, February 5, 1964, 6.

108. Pratley, *Cinema*, 235.

John Wayne sets up a Huey helicopter invasion in The Green Berets. *Courtesy of Batjac Productions and the Academy of Motion Picture Arts and Sciences.*

6

☆

Interventionism in
The Green Berets

Just six months before the premier of *The Green Berets*, the *Washington Post*, along with most major U.S. newspapers, published one of the most dramatic images to ever come out of Vietnam.[1] Also of interest in this issue were four accompanying front-page pieces furnishing an eerie foretaste of the war's future. The top left article cited routine casualty statistics. The specific numbers—232 sent home in body bags and 929 wounded—were anything but routine. The top right story outlined Lyndon Johnson's pronouncement about continued bombing in the North. A scant two months later, the president would stun the nation by announcing (1) his order halting bombing north of the Twentieth Parallel, (2) his refusal to send 206,000 more troops as requested by the military, and (3) his decision not to seek a second term. A third news account at bottom left reported outgoing defense secretary Robert S. McNamara's latest grim assessment of the war, broadly hinting he had come to believe the war was unwinnable. The fourth, located in the middle of the page, detailed Richard Nixon's entry into the Republican presidential race.

The focal point of the front page, however, was the dramatic photograph documenting National Police General Nguyen Ngoc Loan shooting a Viet Cong (VC) officer point-blank in the temple.[2] In the course of the Tet Offensive, a turning point for the Vietnam War, the Communists massacred thousands of government officers and their relatives. The reason given by Loan for the summary execution of the VC: he "killed many Americans and many of my people."[3]

American Associated Press photographer Eddie Adams won a Pulitzer Prize for the haunting image. For many, the picture only reinforced the world's perception of the South Vietnamese government as a brutal dictatorship. Later, Adams would testify that the prisoner had killed Loan's best friend and knifed Loan's wife and six kids. "When they captured the guy, I just happened to be there and took the picture. And all of a sudden I destroy [the general's] life."[4]

President Johnson urged General William Westmoreland to convince a skeptical public that the United States could win the war. On November 16, 1967, although Westmoreland promised "light at the end of the tunnel," swelling carnage counts as well declining trust in public pronouncements—the so-called credibility gap—dimmed any hope of America carrying the day. Vietnam military strategy was clearly not working.

Six weeks later, the Viet Cong dazed the world by launching an offensive that involved simultaneous uprisings by Communists living undercover in the provincial capitals of South Vietnam and timed to coincide with the Asian New Year celebration, traditionally an occasion for a ceasefire. With awe-inspiring coordination, roughly eighty-four thousand Communist troops struck at more than one hundred cities, American air bases, provincial capitals, and district capitals.[5] After "three years of bombing that had unleashed more tonnage on Vietnam than in all of World War II, and after so many ground actions in which Viet Cong and North Vietnamese forces had supposedly suffered demoralizing losses," America could not even secure her Saigon embassy.[6]

The Communists mistakenly assumed the attacks would spark a widespread insurrection, toppling the South Vietnamese government and terminating the hostilities. However, the 4 million war-weary residents of Saigon huddled behind their doors and refused repeated Communist invitations to join in the uprising. After days of blood-spattered street fighting, the offensive failed. Americans and the South Vietnamese did manage to retake the captured capitals, but in the process cities were reduced to rubble and civilian casualties ran high.[7] After a trip to Saigon, Walter Cronkite, America's most trusted newsman, told the nation on February 27, 1968, it seemed to him "more certain than ever that the bloody experience of Vietnam is to end in a stalemate."[8]

Although the Communist price tag for the Tet Offensive is estimated at thirty-three thousand to fifty-eight thousand troops, Hanoi stuck to the official party line that Tet remained "the greatest victory ever." General Vo Nguyen Giap, the architect of the offensive, contended he was prepared to lose, if necessary, ten of his men for every American killed.[9] He also held two other expectations: (1) his attacks would shatter the United States' sense of invincibility, diminishing the American will to fight, and (2) the Tet Offensive would split the enemy alliance by evidencing American vulnerability. The former was realized while the latter was not.

For Americans, however, Tet did raise serious doubts about the loyalty of Nguyen Van Thieu and the Army of the Republic of Vietnam (ARVN). When put to the test, the South Vietnamese troops performed disappointingly, and Thieu's government poked along for months before delivering assistance to devastated regions. ARVN soldiers seemed to have no heart for the fight. In some cases, guards deserted their posts, officers holed up instead of joining the action, and after Communists were flushed out, troops engaged in wholesale looting.

The major casualty of the Tet Offensive, however, was American public opinion. The event seemed to crystallize public dissatisfaction with the war. According to Todd Gitlin, two major tremors jolted the nation after Tet, as seen in two lessons: (1) politically, there can be no more drastic outcome for a policy than to be proven not merely ineffective, but *conspicuously* ineffective, and (2) morally, there can be no more devastating criticism of a president than to call him a liar.[10]

Although Gallup and Harris uncovered a mid-February 5 percent uptick in pro-war opinion, the effect was only temporary.[11] By March, the president's job rating sank to a new low—26 percent approval with 63 percent disapproval.[12] The conservative *Wall Street Journal* observed, "the American people should be getting ready to accept . . . the prospect that the whole Vietnam effort may be doomed.[13] *Time, Newsweek,* the *New York Post,* the *St. Louis Post-Dispatch,* and NBC News got behind deescalation. The early March Gallup polls reported the nation divided into 41 percent "hawks" and 42 percent "doves."[14]

For the first time since the War of 1812, a majority of Americans did not support a war in which the United States was engaged. Although the folks at home wouldn't learn about My Lai (where 347 South Vietnamese civilians were massacred by American troops) for twenty months,[15] a tipping point had been reached—the public was fed up with the lack of progress in Vietnam. Further substantiation arrived when a relatively unknown antiwar Democratic senator, Eugene McCarthy, walked away with 42 percent of the vote in the New Hampshire primary.

Questions widely debated across the nation included (1) Should a superpower such as the United States take on the responsibility of policing the world against Communist aggression? (2) Was the American presence in Vietnam unwarranted imperialism? (3) Would bombing raids within ten miles of Vietnam's northern border whip up a World War III–provoking Chinese intervention? (4) Could South Vietnam ever exist as a stabile democracy? (5) Was Vietnamization more than just theoretically possible?[16]

Tet encouraged American policy critics to redline the decibel level of their arguments. Although the antiwar movement was not an initial impetus for getting the United States out of Vietnam, without its existence and persistence, the body bag tally would have rocketed even higher. Ironically, however, by escalating bloodshed on both sides, the Communists may actually have helped nudge "peace with honor" candidate Richard Nixon into the White House.

May, the goriest month in terms of American fatalities, was at the start of the Paris peace talks.[17] Both sides were just as blocked as they had been twelve months prior, when the North Vietnamese were too preoccupied with plotting the Tet Offensive to give peace a chance. Keep in mind that the vast majority of casualties occurred after these negotiations began.[18] Discussion stalled over Hanoi's demands for a cease-fire and National Liberation Front representation at the bargaining table. By April 30, 1975, the war ended up taking the lives of 58,193 Americans, 220,000 South Vietnamese, more than 1 million North Vietnam military/Viet Cong, and 2 million civilians.[19]

INTERVENTIONISM

World War I not only signposted a crossroads in history, it splintered any consensus the nation enjoyed regarding America's role in the world. Our easy victory in the Spanish–American War, speedy expansion into the Pacific and the Caribbean, and the triumph of President Theodore Roosevelt in negotiating a settlement to the Russo–Japanese War gave Americans a sense that America played the lead on the world's stage.

By 1940, two schools of thought emerged in regard to foreign policy: isolationism and interventionism. The isolationists consisted of cynics who had learned their lesson in World War I and who bought, hook, line, and sinker, the "need-for-expansion" fascist claim, the "democracy-does-not-suit-all" internationalist claim, or the "just-say-no-to-provocation" pacifist claim. Interventionists included idealists who dreamed of "making the world safe for democracy" by ending the totalitarian regimes of Germany, Italy, and Japan, while others, such as Republican nominee Wendell Wilkie, held that entering World War II was in America's economic and security interests.

After World War II, America seemed to take up the burden of peacemaker to the world—first with the Marshall Plan, then with Korea and Vietnam. While diplomatic and military interference by one nation in the affairs of another is considered illegal under customary international law (as well as most treaties), America felt compelled to answer the call when democratic self-determination was involved. The question for the United States was not whether to intervene, but under what circumstances.

Advocates split between intervention to protect "vital national interests" and intervention to call a halt to "human rights" violations. Presidents John F. Kennedy, Lyndon B. Johnson, and Richard Nixon were largely motivated by vital national interests, especially as seen through the lens of Cold War *realpolitik*. Kennedy, the first president to commit combat troops to Vietnam, would "pay any price, bear any burden" to guarantee the march of democracy. Johnson not only became obsessed with winning at all costs but also regarded withdrawal as a sign of weakness that would eventually egg on Communist aggression elsewhere. Although candidate Nixon pledged peace and a shift in policy to Vietnamization, he reversed himself when faced with further advances by the Communists. Nixon told Republican congressional leaders "I will not be the first President of the United States to lose a war."[20] He ended up directing the resumption of air attacks and ordered a hostility-broadening incursion into Cambodia.

The troubles in Korea would have been ignored had the country not fallen into what the American military called "the Asian defense perimeter." When the North Koreans crossed the Thirty-eighth Parallel in June 1950, President Truman was convinced that the Soviets (with Chinese Communist compliance) had promoted the cheeky move. To his mind, Korea was the next step in the Soviet Union's global ideological offensive, which had been rapidly evolving from subversion to armed aggression. Korea was not just a civil struggle, but also presented an international challenge that, if unmet, would result in Communist domination of all of Indochina.

The North Korean invaders had anticipated a speedy success. Their bold initiative was unexpected, their forces were superior, and they gambled that the United States would lodge no more than an impotent moral protest. Truman, recalling the disaster caused by appeasement during World War II, prevailed upon the United Nations Security Council to take military action against the aggressors. He also committed American troops. That summer, United Nations forces under General Douglas MacArthur were initially pushed back, but an amphibious landing at Inchon altered the course of the war. In November, the People's Republic of China entered the fray, shoving American-led forces south in what seemed like déjà vu. In the following months, UN troops slowly but surely scrapped their way back to slightly north of the Thirty-eighth Parallel. A cease-fire terminating the large-scale fighting was inked in July 1951.

Vietnam was fought in America's living rooms, live and in color. The former French colony was cleaved, much like Korea, into a Communist-dominated regime in the north and a non-Communist regime in the south. The Viet Cong guerillas, abandoned when the northern armies withdrew under the Geneva agreement, were later reinforced by North Vietnam regulars and routinely terrorized the South Vietnam peasantry. Despite technical advice and assistance from the United States, authorities in South Vietnam finally threw up their hands and begged for help.

President Eisenhower propped up the Saigon regime with one hundred military advisers, hefty financial backing, and American-made arms. In 1961, President Kennedy upped the ante in an agreement that included American support troops and the formation of the U.S. Assistance Command. By 1962, four thousand troops were stationed in Vietnam and the first body bags came home.[21] At the same time, the United States wormed its way into South Vietnamese politics, actively assisting in the overthrow of the repressive government of President Ngo Dinh Diem.

Presidents from Eisenhower to Nixon took the position that if America didn't fill the vacuum left by the French pulling out, then the Communists would. Further, they maintained, if Communist expansion was not checked in South Vietnam, the rest of the Asian states might topple like a line of balanced-on-end dominoes. However, opponents who knew their Asian history countered, quite persuasively, that the Vietnamese had staved off Chinese aggression for generations, so why should this juncture in time be any different?

McGeorge Bundy, national security adviser to Presidents John F. Kennedy and Lyndon B. Johnson as well as "author" of the Pentagon Papers, feared shirking our commitment to South Vietnam might hazard a larger war with China or Russia. He also predicted in 1965 that if South Vietnam fell "there would be a great weakening in the free societies in their ability to withstand Communism."[22]

Dean Rusk, secretary of state to both John F. Kennedy and Lyndon B. Johnson, mulishly backed American involvement and repeatedly reminded critics of our promise to defend South Vietnam. He would often call on his experience as a Rhodes scholar to draw parallels to an isolationist Britain failing to halt Hitler. If America could choke off the North Vietnamese now, he reasoned, our nation would not have to face greater losses in the future. Yet, in his memoirs Rusk admitted to making two mistakes with respect to the Vietnam War—underestimating the tenacity of the North Vietnamese and overestimating the patience of the American people.[23]

Under President Johnson, American interventionism reached a zenith. As a result of an alleged attack on U.S. destroyers in the Gulf of Tonkin, Johnson ordered immediate air strikes against North Vietnam. The following day, he secured support for a joint congressional resolution empowering the commander in chief to take "all necessary measures" to defend the United States and its ally.[24] After 1965, air raids transpired daily. American bombs smashed highways, bridges, and rail lines, assaulting the landscape as far north as Hanoi. In searching out the elusive Viet Cong in the south, napalm, white phosphorus, and defoliants such as Agent Orange were released via helicopter. Survivors forfeited not only their homes but also their rice.

General Curtis Le May, along with the Greatest Generation, remembered, "in the last thirty years we've lost Estonia, Latvia, Lithuania, Poland, Czechoslovakia, Hungary, Bulgaria, and China." Cardinal Spellman told his constituents that "this war in Vietnam, I believe, is a war for civilization. . . . American troops are there for the defense, protection and salvation not only of our country, but I believe of civilization itself." David

Lawrence, editor of *U.S. News and World Report,* wrote, "What the U.S. is doing in Vietnam is the most significant example of philanthropy . . . that we have witnessed in our times." Senator Strom Thurmond prophesied in 1968, "If we lose in Vietnam, before you know it, the Communists would be up on the beaches of Hawaii."[25]

By 1969, close to 550,000 troops, including South Korean and Thai soldiers, were posted in Vietnam. The decision to escalate the hostilities, to shell military targets while steering clear of civilians, and to avoid direct confrontations with the USSR and China didn't take the nature of the enemy into consideration. The idea behind our "war of attrition" strategy was to inflict maximum destruction on the enemy but incur minimal damage to our troops. America and her allies would mete out massive firepower against the North and Viet Cong–held areas until the revolutionaries found expenditures too dear.[26] What America failed to realize was that the Viet Cong, just as the Communists in Pyongyang, North Korea, were prepared to endure unthinkable casualty counts. According to Colonel Michael Walker, head of the International Security Affairs' Vietnam group, "those guys don't think or fight the way we do. It's a holy war for them. Dying for their country is honorable. The French couldn't beat them after eight years of trying."[27]

When General MacArthur reported to Truman in December 1950, "we face an entirely new war," he could have been referring to Vietnam as easily as Korea. Lacking air power, Hanoi kept up a continuous attack, harassing American troops from the shadows or the shrubbery, then retreating to secret sanctuaries when outflanked or outfought. They pilfered unexploded U.S. ordnance and used the materials in land mines and booby traps. Conventional U.S. outposts, as illustrated by Camp Dodge, or "Dodge City," in *The Green Berets,* were particularly vulnerable to both spies and sabotage. Most of all, Americans had difficulty distinguishing physically between friend and foe.[28]

SUMMARY OF THE PLOT

The Green Berets (1968) begins with a Fort Bragg, North Carolina, press briefing. Colonel Michael Kirby (John Wayne) of the elite U.S. Fifth Special Forces seems to single out George Beckworth (David Janssen) when the *Chronicle Herald* journalist asks some fairly pointed questions about American intervention in Vietnam. Kirby challenges the war correspondent to see Vietnam for himself—specifically Camp Dodge on the Cambodian–Laos border. (Shooting the scene of the electrifying night battle in which the enemy swarms over Camp Dodge is the reason Wayne needed Pentagon assistance to make this movie.) Kirby's crack, handpicked Green Beret unit includes Sergeant Muldoon (Aldo Ray), Doc McGee

(Raymond St. Jacques), Sergeant Kowalski (Mike Henry), Sergeant Provo (Luke Askew), and Sergeant Petersen (Jim Hutton). After witnessing both the sneak attack on the outpost and the atrocities committed by the Viet Cong, Beckwith reverses his attitude and actually joins in the fighting. A secret mission that seems anticlimactic in light of the protracted firefight involves the kidnapping of a prominent North Vietnamese officer, Phan Son Ti (William Olds) through the use of a beautiful Vietnamese model (Irene Tsu) as sexual inducement. In the last reel, Petersen is greased by a brutal booby trap and Kirby has to break the heart-wrenching news to Hamchunk (Craig Jue), the camp's adopted orphan. "You're who we are fighting for," concludes Kirby.

GREEN BERETS: GUTS AND GLORY

The Green Berets was hardly, as critics liked to whine, "just another combat movie." Wayne intended the film to be interventionist, the sort of undiluted propaganda that brought America into World War I, World War II, and Korea. American isolationists were recycling the same tired arguments, namely, that the conflict in Southeast Asia was none of our business, that the South Vietnamese didn't really want our assistance, and that the United States could hardly be expected to police the entire globe. Americans in general were exhausted with warfare. Korea had proved a wash after the loss of fifty-four thousand American young men. The so-called police action had not changed the pre-1950 map of Korea but did deliver a hammering in the propaganda war. The Communists were able to brag that they had blocked the United States from reestablishing Western imperialist superiority in the East. In fact, America found scant support among the non-Communist Asian powers such as India, Indonesia, and Burma. However, deterring the aggression of the North Koreans reinforced faith in American military strength and stiffened resolve to check Communist expansion elsewhere.

Wayne tried to decode the "McNamara–Rusk–Rostow" rationale for involvement in Vietnam in *The Green Berets*.[29] The hardboiled Sergeant Muldoon addresses a press conference at the Fort Bragg John F. Kennedy Center, advising the assembled journalists that the Soviets mean to dominate the entire planet. Muldoon heads off a seemingly impertinent question about holding free elections by clearing his throat and launching into an impromptu civics lesson: "The school I went to taught us that the thirteen colonies, with proper and educated leadership, all with the same goal in mind, after the Revolutionary War, took from 1776 to 1787, eleven years of peaceful effort, before they came up with a paper that all thirteen colonies could sign—our present Constitution." He then connects the dots between Vietnam and the Communists by slamming down weapons, ammunition, and equipment captured from the Viet Cong on a wooden table. The Soviet Union, Red China, or one of their allies, he explains, were the manufacturers.

The U.S. Army Special Forces traces its roots back to World War I. Colonel Douglas MacArthur, with just a scout and an unreliable pistol, so-journed far beyond friendly lines to survey the Kaiser's defenses.[30] His courageous and selfless mission earned him the Medal of Honor and ultimately inspired the creation of the Green Berets. Colonel "Wild Bill" Donovan headed up a forerunner of Special Forces, the Office of Strategic Services, during World War II. His organization dealt with intelligence, resistance movements, and sabotage until disbanded by Truman on January 22, 1946. His gutsy and self-sacrificing service earned him all four of the military's highest honors. Colonel Aaron Bank, commander of the Tenth Special Forces Airborne at Fort Bragg, North Carolina, activated the Green Berets on June 11, 1952. Best known for "Operation Iron Cross" (the plan to capture Hitler), Bank, while intelligence gathering in Vietnam, warned his superiors that if the United States didn't back Ho Chi Minh it would end up fighting him. His memo to that effect ended up, obviously unheeded, in some back file cabinet at the Pentagon.

Detractors of the Green Berets, especially those opposed to involvement in Vietnam, have cited evidence of lawlessness, corruption, brutality, a predisposition to political extremism, and the unregulated power of "A" teams stationed in Vietnam, but they couldn't keep most Americans from being impressed with the elite group of counterinsurgents. The Green Berets, who faced death daily with grace and courage, are still recognizable war heroes in America. *The Complete History of the Green Berets* documents a revealing event. A black officer sporting a green beret was standing at attention in a Deep South town as a Ku Klux Klan parade approached. The marchers abruptly turned left and went three blocks out of their way to avoid passing in front of him, such was the power and prestige of the Special Forces image.[31]

The Green Berets are unashamedly elitist. Every soldier is trained as some sort of James Bond spy—able to speak six languages and kill seven ways (without making a sound). The chances for any one person of breaking into the corps, at least according to Barry Sadler's hit song, are 3 percent. The Special Forces seeks out only the most intelligent, creative, self-reliant, hyperaggressive, brave-beyond-reason, and committed warriors. Although the average age is thirty-one, Special Forces soldiers are expected to exhibit the physical prowess of a male a decade younger. Furthermore, Green Berets receive the most comprehensive military training available, including training in intelligence gathering, counterinsurgency, languages, communications, unconventional warfare, fieldwork, arms training, and parachute jumping, all in addition to a recognized military specialty.

George Morton, who commanded the Special Forces in 1961, explained, "Kennedy's concept was to lower the spectrum of violence, to alienate the Vietnamese people from the Viet Cong. We treated it as a problem of human rights, and spreading the wealth. Then Kennedy got assassinated in 1963, and we moved to massive military intervention."[32] Kennedy intended his Special Forces to win the hearts and minds of those behind the lines by sharing expertise and preparing indigenous soldiers to fight for their own independence.

The beret of green felt that now symbolizes the Special Forces was not even a component of the official uniform until President John F. Kennedy authorized the distinctive headgear—over the strenuous objections of the Pentagon. A silver insignia consisting of crossed arrows (symbolizing Native American stealth), an intimidating Commando dagger, and the Latin words *de oppresso liber*, "to free from oppression," also designate membership in the corps.[33]

At the height of the Vietnam War, thirteen thousand men were wearing the beret. By the time Wayne got around to glorifying these "quiet professionals," there were only about three hundred left in Vietnam.[34]

Twelve-member "A" teams schooled South Vietnamese, Cambodians, and Montagnard tribesmen.[35] With America supplying the weapons, rations, and uniforms, each of the one hundred base camps in Vietnam housed five hundred to seven hundred men. Since the Special Forces believed indigenous soldiers would prove more steadfast if protecting their own families, their women and children lived alongside the soldiers.

Green Beret teachers, however, were often forced to become Green Beret warriors. "Puff, the Magic Dragon," a C47 airplane armed with Vulcan cannon and other armaments, became common only after 1962.[36] Without adequate firepower, base camps could be overrun on a regular basis. "Mike Forces," mobile strike teams, stepped in when isolated camps were threatened by sneak attacks.

After John Wayne trekked through Vietnam, he acknowledged, "When I saw what our boys are going through—hell—and how [their] morale was holding up and the job they were doing, I just knew they had to make this picture."[37] Colonel Michael Kirby, although purportedly a composite character, was modeled after the most decorated combat colonel in the Vietnam War, Colonel Francis J. Kelly. Wayne bunked with Kelly for two weeks while preparing for the role of Kirby. One of the top three guerilla warfare experts before his retirement in 1972, Kelly was a complicated chap who passed away in 1997. His wife confessed, "You would think he was a real SOB, and he probably was in his day, but he [also] was . . . the sweetest, most genuine man, and he loved people.[38] His last act for the Green Berets was to propose the construction of a Washington, D.C., memorial for women who made the ultimate sacrifice in Vietnam.

Designated by some as "the war without songs," Vietnam doesn't bring to mind such hits as World War I's "Over There" or World War II's "This Is the Army, Mr. Jones," but "The Ballad of the Green Berets" summed up Vietnam for John Wayne. The pop tune shot to the top of the charts for five weeks in 1966 and sold more than 9 million singles and albums. Staff Sergeant Barry Sadler was a Special Forces medic who penned the ditty while recovering from a leg wound. Later, picking out a few chords on an old Harmony guitar, Sadler managed to produce an album that vaulted him into a guest appearance on the Ed Sullivan show. It was a time when America was proud of the crack Kennedy forces and when words such as "grunt," "click," "Charlie," and "frag" had infiltrated the lexicon.

Wayne decided Robin Moore's memoir, *The Green Berets*, would provide the perfect framework for a Vietnam interventionist film.[39] After dropping in on the Special Forces base at Fort Bragg, the blown-away Duke declared, "If people of the United States were apprised of [the quality of the troops] it would renew their confidence in the ability, the decency and the dedication of our present-day American fighting men."[40] The Harvard-educated Moore claimed to have trained and served with the Green Berets while a freelance writer.

Moore's book was first optioned and then dumped by Columbia before Wayne snatched it up, figuring its bestseller standing couldn't help but advance the film. *The Green Berets* turned out to be a mixed blessing. Although Moore supported the war, he insisted on including scenes that also portrayed the Special Forces in an incompetent and corrupt light.[41] Hawks and doves alike called on the memoir to corroborate their respective points of view.[42]

The Defense Department hated the book and demanded that Moore have nothing to do with the screenplay. The book "was objectionable" to the military, claims Wayne biographer Garry Wills. "On almost all conceivable grounds, [Moore portrayed] the Green Berets as lawless, sadistic, and racist."[43]

Screenwriter James Lee Barrett, an ex-Marine who had written *The Greatest Story Ever Told* and *Shenandoah,* used only a few incidents from the Moore book. He managed to come up with an action-packed script that included the Viet Cong overrunning the camp and the kidnapping of a VC general. Still, the Pentagon stipulated substantial changes in Barrett's screenplay before giving Wayne access to Fort Benning, Georgia, and gobs of gleaming military hardware. The Defense Department's Don Baruch was adamant that a covert mission to North Vietnam was not only "not one that the Green Berets would participate in" but also contradicted the Special Forces' mission.[44] Producer Michael Wayne agreed to jettison that particular episode, since he knew his father wouldn't relish a rejected script, not to mention the ensuing negative publicity.[45] The Pentagon also rejected all references to Vietnam as "a civil war," requiring that American aggression be portrayed as neighborly assistance allowing the South Vietnamese to retain their freedom and develop without interference. Finally, the Defense Department objected to any brutal treatment of prisoners, not only as potential grist for U.S. Vietnam policy opponents but also as a clear violation of the Articles of War. Wayne made all the changes, despite the fact that the film was now open to charges of inauthenticity and American bias. A glaring example can be found when Colonel Kirby (John Wayne) holds back Captain Nim (George Takai), who discovers a traitor in the camp.

Incessant debates with the Pentagon, along with the standard setbacks involved in settling financial and distribution arrangements, delayed the movie's release until July 1968—six months after the Tet Offensive eroded both popular support and trust in the military. Worse still, the thirty-six-month delay left Batjac Productions with a dated story and a rapidly aging star.

A PUBLIC RELATIONS VEHICLE FOR THE PENTAGON

At the end of December 1965, President Lyndon B. Johnson received a piece of correspondence that began, "Dear Mr. President. When I was a little boy, my father always told me that if you want to get anything done, see the top man—so I am addressing this letter to you." The letter was signed by John Wayne and proposed a patriotic movie about Vietnam.

Wayne explained that while he supported the administration's Vietnam policy, he realized the number of like-minded Americans was swiftly declining. Consequently, it was "extremely important that not only the people of the United States, but those all over the world should know why it is necessary for us to be there. . . . The most effective way to accomplish this is through the motion picture medium."[46] He added he could make "the kind of picture that will help our cause throughout the world" while still making money for Batjac Productions.[47] He would "tell the story of our fighting men in Vietnam with reason, emotion, characterization, and action. We want to do it in a manner that will inspire a patriotic attitude on the part of fellow Americans—a feeling which we have always had in this country in the past during times of stress and trouble."[48] To make the picture, Wayne required the cooperation of the Defense Department, and in support of this request, he cited a filmography of more than 235 movies—portrayals of integrity and dignity such as *They Were Expendable, Sands of Iwo Jima,* and *The Longest Day.* He concluded by predicting that *The Green Berets* could be "extremely helpful to the administration" and solicited Johnson's assistance in expediting the project.[49]

By 1965, American troop strength was approaching 200,000. The president was intrigued but he decided to request Jack Valenti's counsel.

"Wayne's politics [are] wrong," allowed Valenti, "but insofar as Vietnam is concerned, his views are right. If he made the picture he would be saying the things we want said."[50]

Not only did John Wayne take it upon himself to write his commander in chief, he also cranked out missives to members of the Senate Foreign Relations Committee (Richard B. Russell, John Sherman Cooper, J. W. Fulbright, Clinton P. Anderson, and George Murphy) urging that Congress remain steadfast in backing the war.[51] Wayne argued "that the Commie guerrillas are ruthless, having killed twenty thousand civic leaders and their families during these years of slaughter."[52] He subsequently used this same line of reasoning through Doc McGeen (Raymond St. Jacques) during the press conference opening the movie. McGeen comments that proportionally, the Vietnamese lost twice as many fighting men in their battle for freedom as Americans lost in World War II. If the equivalent percentage of our leadership had been murdered, McGeen contends, the dead would number 250,000 and would include every teacher, every professor, every mayor, every governor, every senator, and every member of the House of Representatives, plus their combined families. It is not any screenwriter who can put a letter to Congress in the mouth of a cinematic character.

It's a little disingenuous for critics to complain that Wayne didn't present both sides. First, interventionist films are inherently biased. *The Green Berets* was not only supposed to persuade young men to line up at their local recruiting offices, but also was intended to urge their families to cheer them on. Why would Wayne include evidence that might undermine his case? *The Green Berets* didn't pretend to be anything but flag-waving propaganda, just like the films promoting intervention in World War I, World War II, and Korea. Further, Wayne intended his cinematic effort to inspire rather than duplicate the *cinema verité* account of Vietnam already occurring on the boob tube.

Second, a 120-minute film couldn't possibly encapsulate the three decades of Vietnam history that still has academicians quibbling. Moviegoers simply wouldn't sit still for a thorough and nuanced exposition. That's why Wayne chose to highlight the major pro–con issues at the Fort Bragg press conference. Wayne, who substantially shaped the script, wanted to duplicate his own personal Vietnam experience for the audience, especially in scenes like the one in "the little village that has erected its own statue of liberty to the American people." He was especially struck by the prediction that a veritable bloodbath of 2 million souls would result if America abandoned the South Vietnamese. He also wanted to portray the Green Berets as "diplomats in dungarees," lending a hand, dispensing medical attention, passing out toys and soap (just as GIs handed out Hershey bars and chewing gum during World War II).[53] Wayne's detractors, however, maintained "Americanism that fails to extend the vision of the

Declaration of Independence to other nations is a dubious creed. A candy bar or a hug are not adequate reparations for the imperialistic occupation and destruction of a hamlet, or of a country, its people and its culture."[54]

Third, Wayne required the Pentagon's approval in order to research actual conditions in Vietnam and gain access to authentic military equipment. Wayne, with TV news bringing the war into American homes every evening, "couldn't afford to come up with anything less than the real thing."[55] According to Vietnam film expert Jeremy Devine, "To obtain [combat footage] a filmmaker had to garner government cooperation or wait several years for the jetsam of the war to make it to civilian sources. Even though this was no excuse for small-scale production, it did practically hamper any proposed epic presentations," such as *The Green Berets*.[56] The Department of Defense's film directive was not only quite specific, but it was also patently partisan. According to Instruction 5410.5, "The production, program, project, or assistance will *benefit* the Department of Defense or otherwise be in the national interest" (italics mine).[57]

Nevertheless, the Pentagon dangled some alluring bait. The army conducted a Huey helicopter–training program at Fort Benning, Georgia, and while they couldn't provide on-duty soldiers, Wayne would be allowed to film regularly scheduled training maneuvers. The army also brought down a platoon of Hawaiian Americans "on administrative leave" from Fort Devens, Massachusetts, to serve as Asian extras in the film. The jump school colonel seen shooting trap with Wayne in the film was Colonel Bill Welch, the legendary commander of U.S. paratroopers. *The Green Berets* was granted three advisers: a technical consultant to keep military protocol straight, a liaison who arranged for men and gear, and a Pentagon man who kept the Department of Defense continually informed.

Batjac Productions was billed a mere $18,623.64 by the Defense Department, which included eighty-five hours of helicopter flying time and 3,800 man days of military personnel.[58] Batjac also built a $150,000 Vietnamese-type village at Fort Bragg, North Carolina, which is still in use as a training site for jungle warfare.[59] In June 1969, Representative Benjamin Rosenthal of New York demanded a General Accounting Office investigation, charging that the army subsidized the film to the tune of $1 million. Wayne responded by dubbing Rosenthal as "an irresponsible, publicity seeking idiot," adding that if this were the nineteenth century, he might have "horsewhipped" the Congressman.[60]

Interventionist films from World War I to Korea have featured patriotic, morale-boosting messages and the blatant demonization of the enemy. While, deep down, Americans may have realized that our World War I and World War II foes were not really malevolent subhumans, it made everybody feel good to presume they were. During the schizophrenic '60s, however, dramatizing enemy atrocities produced the opposite effect. The problem was that the national feeling of unison legitimizing interventionist films twenty-five years earlier was now conspicuously absent. When the audience drew comparisons, the Green Berets did not always come out as the "good guys."

The "Puff, the Magic Dragon" plane in the film takes only sixty seconds to mow down the Viet Cong with Vulcan cannon. The act of retaliation for the Viet Cong invasion of the camp seemed to some an Old Testament–like visitation of divine justice. Further, Sergeant Muldoon flashes an evil grin as he blows a bridge teeming with VC to kingdom come. His fondness for and expert employment of explosives goes back to a childhood chemistry set. Hollis Alpert, in *Saturday Review,* mused these scenes "made me wonder if John Wayne was attempting to serve the cause of Hanoi by portraying Americans in Vietnam as ruthless, murderous, and sadistic."[61]

The allies were forced to adopt unconventional warfare, fighting in the same reprehensible manner as the enemy, when the National Liberation Front buried land mines, set impaling mantraps, and concealed poisoned "pungi sticks," with points capable of penetrating the heaviest marching boots, on the ground. The movie clumsily tries to underline the notion that VC atrocities were somehow worse than American atrocities. Take the pungi sticks: "It's a little trick we learned from Charlie. But we don't dip them in the same stuff he does." Then there's the sex angle. When Colonel Kirby lacks sufficient evidence to hold a Viet Cong general, the Special Forces concoct a kidnapping scheme using the VC's supposed uncontrolled lust to, quite literally, capture him with his trousers down.

The North Vietnamese Army is represented as a terror machine that systematically robs the mountain district inhabitants of rice, chickens, and young men. An old village chief, who grows to trust the Americans after Doc treats his granddaughter, is murdered before his tribesmen can be brought into Dodge City for protection. The enemy uses the cover of night to sneak into the vulnerable settlement, set the huts ablaze, and abduct all the fighting-age males. In the muted light of dawn, women with soot-blackened faces huddle together and the headman bleeds to death as he hangs from a post. The chief's sweet granddaughter is subsequently discovered in a thicket outside the village, having been savagely assaulted by five Viet Cong—like so many other female family members of resisting chieftains.

THE RELUCTANT WITNESS

Postwar Vietnam films such as the *Deer Hunter, Apocalypse Now, Full Metal Jacket,* and even *Good Morning, Vietnam* paid homage to Wayne's employment of a skeptical journalist to represent the American public. For Wayne, however, to focus on the print media seems odd—after all, Vietnam was a television war. Viewing napalmed children and burning villages proved to be "a picture is worth a thousand words" more effective than lengthy editorials in undermining popular support for the war. Additionally, Wayne could have exploited the fact that TV reporters were permitted far more unregulated access than print journalists.

In essence, the film is a Socratic argument between Colonel Mike Kirby and George Beckworth. When Kirby throws out the challenge "Hard to talk to anyone about this country until they've been over and seen it," Beckworth journeys, in jungle safari polyester, to see Vietnam for himself. He returns to the United States determined to report the truth. Beckworth isn't won over by logic or reason—the kind of nuanced arguments that pundits and politicians might exchange on the opinion pages—but by sheer sentiment. In fact, Beckworth does the one thing objective newsmen are not supposed to—he becomes personally involved with his subject, or at least one little Montagnard girl. When confronted with the atrocities committed against her and her people, the war correspondent falls victim to his emotions. Further, he isn't just persuaded; he is fundamentally changed. You can actually watch his face harden with resolve and the desire for revenge as he exchanges his typewriter for an M-16.

The movie pivots on a couple of ideas about journalism. First, just because an article appears in black and white doesn't make it true—surveys indicate that increasing numbers of American readers believe the press to be untrustworthy, unreliable, and uninformed. When housewife Gladys Cooper remarks, "It's strange that we never read of this in the newspapers, Muldoon responds "well, that's newspapers for you, ma'am—you could fill volumes with what you don't read in them." Second, only actual eyewitnesses should comment about war. The Pentagon, you see, isn't likely to issue impartial assessments of day-to-day activities, and newspaper publishers (think Hearst) are not above promoting a personal agenda. When Kirby asks Beckworth, "What are you gonna say in that newspaper of yours," Beckworth replies, "If I say what I feel, I may be out of a job."

When Kirby reminds Beckworth he can always find employment in the military, the journalist demurs, "I could do more good with a typewriter." According to critic Douglas Brode, to suggest that Beckworth could spread the word and convince the nation to get behind the war effort was just wishful thinking. "In fact," Brode writes, "most of the liberal journalists who visited Viet Nam returned with [an even] stronger conviction that we were engaged in a desperate, disillusioning struggle, and the reports they filed in their papers continued to stir more and more people to question the validity of our current conflict."[62] Whether or not reporters were actually opposed to the war, alleged partiality was subsequently used as a justification for restricting access to conflicts such as Grenada, Panama, and the Gulf War. The Pentagon took a big chance embedding journalists in Operation Iraqi Freedom.

Garry Wills believes that Wayne is actually reversing the real-life experience of most American journalists. The well-known cluster of reporters who filed alarming reports from Vietnam—Neil Sheehan, David Halberstam, Malcolm Browne, Charles Mohr, and Mort Perry—all went there believing the war was both worthwhile and winnable. In fact, Wills found that these journalists began to doubt that Vietnam was winnable long before concluding it was not worthwhile.[63]

DON'T FENCE ME IN

Critics bashed *The Green Berets* as a gung ho World War II retread, too much like the unabashed heroics, willful naïveté, and ham-fisted hawkism in *Sands of Iwo Jima* or *Back to Bataan*.[64] According to *Variety*, "The film is a prime example of anomalies and anachronisms, compounding credibility gaps and generation gaps. Presumably aimed at the dominant young film audience, the picture essentially is trying to tell a war story of today in World War II terminology."[65] Since interventionist films are a specific subgenre of the combat film, why wouldn't *The Green Berets* share characteristics with the World War II interventionist film?

According to son Michael, John Wayne saw the controversy surrounding Vietnam as a natural subject for a film. Beyond that, "it was the story of a group of guys who could have been in any war. It's a very familiar story. War stories are all the same. They are personal stories about soldiers and the background is the war. This just happened to be the Vietnam War."[66]

When the United States entered World War II, the war movie had already been granted structure and substance, and it only required a connection to current events to goose patriotism. During World War II, villains acquired heavy German accents and worked for Hitler. During the Cold War, the bad guys were Communists. Hollywood not only was able to put a human face on hostilities but also employed cinematic language to edify and explain America's involvement. Filmmakers continued to rely on durable stereotypes such as the foe so foul, the sagacious senior officer, and the ethnic cross-section fighting squad managing to accomplish minor miracles via the infectious American spirit.

Why shouldn't Wayne have called on the same interventionist arguments, the same battle film stereotypes, and the same war fiction clichés? Just because a critic might recognize cinematic clichés such as the short-timer "buying the farm" days before shipping home, or the homeless waif tugging at everybody's heartstrings, this didn't minimize their dramatic effectiveness. Like previous interventionist filmmakers, Wayne likewise sought to boost morale, promote self-sacrifice, and bring the nation together.[67] For comic relief, Wayne threw in Sergeant Peterson (Jim Hutton), a gifted supply officer just like the one played by Jack Lemmon in *Mister Roberts* or Tony Curtis in *Operation Petticoat*.

To show how alike interventionist films can be, Sam Fuller's *China Gate* examines Vietnam a full decade before American involvement.[68] Although the flick features a squad of racially balanced Foreign Legionnaires instead of Green Berets, Fuller's cast of characters should sound familiar: a Vietnamese B girl cum spy, a sexually charged Communist general, an adorable native child, and a winsome puppy.

Not only had John Wayne become an expert in producing World War II films, but also the film subject was still popular decades after the peace accords were signed. Linda Dittmar and Gene Michaud argue, "in the same way that the commercial film industry fed America's depression-era audiences images of opulence and prosperity, the Hollywood of the Vietnam era continued to provide a steady diet of representations of World War II, the war most often characterized as the finest example of America's political, moral, and military strength."[69]

Critics also drew parallels between *The Green Berets* and the western. According to *Film Society Review*, "Wayne was able to transfer his [western] cinematic modus operandi to the Vietnam War by singling out a single microcosm within the conflict, then setting the good guys, at great odds, against the bad guys."[70] When you think about it, the western is really a combat film.

However, in depicting Vietnam, according to Albert Auster and Leonard Quart, the combat film cinematic cookie cutter doesn't quite fit.[71] First, the combat film genre usually featured small platoons, not the unique combination of hand-to-hand, guerilla-type fighting coupled with the massive firepower found in Vietnam. Second, combat films didn't usually put civilians in harm's way. In that regard, stock western scenes such as the besieged fort or the circled wagons are actually better suited to the interpretation of Vietnam strike camps. Third, when it comes to depicting atrocities committed by the enemy, vulnerable women and children, essential ingredients in westerns, provoke even more compassion as targets than the men-only enclaves populating combat films.

Since John Wayne appeared in more westerns than movies of any other genre, it is not surprising that he was drawn to a frontier story. "Every country in the world," Wayne said, "loved the folklore of the West—the music, the dress, the excitement, everything that was associated with the opening of a new territory. It took everybody out of their own little world."[72]

Intuitively, Wayne realized the western better represented Vietnam on an allegorical level. This war was essentially a collection of strong, silent types riding in from the prairie to defend freedom-loving farmers against bloodthirsty Communist savages. Further, according to Garry Wills, the western is [better] able to raise serious moral questions because it deals with the clash of different cultures, "not only . . . of Native Americans or Mexicans or Chinese coolies with European colonizers, but . . . of earlier colonizers with later ones."[73]

On the frontier, atrocities, including brutality, torture, and rape, were not uncommon before law enforcement, such as the Texas Rangers or the local marshal, finally arrived on the scene. According to Richard Slotkin, morality is embodied by the frontier's mythic heroes who "stand on the border between savagery and civilization; they are 'the men who know Indians,' and in many ways their values and habits of thought reflect those of the savage enemy. Because of this mirroring effect, the moral warfare of savagery and civilization is, for the heroes, a spiritual or psychological struggle, which they win by learning to discipline or suppress the savage or 'dark' side of their own human nature."[74] The Green Berets not only knew the Viet Cong "Indians" but also, in many ways, echoed their savagery.

Future Vietnam filmmakers followed Wayne's lead. The '70s herded in a host of western-based Vietnam movies in which Vietnam was recast as a romantic wilderness located at the edge of civilization. There, jungle firebases could stand in for frontier forts and cowboy-like heroes could search for adventure, humanity, or themselves.

Nonetheless, loners did not ultimately win the west. Although the three-century-old frontier myth accentuates freedom and rugged individualism, real-life conditions during the 1860s–90s compelled teamwork and barn-raising cooperation among settlers in order to triumph over the wilderness. It was a rare pioneer who could supply all his family's needs. Hamlets mushroomed across the West and the "can-do" spirit that became known as Americanism began to thrive. As in Vietnam, local farmers gathered at cavalry outposts for security. Early frontiersman may not have worn berets, but they acquired languages, became highly proficient with firearms, and schooled themselves in fighting off guerilla-like attacks by both marauding Indians and anarchist outlaws.

For Wayne, the connection between *The Alamo* and *The Green Berets* was so obvious that he quoted from the former while requesting presidential assistance in producing the latter. By choosing the elite Green Berets to provide the scaffold for his scenario, Wayne was also able to connect the dots between John Ford and John Kennedy. According to biographers Randy Roberts and James S. Olson, Wayne in any costume epitomized the archetypal hero of the American western frontier. He was "big, bold, confident, powerful, loud, violent and occasionally overbearing, but simultaneously forgiving, gentle, innocent, naïve, almost childlike. In his person and in the persona he so carefully constructed . . . America saw itself, its past and its future."[75]

Michael Wayne actually identified *The Green Berets* as primarily a "cowboy-and-Indian" film.[76] The clues are obvious, starting with Camp A 107's nickname, "Dodge City," and the line "out here, due process is a bullet," the traditional definition of frontier justice. In fact, the Vietnam outpost itself resembled a fort, with barbed wire and claymore mines substituting for log fortification and cannon. All Wayne had to do was swap red men for yellow, stagecoaches for helicopters, and the Seventh Cavalry for air support. By the end of the movie, Kirby was even able to stride off into a rosy-hued sunset.[77] In fact, the reviewer in *Time* glimpsed more than just the outline of a standard western, noting that the South Vietnamese officers not only sounded like Tonto—"We build many camps, clobber many VC"—but also played a strictly subordinate role to the Duke's Lone Ranger.[78]

THE AMERICAN MYTHOLOGY OF JOHN WAYNE

When 1993 Louis Harris pollsters asked a representative sample of more than a thousand Americans, "Who is your favorite star?" John Wayne came in second, although he had been dead for fourteen years. He was second again in 1994 and first in 1995. From 1949 to 1974, Wayne made the top ten in the Quigley poll (the accepted measure of box-office money-makers since 1931) for twenty-five of the twenty-six years—only missing in 1958, when his *Barbarian and the Geisha* stunk up the theaters.[79]

When Soviet Premier Nikita Khrushchev toured around the United States in 1959, he requested three items on his itinerary: Disneyland, Pennsylvania's Mesta Machine Works, and John Wayne. In his essay "My Heroes Have Never Been Cowboys," the Native American writer Sherman Alexie recalled, "Looking up into the night sky, I asked my brother what he thought God looked like and he said, God probably looks like John Wayne."[80] More than one Vietnam War memoirist admits joining up because he saw himself, like John Wayne, charging up the beach in the *Sands of Iwo Jima*. Ron Kovik, who was tragically paralyzed in Vietnam, claimed that every time he heard the Marine hymn, he thought of John Wayne.[81] As an immigrant, Chairman of the Joint Chiefs John Shalikashvili taught himself English by imitating Wayne movies. Former Speaker of the House Newt Gingrich used the tough-but-fair Wayne character Sergeant John Stryker from *Sands of Iwo Jima* as his role model. As he prepared to straighten out the country's domestic affairs, Richard Nixon admitted to being inspired by Wayne's performance in *Chisum*. Pat Buchanan rallied support for his 1996 presidential bid with Stryker's signature "Saddle up, lock and load." Wayne even made an impression on rock and roll—Buddy Holly took Ethan Edwards's line from *The Searchers* and turned it into the anthem, "That'll be the Day."

Wayne's fans remain unwaveringly committed. The homegrown fan magazine *The Big Trail* is still published bimonthly and seasonal celebrations paying homage to Wayne are scheduled across the country.[82] The Duke has more monuments that most war heroes. There's an impressive equestrian statue in Los Angeles, an oversized striding sculpture at the eponymous Orange County airport, and an eight-foot bronze fronting an Irish pub in San Diego. A foundry in Oregon turns out statuettes for at-home devotions. His films are never off the television screen and are perennial big sellers at the video store. Virtually all of the Vietnam movies churned out during the '80s and '90s contain references to Wayne—the most obvious being Stanley Kubrick's mantra-like mention of Wayne's name in *Full Metal Jacket.* Even though two studios declined to back *The Green Berets,* the decision makers at Warner Bros.–Seven Arts were no fools—Wayne was the box office golden goose who laid only one bad egg in twenty years.[83]

John Wayne even started out "larger than life." When Marion Robert Morrison came into the world in 1907, he weighed more than thirteen pounds.[84] By the time he reached adolescence, he had to stoop to enter a door. He may have been recruited to play football at the University of Southern California, but his physical coordination and grace were not spotted by Hollywood until he took a part-time job moving scenery at Fox Film Studios. According to a *Photoplay* interview, Wayne would start out in the prop department, then move to the lights, and "if they wanted someone to fall off a horse, I'd do that, too, or work on a dress set as an extra for a while. In those days you'd work in every department [to find your] true place in the business."[85] After catching the eye of a casting director, he found permanent employment in westerns and films about college athletes. According to David Thompson, Wayne "had a riveting presence—everything began with that."[86]

One of the advantages of his size and strength was that he was never dwarfed by the landscape, whether Monument Valley or a vast battlefield. Usually garbed in a cowboy outfit or an officer's uniform, he looked out of place in anything else. Yet, off screen the Duke was a bit of a dandy, more accustomed to donning silk suits than denim jeans. He insisted on a daily scrubbing with Neutrogena soap and always appeared meticulously groomed and clad in the finest sartorial splendor. Few knew that the Duke, known for his rough-hewn image, aspired, unsuccessfully it turned out, to Los Angeles' upper crust.[87]

Wayne exerted an easy control over his massive frame, engaging in efficient and fluid movement and using his bulk to invest action with authority. Over the course of his film work, he carefully formulated his signature stance, gestures, and horseback posture. According to Garry Wills, the Duke struck poses that were more than reminiscent of what sculptors call a *contrapposto* lean (the weight shifted to one leg held rigid, while the other is bent and relaxed) and Wills actually matched Duke's major moves on film to sculptures by Michelangelo and Donatello.

Wayne was often cast as a character who bucks tremendous odds. The Duke remained cool and self-possessed as he faced down foes, seeming to psyche out his adversaries with his weighty bearing and spellbinding stride, and without uttering a word.[88] His costars, especially the heavies, had to take advantage of camera angles, lighting, crowds, and costumes to avoid being upstaged by Wayne's powerful presence. He was so sure of himself, however, that he was more than generous with other actors. Since he seemed so indomitable a figure, fans were incredulous when the real-life Wayne surrendered to cancer. Surely, the invincible Duke should have been able to clobber "the Big C."

Wayne's rolling "tough guy" walk remained an inextricable aspect of his smoldering sexuality. His measured phrases seemed to be commands, and his commands were instantly heeded. His craggy face wore a constant expression of partial puzzlement, partial amusement. Critics Gary Arnold and Kenneth Turan observed, "Perhaps no Hollywood actor had a more distinctive appearance—a slightly tilted stance and a loping stride, an emphatic, syncopated way of speaking (which delighted many a mimic, professional and amateur), and an awesome physical presence."[89] Admirers found Duke's gravestone epitaph "Feo, fuerte, y formal" revealing.[90]

At a time when movie men were men, Wayne assumed the role of father figure, a Sergeant Stryker type who simultaneously serves as protector and survival skill instructor to succeeding generations. Authority figures are not ancient and creaky by necessity, but they do seem to need a few odometer miles to command respect. As Wayne matured and his features began to fracture, he not only projected competence and character, he finally cracked the top ten lists of stars. According to journalist Nigel Andrews, "Wayne was special for mid-century Americans because he had been battered into stardom. For its frontline hero, during and after the war, the western world wanted not some overnight pin-up but a man who had been dragged through the movie trenches."[91]

Folks, reaching out for the definition of an American, considered Wayne the real deal. Wayne was not only one of the most recognized icons in the world, but as biographer James T. Campbell puts it, he was also "the seeming quintessence of American manhood."[92] Before his death, he was presented with the same congressional medal awarded to George Washington, Andrew Jackson, and Robert F. Kennedy, which in Wayne's case was inscribed "John Wayne, American." Biographers Roberts and Olson contend, "those who hope to understand America must understand John Wayne's appeal."[93] According to President Jimmy Carter, "it was because of what John Wayne said about what we are and what we can be that his great and deep love of America was returned in full measure."[94]

Yet, biographer Garry Wills poses a provocative question: "What kind of country accepts as its norm an old man whose principal screen activity was shooting other people, or punching them out?"[95]

Answer: a nation of doers. The Duke never played a cerebral individual; his characters were, in fact, downright anti-intellectual. Their method of solving problems always involved action, sometimes violent action. Yet as an actor, Wayne maintained certain, perhaps rigidly held, standards. When Stanley Kubrick tried to sign Wayne as Major Kong, the character eventually played by Slim Pickens in *Dr. Strangelove,* the Duke demurred. The film was a little too pink for his politics.[96] Wayne drew the line at shooting a man in the back, he would never appear as a coward (even turning down Howard Hawks early in his career to avoid such a role), and because Wayne was offended by a script requiring him to slap an American soldier, George C. Scott ended up delivering General Patton's words, "Men, all of this stuff you've heard about America not wanting to fight, wanting to stay out of the war, is a lot of horse dung."

John Wayne taught a generation of men how to stand tall, snatch a kiss, and take a fist on the chin. He represented the ideal American, someone who is patriotic, brave, honest, uncompromising, decent, and strong. Representative Morris K. Udall, a Democrat from Arizona, mused, "If John Wayne was never quite the way we were, he was always the way Americans have wanted him to be."[97] To Admiral Elmo Zumwalt, former chief of naval operations, Wayne was a constant and "one of the five people in my life I thought of as a major male symbol."[98] He filled a need in his audience for someone who exuded steady self-reliance and unshakable adherence to straight-line morality. According to Elizabeth Taylor, Wayne represented, not only to America but the entire world, exactly what people hoped Americans were really like: "tough, strong, loyal, just—and never with arrogance but with true humility."[99]

Wayne's character and charisma were impossible to deny, even to those who abhorred his political philosophy. Ford biographer Joseph McBride commented, "something about John Wane has always stirred deep emotions within me, emotions I have never fully understood. He has that effect on most moviegoers, even the ones who, because their politics take precedence over art, are Wayne-haters."[100] Many liberals cannot forgive Wayne for founding the Motion Picture Alliance for the Preservation of American Ideals and assuming its presidency. In fact, Wayne became a conservative icon simply because he so embodied so many American virtues conservatives consider "endangered," such as "authority, masculinity, [and] love of country."[101]

Feminists aren't usually fond of Wayne, although it would be unfair to characterize his fan base as strictly male. According to Wayne, "I've had three wives, six children, six grandchildren and I still don't understand women."[102]

In Wayne movies, women learn never to expect an apology—they appear grateful to take second place behind a real man and seem to enjoy a good spanking before being bedded down. Wayne, however, discloses his "feminine side" in *The Green Berets.* When Colonel Cai is disgusted by Lin "sleeping with the enemy" to capture the North Vietnamese officer, Kirby attempts an attitude adjustment. He tells Cai that since Lin was, like any other soldier, merely serving her country, Cai should be nourishing her self-esteem instead of allowing his sister-in-law to be consumed by guilt.

For the most part, Wayne preferred the company of men—from his youthful involvement in the Boy Scouts, YMCA, DeMolay, and Sigma Chi to his lifelong association with John Ford and the Young Men's Purity Total Abstinence and Yachting Association. He married three times, always selecting a South American spitfire, but each relationship ultimately failed. The key to his attitude toward women, which swung between wanting to protect and wanting to avoid, probably rests in his mother's flamboyant favoritism toward his younger brother. One can only imagine the loss and abandonment Wayne suffered when she literally gave the sibling his middle name.

While both John Ford and Raoul Walsh claim responsibility for the phenomenon known as "the Duke," there is no doubt that Wayne invented Wayne. "I made up my mind," contended the Duke, "that I was going to play a real man to the best of my ability."[103] Wayne's first theater experience was in high school, where he proved competent enough to make the state Shakespeare competition. After that, directors, writers, producers, cameraman, costumers, friends, and critics offered him assistance along the way. He was single-minded in his effort to create a self so genuine it would envelope him. Opting for naturalism, he modeled his screen persona on both Yakima Canutt, a world champion rodeo cowboy, and Harry Carey, Ford's understated western star.[104] At his best on the range, the actor (who hated horses) was most comfortable as the down-to-earth hombre whom nobody could catch acting.

Critics contend that the Duke wasn't versatile—he always played himself. According to Wayne, "You may say all my parts are the same. That's just what I want you to think. You get lost on the screen if your personality doesn't show through."[105] After viewing Wayne in Howard Hawks's *Red River* (1947), director John Ford had to admit, "that big SOB can act."[106] Whether or not Wayne could readily transform himself into a broad range of characters, the American public was only willing to accept Wayne as the all-American hero, so while Wayne was no Laurence Olivier, Olivier could never be John Wayne.

THE DRAFT DODGER

During a January 1991 congressional debate on the Persian Gulf, Representative Joseph P. Kennedy II argued, "There's a misguided machismo mentality in American now, 'a John Wayne attitude' that says, somehow or another, this is the way we should conduct foreign policy, . . . that Americans can do no wrong and that as long as we're forthright, God will be with us."[107] During Vietnam, American troops called the .45 caliber service pistol "a John Wayne rifle," the hard C ration biscuits "John Wayne cookies," and the two ways of doing a job, "the right way," and "the John Wayne way."[108]

As a young man, Wayne had set his heart on attending Annapolis and becoming a naval officer. "It was a terrible disappointment when I didn't make it," he acknowledged. "In a way I guess I never really got over it."[109] With *Sands of Iwo Jima,* Wayne became synonymous with the defense of the nation,[110] yet the closest the sound stage soldier ever came to military service was a series of USO tours. During a three-week sojourn to Vietnam, the action actually got too close for comfort when Viet Cong snipers fired into the encampment where he was conversing with a group of marines. Wayne tried to make light of the experience, quipping, "They were so far away, I didn't stop signing autographs."[111]

General Douglas MacArthur considered Wayne, more than any other man in uniform, the model of the American soldier. The actor managed to portray every branch of the armed services, including the Seabees, on the silver screen. The Veterans of Foreign Wars bestowed a gold medal on Wayne and the marines gifted him with their "Iron Mike" award.

With the exodus of stars such as Ronald Reagan, Henry Fonda, Clark Gable, and Jimmy Stewart, as well as director John Ford, to the military during World War II, Hollywood was desperate for leading men. Entitled by virtue of his age and four children to an initial deferment, Wayne, biographers Roberts and Olson point out, did nothing illegal in sitting out the war. In an October 1941 letter to his wife, John Ford discussed his disgust with Wayne and Ward Bond's lack of patriotism at a time when the world was descending into darkness. Three months after Pearl Harbor, he dipped his pen in contempt as he pictured Wayne and Bond perched on a mountaintop, keeping their eyes peeled for a potential Japanese invasion of California. "Such heroism shall not go unrewarded," he sneered. "It will live in the annals of time."[112]

Wayne contended he got so banged up doing his own stunts that he actually failed his army physical. Unfortunately, he was never able to produce any paperwork to that effect.[113] Ward Bond, however, was an epileptic, a legitimate 4-F. According to son Patrick, Wayne wanted to enlist, but "he was too old, with too many dependents, plus he had an ear infection from a film he made called *Reap the Wild Wind* [1942], an infection that never left. Every time he'd get in the water it would come back."[114] Bad ear or not, Wayne embarked on a persistent pattern of procrastination that continued ad infinitum. He would skulk to the brink of enlistment but would never sign on the dotted line. Every so often, Wayne would write Ford about joining up as soon as he wrapped another picture, but that moment never arrived.[115]

It may be important to note that Republic's lawyers rather than Wayne himself submitted numerous requests for deferral. When Wayne was classified 1A in 1944, studio attorneys met with the draft board on the grounds that Wayne's films were essential to the war effort. Wayne feared battlefield risks less than the risks to his cinematic career. He observed, firsthand, what happened to actors such as Reagan, Fonda, Gable, and Stewart when they were out of the public eye.

Only once was Wayne confronted outright for failing to serve. He was greeted by catcalls at a USO appearance, but later the GIs personally signed a 107-page, 98-foot-long letter apologizing for their boorish conduct.[116] With the rest of the movie-going public, Wayne could do no wrong and by dodging the largest draft in the country's history, he was able to star in thirteen pictures between Pearl Harbor and Hiroshima.

The Duke, however, did beat himself up—at least psychologically. According to Dennis McLellan, "the absence of a uniform gnawed at his self-respect and sense of manhood."[117] After the war, wife Pilar claimed, he became a McCarthy-era superpatriot who felt compelled to atone by offering up *The Green Berets* as a substitute for actual military service.[118] He hoped the movie "would say every word and bleed every emotion that Presidents from Roosevelt to Kennedy would not permit me to say with a rifle."[119] According to biographer Chester Yosarian, "grunts who served in cavalry, infantry and artillery units were never told that John Wayne was personally *ordered* by three American presidents to withdraw his enlistment papers."[120] Ironically, according to James Kent, the producer/director of BBC's *Unquiet American,* Wayne was probably killed by the very military with which he was so closely identified. He contracted duodenal cancer as a result of filming *The Conqueror* in the desert just ninety miles from a nuclear test site in 1954. Seventy-five percent of the cast and crew from the film succumbed to the same form of cancer.[121]

THE AUDIENCE RESPONDS

Despite being vilified by the critics; shunned by the predominantly liberal Academy of Motion Picture Arts and Sciences, Golden Globe, and New York Critics award voters; picketed by angry antiwar protestors; and written off by a "Vietnam films won't sell" conventional wisdom, *The Green Berets* proved a huge winner at the box office. The film brought in $8.7 million in film rentals during the first six months against a production cost of $6.1 million (including John Wayne's million-dollar salary). Total domestic film rentals amounted to $9.75 million.[122] Foreign distribution and sales to television brought in additional revenue. According to *Variety,* the picture was the tenth biggest moneymaker of 1968, surpassing *2001, Camelot,* and *In Cold Blood.*[123] Only *True Grit* among Wayne's regular starring vehicles took in more money in North America.[124] The film still makes a tidy profit through TV airings and videotape rentals.

The critics were not kind; some were even venomous. Wayne's outspoken, to some reactionary political views, guaranteed that *The Green Berets* would be panned despite popularity with the masses. Wayne argued, "If you stand for something, certain people are going to attack you."[125]

According to Eric Bentley's considered opinion in the 1971 *Film Society Review,* John Wayne was personally responsible for starting the war in Vietnam. Renata Adler of the *New York Times* likewise pulled no punches, calling *The Green Berets* "a film so unspeakable, so stupid, so rotten and false in every detail. . . . It is vile and insane. On top of that, it is dull."[126]

Responding to Adler, Senator Strom Thurmond told the Senate her opening paragraph was enough to convince anyone that *The Green Berets* was worth seeing.[127] In one breath, critic Gilbert Adair, writing from the vantage point of 1981 says, "now it's well nigh impossible to watch *The Green Berets* free of bias," and with the next, he cautions, "but a critic especially must strive to keep an open mind."[128] His loathing for Wayne so colored his thinking that he actually suggested that the Duke fabricated the Viet Cong atrocities in the film so that "Although the My Lai revelations were still to come, one is almost tempted to believe that the ante was upped so that American rapine . . . would be vindicated in advance by the comparison."[129]

Even though it aroused a storm of protest, according to Ivan Butler, "Viewed away from partisan passion, the film appears no more or less nauseating than the great majority of propagandist war pictures."[130] In fact, considering the political climate, *The Green Berets* proved more courageous than interventionist films made without opposition or negative public opinion. "At the very least," Butler points out, "one can have little doubt as to its maker's sincerity."[131]

To Wayne's mind, the negative publicity helped, rather than hindered, the film. "Luckily for me, they overkilled it. *The Green Berets* would have been successful regardless of what the critics did, but it might have taken the public longer to find out about the picture if they hadn't made so much noise about it."[132] The hullabaloo, including boisterous demonstrations outside of theaters, amounted to free publicity and gave the film legs.[133]

Jean Luc Godard asks, "how can I hate John Wayne upholding Goldwater and yet love him tenderly when abruptly he takes Natalie Wood into his arms in the last reel of *The Searchers*?"[134] The answer, of course, is rooted in a paradox—Wayne's politics (which Godard considers indecent) arose out of decent values like loyalty, doggedness, and courage. In *The Searchers,* Godard responded to morality overcoming culture—the same point Wayne offered up in *The Green Berets.*

Wayne's politics were never as reactionary as his left-wing adversaries might like to believe. According to the Duke, "critics [try] to criticize my political inclinations instead of my pictures."[135] *The Green Berets* triumphed, according to Wayne, because Americans both wanted and needed to hear the movie's message.

It may simply have been that the silent majority, who supported the military and loved their country, went to see a picture that reinforced their tenaciously held ideals. Critics, however, saw the film from either an overly distant political stance or an overly distant time period. According to Philip Taylor, "Too little do historians recognize when they are deconstructing film as texts, that the medium of film can play upon audience emotions, which tell us more about ourselves than the film ever can."[136]

Does the success of *The Green Berets* speak more to the popularity of an actor who capitalized on his warrior image or to the state of public support for the war? Wayne admitted, "Sure I wave the American flag. Do you know a better flag to wave?"[137] The point is, no one else was producing Vietnam films at the time, and *The Green Berets'* cinematic artifice, juxtaposed against the television documentation of the war, may well have been a major selling point. Also, Wayne gave folks, who had tried to ignore this conflict in the far-off jungles of Southeast Asia, permission to once again feel the national unity and resolve that underlay World War II. As long as Wayne was fighting for America, albeit in the magical world of make-believe, he was safeguarding a memory of American greatness that many ached to see again.[138]

Timing is everything but never more so than in the release of a movie. Robin Moore's best-seller was set back in 1963, when Vietnam was not only less ambiguous and controversial, but also more exotic and distant. After seemingly endless delays, however, the picture hit the movie theaters only four months after the Tet Offensive, which had shattered America's faith in the military, eroded hope in a speedy resolution, and propelled Vietnam dissent to record-breaking heights.

While *The Hollywood Reporter* dubbed *The Green Berets* "a facile simplification unlikely to attract the potentially large and youthful audience whose concern and sophistication cannot be satisfied by the insertion of a few snatches of polemic,"[139] the reviewer was unaware that in middle America, moviegoers gave Wayne's stirring Vietnam drama a warmhearted reception—often laughing, sometimes applauding, and even cheering a little. According to the *New Yorker*, response was particularly strong at three points during the film: first, when Muldoon tells a housewife that one could fill volumes with what newspapers don't say (that's funny, no matter which side of the political fence you straddle); second, when vicious Viet Cong overrun "Dodge City" and are caught on barbed wire or set aflame by explosives (it's comeuppance time); and third, when in just a few seconds the Vulcan cannon–equipped C47 wipes out enemy forces (a collective chest-welling pride in American ingenuity and know-how swept the theater).[140]

The Green Berets themselves loved the film. Assorted officers interviewed by the *New Yorker* deemed the movie essentially accurate, authentic, and entertaining.[141] Department of Defense consultant Chester Yosarian highlights the cinematic depiction of Special Forces, Saigon nightlife, military protocol, Vietnam vernacular, and the U.S. relationship with the ARVN as a bona fide representation of the way things were in mid-'60s Vietnam.[142] According to a Green Beret sergeant major, "The film was just God, Mother, and the Flag. Now who the hell could have any opposition to that?"[143] Admiration also came from rank-and-file Vietnam vets. According to Michael Lanning, "Anyone who ever wrote or reported that uniformed members of the military did not agree with the content of the film or were embarrassed by it, never sat in a post theater at Fort Benning or Fort Bragg or others around the world and heard the wild cheering that accompanied much of the movie—especially the opening scenes."[144]

Considering what *The Green Berets* was intended to be, an interventionist film promoting American involvement in Vietnam, Wayne accomplished exactly what he set out to do. Over-the-top critics of *The Green Berets* might do well to remember that the Duke's fans divide the world into two groups: those who love John Wayne and those who are just plain wrong about him.

NOTES

1. Film footage of the same incident was carried by NBC news on January 31, 1968.
2. Loan fled South Vietnam after the fall of Saigon in 1975. He opened a restaurant in northern Virginia and died of cancer in 1999.
3. "The Century in the Post," *Washington Post*, February 2, 1999, C13.
4. Jeff McMurdo, "Three Pictures, 2,000 Words," *Ottawa Citizen*, April 28, 2000, A17.
5. Colin McEnroe, "A Page from History: We Were There," *Hartford Courant*, April 28, 1999, F8.
6. Robert Dallek, *Flawed Giant: Lyndon Johnson and His Times 1961–1973* (Oxford: Oxford University Press, 1998), 504.
7. Tet Offensive deaths: 2,000 American soldiers, 4,000 ARVN (South Vietnamese) soldiers, 33,000–58,000 Communist soldiers, and 165,000 civilians.
8. McEnroe, "Page from History," F8.
9. John Morton Blum, *Years of Discord: American Politics and Society, 1961–1974* (New York: Norton, 1991), 293.
10. Todd Gitlin, *The Sixties: Years of Hope, Days of Rage* (New York: Bantam, 1993), 299.
11. Dallek, *Flawed Giant*, 505.
12. Dallek, *Flawed Giant*, 506–507.
13. Blum, *Years of Discord*, 294.
14. Blum, *Years of Discord*, 294.

15. Maurice Isserman and Michael Kazin, *America Divided: The Civil War of the 1960s* (Oxford: Oxford University Press, 2000), 224.

16. "Vietnamization" was allowing the Army for the Republic of Vietnam to take primary responsibility for combat in the South.

17. That month, 2,371 Americans died.

18. Marcella Bombardieri, "Give and Take," *Washington Post,* July 11, 1999, B01.

19. "Vietnam," *Los Angeles Times,* April 11, 2000, A12.

20. Blum, *Years of Discord,* 349.

21. "Vietnam," *Los Angeles Times,* A12.

22. John Kifner, "McGeorge Bundy Dies at 77; Top Adviser in Vietnam Era," *New York Times,* September 17, 1996, A1.

23. Eric Pace, "Dean Rusk, Secretary of State in Vietnam War, Is Dead at 85," *New York Times,* December 22, 1994, A1.

24. The Gulf of Tonkin Resolution was the only explicit legislative branch sanction for American involvement in Vietnam, and it was revoked in 1970.

25. All quoted in Gilbert Adair, *Vietnam on Film: From the Green Berets to Apocalypse Now* (New York: Proteus, 1981), 46.

26. U.S. allies included seventy thousand South Koreans, Thais, Australians, and New Zealanders, as well as 1.5 million South Vietnamese.

27. Donald E. Nuechterlein, *A Cold War Odyssey* (Lexington: University Press of Kentucky, 1997), 124.

28. Phillip L. Gianos, *Politics and Politicians in American Film* (Westport, Conn.: Praeger, 1998), 159.

29. Albert Auster and Leonard Quart, *How the War Was Remembered: Hollywood and Vietnam* (New York: Praeger, 1988), 33.

30. Chester A. Yosarian, " The United States Army's Green Berets' History Reevaluated, Corrected and Respected" (On-line archives of the American War Library, 1996), http://reviews.imdb.com/Reviews/51/5197.

31. See the video *The Complete History of the Green Berets,* from *The Time Machine* series, produced by the History Channel (2002).

32. Henry Allen, "Special Forces, Special Memories," *Washington Post,* November 23, 1982, D1.

33. The Special Forces shoulder patch includes an arrowhead alongside three lightning bolts, symbolizing arrival by land, sea, or air.

34. Auster and Quart, *How the War Was Remembered,* 34.

35. Several hundred thousand Montagnards were not only left high and dry when the United States withdrew from Vietnam in 1973, but they were summarily executed as well.

36. Named for a popular Peter, Paul, and Mary song, it references the white smoke given off by the firing guns.

37. "John Wayne Quotes," www.geocities.com/Colosseum/Field/5754/quot.htm.

38. Manny Gonzales, "Col. Francis Kelly: A Founder of the Green Berets," *Denver Rocky Mountain News,* December 29, 1997, 14B.

39. Alasdair Spark, "The Soldier at the Heart of the War: The Myth of the Green Beret in the Popular Culture of the Vietnam Era," *Journal of American Studies* 18 (1984): 30–39.

40. Philip Taylor, "The Green Berets," *History Today* 45, no. 3 (March 1995): 22.

41. Lawrence H. Suid, "The Film Industry and the Vietnam War" (Ph. D. diss., Case Western Reserve University, 1980), 137.

42. "The Green Berets," *BFI/Monthly Film Bulletin* 35 (September 1968): 131–32.

43. Garry Wills, *John Wayne's America* (New York: Touchstone, 1997), 229.

44. The stated mission of the Green Berets is "reconnaissance, surveillance, and training."

45. Lawrence H. Suid, *Guts and Glory: Great American War Movies* (Reading, Mass.: Addison–Wesley, 1978), 226.

46. Suid, *Guts and Glory,* 222.

47. Suid, *Guts and Glory,* 222.

48. Suid, *Guts and Glory,* 222.

49. Suid, *Guts and Glory,* 222.

50. Suid, *Guts and Glory,* 221.

51. Taylor, *Green Berets,* 21.

52. Taylor, *Green Berets,* 22.

53. Suid, *Guts and Glory,* 223.

54. Linda Dittmar and Gene Michaud, *From Hanoi to Hollywood: The Vietnam War in American Film* (New Brunswick, N.J.: Rutgers University Press, 1990), 27.

55. Suid, *Guts and Glory,* 224.

56. Jeremy M. Devine, *Vietnam at 24 Frames a Second: A Critical and Thematic Analysis of Over 400 Films about the Vietnam War* (Jefferson, N.C.: McFarland, 1995), 39.

57. Michael Lee Lanning, *Vietnam at the Movies* (New York: Fawcett Columbine, 1994), 48.

58. Devine, *Vietnam at 24 Frames,* 44.

59. Frank J. Wetta and Stephen J. Curley, *Celluloid Wars: A Guide to Film and the American Experience of War* (New York: Greenwood, 1992), 199.

60. Devine, *Vietnam at 24 Frames,* 44.

61. Quoted in *FilmFacts* 2, no. 17 (October 1, 1968), 261.

62. Douglas Brode, *The Films of the Sixties* (Secaucus, N.J.: Citadel, 1980), 243–44.

63. Wills, *John Wayne's America,* 232.

64. Larry Langmans and Ed Borg, *Encyclopedia of American War Films* (New York: Garland, 1989), 242.

65. Quoted in *FilmFacts* 2, no. 17 (October 1, 1968), 260.

66. Suid, *Guts and Glory,* 231.

67. See Eben J. Muse, *The Land of Nam: The Vietnam War in American Film* (Lanham, Md.: Scarecrow, 1995).

68. *China Gate* was the first movie to mention the name of Ho Chi Minh.

69. Dittmar and Michaud, *Hanoi to Hollywood,* 2.

70. *Film Society Review* (March–May, 1972), 27.

71. Auster and Quart, *How the War Was Remembered,* 34.

72. "John Wayne Quotes," www.geocities.com/Colosseum/Field/5754/quot.htm.

73. Quoted in Molly Haskell, "The First Action Hero," *New York Times,* March 23, 1997, 13.

74. Steven Mintz and Randy Roberts, *Hollywood's America: United States History through Its Films* (St. James, N.Y.: Brandywine, 1993), 232.

75. Quoted in Steve Neal, "True Grit," *Chicago Sun Times,* November 15, 1995, 35.

76. Suid, *Guts and Glory,* 231.

77. The scene was shot on a west-facing beach. The Duke must have forgotten that Vietnam's coastline looks east.

78. Quoted in *FilmFacts* 2, no. 17 (October 1, 1968), 260.

79. Wills, *John Wayne's America*, 11–12.

80. Joseph McBride, "Hail to the Duke," *AMC Magazine* (July 2001): 5.

81. Ron Kovic, *Born on the Fourth of July* (New York: McGraw–Hill, 1976), 43.

82. *The Big Trail*, named for Wayne's first flick, has been published by Tim Lilley of Akron, Ohio, since June 1984.

83. Allen Eyles, *John Wayne* (New York: Barnes, 1979), 217.

84. His name was changed to Marion Michael Morrison when his mother gave his middle name to his younger brother, Robert Emmett Morrison. "Duke" was the moniker of his pet dog.

85. Quoted in Tony Crawley, *The Wordsworth Dictionary of Film Quotations* (Ware, England: Wordsworth Reference, 1991), 103.

86. David Thomson, "The Way the Duke Walks," *Independent,* May 11, 1997, 26.

87. Julie Salamon, "The Immortal Duke," *New York Times,* September 10, 1995, 7:28.

88. Gary Arnold and Kenneth Turan, "The Duke: More Than Just Hero," *Washington Post,* June 13, 1979, A1.

89. Arnold and Turan, "More Than Just Hero," A1.

90. The Spanish phrase translates roughly as "ugly, strong, and dignified."

91. Nigel Andrews, "Cracked Colossus of the Wild West," *Financial Times,* March 16, 1996, xiv.

92. James T. Campbell, "Print the Legend: John Wayne and Postwar American Culture," *Reviews in American History* 28, no. 3 (2000): 466.

93. Randy Roberts and James S. Olson, *John Wayne: American* (New York: Free Press, 1995), 647.

94. Arnold and Turan, "More Than Just Hero," A1.

95. Wills, *John Wayne's America,* 13.

96. Gene D. Phillips and Rodney Hall, *The Encyclopedia of Stanley Kubrick* (New York: Checkmark, 2002), 89.

97. Eve Zibart, "Everyone's Symbol," *Washington Post,* June 13, 1979, E1.

98. Zibart, "Everyone's Symbol," E1.

99. Arnold and Turan, "More Than Just Hero," A1.

100. McBride, "Hail to the Duke," 5.

101. Campbell, "Print the Legend," 466.

102. Crawley, *Wordsworth Dictionary,* 279.

103. Arnold and Turan, "More Than Just Hero," A1.

104. Wills, *John Wayne's America,* 27.

105. Crawley, *Wordsworth Dictionary,* 196.

106. Ephraim Katz, *The Film Encyclopedia,* 3rd ed. (New York: HarperPerennial, 1998), 1446.

107. Martin F. Nolan, "John Wayne and Foreign Policy," *Boston Globe,* March 3, 1991, B1.

108. Charles Mohr, "U.S. Special Forces: Real and on Film," *New York Times,* June 20, 1968, 49.

109. "John Wayne Quotes," www.geocities.com/Colosseum/Field/5754/quot.htm.

110. Jean-Jacques Malo and Tony William, *Vietnam War Films* (Jefferson, N.C.: McFarland, 1994), 185–186.

111. Suid, *Guts and Glory*, 223.

112. Scott Eyman, *Print the Legend: The Life and Times of John Ford* (New York: Simon and Schuster, 1999), 23–54.

113. Jeff Stricter, "Pilgrim's Progress," *Star Tribune*, July 24, 1997, E1.

114. Eyman, *Print the Legend*, 23–24.

115. Eyman, *Print the Legend*.

116. Yosarian, "Army's Green Berets," http://reviews.imdb.com/Reviews/51/5197

117. Dennis McLellan, "True Duke by the Book," *Los Angeles Times*, September 19, 1995, E1.

118. Yvonne Crittenden, "John Wayne: The Artificial Legend Became Him," *Toronto Sun*, February 4, 1996, C12.

119. Yosarian, "Army's Green Berets."

120. Yosarian, "Army's Green Berets."

121. James Rampton, "Fall of an American Hero," *Independent*, July 5, 1997, 43. Alleged victims included John Wayne, Susan Hayward, Agnes Moorehead, and Dick Powell.

122. Suid, *Guts and Glory*, 234.

123. *Variety*, June 19, 1968, 39.

124. Eyles, *John Wayne*, 221.

125. McLellan, "True Duke," E1.

126. Renata Adler, "Screen: *Green Berets* as Viewed by John Wayne," *New York Times*, June 20, 1968, www.nyt.com/books/97/03/23/reviews/wayne-movie.htr.

127. *Congressional Record*, June 26, 1968, 18856–57.

128. Adair, *Vietnam on Film*, 38.

129. Adair, *Vietnam on Film*, 37.

130. Ivan Butler, *The War Film* (New York: Barnes, 1974).

131. Butler, *War Film*.

132. Suid, *Guts and Glory*, 234.

133. Devine, *Vietnam at 24 Frames*, 45.

134. Andrews, "Cracked Colossus," xiv.

135. Arnold and Turan, "More Than Just Hero," A1.

136. Taylor, *Green Berets*, 21.

137. "John Wayne Quotes," www.geocities.com/Colosseum/Field/5754/quot.htm.

138. "Glory," *New Yorker*, June 29, 1968, 24.

139. *Hollywood Reporter*, June 17, 1968, 3.

140. "Glory," *New Yorker*, 24–27.

141. "Glory," *New Yorker*.

142. Yosarian, "Army's Green Berets."

143. Suid, *Guts and Glory*, 233.

144. Lanning, *Vietnam*, 50.

Gene Evans ponders the horrors of war in The Steel Helmet. *Courtesy of Weiss Global Enterprises, Inc. and the Academy of Motion Picture Arts and Sciences.*

7

☆

Isolationism in
The Steel Helmet

The faces seem drained of color, almost ashen. Draped over each of the nineteen soldiers is a gray poncho that seems to shield the body from an invisible enemy screened by the Korean darkness. The steely figures bear no names. They are just metal militia, arranged at geometric angles and poised on eternal patrol. Sixteen hours a day, confused yet courteous tourists shuffle by this stark tribute to the Korean War. Momentarily unnerved by the tableau, they gather their thoughts and stride purposefully ahead, lingering momentarily at the high point of the memorial to snap pictures, then exiting right and moving on. The Korean War Monument occupies a restful, tree-shaded setting on the national mall, but just like the "Forgotten War" itself, the memorial seems an afterthought, a Washington, D.C., tourist stop just a short stroll away from the more popular Vietnam Veterans Memorial.

HISTORY OF ISOLATIONISM

When Lewis Milestone's *All Quiet on the Western Front* was released in May 1930, *Variety* noted, "Here exhibited is war as it is, butchery. The League of Nations could make no better investment than to buy up the master print, reproduce it in every language, to be shown to every nation every year until the word 'war' is taken out of the dictionaries."[1]

Based on Erich Maria Remarque's personal account of World War I, *All Quiet on the Western Front* movingly and realistically exposes the horror, cruelty, and futility of war. The Academy Award–winning film chronicles the experiences of seven naïve young German soldiers recruited out of high school by an influential professor who can't help lionizing the glory of the Fatherland. It should come as no surprise that Joseph Goebbels denounced the film as both pacifist and antimilitaristic. Remarque was forced to flee Germany because of the controversy surrounding the film.

Considered one of the greatest antiwar films ever made, *All Quiet on the Western Front* quickly secured worldwide acclaim and was dished up as a rationale, especially post–World War I, for American isolationism. Millions viewed the film—*All Quiet* not only echoed but shaped popular opinion. Out of the 10 million drafted during World War II, forty-three thousand (triple the percentage during World War I) refused to go into battle.[2] A 1939 version of the movie, edited to propagandize the case for sitting out the fighting, received a wide showing across America. Like other lifelong pacifists, star Lew Ayres credits the film with crystallizing his passionate viewpoint.

Until World War II, isolationism remained the dominant foreign policy of the United States. In an effort to secure independence and achieve a sense of national unity, the founding fathers cautioned against the potential disruption resulting from preserving attachments to Europe. The United States felt free to pursue isolationism, first, because the Atlantic Ocean provided a daunting physical barrier to attack. Second, the preoccupation of European powers with a succession of imbroglios in Europe allowed the United States to take advantage of America's seemingly unlimited natural resources and become self-sufficient. Third, American foreign policy makers didn't bother themselves with the apparent contradiction between espousing a policy of separation from Europe and a policy of expansion elsewhere.

Despite reliance on war for sovereignty (in the American Revolution), spreading out (the Mexican–American War), and safeguarding the union (the Civil War), Americans tended to envision combat as an aberration rather than an extension of politics.[3] The persistence of a pacifist vision owes much to a "New World" America looking down her nose at the conflict and corruption of the European establishment. Overflowing with hope, the colonists embarked on a quasi-religious mission to establish democracy. Revolution, unfortunately, was a requisite step. John Locke's social contract metaphor assumed that a natural condition of harmony underlies both domestic and international order. He saw war as an unnatural occurrence, artificially constructed by a human agency, as opposed to the desired condition of natural society or legitimate civil association.

In his 1796 Farewell Address, George Washington warned: "Why, by interweaving our destiny with that of any part of Europe, entangle our peace and prosperity in the toils of European ambition, rivalship, interest, humor, or caprice? It is our true policy to steer clear of permanent alliances with any portion of the foreign world. . . . [W]e may safely trust to temporary alliances for extraordinary emergencies."[4]

In contrasting American attitudes toward "entanglements," Michael Woods notes: "Europeans are born entangled, and harbor only the most diffident and complicated dreams of escape from others. Americans, on the other hand are the children of Rousseau [and Locke] to a greater extent than we shall ever chart, and they start from isolation as a primary or desired condition."[5]

Yet, American isolationism didn't last forever. In 1898, the "yellow journalism" of William Randolph Hearst ("You furnish the pictures and I'll furnish the war") roused the American public to ferocious moral indignation after the *Maine* sank under murky circumstances in Havana. The United States handily clinched the ensuing Spanish American War. Our isolationist policy was again swept aside when President Woodrow Wilson interpreted Germans torpedoing passenger ships and sabotaging munitions factories as direct interference with America's rights as a neutral power. The subsequent declaration of war on April 6, 1917, paved the way for the World War I Allies to gamely "make the world safe for democracy."

During the two decades following the "war to end all wars," a noninvolvement policy prevailed. America declined to raise a finger to protect the Loyalists against Franco in Spain or to protect Ethiopia from Mussolini. Japan's invasion of Manchuria and China went unchallenged until Franklin Roosevelt, joining with the League of Nations, ordered an oil embargo. Henry Ford, the unschooled mechanic given to childlike ideas about the world; Charles Lindbergh, the chief spokesperson for the "America First" movement; and Father Charles Coughlin, the radio priest of the 1930s, all took to the airwaves to speak out against American involvement.

Isolationists typically argued that World War I had been a colossal mistake, achieving no lasting peace but costing 10 million lives. They contended that while America had been deluded via wartime propaganda into entering World War I, an older, wiser generation of right-thinking noninterventionists wouldn't prove so gullible this time. Some anti-Semitic naysayers even tried to lay blame for the war on the greed of armaments manufacturers. Proponents gobbled up the fascist claim that the Germans and Italians really needed room to expand, the internationalist claim that democracy was not suited to all nations, and the pacifist claim that there would be no war if just one side refused to be provoked.

Isolationism blew sky high with the American fleet, however, when the Japanese attacked Pearl Harbor on December 7, 1941, a day that continues to live in infamy. At war's end, however, weighing George Kennan's central concept of "containment" (as reflected in the Marshall Plan, the Truman Doctrine, and NATO) on one hand against geographic inaccessibility (because of the Atlantic and Pacific Oceans) on the other rendered the "isolation vs. intervention" question an ideological toss-up. Woods adds that U.S. moral and physical superiority "is at the heart of an American puzzle about our relations with others, for both generosity and selfishness are unilateralist, isolationist attitudes, depending only on our will and our condescension, on our acceptance or refusal of community. We are benign or indifferent gods, ready to do business with humanity only on our terms."[6]

'50s ISOLATIONISM

With Korea, although President Harry Truman and the United Nations were grittily steadfast in an effort to freeze the Communists at the Thirty-eighth Parallel, they were equally resolved to thwart any threat of World War III.[7] When General Douglas MacArthur insisted on far-reaching action—"there is no substitute for victory"—against China (including the use of the atomic bomb) Truman relieved him of his command.

The American people were intractably opposed to intervention so close on the heels of World War II. By March 1951, a Gallup Poll inquired, "What do you, yourself, think we should do now about Korea?" Twenty-three percent thought the United States ought to withdraw and send our boys home while less than half, 43 percent, were convinced America should remain and fight it out.[8] Further, Korea unleashed cynicism about war into the American mainstream. While isolationists undoubtedly fenced with interventionists before the two world wars, the country rallied around the troops once they were dispatched to foreign theaters. Almost from the date of the North Korean invasion, however, criticism of American involvement in Korea picked up steam, eventually predominating the discussion. By 1952, Korea had left such a bad taste in the public's mouth that President Truman, facing almost certain defeat, decided not to seek another term. General Omar Bradley, chairman of the Joint Chiefs of Staff, called Korea "the wrong war, in the wrong place, at the wrong time, with the wrong enemy."[9]

In fact, without a formal declaration of war, Truman was forced to employ the term "police action" to describe our involvement in the Korean conflict. He convinced a reluctant United Nations and fifteen nations (Australia, Belgium, Canada, Colombia, Ethiopia, France, Greece, Luxembourg, the Netherlands, New Zealand, the Philippines, South Africa, Thailand, Turkey, and the United Kingdom) into joining America and the Republic of Korea against the North Koreans and the Chinese Communists.

On June 25, 1950, after a large-scale artillery barrage, the sound of bugles signaled the massed charge of the North Korean People's Army. General Chai Ung Jun and his men poured out of the mountains and punched out the American-sponsored government in South Korea. Previous reports of a North Korean military buildup along the Thirty-eighth Parallel raised no red flags among Western intelligence officers, nor did the warnings of Syngman Rhee, since he cried "wolf" whenever he wanted to acquire more military hardware.

On July 27, 1953, Lieutenant General Nam Il and Lieutenant General William K. Harrison inked a cease-fire at 10:00 AM at Panmunjom, and the last round of the war was discharged about twelve hours later. American forces had struggled in a seesaw conflict that had involved massive intervention by China and years of exasperating negotiations before the armistice. Bottom line: the boundaries of the two Koreas, despite all the death and destruction, had not budged an inch.

According to John Toland, "four million human beings, half of them civilians, died in a brutal contest marked by atrocities on both sides, raging up and down a peninsula the size of Utah."[10] Americans killed in the Korean War totaled 36,516.[11] The American public resented paying such a high price, especially when they learned lives were lost due to post–World War II military unpreparedness, complacency, and the illusion that nuclear weapons and air power alone could deter Communist aggression and ensure lasting peace. While Korea may have been the first hot flash during the Cold War, the conflict proved a blistering blunder for the United States.

After the last shell met its mark, little inhabitable North Korean real estate remained. The tonnage of American bombs dropped on North Korea exceeded all the explosive devices detonated in the Pacific theater of operations during World War II. Seoul, South Korea's capital, had changed hands four times. One-third of South Korea's housing had vanished, along with more than 40 percent of the industry.[12]

In 1950, most Americans were savoring the post–World War II boom and the suburbs were springing to life. For pre–boob tube America, Korea seemed an exotic and remote locale, semishaded in inscrutability and intrigue. Many citizens would have been hard-pressed to pinpoint the country on a map.

At the crossroads of East Asia, the Chinese and the Japanese took turns exploiting the hardy Koreans. Often called the "Irish of the Orient," the Koreans prided themselves on being able to endure grueling circumstances with pluck and humor. Although the Cairo Declaration of 1943 insisted that Korea ultimately become independent, the Yalta Conference called for the Soviets to receive the surrender of Japanese forces north of the Thirty-eighth Parallel, while America settled for the southern zone. This seemingly innocuous pact suggested by President Truman not only obliterated Korea's chances for freedom but also cleaved a formerly unified people into two relentless adversaries.[13]

The Soviets had given their ally tanks, heavy artillery, and early in 1950, the green light to invade. South Korea, dependent on the North for manufactured goods, fuel, and electricity, found themselves sealed off at the border by the Soviets, who cut off all traffic and trade. The UN General Assembly voted for an all-Korea election, a nine-nation commission to supervise, and the departure of respective occupation troops after the formation of a legal government. On May 10, more than 92 percent of the registered voters in South Korea elected a National Assembly with Syngman Rhee as first president of the Republic of Korea.

The Communists elevated Kim Il-Sung as premier of the Democratic People's Republic of Korea. He commanded eight full and two half-strength divisions that had been trained by high-ranking Soviet military advisers. His ground forces totaled 150,000, with 89,000 well-instructed combat troops, and he was supplied with mortars, howitzers, self-propelled guns, antitank guns, and 150 T-34 tanks. In the south were only sixty-five thousand partially trained combat troops, lacking medium artillery and recoilless rifles and armed with M-1 rifles, carbines, mortars, howitzers, and unreliable bazookas. The somewhat pathetic air force of the South Koreans consisted of twenty-two training and liaison planes.[14]

To the American people, the struggle to contain communism remained far less morally urgent than ridding the world of the fascist scourge or, even closer to home, hunting down the sneaks who attacked Pearl Harbor. When the North Koreans overran South Korea, nobody in the Communist world figured the United States would do much beyond some histrionic hand-wringing. After all, when Secretary of State Dean Acheson traced an American defense line in Asia, he left Korea hanging out in no man's land.[15]

Besides, how could the United States be at war when Congress had not given the say-so? Despite goading by MacArthur-led interventionists, the powerful Senate "China lobby,"[16] and news magazines such as the *New Republic, The Nation,* and Henry Luce's *Time,* Americans paid negligible attention. According to a September 1950 Gallup poll, a scant 2 percent answered "Korea" to the query "What do you personally regard as the most important issue which should be discussed in the coming November election campaigns for Congress?" Voters were much more fretful about the Cold War, the high cost of living, and military preparedness.[17]

The handful who were concerned took comfort in the boast of top Korean adviser Brigadier General William L. Roberts that American-prepared South Korean forces were second in quality only to U.S. troops. The five hundred military advisers remaining at the end of June 1949 gave the South Koreans just enough guns and guidance to repel a Communist attack, but not enough to instigate an attack on the north. The United States wasn't quite the Santa Claus the Communists were. The South Koreans got no tanks, heavy guns, or aircraft.

America inched its way into the war with the air force shepherding the evacuation of American civilians, the army shipping weapons and ammunition to the South Koreans, and the navy and air force shelling, initially only in the south, then north of the Thirty-eighth Parallel. Nothing worked. On the fifth day of the war, General Douglas MacArthur advised Truman that, to halt the hostilities, American boots were needed on the ground. Four divisions of the U.S. Eighth Army were pulled in from soft duty in Japan. The occupation forces were woefully short on training, arms, and combat readiness. The regimental combat team on Okinawa didn't prove to be in any better shape. Initial military support by the United States was anything but impressive.

For the army that vanquished Japan and Nazi Germany, the first few hours of combat in Korea were both sobering and humbling. U.S. military leaders figured the mere presence of American troops would bully the North Korean army into retreat, but they hadn't checked the odds—approximately 20,000 of the enemy faced 406 Americans. On July 5, 1950, a North Korean tank column of thirty-three Soviet-built T-34s met Task Force Smith, the first battalion to confront the North Koreans. The Communists simply brushed right past U.S. forces armed with only a handful of antitank shells and World War II–era bazookas that failed to penetrate the thick armor on the Soviet tanks. A few hours later, a mile-long line of tanks and infantry snaked toward the terrified GIs. The Americans were ordered to hold their fire until the North Koreans were within one thousand yards and, oddly enough, the North Koreans were caught by this surprise tactic. Momentarily. After several hours of skirmishing, however, the outflanked U.S. forces had no choice but to fall back. Only 250 Americans survived.[18]

On July 20, American and South Korean troops were routed out of Taejon in a thrashing that led to the embarrassing capture of Major General William F. Dean (the commander of all U.S. troops in Korea). According to David Halberstam, "after three weeks in battle . . . of the almost 16,000 men who had been committed, only half were still able to fight. More than 2,400 men had been lost, either dead or missing. It was one of the worst periods in American military history."[19]

Dean's successor, Lieutenant General Walton H. Walker, managed to assemble a strong defense perimeter in Pusan, but sparring there ran up a fearsome butcher's bill. The United States lost more men in a single day than it did in all of Operation Desert Storm.[20] GIs, however, did eventually learn how to slug it out in Korea. By the end of July, in fact, the number of attackers on the outside of the Pusan Perimeter finally slipped below the number of defenders on the inside.

In Tokyo, MacArthur was cooking up a scheme to catch the North Koreans from behind—an amphibious gamble at Inchon. At five thousand-to-one odds (according to the general himself), the ploy would effectively slash enemy supply lines and entrap the North Korean army.[21] Within two weeks, MacArthur was able to escort South Korean President Syngman Rhee back to what remained of his capital. While the original American objective had been to restore Korea to prewar conditions, to MacArthur it seemed a shame to stay triumph in its tracks. Further, Rhee had no intention of halting his army at the Thirty-eighth Parallel.

MacArthur took a war that was his to win and, through megalomaniacal management by remote control from Japan and an overconfident sense of destiny, turned Korea into a military quagmire. A famous Herblock cartoon pictures a glowering MacArthur with a block-shaped world labeled "East Asia" and George C. Marshall pointing to a conventional globe and saying "We've been using more of a roundish one lately."[22] MacArthur's drive toward the Yalu River, which he believed would end the war, was an unmitigated disaster. The question on most military minds was, How many of the 2nd Infantry Division and the First Marines would get out alive? According to David Halberstam, "by dint of his arrogance, foolishness, and vainglory MacArthur was about to take a smaller war that was already winding down and expand it to include as an adversary a Communist superpower."[23]

Not only did MacArthur fuel McCarthyism, but two more years of blood-spattered, morale-killing hostilities were the price tag for bad judgment. By November 30, 1950, President Truman seriously weighed dropping the bomb, but retreated in the face of stormy protests from European allies. The possibility of victory via atomic war raised an important question: Would the United States press on *at any cost* as it had in World War II?

In the end, stalemate proved an acceptable alternative to unconditional victory. There would be no vigorous push into the enemy's heartland—only stability with two sides so evenly balanced that neither could budge the other. Korea would be the forerunner to other limited military conflicts, notably Vietnam, but also Grenada, Panama, the Persian Gulf, Somalia, Kosovo, Bosnia, Afghanistan, and Iraq.

A central role for foot soldiers had not been expected during a so-called Atomic Age, but the undeveloped Korean terrain did not welcome technology. At first, Americans found themselves too dependent on wheels to brawl with an enemy that had no wheels at all. Floods washed away bridges. Rocky rises laid bare of pine trees by shelling were far too stony to dig proper foxholes. Rice paddies full of human feces made the entire nation stink. The South Koreans, with whom and for whom Americans had been fighting, would periodically ditch their weapons and head for the hills.

Korea's rugged topography, however, was nothing compared to the climate. Soldiers froze, sometimes literally, during the bone-numbing mountain winters. In summer, heat and humidity rebuked with equal intensity. GIs, carrying their worlds on their backs, had to slog through rice paddies and muddy roads during bucketing downpours.

There was no push-button equipment, just recycled World War II surplus. The army was so short of tanks that vehicles serving as Fort Knox monuments were refitted with engines and shipped to Korea. Rusting gear from South Pacific battlefields was hastily refurbished in Japan. Ham-and-egg K rations, which had turned black, along with unpotable water gave the infantrymen incessant intestinal distress.[24]

The litany of inadequacies included unreliable M-1 rifles and mortar shells that failed to detonate. A scarcity of combat boots found many soldiers in sneakers. Spare parts for vehicles and radios were nonexistent. There were no maps. A frustrated Colonel Jay Loveless confessed to breaking into a schoolhouse so he could tear appropriate pages from a geography textbook.[25]

American troops lacked experience. According to Colonel John (Mike) Michaelis, an early hero of the war, "They'd spent a lot of time listening to lectures on the differences between Communism and Americanism and not enough time crawling on their bellies on maneuvers with live ammunition singing over them."[26] Qualified officers were also in short supply and remained so for the duration. The only item in abundance seemed to be promotions. To fill the gaps caused by casualties, the army pulled grunts with gumption out of the ranks and put them in charge.

Chief of Staff Omar N. Bradley later wrote that demobilization and budget-slashing after World War II had reduced the army to a "shockingly deplorable state" in which it "could not fight its way out of a paper bag."[27] Pentagon funding, measured in today's dollars to discount the effect of inflation, sagged at $123 billion in 1949.[28] In 1951, however, when Gallup reported an overwhelming 73 percent of Americans did not believe the United States was as well prepared for the Korean War as it should have been,[29] the budget tripled (to $366 billion), and it peaked at nearly $500 billion the following year. Military spending hasn't dropped below $250 billion since.[30]

Korea was the war that introduced Americans to racial integration in the military for the first time since the Civil War and speeded up the process set in motion by Truman's 1948 executive order. By most accounts, however, black soldiers were not widely accepted in predominantly white units. Even the Chinese Communists segregated black POWs so that the enemy could exploit any underlying gripes and grudges. Sergeant Jerry Morgan, an African American who also served in World War II and Vietnam, rejected the heavy-handed attempts of the Chinese to denigrate America or religion. He also insists that black POWs supported one another far better than their white counterparts. "We didn't lose a man in my squad from the first day of capture to Operation Big Switch—not a single person. There were ten of us . . . when it was a matter of life and death; we had to lean on one another. We had our private spiritual and religious prayer services . . . without the Chinese even knowing it."[31] Yet, of the twenty-one Americans who refused repatriation and chose instead to live in the People's Republic of China, three were African American.[32]

Korea was the war that introduced "brainwashing." In fact, the Communists snubbed the rules, refusing to believe that the Geneva Convention applied to them. Finding corpses with hands tied behind their backs became a gruesome everyday discovery. In addition, villagers were forced to dig great pits and shovel earth over thousands of dead and dying South Koreans. British war correspondent Alan Winnington, after viewing the valley where a thin layer of soil blanketed rotting corpses, wrote: "Through the fissures could be seen among the stinking masses of flesh and bone, hands, legs, grinning skulls stripped to the bone, heads burst open by bullets, wrists tied together."[33] In September 1950, approximately sixty wrist-bound American prisoners were shot in the back of the head after assembling in a Taejon prison yard.[34] U.S. POWs were tortured, starved, death-marched, and slaughtered. Although imprisoned and missing-in-action military personnel would be more of a focus in Vietnam, the Pentagon reported that almost eight thousand American military were summarily executed while prisoners of the North Koreans or their Chinese allies.[35] In answer to the question "What are we fighting for?" Lieutenant General H. B. Ridgway wrote: "The real issues are whether the rule of men who shoot their prisoners, enslave their citizens, and deride the dignity of man, shall displace the rule of those to whom the individual and his individual rights are sacred."[36]

Korea was the war that introduced the inability to tell friend from foe. Operational and intelligence summaries reported instances of North Koreans driving villagers in front of attacking troops or mingling with refugees in order to infiltrate rear areas. According to UN figures, the North Koreans dispatched twenty-five thousand civilian South Koreans.[37] American soldiers sometimes chewed over a bitter choice—fire on civilians or be overrun by North Koreans in disguise. Frank Hackett, an eighteen-year-old private first class landing with the First Marine Division at Inchon, remembers, North Koreans "would lay in the snow, cover themselves, and when the column would go by, they'd start shooting, knowing full well they were going to get killed." He added, "you'd see dead Chinese lying on the side of the road, and it became a habit to stick them with your bayonet" because if they were only "playing dead," a failure to do so "could cost you your life."[38]

During the 1952 campaign, pollsters told Dwight D. Eisenhower that the American people wanted out of Korea. The fighting may have ended in 1953, but civil war continues to this day and thirty thousand U.S. troops are still stationed in Korea. North Korea has become a Stalinist backwater so impoverished—the per capita income is $706—people are starving. South Korea, rebuilt with aid from the United States and other nations, is making vast economic strides—producing goods ranging from automobiles to electronics. The per capita income is a whopping $8,900.[39] The 46 million residents enjoy one of the highest living standards in Asia.[40]

SUMMARY OF THE PLOT

"Film is a battleground: love, hate, action, death. In a word: emotion."[41] Sam Fuller uttered this line, in English, in Jean-Luc Godard's 1965 classic *Pierot Le Fou.* Fuller's *Steel Helmet* (1950), scripted in a week, shot in ten days, and released only six months after the start of the Korean conflict, targeted an audience weary of war. The film opens in the aftermath of a massacre. The credits roll over a bullet-dented U.S. soldier's helmet serving as an antiwar symbol. Then the helmet moves. Underneath, the audience finds hard-boiled Sergeant Zack (Gene Evans)—the sole survivor of his platoon, wasted and left for dead. Zack's hands, bound by his own bootlaces, are cut loose by a ten-year-old South Korean orphan (William Chun) Zack nicknames "Short Round" after the type of shell that "doesn't go all the way."[42] Zack tries to shake his newfound tagalong but the kid sticks, explaining, "when you save someone's life, his heart is in your hands." The two bump into a disoriented infantry patrol, stumbling so noisily around the jungle that they provide an easy target for the enemy. Zack agrees to lead the detachment to a nearby Buddhist temple in exchange for a box of cigars. Each offbeat member of the multiethnic squad has a failure-to-fit-in fable to tell. Private Conchie Bronte (Robert Hutton), Corporal Medic Thompson (James Edwards), Sergeant Buddhahead Tanaka (Richard Loo), and Private Baldy (Richard Monahan) are being commanded by a recent officer candidate school grad, Lieutenant Driscoll (Steve Brodie). A holed-up North Korean officer (Harold Fong), discovered after he stabs a sentry, is taken prisoner. He attempts to undermine the morale of the minorities in the company, but to no avail. When the POW ridicules the childish prayer of Short Round, later the victim of a sniper's bullet, Zack becomes so incensed that he blows the Communist away and is promised a court-martial by Driscoll. The observation post comes under full-scale attack with, at the end, only Zack, Baldy, and Thompson walking away. Despite the fact that Zack doesn't have anything good to say about Driscoll, he leaves his bullet-scarred helmet as a gesture of respect, to mark the dead lieutenant's grave.

A PUBLIC RELATIONS NIGHTMARE FOR THE PENTAGON

Whenever they get the chance, the military will always spin war as a grand and glorious experience. According to Fuller, "They can't let the reality out. It would be a disaster. There are thousands of guys killed in battle and they don't even know their identity—they're blown up. An eyeball there, an arm here, a penis there—that's what you get on the battlefield. When you're at the front, you're in a constant state of tension."[43]

According to screenwriter Clancy Segal, "if it is possible to be an anti-fascist, democratic, war-inspired antiwar peacenik Old Soldier, Fuller fits the bill."[44] To say *The Steel Helmet* was a controversial film is something of an understatement. Fuller remembers a showing of the film at which protestors were so infuriated that they upended the box office.[45] Criticism poured forth from the White House and the Pentagon; even J. Edgar Hoover got into the act.[46] Since it would be at least a decade before actual Korean combat footage would be available to civilian sources, Fuller, with hat in hand, took his project to the Pentagon. He was unceremoniously turned down, either because bureaucrats were just following standard operating procedure (Instruction 5410.5, "The production, program, project, or assistance *will benefit* the Department of Defense [DoD] or otherwise be in the national interest"; italics mine) or because the fiercely independent director wouldn't relinquish *any* control over his film.

The DoD had expressed displeasure with three specific scenes: the American who executes a defenseless North Korean prisoner in a passionate rage, the Nisei who discloses his personal experience in a World War II American internment camp, and the black who divulges being victimized by bigots not only at home but also in the military. While John Wayne in *The Green Berets* readily made the changes required for Pentagon approval, the autonomous Fuller steered clear, despite the money-saving and authenticity-enhancing temptation. No military goodies the Pentagon might care to dangle in front of him were worth compromising his ultimate vision for the film. As it turned out, *The Steel Helmet,* which was more of a character study than a combat film anyway, got away with a single (albeit claustrophobic) set, several carefully controlled but permit-lacking explosions, and a half day of exteriors shot in Los Angeles' Griffith Park.

In 1950, when the film was released, the country was in the full throes of the HUAC investigations. Gene Evans, who played Zack, realized that with the mood of the country so far to the right the picture might raise hackles. "I was deaf on McCarthy and all that stuff, and so was Sam. But there was a lot of sentiment—just as there is again now—that if you don't grab the flag and run out in the street and start waving it and play the drum and bugle, then you are no patriot and you don't love your country."[47]

There are obvious parallels between Fuller's *The Steel Helmet* and Wayne's *The Green Berets:* soldiers can't tell ally from adversary ("If he's running with you he's South Korean, if he's running after you he's North Korean"); there's the poignant relationship between an Asian boy and an American soldier (according to Fuller, "So I thought it might be a very effective scene if Zack blows his top, not because of the enemy or shooting or all that, but because of a kid");[48] and godless communism serves as the evil enemy. According to Nicholas Garnham, Fuller's anti-communism is far from simplistic. Communists fulfill two dramatic purposes in Fuller's movies. First, they function as nightmare figures directly associated with insanity. The North Koreans charging the temple could have been real or they could have resulted from Zack's mental breakdown. Second, Communists operate as a crucial catalyst. When it comes to Short Round, it is the North Korean major who forces Zack to face up to his emotional constipation.[49]

The press reacted to the film with shock and confusion. As Fuller recalls, he was disparaged by a big full-page ad asking, "Would you shoot this [North Korean major]?" and by blistering editorials from both the right and the left: Victor Reisel "said this picture is anti-American, pro-Communist. And the commie paper, the *Daily Worker,* loved it—[because it] shows what beasts the American soldiers are. My mother called me from New York, she said *'Hello, Comrade.'"*[50]

While the DoD may have applauded Fuller's depiction of North Koreans as sneaky and underhanded (masquerading as worshippers or booby-trapping corpses), they drew the line at an American shooting a prisoner of war.[51] The viewing public, however, seemed to have no problem with that scene,[52] and to Fuller's mind slaughtering POWs was an everyday occurrence in Korea—by both sides. He claimed he was merely reporting reality with his camera. In fact, to prove his point, Fuller got his old company commander on the phone to inquire, "Did you ever shoot a prisoner of war?" The answer came back without a moment's hesitation. "Of course," said the commander.

When a cluster of generals tried to broad-brush the film as "Communist indoctrination," they lost all credibility with Fuller. In his autobiography, he recounts being interrogated by these generals about choosing Thompson as the last name of the black medic. Fuller readily admitted he was attracted to the good strong sound of the appellation as well as the obvious association with Turkey Thompson, a contemporary heavyweight fighter. The assembled brass claimed Fuller should have known that "Thompson" was code for "clandestine communist workers in the U.S."[53] Further, when confronted with the claim that there were no Buddhist temples in Korea, he pulled out a map from the Korean consulate with several clearly marked. According to Fuller, "soldiers were trained to fight the fascists during the war. Now the bigoted winds of McCarthyism were blowing across democratic America, spreading the seeds of another kind of fascism. The only way to fight these people here at home was to expose their stupid, reactionary ideas. I was proud to poke holes in their fundamentalist bullshit."[54]

Fuller tried to encapsulate not only the horror, cruelty, and futility of war, but the reigning state of chaos as well. He explains, "Everything goes too fast. Something happens to your nervous system, very abnormal to it, from your head to your fingers. It's worse than when you're driving like hell and suddenly you have to stomp on the brake."[55] As to regulating the battlefield with rules such as the Geneva Convention, he argues, "You can't have law in war. A dogface with an M-1—that is the law!"[56] Fuller has two objections: first, compiling regulations to govern what is an inherently illegal act makes no sense, and second, any attempt to legitimize the stupidity that occurs on both sides is wasted effort.

Since Fuller uses combat not only as an extended metaphor for life but also to comment on the confusion of appearance and reality—snoring that sounds like incoming shells, for example—he concludes that the most rational stance in an irrational world may just be madness. Case in point: Zack grabs the Communist he has shot by the collar and bellows, "if you die, I'll kill you." According to biographer Phil Hardy, "Undeniably, Fuller's fiercely integrationist view of America is founded on contradictions and confusions that he cannot resolve. His hero always chooses America—he [not only] makes a leap of faith but tries to explain why. [But] if he's America's apologist, he's also its educator."[57]

Fuller contended that the Geneva Convention didn't take into account the wartime opportunist who, when he finally runs out of cartridges, sticks his mitts in the air, claiming "That's enough, you can take me prisoner now." As Fuller recalls, he and his fellow combatants did honor one unwritten rule regarding POWs during World War II: "If an enemy surrendered to us while he still had bullets in his gun, we took him in. But if he put his hands up after emptying his gun and killing [our] friends, we'd shoot him. Because, gee, isn't that cute? He's out of bullets and now he wants to make peace with us?"[58]

Despite a seemingly emotionless demeanor, Zack is barely hanging on. With the goading of the Communist POW, he just snaps. According to Fuller, "If you can't stand tension anymore, you can commit suicide or commit violence and insanity. In violence, the irrational forces driving man are turned outward and clash head-on with the similar forces in another."[59] Zack shoots the North Korean not just because he was the enemy but also because he attacks Zack's relationship with Short Round. The North Korean forces Zack to confront the cognitive dissonance between allegiance to another and allegiance to self. Zack's psyche, only willing to acknowledge the latter, splinters under the strain. In fact, by the end of the picture, Zack surrenders his sanity—making a mental sentimental journey back to the beach at Normandy. Permanently.

The second reason the Pentagon was not so crazy about *The Steel Helmet*, in addition to the scene where Zack executes the POW, was that Fuller "brought out the fact that Germany was not the only country that had concentration camps. We didn't gas people, we didn't burn them or starve them to death, but we had concentration camps."[60] While the Japanese American internment camps weren't exactly hush-hush in those days, the extent of an internee's hardship and humiliation would not be widely known until television documentaries such as Walter Cronkite's *Twentieth Century* let the entire country in on FDR's dirty little secret. Feared as potential saboteurs, 112,000 Japanese Americans, 70,000 of them Nisei (American born), were evacuated from the West Coast and placed in ten "reloca-tion centers" where they were confined for up to four years. Amid qualms that an invasion of the West Coast was imminent, President Franklin D. Roosevelt issued Executive Order 9066 on March 18, 1942, which permit-ted civil rights restrictions that would have been unconstitutional during peacetime. The incarcerated Japanese Americans, forced to leave their homes and often separated from loved ones, were not guilty of any wrong-doing—many, in fact, were children. The U.S. government literally tore families apart. Japanese American entrepreneurs were also compelled to abandon their businesses. Individuals merely one-eighth Japanese could be summarily herded onto crowded trains and transported to relocation camps where conditions were cramped, crowded, and callous. In late 1944, the U.S. Supreme Court upheld the legality of the evacuation policy but at the same time ruled that prolonged detention of Japanese Americans (whose loyalty had been ascertained) was against the law.

After World War II, however, America warmed toward Japanese Amer-icans. The abrupt about-face was due in no small part to the dazzling record of the 442nd Regimental Combat Team, composed almost entirely of Japanese Americans much like *The Steel Helmet's* Sergeant Tanaka. These men were the most highly decorated military unit in American his-tory. In 1988, under the Civil Liberties Act, the U.S. government issued 120,000 individual apologies for violations of Japanese American consti-tutional rights along with a financial award of $20,000 in tax-free repara-tions to each eligible internee.

A third reason the Pentagon wasn't happy about *The Steel Helmet* related to racial prejudice against blacks. When the North Korean major taunts Corporal Medic Thompson (James Edwards) with "I just don't understand you. You can't even eat with them unless it's during a war," the black man is mind-blowingly patient, even in his terse response: "some things you can't rush." Even though President Truman ordered the armed forces inte-grated two years before the start of the Korean conflict, military leaders did not hurry to put policy into practice. The armed services just weren't ready for black and white soldiers to share the same foxholes—at least not initially. Bennie Gordon, drafted into the army in the fall of 1951, finished his basic training at Fort Sill, Oklahoma. Although he served in an inte-grated unit, he recalls a white soldier confiding his shock at drilling along-side blacks. It was the first time he had even seen a Negro, "other than in a Tarzan movie."[61] When Charles King reported to Fort Leonard in the au-tumn of 1950, whites hung their helmets on one side of the camp, blacks on the other. Vernon L. Warren remembers traveling with a young white soldier from Detroit and stopping at a Kansas City bus station en route to Fort Riley. The waitress behind the counter scowled and acknowledged that she would be happy to serve Warren's companion, but she would not wait on a Negro. Warren ended up at POW Camp No. 5 along the Yalu

River. He not only remembers prisoners being segregated by race but during the first few days of his thirty-month confinement, Chinese guards actually attempted to scrub the black off his skin. When Warren was finally released, as part of "Operation Little Switch" in the spring of 1953, he weighed one hundred pounds. "You could play the Star-Spangled Banner on my rib cage," he disclosed.[62] By the end of the Korean conflict, 90 percent of black soldiers were assigned to integrated units. The sustained success of African American troops effectively negated the strident shouts of naysayers who insisted that black and white soldiers wouldn't be able to serve together.

The Steel Helmet's Corporal Medic Thompson obtained his medical training on the G.I. Bill after service in World War II, where approximately 1.2 million real-life black men and women served. The fifteen thousand black fighting men of the illustrious 92nd Infantry Division, known as the Buffalo Soldiers, served their country with distinction and pride.[63] Long-standing segregationist policies may have prevented African Americans from entering the Army Air Corps, but in 1941, an all-black army air unit was established at the Tuskegee Institute in Alabama, where a handful of African Americans won their wings.

Black American soldiers, who battled to liberate Europe, did so knowing that in their own country they had yet to share full rights of citizenship, but they volunteered anyway—mostly in a limited support capacity because their white superiors doubted their ability to fight. In fact, only 3 percent were initially assigned to combat duty, but those who went into battle performed valiantly.[64] Any further reservations about blacks evaporated, however, when the enemy decimated white troops. The need for soldiers overpowered the desire to separate the races.

After finally accepting the service of black volunteers, the army failed to honor them with the medals to which they were entitled. While Americans say they believe that heroism comes in all colors, until recently only white soldiers were gifted with military honors, due to shoddy paperwork and military officials who preferred to overlook black bravery on the battlefield. According to federal records, none of the 2,221 African American volunteers who survived the war received recognition for exemplary combat service. Records for only 763 have been located, and among them 50 have subsequently been awarded Bronze Stars, most posthumously. In January 1997, President Bill Clinton conferred the Congressional Medal of Honor on seven black soldiers with his heartfelt apology for the delay.[65]

Many historians now link black participation in World War II with the origin of the civil rights movement. Not only did anti-Nazi propaganda generated during the war boost the disconnect between the ideal of democracy and the reality of racism, but also situating the United Nations headquarters in New York rendered American racial inequality even more conspicuous to the rest of the globe. According to *Magill's Survey of Cinema, Steel Helmet* provides an important footnote to cinematic history because an African American actor (James Edwards) played a medic rather than the customary janitor or Pullman porter.[66]

Fuller did not hesitate to expose topics the military would rather keep under wraps: "If the country did something shameful, it's shameful," he said. "These are problems we Americans should not hide, should not be proud, or ashamed of. Rather, we should recognize and dramatize them."[67]

In addition to the three issues outlined above, the Pentagon probably didn't want the public to know the woeful extent to which our side, especially early in the war, was unprepared. American forces lacked leadership, reliable weaponry, adequate food, and dependable intelligence. In *The Steel Helmet*, Zack is compelled to glean ammunition and weapons from the dead. Lieutenant Driscoll experiences a nasty scare with a substandard hand grenade—fortunately, a cool Buddhahead Tanaka locates the loose pin before the explosive device discharges. If the radioman doesn't keep correcting the bombardment targeting, the Temple lookout post would fall victim to friendly fire—a nightmare theme that highlighted several antiwar movies about Vietnam.

The Pentagon probably didn't want the public to know the extent to which U.S. soldiers toted their own cultural prejudices with them to Korea. Early in the picture, Sergeant Zack calls Short Round a "gook." The boy responds, "I am not a gook. I am Korean." American soldiers were regularly perplexed when a Korean would say, "Me no gook. *You* gook." In Korean, the word "Miguk" means "American." Both Zack and Medic Thompson rip Short Round's handwritten prayers off his back, disregarding the sacredness of the Buddhist custom. Zack not only uses the contemptuous phrase "eat rice" instead of "hit the dirt" but also flips off a "don't take any wooden yen" when he should know that the South Korean currency is the won. When Private Conchie Bronte plays "Auld Land Syne" on the chaplain's organ, Zack is chagrined to find Short Round proudly warbling along in his native language. He has no idea the boy is singing the South Korean national anthem. Even though World War II veteran Tanaka regularly offers sage advice, Driscoll routinely disregards it. Zack observes there is something about the way Buddhahead's eyes are slanted that keeps the officer from paying heed. Finally, Fuller uses the North Korean officer's demise to present the most persuasive argument against communism. By asking Medic Thompson for a prayer, the POW trades the Communist ideology for the spiritual comfort of Buddhism. In other words, when faced with the Grim Reaper and the question of an afterlife, political philosophy is just plain irrelevant. The adage "there are no atheists in foxholes" hovers unspoken in the air.

American soldiers, still clammy with sweat from Cold War paranoia, don't realize that communism itself comes in different flavors. When Zack

warns Lieutenant Driscoll, "There's nothing out there but a lot of rice paddies crawlin' with Commies, waitin' to slap you between two hunks of
rye bread and wash you down with fish eggs and vodka," he illustrates a
confusion that is later corrected by the POW, who asserts "I am not a Russian! I am a North Korean Communist."

Hot or cold, war is never an answer for Fuller. The final seven words in
his inarguably isolationist film are "there is no end to this story." In his
inimitable tabloid journalistic fashion, Fuller cuts to the crux. He explains,
"That's what I want to show: that this was *not* the end. Wars go on and on
and on. [And war itself is just] impossible."[68]

FULLER AS ZACK

Not only is the hard-nosed soldier who sticks a cigar stub in his mouth
without benefit of a match a time-honored movie cliché, but also an un-
lighted Romeo y Julieta stogie was the signature prop of Sam Fuller. Just
like Sergeant Zack, Fuller's spirit was twisted by the brutality of World
War II. They both scrapped as "dogfaces" with the 16th Regiment of the
First Infantry Division from North Africa to Sicily to France to Germany
to Czechoslovakia. On D-Day, Fuller, like his fictional alter ego, was im-
mobilized by German bombardment for three hours on Omaha Beach, a
sweep of sand Fuller portrays as "lined with the intestines of men." Fuller
earned the Bronze Star, the Silver Star, and the Purple Heart the hard way,
storming beachhead after beachhead. Even the director's noncombat
films evidence his obsession with war. The gangsters in *House of Bamboo*
and *Underworld USA* command their criminal enterprises exactly like military operations. Even in *The Crimson Kimono,* love is a battleground and
everyone gets wounded.

Fuller recorded his infantry experiences in diaries, which he later used
to script his films. Perhaps *The Steel Helmet,* and later *The Big Red One*,
helped to exorcise Fuller's demons. Daniel Selznik noted the similarity
between *The Big Red One* officer who inspires confidence in his soldiers,
despite devastating setbacks, and Fuller, whose devotion encouraged the
production company through terrorist threats and oppressive summer
heat: "Fuller is a born Boy Scout leader," Selznik writes, "the kind who
can get everyone else to hike the last mile because he is leading the way."[69]

Who is Zack? He seems cold-hearted, self-centered, and only interested
in getting out of Korea alive—he's the typical unsympathetic Fuller anti-
hero. Critic Nora Sayre considers Fuller's protagonist so over the top she
writes, Zack is "so exuberantly sadistic that we can't ever side with him:
foul to his men and to all Koreans, he seems to personify the derangement
that perpetuates a fruitless war."[70] The last thing Fuller wanted Zack to
be, however, was a hero. He refused to cast John Wayne in *The Big Red*

One, not because of Wayne's politics, but because the Duke was "a symbol of a kind of man I never saw in war. He would have given it a heroic touch that I hate in war movies."[71]

Zack may be the World War II retread who mocks all proprieties, but his in-the-trenches seasoning and survival savoir-faire are grossly underestimated by Driscoll. When the dead body of an American GI is discovered, the lieutenant orders the removal of his dog tags. Zack barks, "Leave him. A dead man is a dead man. Nobody cares." Sneering at this admonition, Driscoll has the tags removed anyway, and a soldier is instantly blown to bits. From that moment on, Zack moves from monster to mentor.

Fuller, however, teases out the inherent limitations when one weighs each decision against the counterweight of merely staying alive. When the audience first meets Zack, his arms are tied behind his back and he is slithering on his stomach through a field littered with cadavers. The camera pulls back and involves the viewer in the sheer physicality of effort it takes to survive. Cut free by the South Korean orphan, Zack tends his wounds without a word. According to Fuller, "you see, everybody in a war acts to save himself."[72] Not until Zack has dealt with his leg injury (a threat to his survival) does he turn to acknowledge his liberator. Even then, however, Zack immediately tries to disengage, to retreat back to his cynical comfort zone. He then attempts to cancel his debt to Short Round by offering him chocolate—the relationship must operate on a strictly quid pro quo basis. When he finds he hasn't any chocolate in his pack, he resorts to alternative distancing defense mechanisms.

Zack is not so much bigoted as feelings frozen, petrified of getting too close to anyone who might die or abandon him. According to Fuller, "the only emotion you have is 'when do I get out of here, and when does somebody replace me?' That's the only emotion you ever experience in war."[73]

The Steel Helmet marks the first time Fuller employed characters and dialogue taken directly from his journals. According to biographer Lee Server, "no auteurist phrenology is needed to determine Fuller's influence on his work."[74] The real-life Anthony D. Zack, who served in Europe and North Africa with Sam Fuller and succumbed to cancer at eighty-four, was delighted to give his name to *The Steel Helmet*'s central character. He never regarded himself as anyone special; in fact, he used to maintain, "The real heroes [in World War II] are dead."[75]

Fuller's war movies are tough and gritty. He captured the lingo ("no bullets, they were all swackled by the enemy") as well as the bone-weariness of men incessantly under siege ("first we'll eat and then we'll bury them"). The viewer can't help but identify with the combatants as they scrunch down—grungy, groggy, and grouchy. Fuller insists, "I can't see any way of making people taste revulsion towards violence, whether it's a gangster or war background, without disrobing it to the fullest."[76]

Zack's sanity-preserving sarcasm is most evident when he tells Driscoll's squad, "Nobody knows where you are except the enemy." Yet, while Zack might be suffering under the delusion he is a rock-hard professional, he does manage to expose his soft emotional underbelly to the South Korean orphan. In fact, losing Short Round robs Zack of the cynical self-absorption that has previously enabled him to keep the nightmare of Normandy at bay. Zack loses his heart and his mind.

The burly Gene Evans won his first starring role not because of his acting ability, but because he had served in the combat engineers during World War II—"cleaning up what [*The Big Red One*] infantry couldn't."[77] Fuller was pretty impressed that the much-decorated soldier had spent D-Day plus two on Omaha Beach, but what really convinced Fuller to cast Evans as Zack was his ability to properly rack back an M1.[78]

Just as Driscoll's unit was rocked by Zack's legendary temper, Evans remembers being bowled over by the fit Fuller threw when producer Murray Lerner tried to replace Evans with another actor. "Fuller just went absolutely crazy. He came boiling back down to the sound stage" and boycotted his directorial duties until the powers that be came to their senses.[79] As with Zack, when Fuller blew his stack there were prodigious consequences.[80]

Fuller used Zack's dented helmet to symbolize "survival."[81] In fact, the actual artifact meant the world to Sam Fuller, who presented the prop to Gene Evans as a Christmas gift. Evans was actually miffed—he had been expecting an expensive present, something commensurate with Fuller's $40,000–$50,000 weekly salary. Decades later, at a University of Southern California Fuller Film Retrospective, Evans, who appeared as a "special guest," arrived toting a mysterious paper bag. "What have you got in the sack?" queried Fuller. "Everybody in the place is looking at that damn sack," says Sam, "and nobody's looking at my cigar." Evans pulled out the helmet, allowing that since he'd enjoyed the keepsake for several decades, he decided it was time to give it back. Fuller was so emotionally wrought, Evans reported, he could scarcely speak.[82]

Fuller was a man of unwavering ethics and constant values. Like Zack, when Fuller claimed you as a friend, his loyalty never deviated. Gene Evans remembers, "There were guys he took from picture to picture who just couldn't get a job otherwise. I mean, they were no good. But he would manage to place them in his pictures where they couldn't do any harm."[83] According to Tim Robbins, Fuller could have spent the war at a desk job, well out of harm's way, but he categorically refused on moral grounds.[84] Probably his greatest reason for remaining at the front, according to Robbins, was that he was a born journalist who didn't want to miss the opportunity to see history unfold. Further, he would never have been content to scribble meaningless press releases for generals—that just wasn't his calling.[85]

A WAR FILM WITH A DIFFERENCE

War was Fuller's favorite cinematic subject. According to the director, "The drama of war is not in the fighting. It's an emotional thing. And the emotion can be very intense, because you have to be insane to squeeze a trigger at another human being."[86] He explored the madness of war in *Fixed Bayonets, Hell and High Water, China Gate, The Big Red One,* and *Merrill's Marauders.* His direct and unsentimental attitude toward the battlefield brought him to several inflexible cinematic rules: (1) leave the soldiers dirty, tired, and unshaven; (2) never put girls in war films; (3) never let actors parade around and show off; (4) don't stop the action when someone is hit or killed, carry on; and (5) never allow a G.I. to bring out his wallet to look at his fiancée's photograph—this *never* happens in real life.[87] Fuller's favorite Hollywood war films were John Ford's *The Informer* and William Wellman's *The Story of GI Joe.*

Not only does Fuller include the requisite antiwar horror, waste of life, and senseless violence in *The Steel Helmet,* but he also takes pains to counter the exhilaration, adventure, and camaraderie that interventionist films employ to rouse young men into queuing up at armed services recruiting offices. Fuller pulls no punches: "I don't like propaganda films. I never made a hurrah picture about war."[88] In fact, he strenuously objected to the gung ho finale the studio gave *Merrill's Marauders.* "My ending," claimed Fuller, "does not try to induce you to join the Army."[89] General George Patton III was disappointed in *The Big Red One* for its failure to exhibit "recruitment flavor." "That's exactly what I wanted him to say," contends Fuller, "because there are no heroics in my pictures. These are the survivors of war and they do what they have to do to stay alive."[90]

Combat films provided Hollywood with a socially acceptable means of bringing violence to the screen. While the Motion Picture Production Code (MPPC) opposed brutal killing and mass slaughter, films in which aggression was directed against enemies of the United States got a thumbs-up from the MPPC. There was certainly enough butchery and carnage in *The Steel Helmet* to hold an audience's attention, but to Fuller, war was literally hell and he stopped short of gratuitously glorifying battle. His soldiers do not die a sanitized death with "America the Beautiful" on the sound track. According to Fuller, "In the movies it is almost impossible to show a real war, to photograph battle. There is smoke everywhere. And the average moviegoer does not want to see real war. Men afraid, men vomiting, men [defecating] in their pants, men shooting men on their own team."[91]

Rarely, Fuller felt, had the movies synthesized anything like the jumble of misery, unpredictability, and immorality of actual combat. In a 1946 letter, Fuller calls Lewis Milestone to task about *A Walk in the Sun:* "Why a man of your caliber [sic] should resort to a colonel's technical advice on what happens to a platoon is something I'll never figure out. Some day there'll be an *All Quiet* on the American doggie and I'm going to do my best to be the doggie to write it."[92] That aspiration, of course, was realized in *The Steel Helmet.*

Despite being rushed into production, *The Steel Helmet* rises above the battlefield formula film, which typically features a steadfast officer rallying a badly outnumbered unit against a seemingly indomitable enemy. *The Steel Helmet* was one of the few pre-Vietnam films to criticize the future instead of just rehashing the glories of the past. By pitting a weathered World War II veteran against an untrained ninety-day wonder, Fuller mirrors the commitment clash between lifers and short-termers that actually occurred early in the Korean conflict. While Fuller's cinematic goals may have been restricted by a miniscule budget, he invested his modest production with authentic detail, offbeat characters, and compelling intensity. No wonder the sleeper became a sensation, stirring up controversy and racking up a fortune for the unknown director. The scene in which Zack locates an enemy sniper by tracing his line of fire is so realistic, according to war film expert Paul M. Edwards, it was later used by military training schools.[93]

The mute soldier, who speaks up only when he is knifed in the back, reflects America's confusion, if not alienation, in Korea and demonstrates exactly why the "Forgotten War" never proved a popular subject for Hollywood filmmakers. In *The Hunters* (1958), the Robert Mitchum character sums it up best: "Korea came along too soon after the real big one. It's hard to sell anyone on it." Korea was not a war—it was a police action—the goal being a negotiated settlement. World War II, by contrast, was a moral struggle between good and evil that was sustained until victory was achieved. Fuller not only encapsulated America's impatience with such befuddling nuances, but also captured the budding sense of defeatism vexing the country.

While *The Steel Helmet* is not exactly a religious film, the screen-filling Buddha presents an undeniable spiritual presence and Short Round's meticulously brush-stroked prayers prove pivotal to the plot. Fuller specifically positioned the plasma packet in the palm of the golden figure. "I wanted to show the blood running out of His hand into the Commie. I thought it would be very touching to have death there in the lap of his God, [even though] within minutes that whole temple is going to be obliterated. But still the Buddha remains."[94] Fuller was, in fact, mindful of the three-times-larger-than-life statue in Kamakura Japan (seen in *The House of Bamboo*) that emerged unscathed during a devastating earthquake. "That's the flavor I tried to get with the Buddha in *Helmet*."[95] Zack even makes an attempt to spin the prayer wheel in which his little buddy placed so much stock. When the American soldiers first enter the temple, even though they may not understand much about Korean culture, they do doff their helmets in respect. In fact, Lieutenant Driscoll orders the squad to leave the house of worship exactly as they found it—an impossibility, of course, once the shelling starts. The inclusion of a conscientious objector among the Americans is an attempt to balance eastern and western beliefs. Before Vietnam, the United States granted either exemption or noncombatant service (Conchie Bronte serves as the chaplain's assistant) to members of recognized pacifist religious sects. Bronte tells Zack that he had been studying for the priesthood but decided to come to Korea because "if one's house is in danger, you fight for it." For Fuller, religion also exemplified universality of allegiance, an overarching theme in *The Steel Helmet*.[96]

THE AUDIENCE RESPONDS

The Steel Helmet, according to Fuller, "had everything [going] against it— no names, one set, no girls, no romance," but it proved to be box-office magic.[97] Filmed at a cost of $105,000, it was the first independently produced picture to play Loew's State Theater in New York City and ended up grossing more than $6 million.[98] Fuller deservedly won the Writer's Guild of America Award for best-written American low-budget film in 1951.[99]

According to *Variety*, Lippert Pictures had a sure money film. "It pinpoints the Korean fighting in a grim, hard-hitting tale that is excellently told. . . . Even without actual battle scenes, Fuller gets in a full flavor of combat, the U.S. Infantry, and the men who are the foot soldiers."[100]

Even Bosley Crowther of the *New York Times* was impressed. "The writer–director–producer," according to Crowther, "has sidestepped the romantic war clichés and has taken a distinctly melancholy and dismal view of the business at hand. The country is hostile, the situation is precarious, the organization appears uncomfortably loose, and the soldiers, while not exactly cowards, are nobody's fearless buckaroos. In short, Mr. Fuller has managed to work into his modest film a great many implications of ineffectualness in the Korean War."[101]

The Steel Helmet suggests and, perhaps to a degree, helped determine the attitude Americans would assume toward the two conflicts following World War II. In the second war to end all wars, we had oozed self-assuredness and solidarity. During Korea and Vietnam, however, the national emotion would snake from suspicion to scorn.

The credit "Written, Produced, and Directed by Sam Fuller" ensured that the original Hollywood hyphenate's films would approximate, as closely as possible, his highly personal cinematic vision for more than four decades. Andrew Sarris considered Fuller an "authentic American primitive." While his detractors recoil at his extreme view of human behavior, his fans contend his films vibrate off the screen. Fuller films take an audience by the scruff of the neck and give a teeth-rattling shake. While Fuller's fans appreciated his ability to turn the most formulaic genre into an engaging psychological study, he recapitulated his career in these eleven words: "I made pictures the way I thought I should make them."[102]

NOTES

1. Quoted in Andrew Kelley, "*All Quiet on the Western Front:* Brutal Cutting, Stupid Censors and Bigoted Politicos, 1930–1984," *Historical Journal of Film, Radio, and Television* 9, no. 2 (1989): 135–50.

2. Howard Zinn, *A People's History of the United States: 1492–Present,* revised ed. (New York: HarperPerennial, 1995), 409.

3. See Carl von Clausewitz, *On War,* edited and translated by Michael Howard and Peter Paret (Princeton, N.J.: Princeton University Press, 1984).

4. George Washington, "His Farewell Address," in *The World's Famous Orations,* edited by William Jennings Bryan, vol. 7 (New York: Funk and Wagnalls, 1906), 106.

5. Michael Wood, *America in the Movies: Or, "Santa Maria," It Had Slipped My Mind* (New York: Basic, 1975), 39.

6. Wood, *America,* 30.

7. The UN resolution called for action "to repel the armed attack and to restore peace and security in the area."

8. *Public Opinion Online* (Roper Center at the University of Connecticut, 1990), QUESTION ID: USGALLUP.51-472, QK07.

9. Marvin Seid, "Cold War First Turned Hot in Korea," *Los Angeles Times,* November 6, 1999, B8.

10. John Toland, *In Mortal Combat: Korea, 1950–1953* (New York: Morrow, 1991), 7.

11. Steve Vogel, "Miscount Etched in History," *Chicago Sun–Times,* June 25, 2000, 39.

12. Seid, "Cold War," B8.

13. On August 10, 1945, John J. McCloy, the assistant secretary of war, told two War Office colonels (Dean Rusk and Charles Bonesteel) to come up with some sort of demarcation line. Poring over a schoolboy map of Korea, they fixed on the Thirty-eighth Parallel.

14. Toland, *Mortal Combat,* 18–19.

15. In a January 12, 1950, speech, Dean Acheson excluded South Korea from the Pacific defensive perimeter.

16. Senator Styles Bridges of New Hampshire claimed that (Nationalist) China asked for a sword and we gave her a dull paring knife.

17. *Public Opinion Online* (Roper Center at the University of Connecticut, 1990), QUESTION ID: USGALLUP.50-461, QK04A.

18. David Owens, "406 vs. 20,000," *Hartford Courant,* June 25, 2000, A7.

19. David Halberstam, *The Fifties* (New York, Fawcett Columbine, 1993), 75.

20. On September 5, 1950, the army and marines reported 137 killed, 511 wounded, and 587 missing.

21. The Inchon Landing occurred on September 15, 1950.

22. See Stanley Weintraub, *MacArthur's War: Korea and the Undoing of an American Hero* (New York: Touchstone, 2000), 350.

23. Halberstam, *Fifties*, 106.

24. Weintraub, *MacArthur's War*, 64.

25. Weintraub, *MacArthur's War*, 65.

26. Quoted in Halberstam, *Fifties*, 74.

27. Michael Dobbs, "Shoot Them All," *Washington Post*, February 6, 2000, W06.

28. David Wood, "Military Policies, Tactics Rooted in Korean War," *Times–Picayune*, June 25, 2000, A08.

29. *Public Opinion Online* (Roper Center at the University of Connecticut, 1990), QUESTION ID: USORC.51APR, R05.

30. Wood, "Military Policies," A08.

31. Lewis H. Carlson, *Remembered Prisoners of a Forgotten War* (New York: St. Martin's, 2002), 144.

32. Clarence Adams, William Wite, and Larance Sullivan.

33. Quoted in Toland, *Mortal Combat*, 127.

34. Carlson, *Remembered Prisoners*, 97.

35. Dobbs, "Shoot Them All," W06.

36. H. B. Ridgway, "Why We Are Here" memorandum, Headquarters Eighth United States Army Korea Office of the Commanding General (January 21, 1951), 1. The protégé of George C. Marshall, Ridgway replaced General Walton Walker as commander of the Eighth Army on December 23, 1950, when Walker perished in a jeep accident.

37. Ridgway, "Why We Are Here."

38. Steve Vogel, "Veterans Still Feel the Hidden Wounds; Soldiers Went from Frostbite to Cold Shoulder," *Washington Post*, June 21, 2000, B01.

39. "North Korea Effort Must Be Halted," *Ventura County Star*, December 28, 2002, B8.

40. Robert J. Caldwell, "History's Heroes," *San Diego Union–Tribune*, June 25, 2000, G1.

41. Samuel Fuller in Jean-Luc Godard's film *Pierrot le Fou*.

42. The name "Short Round" was also adopted by Steven Spielberg for his cute Asian kid in *Indiana Jones and the Temple of Doom*.

43. Lee Server, *Sam Fuller: Film Is a Battleground* (Jefferson, N.C.: McFarland, 1994), 21.

44. Clancy Segal, "The Macho Man of the Movies," *Los Angeles Times Book Review*, November 17, 2002, R3.

45. Server, *Sam Fuller*, 54.

46. Server, *Sam Fuller*, 34.

47. Server, *Sam Fuller*, 105.

48. Eric Sherman and Martin Rubin, *The Director's Event: Interviews with Five American Film-Makers* (New York: Atheneum, 1970), 130.

49. Nicholas Garnham, *Sam Fuller* (New York: Viking, 1971), 116.

50. Server, *Sam Fuller*, 27.

51. Could Fuller have reversed, for poetic purposes, the embarrassing capture of the American major general William F. Dean, the commander of U.S. troops in Korea?

52. Michael Lee Lanning, *Vietnam at the Movies* (New York: Fawcett Columbine, 1994), 31.

53. Samuel Fuller, with Christa Lang Fuller and Jerome Henry Rudes, *A Third Face: My Tale of Writing, Fighting, and Filmmaking* (New York: Knopf, 2002), 263.

54. Fuller, *Third Face,* 264.

55. Server, *Sam Fuller,* 28.

56. Server, *Sam Fuller.*

57. Phil Hardy, *Samuel Fuller* (Westport, Conn.: Praeger, 1970), 32.

58. Nigel Andrews, "Fuller's Law of Film-Making," *Financial Times,* August 8, 1992, XIII.

59. Garnham, *Sam Fuller,* 146.

60. Server, *Sam Fuller,* 27

61. Bill Smith, "Black History Month; Minorities in Uniform," *St. Louis Post–Dispatch,* February 20, 2002, A1.

62. Smith, "Black History."

63. The name "Buffalo Soldiers" was taken from all-black units that fought on the frontier and in World War I.

64. "Fighting Hitler and Jim Crow," *Times–Picayune,* February 4, 2001, 6.

65. Steve Vogel, "Black GIs Get Belated Recognition; Medals Awarded to Soldiers Who Volunteered for Combat in Second World War," *Washington Post,* November 6, 2000, B03.

66. Frank N. Magill, ed., *Magill's Survey of Cinema,* second series, vol. 5 (Englewood Cliffs, N.J.: Salem, 1981), 2273.

67. David Sterrit, "Sam Fuller's World War II," *Christian Science Monitor,* July 21, 1980, 19.

68. Sherman and Rubin, *Director's Event,* 132.

69. *Contemporary Authors Online* (Gale Group, 2000). Reproduced in *Biography Resource Center* (Farmington Hills, Mich.: Gale Group, 2001), www.galenet.com/servlet/BioRC.

70. Nora Sayre, *Running Time: Films of the Cold War* (New York: Dial, 1982), 184.

71. Server, *Sam Fuller,* 21

72. Quoted in Sterrit, "Fuller's World War II," 19.

73. Sherman and Rubin, *Director's Event,* 130.

74. Server, *Sam Fuller,* 2.

75. Alana Baranick, "Anthony Zack Inspired Character in War Film," *Cleveland Plain Dealer,* January 7, 2000, 7B.

76. Ezra Goodman, "Low Budget Movies with POW!" edited by Gene Brown, *The New York Times Encyclopedia of Film* 8 (New York: New York Times Books, 1984), NYT (Feb 28, 1965B).

77. Server, *Sam Fuller,* 65.

78. Server, *Sam Fuller,* 66.

79. Server, *Sam Fuller,* 104.

80. Server, *Sam Fuller,* 66.

81. Fuller, *Third Face,* 256.

82. Lee Server, "The Man in the Steel Helmet," *Film Comment* 30, no. 3 (May 1994): 73.

83. Server, "Man," 71.

84. Robbins produced a documentary for the British Film Institute about Fuller entitled "The Typewriter, the Rifle and the Movie Camera" in June 1996.

85. Tim Robbins, "Sam and the Search for Truth," *Guardian,* February 25, 1970, T8.

86. Quoted in Sterrit, "Fuller's World War II," 19.

87. Goodman, "Low Budget Movies."

88. Server, *Sam Fuller,* 52.

89. Server, *Sam Fuller,* 52.

90. Server, *Sam Fuller,* 52.

91. Server, *Sam Fuller,* 20.

92. Server, *Sam Fuller,* 2–3.

93. Paul M. Edwards, *A Guide to Films on the Korean War* (Westport, Conn.: Greenwood, 1997), 11.

94. Sherman and Rubin, *Director's Event,* 132.

95. Sherman and Rubin, *Director's Event,* 132.

96. Hardy, *Samuel Fuller,* 12.

97. Goodman, "Low Budget Movies."

98. John Hart, "Sam Fuller Documentary Irresistible," *Seattle Times,* June 28, 1996, F8.

99. Magill, *Magill's Survey,* 2273.

100. *Variety,* January 3, 1951.

101. Bosley Crowther, "Steel Helmet," *New York Times Film Reviews* 21, no. 5 (January 25, 1951): 2490.

102. *Contemporary Authors Online.*

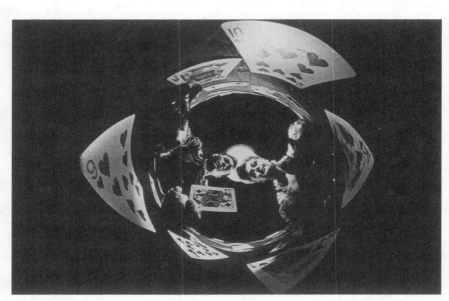

Angela Lansbury controls Communist assassin Laurence Harvey in The Manchurian Candidate. *© 1962 Frank Sinatra Trust Number 10. All Rights Reserved. Courtesy of MGM CLIP+STILL and the Academy of Motion Picture Arts and Sciences.*

8

☆

Cold War Hawkism in
The Manchurian Candidate

With Senator John McCain sprinting from an unlikely long shot to George W. Bush's worst political nightmare in the 2000 primary campaign, references to the *Manchurian Candidate*'s assassin, who was spurred into posthypnotic action by the turn of a playing card, found their way into news magazine profiles as well as *Saturday Night Live* sketches. In fact, when McCain was asked why he decided to toss his chapeau in the presidential ring, an apparent abrupt shift from his 1996 position, he deadpanned "I was sitting in a room and Angela Lansbury turned over a queen of diamonds." *Newsweek*'s Jonathan Alter allowed that this sort of droll response helped explain McCain's wild popularity with the press.[1] Suggesting that McCain had been brainwashed, like the Laurence Harvey character in the film, during his nearly six-year sojourn at the Hanoi Hilton was obviously a political ploy to blunt the senator's potent personal story and attractive reformist message. It worked—not nearly enough Republican voters believed McCain was playing with a full deck. They backed the $100 million–funded George W. Bush instead.

Author Thomas Doherty claims that the prejudice haunting a redeemed captive such as McCain harkens back to colonial days, when POWs were considered "tainted by prolonged contact with the enemy."[2] A similar notion won over army psychiatrists examining returning Korean War POWs. The good doctors figured that the only way American soldiers could have collaborated with the enemy had to be brainwashing—those godless Communists had somehow conditioned our boys to act against conscience and country.

COLD WAR HAWKISM

All Americans became anti-Communists during the Cold War—four decades (1947–89) of intense military strategy and political free-for-all hostility that started to simmer right after the shock of Hiroshima's instantaneous destruction.[3] The chilling realization that mankind now possessed the means of self-annihilation was just beginning to sink in as the United States and her Western European allies started to face off against the USSR and Communist countries. While American journalist Herbert Bayard Swope coined the term "Cold War" for a 1947 speech by financier Bernard Baruch, it took nearly a decade for the phrase to claim a place in the national lexicon. According to a January 5, 1951, Gallup poll, to the question "Will you tell me what the term 'cold war' means?" 47 percent found an answer from among "a war without shooting," "a war of nerves," "propaganda," "threats," "agitation," "war mongering," "war scare," or "diplomatic war." Interestingly enough, however, some 29 percent of those who responded had no idea what the phrase meant.[4] By December 1955, however, 56 percent of those polled were able to clearly define the term.[5]

Explanations of the causes of the Cold War vary among political scientists: traditionalists argue that Americans awoke somewhat sluggishly to the threat of an aggressive Soviet Union; soft revisionists, such as Donald Fleming, maintain that anti-Communists in the Roosevelt and Truman administration sabotaged Roosevelt's plan for a postwar alliance with the USSR; while hard revisionists such as William A. Williams contend that expanding American capitalism, which demanded an international marketplace, led to the Cold War.[6] A fourth group, the postrevisionists, claim neither Truman nor Stalin were looking for trouble but conflict between the only two powers left standing after World War II was clearly inevitable. As early as the nineteenth century, Alexis de Tocqueville prophesied that Russia and the United States would rise to the top as global powers. It didn't take a rocket scientist to figure out suspicion and mistrust between the two would be exacerbated by ideological differences. The Marxist–Leninists among the Soviet leadership assumed that capitalism would inevitably seek out the destruction of the Russian system. In the United States, a long-standing hatred of communism fueled the outlook that the USSR was hell-bent on world conquest.

Soviet employment of military force to establish Communist governments in Eastern Europe smacked up against America's insistence on the right of self-determination while further swelling suspicion that the USSR, after dominating Eastern Europe, would attempt to communize Western Europe as well. The USSR had incurred colossal losses in the war against Nazi Germany and considered Eastern Europe, thrust behind an "Iron Curtain," a buttress against another incursion from the West.[7]

Several issues that defied negotiation or appeasement contributed to the onset of the Cold War. America held that Stalin broke his word with respect to holding free elections in Poland. The abrupt end of the lend-lease aid program in May 1945 further soured the economic relationship between the United States and the USSR. Further, the two countries continued to squabble over the reconstruction of Germany, the establishment of a Soviet occupation zone in Japan, and the Soviet Union's intention to build an atomic bomb. Finally, even the United Nations couldn't reconcile the intense ideological clashes that contaminated communication between the former allies.

Truman lacked savoir-faire about foreign affairs, to say the least. Like most Midwestern politicos, he espoused both isolationism and anticommunism. While he stopped short of unequivocal opposition to World War II, for obvious reasons, it had been his expectation that the Germans and the Soviets would knock each other off without significantly involving the United States. He even advocated financial aid to Germany in the event the Soviet Union overwhelmed Hitler's forces.

As president, Truman gradually evolved into a Cold War hawk, eventually taking a hard line against the Soviets. There were few serious dialogues and no summit talks between the superpowers between 1945 and 1955. During the first year of the Truman administration, however, his advisers patched together a crazy quilt of accommodation and concession, despite increasing Soviet aggression in Eastern Europe. Without sufficient erudition in foreign affairs, Truman allowed his advisers, primarily two liberal internationalists, George C. Marshall and Dean G. Acheson, to flesh out his foreign policy.

Truman did sign off on "the buck stops here" decisions as necessary. When, for example, the USSR began to bulldoze Greece and Turkey in March 1947 and Britain, severely weakened by World War II, seemed to forfeit her position as a global leader, Truman broke from traditional foreign policy and decided to fill the void by promising the besieged nations economic and military aid. He knew his proposal (now known as the Truman Doctrine) would be a tough sell. Largely unconvinced that the nation should foot another country's bills as well as ignorant of the swift decay in American–Soviet relations, Congress and the American people were under the mistaken impression that Stalin remained an ally.

In a meeting with a congressional delegation on February 27, 1947, instead of rationalizing aid to Greece and Turkey as the only humanitarian course, Under Secretary of State Acheson discreetly sketched out the need to curb Soviet expansionism.[8] Thus, pledging to pick up the tab for countries opposing communism, in essence he appended an anti-Communist proviso to Truman's policy of liberal internationalism.

Truman, savvy speechmaker that he was, saved the scary specter of communism as the finale to his famous March 12, 1947, address. With the unsavory prospect of totalitarianism hanging like a Damoclean sword, Truman broached his request for a $400 million aid package as well as a contingent of American military personnel to train Greek and Turkish armies. While some grumbles rumbled forth from both the pacifist left and isolationist right, most queued up behind the president.

To avert the lingering despair and economic destitution in countries devastated by World War II, and taking a lesson from the unsuccessful punitive postwar measures of World War I, the revolutionary Marshall Plan was announced in June 1947. The proposal, seemingly nothing less than splurging scarce economic resources in order to breathe life into an enemy, later proved a mix of creative charity and shrewd statesmanship. The measure extended $17 billion in loans and grants to rebuild the uncertain economies of Western Europe, including West Germany. Secretary of State George C. Marshall provided a sufficient number of strings to ensure that the Soviets, who were likewise eligible for aid, would categorically refuse any capitalist largesse. If the Russians had pinched their noses and offered their palms, undoubtedly a zealously anti-Communist Congress would have withdrawn support posthaste. While the Communists spurned the loot as yet another example of American imperialism, the European democracies cheered and submitted some $22.3 billion in recovery requests. Truman ended up signing the Foreign Act (implementing the Marshall Plan) on the heels of awe-inspiring congressional backing.

The Kremlin didn't take all this show of Western economic muscle sitting down. Stalin ratcheted up control over the international Communist movement and purged the national party of any leaders who might assert independence from Moscow. In February 1948, the democratic government of Czechoslovakia, after indicating interest in Marshall Plan money, was instantly transformed into a Soviet satellite by a Communist coup. Relations between America and the USSR ultimately reached rock bottom. Truman started hearing echoes of Adolph Hitler in Stalin's speeches. By May, Soviet authorities had blocked all Western land-access routes to Berlin, in the first of three crises involving the divided German city. Only the success of British and American air cargo supply planes reduced Cold War pressures between the superpowers—eventually the Soviets lifted the blockade on September 30, 1949. Although intended to cleave the three Western powers, it not only solidified resistance to the Soviets but also stepped up the establishment of West Germany.

To Truman, the Cold War posed no mere theoretical debate about philosophical systems; the Soviet Union presented a clear and present danger to the United States as well as the rest of the free world. To counter that threat, Truman was raring to rebuild American military strength. From the beginning of his presidency, he pushed for an organizational shake-up of the military. By signing the National Security Act on July 25, 1947, Truman was able to consolidate the constantly wrangling War and Navy Departments, throw the Central Intelligence Agency (CIA), the National Security Council (NSC), and the U.S. Air Force into his new Defense Department mix, and top off the hierarchy with a cabinet-level Secretary of Defense, who was obliged to command in consultation with the newly formed Joint Chiefs of Staff.

In April 1949, the Western powers launched a military agreement establishing the North Atlantic Treaty Organization (NATO), calculated to create a military counterbalance to Soviet forces in Europe. In the next few years, the Europeans would upgrade their defenses under the command of General Eisenhower. With the Marshall Plan and NATO, Western Europe acquired an economic and military wallop against communism. Yet, two shock waves hammered away at American morale in 1949: the Soviet Union got the bomb and China (except for Taiwan) fell to Communist Party forces under Mao Zedong.

American foreign policy under Truman was based on "containment," a term initially employed by the U.S. diplomat and Soviet expert George Kennan to argue that Soviet expansionism might be restrained by responding to Communist pushes wherever they occurred. The Cold War, reasoned Arthur M. Schlesinger Jr. in *The Vital Center,* was a clash between freedom and totalitarianism.[9] Rendered attractive to both doves and hawks by this moral underpinning, containment sustained anti-Communist resistance until, at last, the Soviet empire crumbled in August 1991. The United States also sought to cut short Communist gains via crushing military superiority, by forging new alliances in Asia (the Southeast Asia Treaty Organization) and in the Middle East (the Central Treaty Organization) and offering economic and military support to nations threatened by Communist molestation or subversion.

On January 31, 1950, President Truman asked his advisers to reexamine the country's objectives in the Cold War. National Security Council Document 68, which hit the president's desk on April 7, 1950, has been dubbed "the blueprint of the Cold War." Prepared by Paul Nitze, a forty-three-year-old hawk heading up the State Department's Policy Planning Staff, NSC-68 called for an unprecedented escalation of defense spending, despite budget constraints. The memo laid out an approach to Soviet relations that would guide American policy makers for decades. Phrased in language Nitze would later admit was "extreme," NSC-68 rendered compromise impossible and opened the door to undercover acts. Contending without equivocation that the objective of the Kremlin was to impose absolute authority over the world, the document predicted (without offering any substantive evidence) that the Soviets would attack in five years. NSC-68 also overturned George Kennan's original "strong point" strategy, which limited the containment of Soviet expansionism to a few essential industrial and military centers in Western Europe, the Middle East, and Japan. NCS-68 further pitted the fundamental purpose of the United

States "to assure the integrity and vitality of our free society, which is founded upon the dignity and worth of the individual," against the Communist intent "to retain and solidify their absolute power, first in the Soviet Union and second, in the areas now under their control."[10] The document further contended that the Soviets were working toward "the complete subversion or forcible destruction of the machinery of government and structure of society in the countries of the non-Soviet world and their replacement by an apparatus and structure subservient to and controlled by the Kremlin."[11] Undergirding NSC-68 was the assumption that every inch of land conceded to the Communists hacked away at America's credibility with the rest of the world. Later, it turned out that NSC-68 estimates of Soviet troop strength and missile-building capacity were exceedingly exaggerated. According to former secretary of state Henry Kissinger, the document "was based on a flawed premise that we were weaker than the Soviets and had to build from positions of strength. In fact, we were stronger than they were."[12] Yet, according to a March 3, 1950, Gallup poll, 40 percent (to 28 percent) of the respondents believed the United States was losing the Cold War to Russia.[13]

The North Korean invasion of South Korea on June 26, 1950, marked the launch of the Cold War. The initial humiliating reverses, the countless Chinese troops, and the failure of the Truman administration to bring the war to a triumphant close caused nagging qualms about the Soviet Communists on the domestic front to evolve into unqualified hostility (see McCarthyism). According to Joseph S. Nye, "the effect of the Korean War was like pouring gasoline onto a modest fire."[14]

While one might expect that Korea would have been the top issue in the November 1950 election campaign for Congress, in an August 25, 1950, Gallup poll asking what the most important campaign issue was, the highest percentage (17 percent) of respondents answered "Cold War," more than double the number (6 percent) concerned with the Korean Conflict.[15] Johns Hopkins psychiatrist Jerome D. Frank considered the Cold War a collective sickness infecting both superpowers. The United States was mired in a descending spiral of suspicion with the Soviets, Frank argued, that eventually became a self-fulfilling prophecy: "We act toward an enemy in such a way that he is moved to react toward us in a way we predicted and dreaded."[16]

In the wake of Korea, when twenty-one Americans refused repatriation, choosing instead to reside in the People's Republic of China, and hundreds came home accusing each other of collaborating with their captors, public officials turned to brainwashing as the only possible explanation. Army psychiatrist Major William E. Mayer reported that approximately one-third of all American POWs surrendered to Communist programming.[17] For fifty years, the media, general public, and scholars have not only heaped ignominy on former Korean War prisoners but have also mistakenly classified them as "brainwashed," subjecting them to reeducation sessions and constant badgering by FBI agents.

America had learned its lesson by Vietnam, however, and during basic training prepared her troops for possible Communist indoctrination. Doherty cites the testimony of Lieutenant Commander Richard Stratton, a POW who had not only seen *The Manchurian Candidate* but also so convincingly mastered Laurence Harvey's vacant stare and robotic body movement that the media, invited to witness his "defection," immediately picked up on the idea that he had not turned traitor but was merely spoofing the film. Subsequent newspaper articles and newsreel reports, detailing North Vietnamese attempts to force American POWs in front of the camera, blew away any propaganda potential for the Reds.

Born of McCarthyesque paranoia and crackpot Freudianism, the term "brainwashing" was coined by a CIA propaganda operator who worked undercover as a journalist. Edward Hunter, who was fond of asserting that the Soviets "brainwashed" prisoners the way Pavlov had conditioned dogs, borrowed the literal translation of the Chinese *xi nao* (meaning "thought reform") to describe supposed Communist mind control.[18] Brainwashing is usually understood as the process of intentionally subjecting individuals to physical and psychological privation in order to "adjust" their thoughts, attitudes, and actions. It differs from indoctrination, not only by including coercion (which undermines free will), but also in its radical intent to cleanse the mind totally of one set of ideas and replace them with another.

When the Chinese Communists came to power in 1949, they sought to bring dissidents around to their way of thinking by requiring the confession of past crimes and the acceptance of Communist beliefs. Americans had recently read not only about Hungarian Cardinal Josef Mindszenty, who responded like a zombie at his trial, but also about other Soviet defendants reciting far-fetched declarations of guilt in a dull, cliché-ridden monotone. Americans were already alarmed at the prospect of Communist mind manipulation and Hunter's new word, "brainwashing," seemed to make it real.

When the Chinese government first launched a propaganda offensive featuring confessions by captured U.S. pilots, Americans were told that the recorded statements were false and forced. By the end of the Korean War, however, officials announced that seven out of ten U.S. prisoners held in China had either "confessed" or signed petitions calling for an end to the American war effort in Asia.[19]

CIA Director Allen Dulles and the heads of the other American security agencies became almost frantic in their efforts to find out more about Soviet and Chinese brainwashing techniques. Under pressure for answers, Dulles turned to Dr. Harold Wolff, a world-famous neurologist partnered with Lawrence Hinkle of Cornell University Medical College in New York

City. The Wolff–Hinkle report, considered the definitive work on the subject, flatly denies that the Soviets and the Chinese exercised any out-of-the-ordinary mind control methods—no drugs, hypnosis, exotic hardware, or futuristic technology. Furthermore, the Communists used no psychiatrists or other behavioral scientists to devise interrogation techniques—their stock in trade was basic, albeit brutal, police methods.

Sleep and food deprivation, intense physical discomfort or torture, isolation from familiar surroundings, the constant fear of being summarily executed, and a prison routine requiring absolute obedience shoved most prisoners into a cooperative frame of mind. A marine colonel interviewed by Lewis H. Carlson confessed to trumped up charges of conducting germ warfare once his interrogators threatened to take the lives of his children—the Communists not only knew their names but also where they went to school.[20]

Positive reinforcement followed small steps toward reeducation and included more food, better living conditions, and the promise of eventual freedom. According to five physician POWs sent back to Fort Benning, Georgia, "It was made painfully clear to each prisoner that living conditions would be improved only so long as there was no resistance to the study program."[21]

Indoctrination also utilized social pressure to foster the acceptance of new ideas, including mutual criticism sessions that played on the generalized guilt feelings experienced by most human beings. The Communist captors attempted to sow dissension by placing ranking POWs in the most degrading jobs and encouraging enlisted men to not only call officers by their first names but regularly shun or disobey them.[22] Before they were segregated from the enlisted men, however, some officers ordered their men to cooperate with camp officials, particularly when they surmised such conduct would save lives. According to sociologist Albert D. Biderman, however, "it was not brainwashing that was the primary reason for collaboration but a sense of survival."[23]

American soldiers were ill equipped to deal with psychological warfare. Almost to a man, enlisted men as well as noncommissioned officers later admitted they were not sufficiently trained to defend their country's principles when the Communists denigrated the United States during propaganda sessions.[24] Captain Louis N. Rockwerk, in response to the question "What could we have done to better prepare our men for captivity?" declared, "Teach them Americanism. Teach them the values of our country."[25]

Published accounts of the POW controversy reached millions of readers but, according to Carlson, it was Hollywood, especially *The Manchurian Candidate*'s heavy-handed portrayal of brainwashing, that did the most to stigmatize Korean War POWs.[26] GIs had to compete with make-believe heroes who waged "incessant war on their dim-witted captors, escaped when possible, sabotaged and killed when necessary, and retained not only a faith in God but in the superiority of the American way of life."[27]

Korean detainees invented categories to describe levels of disloyalty— "Progressives" (sell-outs who grossly collaborated with the enemy), "Rats" (whose sole motivation was to help themselves at another's expense by spying or willingly spreading Communist propaganda), and "Reactionaries" (rigid adherents to the military code who preferred death before disclosure of anything more than name, rank, and serial number). Lloyd Pate, only sixteen years old when captured on January 1, 1951, estimated that only 5 percent of the prisoners were Progressives, 5 percent were Reactionaries, and 5 to 10 percent were Rat informers. To his mind, that left some 80 percent who were not much different from contemporary Americans— namely, unapologetically apolitical.[28] Unwilling to stick their necks out, American POWs merely tried to endure some pretty unendurable circumstances. Although a few were strong-armed into signing petitions or writing articles, most sat passively through Communist lectures and discussions.[29] Furthermore, prominent social scientists argued that Korean War prisoners differed little from detainees during earlier wars.[30] Cold War paranoia seemed to particularly single out Korean captives for censure.

In the one-hundred-mile Tiger Death March, the worst of the forced walks to internment camps, prisoners suffered a fatality rate of 65 percent. On Halloween 1950, 845 North Korean–held prisoners, including eighty noncombatants, left Manpo for Chunggang, near the Yalu River. Before moving north, the detainees had already suffered the effects of bitter cold and laughably insufficient shelter, filthy clothing, contaminated water, inadequate health care, lice and other pests, boredom and lethargy, debilitating diarrhea, uncertainty about the future and, above all, acute hunger. Father Philip Crosbie calculates the toll: "A few months ago they could have made the march with ease. Captivity had transformed their vigorous young bodies into feeble, tottering skeletons."[31]

Once debriefed, former POWs provided ample evidence that Communist mind control, if it worked at all, only worked as long as the prisoner was locked up. None of the twenty-one who refused repatriation remained in China and all eventually fell away from the Communist ideology. According to J. Robert Moskin, "Under the chaos and harsh realities of life in China, the effects of Communist brainwashing wore off. Most of the American defectors found the regimentation, the conformity, and the Puritanism unbearable."[32]

Akira Chikami, taken into custody in August 1951, questions, "Were we brainwashed because we had to sit there in a class listening to people talk about germ warfare, an unjust war, and all this kind of nonsense? That doesn't brainwash you."[33] Billy Joe Harris, who describes himself as a "tough, old, Missouri country boy," put it best, "I'm here to tell you when you come from a land of plenty and you go into a country like that where they can't even feed you enough to keep you alive, how in the world did they expect to cram Communism down your gullet?"[34]

Journalist Eugene Kinkead, the most notorious among Korean War POW critics, had to admit, "The prisoners, as far as Army psychiatrists have been able to discover, were not subjected to anything that could properly be called 'brainwashing.'"[35] Further, Communist indoctrinators could not hold sway over their subjects like the sinister puppet master depicted in *The Manchurian Candidate*. They could not create remote-control assassins. Nonetheless, brainwashing did create, according to army psychiatrist Major William E. Mayer, "a substantial loss of [self-]confidence."[36] What probably caused the most damage to morale, however, was the fact that there were no parades, no medals, and no "welcome home, soldier" greetings for Korean War detainees. According to Robert Jones, who suffered severe frostbite, the ravages of beriberi, an infection from battlefield wounds as well as what he considered the ultimate insult—being mistaken for dead and discarded under a pile of corpses—"those American [psychiatrists] weren't interested in a damn thing except did we collaborate."[37]

Amid Cold War hysteria following the end of the Korean conflict, a widely circulated intelligence report, never verified, asserted that the Russians had purchased the world's supply of LSD. Perhaps brainwashing might have lasted if enhanced by a powerful psychedelic; perhaps not. Paranoia-driven America, however, couldn't allow an LSD gap. Enter Sidney Gottlieb, the CIA master of mind control whose sensory deprivation, audio repetition, electroshock therapy, and hypnotic suggestion programs remain a zenith for rogue government agencies careening off kilter. According to his biographer, he "reflected the same polarities that defined the Cold War, the virtues and vices of extreme patriotism, the promise and perversion of science."[38]

Gottlieb oversaw a vast network of psychological and medical experiments conducted in hospitals, universities, research labs, prisons, and safe houses. So as not to "skew the results," most were carried out without the knowledge or permission of the subjects. In addition, any person who came within the purview of the CIA was fair game for testing. The most notorious Gottlieb project was MK-ULTRA, created in 1953 and intended, in Gottlieb's words, to explore the effects of LSD as well as "various techniques of behavior control in intelligence operations."[39] Ultimately, however, Gottlieb gave up on LSD, concluding that as "an intelligence tool" the drug was inherently undependable as well as morally abhorrent to those in American intelligence.[40]

SUMMARY OF THE PLOT

The Manchurian Candidate (1962) was rereleased theatrically in 1987, when for unspecified reasons Frank Sinatra decided to allow the film to be shown at the New York Film Festival. Sinatra supposedly withheld the film from distribution for almost a quarter-century to honor John F. Kennedy's memory.[41] Conjecture has it that there are obvious parallels between Raymond Shaw (Laurence Harvey) and Lee Harvey Oswald— notably as brainwashed ex-soldiers supposedly controlled by the Soviets and employing sniper rifles as the weapon of choice. In addition, before murdering John F. Kennedy, Lee Harvey Oswald had allegedly watched *Suddenly* (1954), a thriller starring Sinatra as the ringleader of a gang hired to assassinate the president. After it was turned down by all the major studios, United Artists picked up *The Manchurian Candidate* after Sinatra, reassured that President Kennedy harbored no objections, agreed to play the lead.[42]

The Manchurian Candidate, based on the 1959 Richard Condon bestseller, begins with veteran army major Bennett Marco (Frank Sinatra) being haunted by recurring nightmares following his Korean War stint.[43] Raymond Shaw (Laurence Harvey) likewise returns from Korea. He has been awarded the Congressional Medal of Honor but Marco, who was Shaw's commanding officer, as well as other members of the platoon can't articulate just what Shaw did to warrant the country's highest military honor. Shaw distances himself from his overly protective mother (Angela Lansbury) and McCarthyesque stepfather Senator John Iselin (James Gregory) and embarks on a journalistic career.[44] When his "American control" (his own mother, a highly placed Communist agent) suggests he play a game of solitaire, a posthypnotic suggestion triggered by the queen of diamonds kicks off his programming and he murders, without mercy or memory, his boss Holborn Gaines (Lloyd Corrigan), a liberal Republican with a weakness for women's nightwear. Next on the hit list are Shaw's new bride Jocie (Leslie Parrish) and her Adlai Stevenson–like father, Senator Thomas Jordan (John McGiver). Marco suspects that not only was his unit brainwashed during their tour of duty, but also that the highly decorated Sergeant Shaw has been transformed into a guiltless political assassin. Marco, bolstered by the love of a "good woman," Rosie (Janet Leigh), pieces together the clues and ascertains the remote-control assassin's trigger, his next target, and the American traitors behind a sinister Communist plot to put a Red in the White House.

HAWKISM IN *THE MANCHURIAN CANDIDATE*

Once war hero John F. Kennedy was elected to the presidency, he yearned to lead, to invigorate a nation that had been lulled into languor during the Eisenhower years. The ringing tone of his inaugural announced, "let every nation know, whether it wishes us well or ill, that we shall pay any price, bear any burden, meet any hardship, support any friend, oppose any foe to assure the survival and the success of liberty."[45]

The most distinctive feature of JFK's foreign policy, as outlined by Walt Rostow, was its unapologetic emphasis on the Third World.[46] JFK agonized that "those people in the huts and villages" would prove inherently vulnerable to Communist subversion.[47] He argued, "I know full well that every time a country, regardless of how far away it may be from our own borders . . . passes behind the Iron Curtain, the security of the United States is thereby endangered."[48] While JFK might have preferred the Peace Corps, Food for Peace, the Agency for International Development, and the Alliance for Progress to military intervention, he realized that Communist insurgencies might prove so unyielding they would require missiles instead of meals. During the 1960 campaign, Kennedy declared, "Washington is the capital of the free world, [and] the president must be its leader."[49]

With both sides stockpiling nuclear weapons, ensuing Soviet–American confrontations, which had replaced any attempt at coexistence, were rendered all the more chancy. The Berlin Wall evolved from a temporary partition to a permanent barrier. The level of risk underscored by the Berlin crisis of 1961 and by the Cuban Missile Crisis of 1962 failed to shake the hawk-in-chief's resolve. JFK simply balked at yielding to Soviet intimidation, even if it brought the world closer than it had ever been to nuclear conflagration. In fact, a post–Cuban Missile Crisis Khrushchev was so struck with JFK's aggressiveness that he reported to the Supreme Soviet in December 1962, "If [the United States] is a 'paper tiger' . . . those who say this know that this 'paper tiger' has atomic teeth."[50]

As a Cold War hawk, Kennedy went on to pursue a diplomacy that, in its keenness to tackle all Communist challenges to American power, exceeded the militancy of former presidents. When Premier Khrushchev announced the Soviet intention to support "wars of national liberation" against non-Communist regimes around the world, Kennedy responded by reshaping American armed forces and intelligence policies to create a "flexible response" to counter Communist revolt. Not wanting to show any sign of weakness to the Soviets, in the spring of 1961 Kennedy approved a CIA plan dispatching a group of Cuban émigrés (some of whom would later be linked to the Watergate break-in) to storm the Cuban coastline, charge into the mountains, and inspire a revolt of indigenous anti-Castro forces—the miserable fiasco now known as "the Bay of Pigs."

Word of the proposed American-backed coup, however, had circulated for months throughout Central America, thus eliminating the requisite element of surprise. Castro's modest air force simply met the invaders at the beach and cleared them away. Kennedy took four days to admit to the American people what the world already knew—the Bay of Pigs was an American operation, conducted in secrecy and without benefit of congressional sanction. Sensing the young American president was prone to blunder, Soviet leader Nikita Khrushchev embarked upon a series of chal-

lenges that would eventually include building the Berlin Wall, testing nuclear devices three thousand times more powerful than the Hiroshima
bomb, and in an attempt to discourage another American invasion, arm-
ing Cuba with nuclear-tipped missiles aimed directly at the United States.
Vietnam would provide an additional test of Kennedy's skill at international affairs. By November 1963, JFK had substantially augmented the
American military commitment to South Vietnam. According to William
O'Neill, "partly it seems, [Kennedy] enlarged the American presence to
impress Premier Khrushchev with his resolution."[51]

By June 1962, only 28 percent of those polled by Gallup believed that
the West was ahead of Russia in the Cold War.[52] Five months later, about
the time *The Manchurian Candidate* was released, Gallup reported that of
all the problems facing the country, the Cuban situation (37 percent) filled
American citizens with the most trepidation.[53] By mid-October, the
United States gathered conclusive proof that Soviet offensive missiles
were being deployed in Cuba. This "material change in the balance of
power" was unquestionably intolerable to President Kennedy, but he
would carefully weigh his options as he moved to manipulate
Khrushchev into dismantling his weapons. The Joint Chiefs of Staff encouraged an air strike. Others, including the president's brother, Attorney
General Robert F. Kennedy, not only opposed the idea of a surprise attack
"reminiscent of Pearl Harbor" but also feared overkill might make Fidel
Castro a martyr throughout Latin America.

After nearly two weeks of intense debate, President Kennedy opted for
a blockade ("quarantine") to be lifted once Soviet missiles were carted
away. He also warned that a Cuban assault would be countered by a strike
on the Soviet Union. American intercontinental ballistic missiles at silos
situated across the West were prepared for delivery. Fleets of nuclear-
armed *Polaris* submarines approached Soviet waters. The air force was put
on DEFCON 2, the highest alert ordered during the post–World War II era.
Diplomatic messages shuttled back and forth between Kennedy and
Khrushchev. Pope John volunteered as peacemaker. Soviet ships inched
toward the five-hundred-mile arc formed by sixteen navy destroyers and
three cruisers to prevent access to the east coast of Cuba. While the world
sat dumbstruck by the impending menace of nuclear holocaust, the grip-
pingly tense, thirteen-day face-off concluded with Khrushchev backing
down. When word reached Kennedy and his advisers, Dean Rusk exclaimed, "We're eyeball to eyeball, and I think the other fellow just
blinked."[54] Humanity had hung in the balance. The Soviet Union and the
United States had edged so close to the nuclear brink that they jolted each
other into an unprecedented phase of cooperation. Into this agonizingly
anxious atmosphere, *The Manchurian Candidate* was released.

While much McCarthy-bashing goes on in the movie, make no mistake,
the Commies are the bona fide bad guys and *The Manchurian Candidate* is

a hawk film. Even though red-baiters are lampooned as hypocritical id-
iots (unforgiving Hollywood can't seem to help itself in this regard), it is
the savvy Communists, who have seemingly mastered mind control, who
are actually able to ingratiate themselves into the hallway just outside the
Oval Office. Both Richard Condon and George Axelrod were earnestly
persuaded not only that the Red Menace was real, but also that the Russians and the Chinese were capable of outfoxing American security. They
believed it was time to be very, very scared.

   The Manchurian Candidate took on post-Korean America's nastiest com-
munal fears and painted a scenario direr than shrinks who harassed former Korean POWs faced in their worst nightmares. Take the night maneuver that introduces the film: Shaw's platoon is advised by Chunjin
(Henry Silva), the traitorous local interpreter, to walk in single file—a tac-
tically indefensible strategy—yet like a dim-witted flock of sheep, they
comply.[55] Consequently, they are ambushed, knocked unconscious, and
transported via helicopter into Manchuria, where Raymond is turned into
a guilt-free assassin. Yen Lo exhibits Raymond's dispassionate killing capacity by instructing Shaw to execute Ed Mavole (Richard La Pore) with
a white scarf. The audience is horrified as Major Marco yawns and the rest
of the men sit stupidly and stare. If that isn't enough, the presentation
continues as Lo calmly directs Shaw to point his pistol toward the smiling
face of the platoon's favorite, Bobby Lembeck (Tom Lowell). The men are
subsequently conditioned to remember Shaw as "the bravest, kindest,
warmest, most wonderful human being" ever known.

   Shaw's editor, Holborn Gaines, is dispatched in yet another "demonstration." When Senator Thomas Jordan boldly announces his plans to
block Iselin's nomination as vice president, Jordan and daughter Jocie are
targeted, but the most significant bull's-eye is yet to come: "You are to
shoot the Presidential nominee through the head," instructs Mother.
"And Johnny [Iselin, her husband and co-conspirator] will rise gallantly
to his feet and lift Ben Arthur's body in his arms, stand in front of the microphones and begin to speak. The speech is short, but it's the most rousing speech I've ever read. It's been worked on here and in Russia on and
off for over eight years. I shall force someone to take the body away from
him. And Johnny will leave those microphones and those cameras with
blood all over him, fighting off anyone who tries to help him, defending
America even if it means his own death, rallying a nation of television-
viewers into hysteria to sweep us up into the White House."

   In addition, only shifty Soviets were capable of co-opting one of America's most cherished traditions, the Congressional Medal of Honor, to politically position an assassin. According to Condon, "A theater commander who later became President and a President who had formerly
been an artillery captain both said that they would rather have the right
to wear the Medal of Honor than be President of the United States."[56]

Yet, while the Communist threat is treated seriously for the most part, at times the movie also delivers up some anti-Communist cant with chuckles. Screenwriter George Axelrod, who admits to being a conservative, administers a couple of healthy pokes at the Reds' attraction to capitalism when he has Yen Lo complain that his wife has burdened him with an appallingly long Macy's shopping list. Zilkov (Albert Paullson) boasts that the rest home (where Raymond's links are being retested) is presently operating in the black.

According to Peter Roffman and Jim Purdy, America "is so free and open that people have become too trusting, taking everyone, including the Communists, at their word."[57] The film teaches that, like the pod people in *Invasion of the Body Snatchers*, Commies can disguise themselves as anyone—from a capable houseboy to a hyperpatriotic senator's wife.

THE FIRST PSYCHOPOLITICAL THRILLER

The Manchurian Candidate shifted Hollywood's idea of what mass market film audiences would accept in terms of style and subject matter.[58] By punctuating Condon's signature sneer with pop psychology paranoia images, Frankenheimer conjures up not only the first psychopolitical thriller but also a meritorious merger of surrealistic symbolism and '50s reality. Within a year of the film's release, the country would begin to implode with assassinations, race riots, and antiwar demonstrations. As Janet Maslin allowed, "There was so much that we had the good luck not to know in 1962. . . . [A] lone assassin, perhaps under the influence of a foreign government, can indeed shoot an American political leader."[59]

With respect to the psychological aspect of the psychopolitical thriller, Bosley Crowther in his *New York Times* review pointed out, "We are asked to believe that, in three days, a fellow could be brainwashed to the point that two years later, he would still be dutifully submissive to his brainwashers' spell."[60] Yet, according to critic Nora Sayre, fears aren't always based on facts.[61]

The Manchurian Candidate brand of mind control goes far beyond what the Communists were actually doing during Korea. In fact, the movie's Yen Lo more closely resembles the CIA's Sidney Gottlieb than the bullies who tried to brainwash American POWs. Supposedly building on the work of Pavlov, Lo seeks to implant an overriding motive, namely, total submission to the operator, in the subject's mind. In addition, the subject is led to believe he is playing a game or acting a part. "The first thing a human being is loyal to," observes Yen Lo, "is his own conditioned nervous system."[62] Lo further realizes he will have to set up some sort of remote-control device that will allow a secondary or even tertiary party to direct behavior.

The modern practice of hypnosis began with Franz Mesmer, an eighteenth-century Viennese physician who experimented with the power of suggestion. Accepted as a valid medical therapeutic technique and recognized by the American Medical Association, hypnosis is not sleep but heightened concentration that focuses a person's attention on a particular behavior—say, to stop smoking. Posthypnotic suggestions allow the subject to be reminded of that goal by an object in the environment. For example, a posthypnotic suggestion can condition the subject to be nauseated by cigarette smoke. If the posthypnotic suggestion is not enforced, it eventually wears off.

As Yen Lo lauds the mind-bending power of hypnotic suggestion, he allows, "I am sure you've all heard the old wives' tale that no hypnotized subject may be forced to do that which is repellent to his moral nature, whatever that may be. Nonsense, of course." Despite the fictional Yen Lo's boast, Yvonne Rill contends that hypnosis cannot cause someone to act against his or her own will, work as a truth serum, or create permanent amnesia.[63] Ordinary hypnotic suggestions never directly order subjects to do anything—instead they are phrased passively, tacitly inviting the subject to participate in a make-believe role.

Lo initially uses powerful drugs to brainwash Raymond Shaw, causing his subject to descend into "deep unconscious." During the eleven-hour procedure, Lo implants and tests an elaborate network of conditioned links. A second deep unconscious descent, induced by light this time, lasts almost eight hours. During that time, Lo inserts additional links—first, those that will motivate individual assignments and, second, an amnesia mechanism that will cause assignments to be forgotten by the conscious mind and that precludes Shaw from consciously weighing the rightness or wrongness of his behavior.

Shaw is the ideal remote-control killer candidate. A crack shot since childhood, Shaw is not merely capable of killing an enemy solider—he already had. There is no initial aversion to homicide. "A marvelous outlet for his aggressions," observes Lo. Since Lo's brand of conditioning renders the subject incapable of remembering what he has been told to do, the morality issue is moot. Deep unconscious conditioning, which has yet to be perfected in the real world, permits Lo to fabricate the perfect assassin—an individual who murders without guilt, without fear of capture, and without the possibility of confessing to the authorities. As Lo instructs, "Raymond will remain an outwardly normal, productive, sober, and respected member of the community. And I should say, if properly used, entirely police-proof. His brain has not only been washed, as they say, it's been dry-cleaned."

The rub, of course, is that not all of the members of the Raymond's unit are as thoroughly conditioned as he is. Sigmund Freud wrote, "There are dreams as distinct as actual experiences, so distinct that for some time after waking we do not realize that they were dreams at all."[64] *The Manchurian Candidate* posits the reverse. The experiences of Major Bennett Marco and Corporal Al Melvin are as distinct as actual dreams, so distinct that for some time after sleeping they do not realize that they were experiences at all. A sweating, heart-pounding Marco invariably awakens from frightmares in which Ed Mavole is strangled by Shaw. Melvin's fitful slumber dissolves into the second garden party sequence, in which Raymond is coolly directed to shoot "mascot" Bobby Lembeck "through the forehead." The confusion between reality and dream world unravels when Marco rings the bell at Raymond Shaw's apartment door and instantly recognizes Chunjin as the translator who led the platoon into an ambush.

Armed with a forced deck, Marco visits Shaw in a hotel room overlooking Madison Square Garden.[65] He poses the activating question, "How about passing the time by playing a little solitaire?" With the first red queen, Marco becomes Shaw's new controller. He now possesses the ability to render Yen Lo's amnesia mechanism inoperative and unlock the truth. He finds out the unit was captured by a Russian Airborne Unit and flown to a town called Tomwa. For the next three days, they were brainwashed by a team from the Pavlov Institute in Moscow. Raymond, without any emotion whatsoever, recounts the garden party at which "I strangled Ed Mavole and shot Bobby Lembeck." After Marco directs Shaw to deal out a second red queen, Raymond, almost lethargic, reports, "Then I killed Mr. Gaines. It was just a test. That business about jumping in the lake [at Jilly's]—it really did happen. It was an accident. Something somebody said in the bar accidentally triggered it." Another queen reveals the murder of Senator Jordan. Mercifully, Marco instructs Shaw to forget everything that happened with his wife and father-in-law before he poses the big question, namely, "what have they built you to do?" Shaw does not know. At that, Marco fans a fistful of red Queens in front of Shaw's face, peeks out in a space between the cards, and commands: "Fifty-two red queens and me are telling you . . . it's over."

When Yen Lo selects the queen of diamonds to trigger Raymond's programming, he makes an inspired choice. Not only are playing cards readily available but also, according to Lo, "they offer clear, colorful symbols that, in ancient, monarchical terms, contain the suggestion of supreme authority."[66] The black army intelligence psychiatrist (Joe Adams) is able to deduce that the solitaire game serves "as some kind of trigger mechanism" and advises Marco to concentrate on the face cards "because of their symbolic identification with human beings."[67] Suddenly, Marco flashes back to Manchuria: "I can see that cat standin' there smiling like Fu Manchu" and saying "The queen of diamonds is reminiscent in many ways of Raymond's dearly loved and hated mother and is the second key to clear the mechanism for any other assignment." While Raymond may be in love with Jocie, he didn't have the chutzpah to oppose his mother's wishes as an adolescent. The fact that Jocie shows up at the masquerade ball dressed in a playing-card costume seems to propel him toward the altar at warp speed.[68] Her gigantic queen of diamonds literally trumps his mother's regulation-size playing card.

Fortune-tellers, who claim to draw on a combined knowledge of astrology, numerology, and certain other occult wisdom, tell us that those whose birth dates are assigned the queen of diamonds frequently fret over finances, although they can't help overindulging expensive tastes.[69] They can be ruthless when crossed and tend to be control freaks. Headstrong and proud, those born under the queen of diamonds share a fear of abandonment, are willing to grab power without hesitation, and often marry more than once.[70] These characteristics fit Eleanor Shaw Iselin like a custom-made leather glove. Setting her sights on the Oval Office, her wildly extravagant fancy dress ball, her legendary temper, her ice-queen demeanor,[71] and her domination of men reflect the typical queen of diamonds profile. While the movie doesn't make obvious Eleanor's incestuous relationship with her son (actually a recycling of her sexual attachment to her father), the audience is shocked when she kisses Raymond sensuously on the mouth.[72] Further, patriotism is linked to the queen of diamonds as the credits roll over a composite "stars-and-stripes" female face card.

With respect to the political aspect of the psychopolitical thriller, a *Time* critic alleged that Richard Condon had grabbed the political parties "by their tails and swung them around his head like a couple of dead cats."[73] Actually, Johnny Iselin, Holborn Gaines, and Senator Thomas Jordan are all Republicans—although Condon usually juxtaposes the right-wing Iselin against the more liberal Gaines and Jordan to introduce conflict. According to Hal Hinson of the *Washington Post*, "In truth, the film, which takes off on McCarthyism and the anti-Communist hysteria of the '50s, is an exceedingly loopy satire of the entire American political circus and could be viewed as offensive to the sensitive-souled in either camp."[74] Indeed, the film was picketed in Orange County, California, for being pro-Communist, while Paris protestors denounced it as right-wing propaganda. The British Film Institute dubbed *The Manchurian Candidate* both the American and un-American film of the year.[75] Margot Henricksen concludes that in "the end the film collapsed all distinction between anticommunism and communism: both systems emerged as examples of political repression."[76] Andrew Sarris contended that the plot was "particularly resourceful in treating the 'Communist Menace' as both a red herring and a man-eating shark."[77]

When both the American Legion and the Communist Party lodged protests, Frankenheimer admitted to encouraging both.[78] In taking aim at the political right and left, *The Manchurian Candidate* designates them as treacherous mirror-image twins. Take the scene in which a seemingly somnambulistic Raymond enters the Jordan household and stumbles upon the senator fixing a midnight snack. Shaw calmly pulls out a revolver equipped with silencer (to better silence the opposition, my dear) and conceals the weapon at his side until the senator removes a carton of milk from the refrigerator. As Shaw fires, what Frankenheimer means to be the liberal "milk of human kindness" flows in a single stream from a bullet traversing the container. Now contrast that sequence with Senator Iselin's complaint that he can't keep the number of Communists in the Defense Department straight. Mrs. Iselin softens and inquires, "Would it really make it easier for you if we settled on just one number?" Inspired by the tomato ketchup with which her husband is dousing his steak, she comes up with 57—the exact number of pickle varieties produced by Heinz & Co. Yet, given the paranoid tenure of the time, the film is generally interpreted as seconding the hawkish motion to pay any price, bear any burden, meet any hardship, support any friend, and oppose any foe to assure the survival and the success of liberty.

No one questions this film's credentials as a thriller—the viewer is jolted from one scene to another as if trapped on a speeding train undergoing relentless rerouting. Magill notes "The tactic of keeping the audience in the dark as to whether Raymond's mind has been 'cleared' generates almost unbearable suspense."[79] Condon, in Roderick MacLeish's estimation, "is one of the living masters of [the thriller] genre."[80] According to *Variety*, "the picture moves forward with a constantly increasing tension and momentum which never allow for audience second-guessing of the macabre plot twists or coincidences."[81]

ANATOMY OF AN ASSASSIN

Had it not been for Jocasta, Oedipus would have languished in obscurity instead of becoming the tragic hero of Greek mythology and the namesake of Freud's most infamous complex. None of the discoveries of psychoanalytical research has evoked such furious opposition as Freud's contention that males are psychologically destined to direct their first sexual impulses toward their mothers. Given the clout of the production code, the film version of *The Manchurian Candidate* could only hint at a sexual relationship between Raymond and his mother. Frankenheimer accomplishes this by having Mommy Dearest grasp her son's face with perfectly manicured fingers while smothering his visage in kisses. She ends with a warm, seductive smooch on the lips. According to the book, however, Raymond's mother takes him to her bed only once and he is definitely *under orders*. She purrs "When you smile, Raymond dearest, for that instant I am a little girl again, and the miracle of love [with Daddy] begins all over again."[82] It seems the only man Raymond's mother ever loved was her own father and their relationship ended only because of his demise.

Neither the poets nor philosophers of ancient Greece suffered any difficulty in distinguishing between voluntary and involuntary behavior. The reason that *Oedipus Rex* moves the reader is because the protagonist is definitely not a free agent—he is a victim of fate. The audience would have no sympathy for, and therefore no identification with, a character who chooses to violate the major taboos (patricide and incest) promulgated by Greek society. Thus, Sophocles has no choice but to rule out any *conscious* desire by Oedipus for his mother. In the play, Jocasta speaks of desires playing out in dreams, not mindful enactment.[83] According to Freudian scholar Harold Bloom, not only does Oedipus lack a tragic flaw, he doesn't suffer from "that masterpiece of ambivalence—Freud's Oedipal complex."[84]

Likewise, Raymond holds no incestuous feelings for his mother. In fact, he rarely speaks of his mother with anything but contempt.[85] When Mrs. Iselin deftly turns a hero's welcome for her son into a photo op for her husband, Raymond makes no move to hide his disgust. To his mind, she has sullied the Congressional Medal of Honor—the only prize "that brings generals to their feet." Over champagne, while a record player sings out "The Twelve Days of Christmas," Shaw painstakingly details a miserable childhood under the domination of his ice queen mum. "My mother, Ben, is a terrible woman. . . . [A]fter what she did to Jocie and me [breaking up the young couple], that's when I began to hate her." Mrs. Iselin finds Raymond's romantic relationship with "that Communist tart" more than a tad threatening. To compel her son to write a "Dear Jane" letter (confessing trumped-up homosexuality) she leans heavily on maternal guilt, thinly disguised as anti-Communist ideological doctrine.

According to Freud, in addition to incestuous feelings toward the mother, the Oedipal complex includes hostility toward the male parent. On the contrary, Shaw adored his biological father. When Daddy committed suicide as a result of losing his wife to his law partner (Johnny Iselin), Raymond was inconsolable.[86]

During the Cold War, America turned to psychology to answer the seemingly unanswerable questions—especially what to do about the nameless dread that deluged the national unconscious. From 1940 to 1964, America saw a sixfold increase in the number of practicing shrinks.[87] Psychoanalysts became pop culture heroes who worked mind-blowing wonders with damaged personalities. The isolated '50s mom became increasingly dependent on experts like Dr. Benjamin Spock, who tossed around Freudian terms such as "ego," "oral gratification," and "repression," while television and novels represented psychotherapists as astute and compassionate. By the mid-'60s, however, the analyst's couch became the butt of bad jokes and the media started characterizing psychologists as crazier than their patients. In *The Manchurian Candidate*, Jocie initially speculates that her father's obsession with slithering reptiles might be totally Freudian but eventually concludes, with apologies to Sigmund, that sometimes a snake is just a snake.

Psychoanalytic therapy, especially in light of the huge advances in pharmacology and the behavioral sciences, simply did not live up to its grandiose claims. Mothers tossed baby care books, filled with permissive advice about weaning, thumb-sucking, masturbation, and toilet training, on the trash heap. Yet, something was definitely wrong with the young men in America. Psychologists quickly pointed the finger at American mothers, who were saddled with the blame for everything from juvenile delinquency to homosexuality. In fact, a U.S. Army study actually concluded that American Korean War prisoners didn't stack up to captives from Great Britain and Turkey due to "some failure in childhood and adolescent training—a new softness."[88] Major William E. Mayer laid the blame for America's poor showing at the feet of "domineering mothers."[89] In 1942, Philip Wylie, the author of *Generations of Vipers*, zeroed in on "momism" as the reason American males were deficient in manliness. Wylie not only accused good old Mom of retarding the logical development of her sons, but also concluded that overindulgent American mothers simply weren't up to the job.[90] Edward Strecker echoed Wylie's assumptions in *Their Mother's Sons*.[91]

More germane to a discussion of *The Manchurian Candidate*, however, is the notion that Oedipus, like Raymond Shaw, was driven not only to discover the truth, but also to accept full responsibility for his actions at whatever cost. Shaken by the abominable crimes they have unwittingly committed, both Oedipus and Shaw try to right wrongs resulting from the irreversible chain of events their respective mothers have set in motion. Oedipus sees no other course but to gouge out his eyes. Accompanied by his faithful daughter Antigone, he flees the city, wandering as a blind beggar throughout Greece until death releases him. Whether resulting from Marco's deprogramming effort or the shock of personal realization, Shaw finally wrests power away from his American control. Instead of shooting Benjamin K. Arthur as Eleanor has instructed, he captures his stepfather's forehead in his crosshairs and we see Iselin slump to the floor. Efficiently reloading the rifle, he lines up Mother, and we see her collapse like a rag doll. He pauses briefly to don the Congressional Medal of Honor and then turns the weapon on himself.

Not just anyone could serve as the Communist-manufactured gun. Choosing an individual adept at killing, with or without a weapon, is a given. "Raymond," according to Condon, "had made tech sergeant because he was a bleakly good soldier and because he was the greatest natural marksman in the division."[92] The assassin would also have to forge vital political connections. Raymond's mother is known as a dominant wheeler-dealer in the nation's capital. Also, as a distinguished journalist and stepson of a U.S. senator, Shaw would be welcome not only anywhere in Washington, D.C., but also, more important, in the inner sanctum of either major political party.

As to requisite psychological characteristics, it is highly desirable for the assassin to lack emotion—feelings just might interfere with the wiring Lo installs in Shaw's subconscious. As Marco describes Shaw in the book, "His fingernails gleamed. His shoe tips glowed. His color shone. His teeth sparkled. The only fault with the lighting circuit was behind his eyes."[93] The inability to express passion, however, doesn't make for a very likable individual. In the precredits sequence, Sergeant Shaw, pausing beneath a portrait of General Douglas MacArthur, reins in his platoon's late night partying in a Korean brothel.[94] The men, dripping with disdain, observe: "It's just our Raymond. Our loveable Sgt. Shaw."

Further, highly intelligent individuals make good hypnosis subjects because of their inherent ability to concentrate without distraction. Not only is Shaw smart, he is also highly suggestible, making him a perfect prospect for mind control. During the garden party demonstration, when asked whom he dislikes the least, Raymond chooses Marco. "Look how he is drawn to authority," gushes Lo. In addition, the Communist has no trouble establishing the deep conscious conditioning connections necessary for total manipulation after Shaw has spent years being "brainwashed" by his own mother. Finally, it is no accident that Mrs. Iselin is chosen as his American control. Lo needs an individual who will have no trouble issuing orders and who will not draw unwarranted attention when she makes periodic visits to Shaw.

Shaw is also easily manipulated because he is seething with resentment. Raymond's favorite story, especially when under the influence of alcohol, involves the betrayal and humiliation of his father by his monster of a mother. Hooking into resentment, according to Yen Lo, is the key to creating the perfect killer.[95] In the movie, the African American psychologist observes: "the human fish swim . . . [and] develop psychic injuries as they collide with one another. Most mortal of all are the wounds gotten from the parent fish."

What keeps Raymond from experiencing the same nightmares experienced by Marco and Melvin? Surely, reality must also have slipped into his dreams at some point. Even if it did, however, the man who couldn't stand to be touched simply wouldn't admit that anybody or anything had crawled inside his head. It's worth noting that Oedipus gouges out his eyes in order to cut himself off from all contact with humanity. According to Greek scholar E. R. Dodds, "if he could choke the channels of his other senses, he would do so."[96]

Finally, only those who have something to lose are able to experience fear. According to Marco, Shaw "was a marooned balloonist, supported by nothing visible, looking down on everybody and everything, but yearning to be seen so that, at least, he could be given some credit for an otherwise profitless ascension."[97]

Raymond's marriage to Jocie does radicalize him in that regard. Marco doesn't even recognize the blissful, jovial, lovable Raymond who has taken to making jokes.[98] When Mrs. Iselin orders Raymond to kill Thomas Jordan, the elimination of Jocie (which he is programmed to do because she is a potential witness) is an added bonus—the red queen would have to suffer no more competition.

CONDON'S ALTER EGO: MAJOR MARCO

As the son of an attorney, Richard Condon might have been the richest kid on his block, but with D's and F's on his De Witt Clinton High School report cards, no college recruiter ever came to call. Like Major Bennett Marco, however, Condon became a voracious reader. When the audience is first introduced to Marco, in fact, the camera pans from his fruit salad–decorated army uniform to a twin bed snowed under by hefty volumes. As the Colonel (Douglas Henderson) enters Marco's bachelor digs, he is so staggered, he stammers, "My God, where did you get all the books?" While Marco admits that the towers of tomes make for "great insulation against enemy attack," the truth is, like Condon, Marco can't help indulge a catholicity of interests and is proud to admit there isn't a best-seller in the stack.

Condon called New York home for forty-two years. He grew up across the East River from Manhattan in Washington Heights—a melting pot for Germans, Italians, and Irish. There the prickly realist was able to observe political corruption at work, but from a proper distance. His adolescence coincided with the New Deal and Tammany Hall Democrats. As a fifteen-year-old, he was paid to herd drunks out of Third Avenue saloons and into the polling booths. Like Joseph Heller, William Burroughs, Norman Mailer, Thomas Berger, Ken Kesey, and Thomas Pynchon, Condon wrote about a world in which politics had run amok. *Extrapolation* contributor Joe Sanders once observed: "In Condon's novels, politics is a device by which a few clever people manipulate many others to gain their selfish ends."[99]

Most of the material for Condon's blend of "mythologized fact" or "fiction of information" is colored by a hawkish worldview. Condon is the literary version of the psychiatrist in the *New Yorker* cartoon who informs his client, "I'm afraid you're not paranoid. People really are out to get you." According to Condon's Law, when you don't know the whole truth, the worst you can imagine is bound to be close. A critic for the *New York Review of Books* contended that Condon "isn't an analyst but an exploiter of our need to believe the worst."[100]

Near the end of this life, Condon observed that the film version of *The Manchurian Candidate* was the sweetest screen translation ever made of one of his books. The man who always took communism seriously was bowled over that the United Artists film adhered so closely to his cautionary tale.[101] The major difference between the book and the film primarily resulted from moral restrictions spelled out by Hollywood's Hays office. In the best-seller, the hawkish Marco actually orders Shaw to assassinate his parents and Raymond's mother, robed in red Chinese (communist) silk sheath, seduces Shaw while he's under a queen of diamonds trance. However, more important to Condon was the preservation of his message, namely, that mass manipulation, under various guises, is real and should scare the hell out of everybody. As a twenty-year movie publicist for Walt Disney, Twentieth Century–Fox, Paramount, and United Artists, Condon considered himself an expert propagandist, but he feared the "Countless murders [that] have been committed while under the continuing hypnosis of patriotism, religion, exclusionary societies, and self-righteous tribal innuendo."[102]

Yet, Condon had his warm and fuzzy moments. While working as a copywriter for an advertising agency, he met a model named Evelyn Hunt, whom he married in 1938. She was not only a "Powers Girl" who helped him enter the movie business, but also made him the grateful beneficiary of her devotion.[103] In *The Manchurian Candidate*, Condon writes, "There is an immutable phrase at large in the languages of the world that places fabulous ransom on every word in it: 'The love of a good woman.' The six words shine neither with sentiment nor sentimentality. They are truth; a light of its own; unchanging."[104] Marco declares Eugenie Rose Cheyney (Janet Leigh), who Condon modeled after his own wife, such a woman. Their "cute meet" encounter on a Washington-to-New York train has been described by *Variety* as "one of the great love scenes since [Humphrey] Bogart and [Lauren] Bacall first tossed non-sequiturs at one another in *To Have and Have Not*."[105] Filmed in a prolonged two-shot, the couple's clever conversation spans local geography, the meaning of names, and cryptic references to all matters Arab. The exchange ends with the instantaneously smitten Rosie attempting to "brainwash" Marco with her address and phone number.[106] At first, the audience might well wonder if the whole tête-à-tête is some sort of cryptic code between a mind-controlled Marco and his American operative, but they quickly realize that Condon is merely reporting a romantic incident between two incredibly well-read and witty intellectuals.

THE LAST RESORT OF THE SCOUNDREL

According to Dr. Samuel Johnson, patriotism is the last resort of the scoundrel. Patriotism is likewise the last resort of the parodist—that is, if you can handle the ham-handed spoofing in *The Manchurian Candidate.* At the time Condon penned his best-seller, Senator Joseph McCarthy met his maker and left behind a nasty gash on the body politic. Condon points out, "It's the villains that make good literature, because they're the only ones in the story who know what they want."[107] McCarthy, like Johnny Iselin, always knew what he wanted—he just overreached his grasp.

When Senator Jordan informs Mrs. Iselin he will fight her efforts to position her husband in the vice-presidential spot in the primary, he adds, "I think if Iselin were a Soviet agent he couldn't do more to harm this country," an echo of Truman on McCarthy. According to Hal Hinson, "What the movie suggests, in the most offhandedly outrageous manner, is that it is possible for a Red-controlled stooge to reach high office while niftily avoiding detection by presenting himself as a rabid anti-Communist. And it's this wry, cold-blooded attitude toward American political foibles that may have provoked such controversy at the time of its original release."[108] However, as Korean POWs learned, American citizenship spoils one for residence in any other country, especially those totalitarian regimes in which the citizen is expected to follow orders without question and to subsume his or her own desires to the supremacy of the state. In fact, once in power, Mrs. Iselin plans to grind her Red superiors "into the dirt [for] what they did in so contemptuously underestimating me."

Not only does *The Manchurian Candidate* resurrect McCarthy to ridicule him, but it also employs a plethora of patriotic symbols to further poke fun at politicos in general. Every scene with the liberal Republican senator Thomas Jordan includes a larger-than-life representation of the American eagle. As Shaw assassinates the senator, the camera angles around to catch a wood-carved eagle seemingly suspended over Jordan's head. The bird is looking to the left, in the direction of the talon that resolutely grasps a Cold War dove-loving olive branch.[109] While in America the eagle has come to represent freedom, soaring down from lofty mountains where it makes its home, there are those who contend that the eagle also possesses a dark side. Both Benjamin Franklin and John James Audubon argued that the bald eagle was actually a bird of bad moral character, remorselessly stealing the labor of the fishing hawk and cowardly fleeing from the diminutive kingbird. Jordan accumulates enemies as well. He ends up suing Raymond's mother for defamation and slander, winning $65,000 and court costs—which he promptly donates, as a symbolic slap in the face, to the American Civil Liberties Union.[110]

Every time the audience glimpses the far right-wing Republican senator Johnny Iselin, they should also see a hawk (that is, a bird) looming in the background, but instead Frankenheimer insisted on coupling Iselin with a political hawk, Abraham Lincoln, founder of the GOP and advocate of military force during the Civil War. Big John doesn't just aspire to sleep in the Lincoln bedroom; he is determined, like his role model, to make the entire White House his home.

The audience first encounters Iselin when his visage is reflected in the glass fronting a Lincoln portrait. He actually seems to be speculating whether or not he might be the reincarnation of Honest Abe. The Iselins display busts, photographs, and paintings of the sixteenth president in every room—there is even a Lincoln lamp in the library. When you spot Iselin at the fancy dress ball, he is decked out in an artificial beard and stovepipe hat. Scooping out a great expanse of caviar (artfully arranged into the Stars and Stripe), he excuses his desecration with the words, "It's all right, it's *Polish* caviar." At the same party, he employs his wife's Bo Peep staff to engage in a limbo competition—no one bothers to ask him "how low can you go?" He seems to be the undisputed champion.

Iselin and Lincoln shared more commonalities than one might think. Neither could be called "handsome" by any means. As was Lincoln, Iselin is basically a passive individual, driven toward higher office by a politically ambitious woman. From his earliest days, Lincoln sensed his destiny was controlled by some higher power, while Big John Iselin is a superstitious Catholic who knows marriage to Raymond's mother "was an impious thing"[111]—a belief that brings about impotence and a mounting dependence on the bottle. Iselin, like Lincoln, is an attorney, subject to debilitating bouts of depression, and eventually a victim of an assassin's bullet.

ONE NATION UNDER TELEVISION

During Raymond and Jocie's honeymoon at the Bedford Village Inn, Jocelyn clicks on the television, prompting a sarcastic observation from Raymond: "Have you noticed that the human race is divided into two distinct, irreconcilable groups—those who walk into rooms and automatically turn television sets on, and those who walk into rooms and automatically turn them off?" During the early '60s, progressively more Americans were clicking sets on, preferring the convenience of staying home to watch free entertainment to forking over money for a movie ticket.

Film, which requires a conscious suspension of disbelief, has always been considered "larger than life." However, when television took over the living room (Bob Hope referred to TV as that piece of furniture that stares back at you), viewers felt like they were somehow eavesdropping on reality. In addition, the one-eyed monster, exerting more influence on human behavior than the classroom, the church, and city hall, fused the nation into a single marketplace. The postwar economy purred, its motor gassed up not so much by bigger and better products but by bigger and better advertising campaigns. Television, via the cadence of a clever jingle or the splash of spellbinding imagery, was the home appliance used to sell other home appliances. By the mid-'60s, Mr. and Mrs. America found themselves regularly brainwashed by the incessant thirty-second seductions sandwiched between regular programming.

Two scenes involved live television in *The Manchurian Candidate*—a high decibel confrontation between Iselin and the secretary of defense with a TV screen acting as intermediary and the news coverage of the Republican convention at Madison Square Garden. Frankenheimer, whose flair for interior drama and fluid camera work directly evolved from TV, was able to demonstrate, in a very visual way, the emerging role of television in shaping public opinion. In the Senate hearing room, crammed with reporters, technicians, film camera equipment, and television monitors, the secretary of defense (Barry Kelley) announces he will be making cuts in the defense budget. Senator Iselin, an uninvited guest, grandstands in the background, delivering bombastic blasts at the secretary as Mrs. Iselin, observing her husband's televised image on the monitor next to her, nods and glows. According to Gerald Pratley, "In one shot we see Angela Lansbury, the mastermind, in the foreground, her senator husband, the puppet, in the background and the Secretary, the subject of the Senator's accusation of Communists in the defense department, angrily reacting on the TV screen—everything combined in one frame reflecting the whole shot, yet filled with conflict and movement."[112] Iselin then announces, "I have here a list of the names of 207 persons who are known by the Secretary of Defense as being members of the Communist Party"; he demands an immediate response—intimating that there's been some sort of cover-up. He and the secretary harangue each other with dialogue that, according to Frankenheimer, is completely ad libbed. When the secretary calls for the sergeant at arms to "throw that lunatic out of here," although the secretary is seated in the front of the room, when he points to Iselin the TV monitor shows his hand movement in reverse, a symbolic representation of what Janet Maslin called "the ability of television to distort images."[113]

Frankenheimer admits that the scene in the Senate hearing room would have been impossible "if I hadn't directed live television. . . . [U]ntil then, scenes showing television sets faked the picture you saw on the screen."[114] TV also sharpened Frankenheimer's quasi-documentary technique, especially the striking two- and three-shots in which a (usually) silent character looms large in the foreground while others, in deep focus, converse in the background. This modus operandi proves especially effective during Marco's dream sequence, when huge hands play solitaire with invisible cards. A compelling image to begin with, the action also supplies the answer to a question posed in a later scene—"What was Raymond doing with his hands?"

According to Frankenheimer, today's movies, with background swirling wildly out of focus, often confuse the audience. "In my action scenes, everything—everything—is in focus. You have to geographically orient your audience. . . . [T]he viewer needs to know the physical relationships between the people in the scene."[115] Nowhere is Frankenheimer's grounding in physical reality technique more effective than in the Madison Square Garden sequence. Due to financial restrictions, Frankenheimer filmed Laurence Harvey making his labyrinthine route to the sniper's perch—tramping up empty aisles, jostling along backstage hallways, striding from one end of a bustling kitchen to anther, ascending the stairs, treading lightly across a balcony catwalk, and sneaking into the claustrophobic projectionist's room—in an empty auditorium. Undersized sets crowded with extras (staged according to photographs of the 1960 Democratic convention) were intercut with stock crowd footage in order to supply the kitschy carnival montage that characterizes a political rally.

Originality usually results from an artist's attempt to unravel a vexing predicament. Filming the dream sequences in *The Manchurian Candidate* provided Frankenheimer with ample opportunity to do some highly creative problem-solving. While Condon employs flashbacks in the novel, Frankenheimer welcomes the audience to the recurring nightmares of Marco and Melvin by having the camera make a slow, 360-degree tracking shot around the room. In the Marco sequence, first Mrs. Henry Whittaker is lecturing on "Fun with Hydrangeas" as the platoon fights slumber.[116] The camera next reveals a dozen or so Sunday best–dressed matrons. Whittaker is abruptly replaced by Yen Lo, who waxes philosophical on the powers of hypnotism. As the images switch surrealistically between the soldiers' delusionary point of view and the rock-hard reality of the Research Pavilion in Manchuria, the audience learns that Shaw's platoon has been programmed to imagine they are actually attending a ladies' garden club party in New Jersey's Spring Lake Hotel. With the Melvin dream sequence, the camera makes a similar trek around the room, but all the ladies, including Whittaker, are portrayed by African Americans—just as a black corporal might envision under hypnosis.[117] Frankenheimer filmed each dream sequence six different times and then dispatched George Axelrod to the editing room with a script and permission to choose the images that best conveyed the story. His selections from the pool of all possible permutations became the working print.

Another calamity arose when Frankenheimer couldn't figure out how Marco discerns Shaw's hiding place in the immense reaches of Madison Square Garden. Frankenheimer admits he ripped off (or paid homage to) *Foreign Correspondent* (1940) in cracking this crisis. In Alfred Hitchcock's film, when Johnny Jones (Joel McCrea) observes that all of the windmills, save one, are rotating in the same direction, he surmises that the Nazis, requiring electrical power for their radio, have holed up in the oddball windmill. In *The Manchurian Candidate*, as the lights go down during the presidential candidate's rousing speech, Marco notices that one lamp remains lit. A single shaft of light streaming out of a tiny window in the projectionist's perch gives away Shaw's location.

Finally, in the scene in which Marco, armed with a forced deck, attempts to deprogram Raymond Shaw, Frank Sinatra has to deliver the "fifty-two red queens and me" speech—a lengthy, complicated, and emotionally taxing monologue. While Sinatra was not resistant to doing more than one take, according to Frankenheimer, he did his best work the first time around. When the director learned that the assistant cameraman had failed to focus the close-up camera, he was incensed. Sinatra's performance had been flawless. Despite several attempts to recreate the magic, Frankenheimer finally had no choice but to use the blurry take. Critics continue to praise the director for his genius in shooting the scene from Shaw's "brainwashed" point of view.

THE AUDIENCE RESPONDS

All the major studios turned down *The Manchurian Candidate*. But today the film is pegged at number sixty-seven on the American Film Institute's Best 100 Films list. Although in 1962 *Variety* gushed of *The Manchurian Candidate* that "every once in a rare while, a film comes along that works in all departments with story, production and performance so well blended that the end effect is one of nearly complete satisfaction," the film, shot in thirty-nine days on a modest $2.5 million budget, failed miserably at the box office.[118] *The Manchurian Candidate* was produced by M. C. Productions, a partnership consisting of Frank Sinatra, John Frankenheimer, and George Axelrod, with 50 percent of the film's revenues going to Sinatra and 25 percent each to the director and the screenwriter. "In addition," claims Axelrod, "Frank was paid $750,000, Larry Harvey got $250,000, and Janet Leigh got $25,000."[119] United Artists would eventually write off the film as a loss.

Frankenheimer laments, "We got fabulous reviews, but United Artists never got behind the movie. They reneged on all the promises they made to Sinatra, Axelrod and me."[120] Arthur Krim, then head of the studio as well as national finance chair of the Democratic Party, may have been right when he refused to approve the project, believing the picture would prove politically explosive.[121] According to Gerald Pratley, "Although Condon's book (which Axelrod follows faithfully) had been published, it is not outspoken books that upset politicians, churches, pressure groups and the like, but outspoken movies."[122] Even Bosley Crowther verbalized his misgivings: "with the air full of international tension, the film *The*

Manchurian Candidate pops up with a rash supposition that could serve to scare some viewers half to death—that is, if they should be dupes enough to believe it, which we solemnly trust they won't."[123]

It's easy to understand why Americans shunned the film. The specter of political assassination, however farfetched it may have seemed prior to November 22, 1963, was too horrifying to consider. President John F. Kennedy's New Frontier earmarking funds for the poor, elderly, education, civil rights, and the space program inspired hope and confidence in the future. A dark movie on the eve of one of this country's brightest economic periods couldn't help attracting a nominal audience.

Most critics, however, loved the film. *The Saturday Review* called the movie "enormously effective" and applauded John Frankenheimer for filling "every restless shot with an unrelenting tension, [alternating] the subtleties of psychological warfare with flare-ups of frightful violence, and at the same time [maintaining] a tone that is seemingly as detached and objective as a newsreel."[124] *The New York Herald Tribune* advised the viewer to "just settle back and let yourself be treated to one of the brightest fantasy thrillers in a long while."[125]

The film was simply ahead of its time. As the Cold War ramped up, America would grow increasingly obsessed with conspiracy theories. George Axelrod, who adapted the novel for the screen and coproduced it, once observed, "The movie went from failure to classic—without passing through success."[126] He went on to add, "When I saw it at the [1987] New York Film Festival, it was a smash."[127] In fact, *The Manchurian Candidate* has made a tidy profit on video and DVD rentals since its rerelease.

Just think—it only took twenty-five years for a classic to come in from the cold.

NOTES

1. Jonathan Alter, "The Old Order Closes Ranks," *Newsweek* (February 21, 2000): 30.

2. Thomas Doherty, "He's a Candidate, but Not Manchurian," *Los Angeles Times*, February 11, 2000, D7.

3. Many American Communists became disillusioned once they found out about Stalin's atrocities. Fear of being investigated by HUAC took care of the rest.

4. *Public Opinion Online* (Roper Center at the University of Connecticut, 1992), QUESTION ID: USGALLUP.51-469, QK09A.

5. *Public Opinion Online* (Roper Center at the University of Connecticut, 1989), QUESTION ID: USGALLUP.55-557, QK007A.

6. On the role of anti-Communists in the Roosevelt and Truman administrations, see Donald Fleming, *The Cold War and Its Origins* (New York: Doubleday, 1961). For the hard revisionist point of view, see William A. Williams, *The Tragedy of American Diplomacy* (Cleveland: World, 1959).

7. Winston Churchill delivered the "Iron Curtain" speech, in which he coined the term, at Westminster College in Fulton, Missouri, on March 5, 1946.

8. Benjamin Frankel, ed., *The Cold War, 1945–1991,* 3 vol. (Gale Research, 1992). Reproduced in *Biography Resource Center* (Farmington Hills, Mich.: Gale Group, 2001), www.galenet.com/servlet/BioRC.

9. See Arthur M. Schlesinger Jr., *The Vital Center: The Politics of Freedom* (Boston: Houghton Mifflin, 1949).

10. Richard Gid Powers, *Not Without Honor: The History of American Anticommunism* (New York: Free Press, 1995). 212.

11. Powers, *Not Without Honor,* 212.

12. Schlesinger, *Vital Center;* Powers, *Not Without Honor,* 212.

13. *Public Opinion Online* (Roper Center at the University of Connecticut, 1991), QUESTION ID: USGALLUP.032250, R10B.

14. Joseph S. Nye Jr., *Understanding International Conflicts: An Introduction to Theory and History,* 3rd ed. (New York: Longman, 2000), 118.

15. *Public Opinion Online* (Roper Center at the University of Connecticut, 1993), QUESTION ID: USGALLUP.50-460, QTP03A.

16. Tristram Coffin, *Senator Fulbright: Portrait of a Public Philosopher* (New York: Dutton, 1966), 28–29.

17. William E. Mayer, "Why Did Many GI Captives Cave In?" *U.S. News and World Report* 24 (February 1956): 57.

18. See Edward Hunter, "Brain-Washing' Tactics Force Chinese into Ranks of Communist Party," *Miami News,* September 1950.

19. Hearings before the Senate Permanent Subcommittee on Investigations, 84th Congress, June 19–27, 1956.

20. Lewis H. Carlson, *Remembered Prisoners of a Forgotten War* (New York: St. Martin's, 2002), 37.

21. Quoted in Carlson, *Remembered Prisoners,* 179.

22. T. R. Fehrenbach, *This Kind of War* (Washington, D.C.: Brassey's, 1998), 318–19.

23. Albert Biderman, *March to Calumny: The Story of the American POWs in the Korean War* (New York: Macmillan, 1963), 75.

24. Carlson, *Remembered Prisoners,* 278.

25. Carlson, *Remembered Prisoners,* 148–49.

26. Carlson, *Remembered Prisoners,* xiii.

27. Carlson, *Remembered Prisoners,* 2.

28. Carlson, *Remembered Prisoners,* 200.

29. Raymond B. Lech, *Broken Soldiers* (Urbana: University of Illinois Press, 2000), 4.

30. See Albert Biderman, *March to Calumny: The Story of the American POWs in the Korean War* (New York: Macmillan, 1963); Walter Hermes, *United States Army in the Korean War: Truce Tent and Fighting Front* (Washington, D.C.: U.S. Government Printing Office, 1966); S. L. A. Marshall, *Pork Chop Hill: The American Fighting Man in Korea* (Nashville: Battery, 1986); *The River and the Gauntlet* (Westport, Conn.: Greenwood, 1953); David Rees, *Korea: The Limited War* (New York: St. Martin's, 1964); *The Korean War: History and Tactics* (New York: Crescent, 1984); and Russell Weigley, *History of the U.S. Army* (New York: Macmillan, 1967).

31. Carlson, *Remembered Prisoners,* 76.

32. Morris R. Wills, as told to J. Robert Moskin, *Turncoat: An American's 23 Years in Communist China. The Story of Morris R. Wills* (Englewood Cliffs, N.J.: Prentice–Hall, 1968), 13.

33. Carlson, *Remembered Prisoners*, 42.

34. Carlson, *Remembered Prisoners*, 191.

35. Eugene Kinkead, "The Study of Something New in History," *New Yorker* 26 (October 1957): 114.

36. Mayer, "GI Captives," 57.

37. Carlson, *Remembered Prisoners*, 213.

38. Carlson, *Remembered Prisoners*, 40.

39. Ted Gup, "The Coldest; Sid Gottlieb," *Washington Post*, December 16, 2001, W09.

40. Gup, "Coldest."

41. According to George Axelrod, when the press pounced on the similarities between the Raymond Shaw character and Lee Harvey Oswald, Frank Sinatra, the film's producers, and United Artists decided to pull the movie. According to Frankenheimer and Condon, however, although the film continued to play on television, it had failed to make a dent at the box office and disappeared from movie theaters by the time Kennedy was killed.

42. JFK only wondered who would be playing the mother.

43. As a partner in the film, Sinatra took the opportunity to make a number of behind-the-scenes decisions. Jilly's Bar and Grill belonged to a Sinatra crony. In another scene, Sinatra brandishes a record album by Mabel Mercer, his artistic mentor. Sinatra's personal plane is used to "transport" Shaw and family to the nation's capital.

44. Frank Sinatra initially wanted Lucille Ball in the role of Mrs. Iselin. According to Angela Lansbury, it was the Oedipal thing between Berry-Berry and his mother in *All Fall Down* that prompted John Frankenheimer to cast her in one of those great roles that every actress dreams about.

45. Theodore C. Sorensen, *Kennedy* (New York: Bantam, 1966), 276.

46. See W. W. Rostow, *The Stages of Economic Growth: A Non-Communist Manifesto* (Cambridge: Cambridge University Press,1960).

47. Sorensen, *Kennedy,* 276.

48. Quoted in Frankel, *Cold War,* www.galenet.com/servlet/BioRC]

49. Quoted in Powers, *Not without Honor*, 309.

50. Quoted in Frankel, *Cold War,* www.galenet.com/servlet/BioRC.

51. William O'Neill, *Coming Apart: An Informal History of America in the 1960's* (Chicago: Quadrangle, 1971), 79.

52. *Public Opinion Online* (Roper Center at the University of Connecticut, 1989), QUESTION ID: USGALLUP.62-659, R051.

53. *Public Opinion Online* (Roper Center at the University of Connecticut, 1989), QUESTION ID: USGALLUP.62-665, R004.

54. Tom Bennett, "Dean Rusk: 1909–1994," *Atlanta Constitution*, December 22, 1994, A8.

55. It is no wonder that Mrs. Iselin, the top Communist operative in the United States, chooses the costume of Little Bo Peep.

56. Richard Condon, *The Manchurian Candidate* (New York: Jove, 1988), 53.

57. Quoted in Steven Mintz and Randy Roberts, *Hollywood's America: United States History Through Its Films* (St. James, N.Y.: Brandywine, 1993), 201.

58. Douglas Brode, *The Films of the Sixties* (Secaucus, N.J.: Citadel, 1980), 93.

59. Janet Maslin, "Candidate Runs Again and Wins," *New York Times,* April 24, 1988, H23.

60. Bosley Crowther, "Screen: *The Manchurian Candidate,*" *New York Times,* October 25, 1962.

61. Nora Sayre, *Running Time: Films of the Cold War* (New York: Dial, 1982), 3.

62. Condon, *Manchurian Candidate,* 30.

63. Tracy Bruce, "Hypnosis Can Increase Concentration, Practitioner Says," *St. Louis Post-Dispatch,* February 1, 2001, 3. Yen Lo continues, "you note-takers might set down a reminder to consult Brenmen's paper, 'Experiments in the Hypnotic Production of Antisocial and Self-injurious Behavior' or Wells' 1941 paper which was titled, I believe, 'Experiments in the Hypnotic Production of Crime' or Andrew Salter's remarkable book, *Conditioned Reflex Therapy,* to name only three."

64. Sigmund Freud, *A General Introduction to Psychoanalysis* (New York: Pocket Books, 1924), 95.

65. A forced deck is composed of fifty-two identical cards—on this occasion, all are the queen of diamonds.

66. Condon, *Manchurian Candidate,* 46. Biblical matriarch Rachel was the model for the queen of diamonds face card.

67. Frankenheimer claims the script only called for a psychiatrist—it was his idea to cast an African American.

68. Frankenheimer recalls that the costume was left over from a 1959 *Playhouse 90* production of Hemingway's *Snows of Kilimanjaro.*

69. "The Queen of Diamonds Person," www.sedonacardsofdestiny.com/Diamonds/_qd.htm.

70. "Atlantean Cards of Destiny," www.askclaudia.com/cards/qd.htm.

71. "Ice" is a colloquial term for diamonds.

72. Thirty-seven-year-old Angela Lansbury was only three years older than Laurence Harvey, the actor who played her son.

73. *Contemporary Authors Online* (Gale Group, 2000). Reproduced in *Biography Resource Center* (Framington Hills, Michigan: Gale Group. 2001), www.galenet.com/servlet/BioRC.

74. Hal Hinson, "Return of the Candidate," *Washington Post,* February 13, 1988, B1. *The Manchurian Candidate* does not technically qualify as a satire, nor did Condon intend it to be—he categorized the book as a political thriller, despite critics confusing the McCarthy parody with true satire.

75. *BFI Monthly Film Bulletin* 29 (December 1962): 168.

76. Margot Henriksen, *Dr. Strangelove's America: Society and Culture in the Atomic Age* (Berkeley: University of California Press, 1997), 268.

77. Andrew Sarris, "Film Fantasies, Left and Right," *Film Culture* (Fall 1964): 33.

78. The American Film Institute Seminar with John Frankenheimer held Feb 5, 1975, at the Center for Advanced Film Studies, Beverly Hills, CA., transcript at the Library of Congress.

79. Frank N. Magill, ed., *Magill's Survey of Cinema* (Englewood Cliffs, N.J.: Salem, 1981), 1525.

80. *Contemporary Authors Online.*

81. *Variety,* October 17, 1962, 6.

82. Condon, *Manchurian Candidate,* 286.

83. Sophocles, *Antigone, Oedipus the King, Electra,* translated by H. D. F. Kitto (Oxford: Oxford University Press, 1994), 81.

84. Harold Bloom, ed., *Sophocles' Oedipus Rex* (New York: Chelsea House, 1988), 1.

85. Marco is not put off by Shaw's stories about his mother. In fact, he claims "it's rather like Orestes [who killed his mother after she murdered Agamemnon] griping about Clytemnestra."

86. Condon, *Manchurian Candidate,* 60.

87. Todd Gitlin, *The Sixties: Years of Hope, Days of Rage* (New York: Bantam, 1993), 17–18.

88. Kinkead, "Study of Something New," 154.

89. William E. Mayer, "Why Did Many GI Captives Cave In?" *U.S. News and World Report,* February 24, 1956, 60–65.

90. Philip Wylie, *Generation of Vipers* (New York: Rhinehart, 1942), 199–208.

91. See Edward Strecker, *Their Mother's Sons* (New York: Lippincott, 1951). See also Hans Sebald, *Momism: The Silent Disease of America* (Chicago: Burnham, 1976).

92. Condon, *Manchurian Candidate,* 23.

93. Condon, *Manchurian Candidate,* 173.

94. A bar girl is reading *Movie Life.* The cover picture features Janet Leigh and Tony Curtis.

95. Condon, *Manchurian Candidate,* 40.

96. Quoted in Bloom, *Oedipus Rex,* 42.

97. Condon, *Manchurian Candidate,* 10.

98. At the Iselin's fancy dress ball, Raymond is costumed as a South American gaucho.

99. *Contemporary Authors Online.*

100. *Contemporary Authors Online.*

101. Hinson, "Return of the Candidate," B1.

102. John Lahr, "A Fairy-Tale for the Future: The Novel and Film *The Manchurian Candidate* Defined American Propaganda and Paranoia in the Age of McCarthy," *Independent* (London), July 21, 1991, 16.

103. See the film *The Powers Girl* (1942), in which actress Anne Shirley attempts to break into the famed modeling school.

104. Condon, *Manchurian Candidate,* 194.

105. *Variety,* October 17, 1962, 6.

106. In the book, Marco had fallen in love with a white Carrara marble statue of an Arab woman he found in a magazine twenty-three years earlier. In the movie, Marco reads *The Ethnic Choices of the Arab.* The question could also be an oblique reference to reincarnation.

107. Mel Gussow, "Richard Condon, Political Novelist, Dies at 81," *New York Times,* April 10, 1996, 16.

108. Hinson, "Return of the Candidate," B1.

109. On the presidential seal, originally the eagle's head faced the talon holding the bundle of thirteen arrows, symbolizing the power of war, but on October 25,

1945, President Truman issued an executive order that specified that the eagle face in the opposite direction.

110. George Axelrod, at the insistence of John Frankenheimer, added a piece of dialogue revealing that Eleanor Iselin, who called Jordan a "Communist" on a radio program, seems to label anyone who disagrees with her as a "Red."

111. Condon, *Manchurian Candidate,* 66.

112. Gerald Pratley, *The Cinema of John Frankenheimer* (London: Zwemmer, 1969), 87.

113. Janet Maslin, "Candidate Runs," H23.

114. Pratley, *Cinema,* 226–27.

115. Joe Holleman, "John Frankenheimer Is a Master When It Comes to Making the Heart Race," *Post–Dispatch,* February 28, 2000, D1.

116. According to Frankenheimer, the speech was taken word for word out of a seed catalog.

117. Frankenheimer was surprised that no viewer seemed to notice that the bellboy was white in this dream sequence.

118. *Variety,* October17, 1962, 6.

119. Roderick Mann, "The Return of The Manchurian Candidate, Classic Re-released after Long Disputes," *Los Angeles Times,* February 12, 1988, 6:1.

120. Aljean Harmetz, "Manchurian Candidate, Old Failure Is Now a Hit," *New York Times,* February 24, 1988, C19.

121. Joel E. Siegel, "Grinning toward Bethlehem," *Washington City Paper,* February 19, 1988, 21–22.

122. Pratley, *Cinema,* 83–84.

123. Crowther, "Screen."

124. Arthur Knight, *Saturday Review* (November 27, 1962).

125. Paul V. Backley, *New York Herald Tribune,* November 25, 1962.

126. Harmetz, "Manchurian Candidate," C19.

127. Mann, "Return," 6:1.

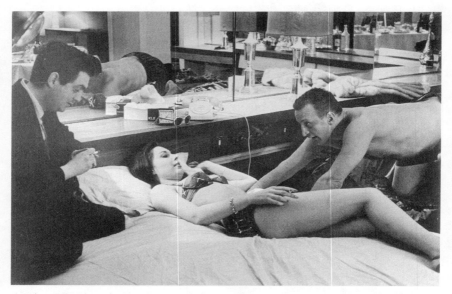

Stanley Kubrick and George C. Scott discuss the coverage area of Tracy Reed's bikini in Dr. Strangelove. © 1991 Columbia Pictures Industries, Inc. Courtesy of Columbia Pictures and the Academy of Motion Picture Arts and Sciences.

9

☆

Cold War Dovism in
Dr. Strangelove, or:
How I Learned to Stop
Worrying and Love the Bomb

Winston Churchill, in a prescient 1924 address entitled "Shall We Commit Suicide?" referred to the foes of democracy when he predicted "it is probable—nay, certain—that among the means which will next time be at their disposal, will be agencies and processes of destruction wholesale, unlimited, and, perhaps, once launched, uncontrollable."[1] During the Cold War, the United States and Russia created an atomic arsenal capable of wiping out the world.

During the past fifty-five years, the *Bulletin of the Atomic Scientists* has been utilizing the upper left quadrant of a clock face to indicate the level of nuclear peril facing the planet. When Maryl Langsdorf, artist and wife of a Manhattan Project physicist, was asked to design a cover for the June 1947 issue, she visualized the minute hand closing in on midnight to symbolize an impending apocalypse as well as a military-type countdown. Each subsequent cover showed the minute hand moving closer or further away from the witching hour in line with the *Bulletin*'s interpretation of world events. In 1964, when *Dr. Strangelove, or: How I Learned to Stop Worrying and Love the Bomb* came out, the doomsday clock read 11:53. The *Bulletin* pointed to China's acquisition of nuclear weapons as well as conflicts brewing in the Middle East, the Indian subcontinent, and Vietnam as reasons for the high-risk assessment.

Last year, the doomsday clock returned to, and throughout 2003 it has remained at, seven minutes to midnight, ironically (despite decades of ups and downs) at precisely the same instant at which the timepiece debuted. It is troubling to note that 2002 marked the third advance of the minute hand since the end of the Cold War in 1991. The *Bulletin* contends that little improvement has been made with respect to global nuclear disarmament—

more than thirty-one thousand nuclear weapons are still maintained by the
eight known nuclear powers, meaning a decrease of only three thousand
since 1998. Furthermore, not only has the United States rejected a series of
arms control treaties, but it has also announced a withdrawal from the
Anti–Ballistic Missile Treaty. Despite the failure to uncover weapons of
mass destruction in Iraq, the *Bulletin* contends that the entire planet still
lives in fear that terrorists will locate and deploy nuclear arms.

Beeping *Sputniks I* and *II* circling the planet in 1957 brought with them
the chilling realization that the same intercontinental missiles that
launched the satellites could just as easily boost a nuclear warhead toward American soil. Pressure to develop the H-bomb increased after the
Soviet Union detonated its first atomic bomb and one of the physicists on
the Manhattan Project was accused of being a Russian spy. After intense
debate, on January 31, 1950, President Harry S. Truman rendered one of
the most sweeping decisions during his or any presidency—the United
States would proceed with work on all forms of atomic weapons, including the so-called super H-bomb. American Catholic bishops were guilty
of only venial hyperbole when they warned, "We are the first generation
since Genesis with the capability of destroying God's creation."[2]

ASCENT OF THE DOVES

In 1973, then U.S. Secretary of State Henry Kissinger observed: "there is
almost always a crisis in the division between doves who seek evidence
for delay, wrapping their hesitation in the mantle of 'diplomacy,' and the
hawks who want pre-emptive action."[3] By 1964, even if the Office of
Civil and Defense Mobilization's estimate that there were a million
bomb shelters in the United States[4] wasn't inflated, the Cuban Missile
Crisis had thrust the country into palpable and pervasive terror that
contributed to the growing peace movement.[5] When *Dr. Strangelove* was
released that year, Cold War doves had become increasingly prominent
for several reasons.

First, October 1962 marked the closest brush Planet Earth had with total annihilation. During their fevered thirteen-day exchange, Nikita
Khrushchev wrote John F. Kennedy, who was giving fifty–fifty odds of
nuclear war, "Be careful as we both tug at the ends of the rope in which
we have tied the knot of war."[6] Initially, JFK favored a military response,
including an air strike, coordinated and executed by superhawk General
Curtis LeMay, who believed the Cuban Missile Crisis provided an ideal
opportunity to simultaneously get the missiles and the Communists out
of Cuba. "During that very critical time," claimed LeMay, "in my mind,
there wasn't a chance that we would have gone to war with Russia because we had overwhelming strategic capability and the Russians knew

it."[7] What LeMay didn't know was that twenty American cities were bull's-eyed by one- to three-megaton hydrogen warhead–armed ballistic missiles. In addition, local Soviet commanders in Cuba were quarterbacking not only tactical nuclear weapons but also forty-three thousand Soviet military personnel (rather than the ten thousand estimated by the CIA). If Kennedy had listened to LeMay and invaded Cuba, millions of Americans would have been exterminated in retaliation.[8]

The crisis was averted when the Soviet Union signed off on the removal of nuclear weapons from Cuba in exchange for the United States' removal of nuclear weapons from Turkey six months later.[9] John Kenneth Galbraith conveyed the paranoia skulking at the edges of Camelot by saying "no student of social matters in these days can escape feeling how precarious is the existence of that with which he deals. . . . The unearthly light of a handful of nuclear explosions would signal [Western man's] return to utter deprivation if, indeed, he survived at all."[10] In a national address on the Limited Test Ban Treaty on July 26, 1963, JFK contended "A full scale nuclear exchange, lasting less than 60 minutes . . . could wipe out more than 300 million Americans, Europeans, and Russians, as well as untold numbers elsewhere. And the survivors—as Chairman Khrushchev warned the Communist Chinese—'the survivors would envy the dead,' for they would inherit a world so devastated by explosions and poison and fire that today we cannot conceive of its horrors."[11] Albert Einstein, whose $e = mc^2$ ushered in the Atomic Age, was once asked how World War III would be fought. His answer was terse and tough. While he admitted to having no idea what sort of weapons would be used in World War III, he felt pretty sure that the war after that would be waged with sticks and stones.

Second, the antinuclear movement, which originated in "Ban the Bomb" protests, was clearly gaining momentum. As far back as 1955, pacifists, artists, and intellectuals had been demonstrating against civil defense drills and bomb tests, occasionally cooling their heels in the pokey as a consequence of acting out their moral witness. Their argument was simple—here, in one horrifying atomic strike, either America or the Soviet Union could unshackle the equivalent of one million tons of TNT. Compare that to all of World War II, when only three million tons of TNT were employed.[12] Sheer terror at the destructive potential of nuclear weapons hit the American people between the eyes. Not only was the H-bomb an exponentially ramped-up alternative to conventional warfare, but it also menaced the very existence of humanity, not just those who were involved in the immediate conflict. The Castle Bravo nuclear test in the Pacific was a perfect case in point. According to historian Martha Smith, heated protests by such nations as India, Japan, Canada, Great Britain, Italy, and France followed after a fifteen-megaton thermonuclear explosion on March 1, 1954.[13]

Nuclear activist A. J. Muste was responsible for pulling together the Committee for Nonviolent Action (militants who sailed small boats into Pacific bomb-test zones or violated perimeters of missile bases) as well as the blue-ribbon National Committee for a SANE Nuclear Policy (an organization which found a fervent following on college campuses). Even conservative Harvard boasted a student SANE (Committee for a Sane Nuclear Policy) chapter by 1959. The Student Peace Union, a spin-off of the American Friends Service Committee, went national in 1960. Galvanized by reports of fallout adding strontium 90 to cow's milk, fifty thousand American mothers demonstrated against the resumption of nuclear tests on November 1, 1961. The next year, a two-day Washington peace march during a blinding snowstorm drew, by various accounts, between four and eight thousand students.[14] Dr. Linus Pauling's antinuke petition signed by eleven thousand scientists eventually nudged President Kennedy into initialing the 1963 Atmospheric Nuclear Weapons Test Ban Treaty. Eventually, even mainstream America questioned the morality of nuclear weapons.[15] When reporters grilled J. Robert Oppenheimer about the ethics of the Los Alamos team achievement, he answered, in words that would return to plague him, "a scientist cannot hold back progress because of fears of what the world will do with his discoveries."[16]

Third, as body bags from Vietnam started arriving home in greater numbers, it looked like doves were dead right. Lyndon Baines Johnson's landslide victory in 1964 hinged on the electoral promise that the president would not be dispatching American boys thousands of miles away to do what Asian boys should do for themselves.[17] For the United States, the 1968 Tet Offensive raised serious doubts about the competence of Nguyen Van Thieu and the Army of the Republic of Vietnam. Snowballing carnage counts dimmed any hope that America would not be able to end, much less win, the Vietnam War.

Fourth, many film folk blacklisted as a result of the HUAC hearings of 1948 and 1952 headed back to work. Anti-Communists who had formerly served as reasonable and responsible proponents of the movement were becoming bogged down in the muck and mire associated with Joseph McCarthy and his ilk. When they tried to raise the alarm that Soviets were covertly funding Western antinuclear groups, they found their voices marginalized and their words of warning, which later proved to be true, raining down on deaf ears.[18]

Fifth, accidental atomic war was quite possible in 1964. Cold sweat–producing scenarios, according to the experts, may have seemed highly improbable because of the plethora of preemptive precautions taken on both sides, yet, because of a climate of mutual suspicion the chances for nuclear holocaust spiked.[19] Take, for example, a false alarm on a warning system. An alarm, false or otherwise, would automatically trigger an increased level of readiness ("Condition Red" in *Strangelove*) while the validity of this information was being checked out. Russia would detect our heightened DEFCON level, and they would also take appropriate action, including an increased security rating. Their heightened defense condition would tend to confirm the original false alarm and the spiral would continue. When one takes into account that the time available to decide whether or not to respond to a Soviet attack ranged from an upper limit of twenty minutes to no time at all, it's a wonder that the planet is still here.[20] During the intense thirteen days of the Cuban Missile Crisis alone, Scott D. Sagan charted *seven* mishaps that, had both sides exercised less caution or common sense, might have escalated into full-fledged thermonuclear war.[21] First, on October 24, 1962, the explosion of a Soviet satellite was initially interpreted as a massive intercontinental ballistic missile (ICBM) attack launch. Second, on October 25, a guard at the Duluth Sector Direction Center, spotting a figure climbing a fence, activated the "sabotage alarm.[22] "Unfortunately, the alarm was misread at Volk Field Wisconsin as an order to dispatch a squadron of nuclear-armed F-106A interceptors. Third, an October 26 test launch at Vandenberg Air Force Base in California proceeded, despite a DEFCON 3 requirement directing all ICBMs to be fitted with nuclear warheads. Russian observers, cognizant of the warhead changeover, were not aware that the Titan missile being test-launched was unarmed. Fourth, the radar warning station at Moorestown, New Jersey, was not notified that an October 26 test launch of a Titan-II ICBM was going to take place in Florida and jumped to the conclusion that America was being attacked.[23] Fifth, at Malstrom Air Force Base, Montana, no armed guards were available to transport a solid fuel Minuteman-1 missile being readied for deployment on October 26, so equipment and codes were placed in the silo—giving a single operator the ability to send off the fully armed missile. Sixth, on October 28, Moorestown radar operators, confused by a test tape (simulating a missile launch from Cuba) being run at the same time that a satellite was spotted over the horizon, informed the national command post that a nuclear attack was underway. Seventh, on the same day, operators at Laredo, Texas, a newly operational radar-warning site, misidentified an orbiting satellite as two Russian missiles targeted for Georgia.

A sixth, and final, reason Cold War doves cemented their ascendancy was détente between Russia and America. Relations between the superpowers started to thaw following the 1953 death of Joseph Stalin, who seemed to find Lenin's bloody footprints a perfect fit for his size-ten jackboots. Documents declassified in September 1998 disclosed a Communist system worse than critics alleged, confirming the full atrociousness of Stalin's purges, genocide, and forcible relocations. Both Russian and Western experts concur that Stalin's policies before World War II cost between 17 and 22 million lives in the Soviet Union.[24]

In addition, ever since the superpowers had realized that their nuclear arsenals were sufficient to destroy the earth several times, their leaders had pondered the possibility of unintentional nuclear war and built pro-gressively more sophisticated safeguards into their nuclear weapon de-livery systems. Further, after the Cuban Missile Crisis, Moscow and Washington established a "hotline" to allow instant communication be-tween Soviet and American leaders.

Advocates of "live and let live" appeasement, especially in academic circles, scoffed at the supposedly "outworn" anti-Communist principles guiding Cold Warriors. Americans, through various exchange programs, were discovering for themselves that all Russians weren't iron-faced, red-eyed monsters. Stewart Udall, the first member of Kennedy's cabinet to visit Russia, and the poet Robert Frost embarked on an eleven-day tour of the Soviet Union in 1962. They shook hands with Soviet premier Nikita Khrushchev as well as engineers and resource developers. "The center of cold war thinking was that the Soviet Union was a monolith and it was reaching out to dominate the world, " claimed Udall. "I didn't see any hostility. I didn't sense any."[25]

DWIGHT D. EISENHOWER: THE "D" STANDS FOR DOVE

If the celebrity panel on the '50s television show *What's My Line?* had to de-duce the identity of America's Cold War dove president, military man ex-traordinaire General Dwight D. Eisenhower would have been their last guess. Ike, however, did more to diminish tensions with the Soviet Union than either his predecessor, Harry Truman (who warned against the dangers of nuclear warfare in his parting address), or successors John Kennedy and Lyndon Johnson. Although he selected a hawk (John Foster Dulles) to serve as secretary of state, Ike barred the hardliner from taking any action that would lead to a U.S.–Soviet confrontation. Eisenhower's personal papers re-veal that, without exception, Dulles took his orders from the Oval Office.[26]

Although Ike made good on his 1952 election promise to visit Korea, he refused to take military action against the People's Republic of China to jump-start the stalemated peace talks. Eisenhower's solution was to in-sinuate through third-country intermediaries that he stood ready to push the atomic button should the need arise. The same empty threat worked in mid-May, when negotiations again reached an impasse. Not only had Eisenhower's atomic game plan cleverly wooed public support via the in-herent promise of "no more ground wars like Korea," but Eisenhower, by finally bringing the Korean conflict to a halt, subsequently prevented war from erupting in either Asia or Europe. Later in his presidency, Ike would take the first baby steps toward closing the Cold War by opening summit negotiations with Khrushchev.

While no one could deny that Eisenhower had pulled off the cease-fire in Korea by playing the bomb card, many didn't share Ike's fixation on nukes. The military and Democratic leadership accused Ike of squirreling all the nation's defense eggs in one basket. The Republican right wasn't pleased either, grousing that without beefing up conventional warfare components, Ike merely posited halfway measures. Meanwhile, America's European allies were raising a stink—they assumed American atomic saber rattling would make their turf a target for reprisal by the Soviets.[27] The first item on Eisenhower "to do" list had been a reevaluation of the nation's defense strategy. In a basic national security policy shift called the "New Look," Eisenhower utilized nuclear superiority not only to deter the Russians ("If you attack me, I may not be able to prevent it, but I can retaliate so powerfully that you will not want to attack in the first place"), but also to shrink the defense budget and the number of conventional forces. He reasoned that nukes delivered national security at an affordable price or offered, so to speak, "more bang for the buck." John Lewis Gaddis, who perceived the entire Cold War as a period of extended superpower stability, offered this explanation: Eisenhower's "criticism of . . . NSC-68 [Paul Nitze's "blueprint of the Cold War], was that it was going to bankrupt the country. And Eisenhower wasn't sure which was worse: the bankruptcy of the country or a victory for Communism."[28]

When General Matthew Ridgway objected to the president's defense reduction plan, Eisenhower replaced him with General Maxwell Taylor (who likewise got the heave-ho when he resisted). Understandably, there was no place in Ike's administration for Paul Nitze, so Nitze joined an ad hoc study team assessing Cold War strategy. The group contended that the Soviets would boast a strategic advantage called the "missile gap" within a few years and advocated tripling the defense budget as well as funding a $40 billion fallout shelter program. Ike, who thought the rationale sounded more like science fiction than science fact, junked the group's recommendations.[29] Nitze, not to be deterred, leaked the report to the press. Opportunistic Democrats exploited the document to inflame already extant anxiety in the land of the free and home of the brave. In 1960, John F. Kennedy hurtled into office on the "missile gap" express. Even though Kennedy would determine, early in his term, that no arms gap existed (America maintained a handy seventeen-to-one superiority),[30] he still instigated a whopping defense buildup. As each new weapon and delivery system was fleshed out, the policy differences between doves and hawks widened. The essential point of disagreement coalesced around the hawk need to outgun Moscow in every weapons category while doves insisted on negotiating with the Russians to shrink and control nuclear arms.

Unbeknownst to his critics, Ike was dead set against the use of nukes. It started with his mother Ida, who was not only deeply religious but also an inflexible pacifist. Additionally, while in the military, Ike witnessed firsthand the incredibly destructive power of nuclear devices. Such knowledge, admitted the general, tended to amplify the attractiveness of peace. According to General Andrew Goodpaster, Ike had predicted that with a nuclear war, "we would need bulldozers to push the bodies off the streets. . . . [T]his just makes no sense at all."[31]

When Admiral Robert B. Carney gave an off-the-record interview just hinting at using atomic weapons, he got the "Ridgway treatment" from Ike and found himself shut out of a second term as chief of naval operations. Ike also privately lectured his chiefs against intimating, in any manner, that the United States was looking for war.

Eisenhower met with the new Soviet leader Nikita Khrushchev and together they cobbled together a "peaceful coexistence" in which dispute resolution alternated between productive talks and diplomatic pouch-passed intimidation. At the Twentieth Party Congress in February 1956, two months after the successful test of the Soviet hydrogen bomb, Khrushchev maintained that the world faced either coexistence or the most destructive war in history. From his very first briefing on nuclear weapons (September 1953) Khrushchev began to understand, on a personal level, that proliferation would inevitably lead to total destruction. "When I was appointed First Secretary of the Central Committee and learned all the facts of nuclear power, I couldn't sleep for several days," he confessed. "Then I became convinced that we could never possibly use these weapons, and when I realized that I was able to sleep again."[32] It was a shared terror at what the other guy could do that helped produce a three-decade standoff between the powers. With the risk of global annihilation, the leadership of both the Soviet Union and the United States grasped that (1) the seemingly permanent Cold War needed to be addressed as an issue of mutual concern; (2) despite bitter ideological differences, both superpowers wanted to avoid nuclear war; and (3) improved communication, whether in the form of bilateral talks or the installation of a hotline, was the primary key to global survival.

The Soviets proposed a moratorium on nuclear weapons testing in 1956. Ike okayed the deal on principle but negotiations sputtered along, with each side insisting on the completion of a seemingly endless series of exceptions before the ban took effect. Furthermore, a rash of charges and countercharges of bad faith and deception clouded the air. By late 1958, however, both sides settled on a voluntary moratorium that, with various conditions attached, was later renewed under John F. Kennedy as the Nuclear Test Ban Treaty of 1963, a major turning point in the Cold War that encouraged the *Bulletin of the Atomic Scientists* to set the doomsday clock back to twelve minutes before midnight. Nevertheless, ideological rivalry, competition for influence, and the arms race remained the only game in town, as Khrushchev reopened the question of Berlin with a high-octane, six-month deadline on negotiations. Plans for a Paris summit to confab over the Berlin Crisis fell apart, however, when the Soviets shot down a

U.S. U-2 plane. Honest Ike, who didn't think much of spy planes any-way—as far as he was concerned, you don't risk peace for information available via alternative methods—got caught with "lost weather plane" egg on his face.[33] Decades would elapse before historians could appreci-ate Eisenhower's efforts to contain the Cold War.[34]

KENNEDY MELLOWS

Historian John Lewis Gaddis contends the Cuban Missile Crisis marked the end of the Cold War. Although the Soviets still tried to compete with respect to stockpiling nuclear weapons, their faith in the Communist ide-ology was on the wane and the West had won.[35] On June 10, 1963, Kennedy, a reputed hawk, served up an astonishingly conciliatory ad-dress on American–Soviet affairs.[36] Bemoaning the fact that the super-powers seemed suspended in an endless spiral of suspicion, he broadcast his backing for a comprehensive test ban treaty to be hashed out during a series of high-level talks.

In addition, Kennedy's innovative defense policy, the Single Integrated Operational Plan, constituted an abrupt shift from Eisenhower's "massive retaliation." Introduced by Secretary of Defense Robert S. McNamara, Kennedy's plan coordinated the various branches of the military and cur-tailed strikes on major population centers. Kennedy prayed that making cities "off limits" would somehow permit both sides to call a halt to the indiscriminate slaughter of civilians. As part of a "flexible response" that would mete out military response in proportion to the level of threat, the Kennedy administration beefed up American conventional forces, rea-soning that a "limited war" approach could counter Soviet aggression without immediate recourse to nuclear weapons.

In negotiating the Nuclear Test Ban Treaty of 1963, Kennedy was struck by the irony that "Mr. Khrushchev . . . would like to prevent a nuclear war but is under severe pressure from his hard-line crowd, which interprets every move in that direction as appeasement."[37]

SUMMARY OF THE PLOT

Dr. Strangelove, or: How I Learned to Stop Worrying and Love the Bomb (1964) not only is the most memorable satire on the nuclear age, but it also made unbearable horror unbearably humorous.[38] General Jack D. Ripper (Ster-ling Hayden) calls British group captain Lionel Mandrake (Peter Sellers) to his office to inform him that Burpelson Air Force Base is now at "Con-dition Red" and that all radios are to be confiscated. Obsessed with the notion that the Russians are trying to dilute "precious bodily fluids" via fluoridation, Ripper initiates "Plan R," a safeguard retaliatory arrangement designed for use in the event that the president has been incapacitated. Ripper, however, is hoping to capitalize on the Soviets interpreting American planes in USSR airspace as a preemptive strike so he can precipitate World War III. Once Mandrake discovers a civilian radio broadcast, he realizes Ripper is bonkers and he tries to trick the general into revealing the recall code.

Meanwhile, a hapless, hopeless President Merkin Muffley has to contend with a drunken Soviet Premier Dmitri Kissof as well as a gung ho General Buck Turgidson (George C. Scott), who pushes for an all-out attack. Pandemonium breaks out in the War Room when Ambassador de Sadesky (Peter Bull) informs the president that the Soviet Union has constructed a doomsday device, a new Russian weapon programmed to automatically detonate in the event of nuclear attack. As the world hangs in the balance, the big brass gathered in the War Room hatches a plan to assist the Russians in shooting down American B-52s. Mandrake figures out the secret recall combination only to be hassled by homophobic Colonel Bat Guano (Keenan Wynn). Such are Mandrake's powers of persuasion, however, that he eventually talks Guano into liberating change from a Coke machine so he can telephone the White House. Guano, who still harbors reservations about Mandrake's credibility, shoots back, "You're gonna have to answer to the Coca-Cola Company."

Eventually, all the B-52s are accounted for except *The Leper Colony*, commanded by Major T. J. "King" Kong (Slim Pickens), a crafty, good-old-boy Texan who manages to evade USSR fighters as he heads for Laputa, a designated target deep inside Russia.[39] Back in the War Room, the wheelchair-bound ex-Nazi, Dr. Strangelove, suggests mineshafts could save top government officials from extinction.

Meanwhile, Kong discovers that the bomber bay doors are jammed. After hastily rewiring the circuitry, Kong inserts an alligator clip into the patch panel and the latch releases at the last possible moment. He rides the bomb down like a cowboy on a bucking bronco. The exploding "Hi There" missile triggers the doomsday machine and the world ends in a series of dramatic mushroom clouds.

DOVISM IN *DR. STRANGELOVE*

Writing from the vantage point of the present, film expert Robert Kolker claims, "Part of the complexity of *Dr. Strangelove* is that it presents its [end of the world] prophecy as comedy, provoking laughter and fear."[40] Writing from the vantage point of 1964, Bosley Crowther begs to differ. *Dr. Strangelove* was "beyond any question, the most shattering sick joke I've ever come across."[41]

You Can't Be Serious

Laughter, at least for Stanley Kubrick, proved the only sane response to the madness of MAD.[42] Critic Lewis Mumford seemed to resonate with Kubrick's message: "What the wacky characters in *Dr. Strangelove* are saying is precisely what needs to be said; this nightmare eventuality that we have concocted for our children is nothing but a crazy fantasy, by nature as horribly crippled and dehumanized as Dr. Strangelove himself."[43] According to Roger Ebert, "Kubrick made what is arguably the best political satire of the century, a film that pulled the rug out from under the Cold War by arguing that if a 'nuclear deterrent' destroys all life on Earth, it is hard to say exactly what it has deterred."[44]

Director Barry Sonnenfeld, known for his smart comedies,[45] believes Kubrick succeeded by placing ridiculous characters in an absurd situation but directing his actors to play it straight.[46] Ebert agrees, adding "*Dr. Strangelove*'s humor is generated by a basic comic principle: People trying to be funny are never as funny as people trying to be serious and failing"[47]

Further, Kubrick's genius, according to Sonnenfeld, was permitting the audience to decide where the laughs were located. By favoring wide shots over close-ups, Kubrick kept the camera neutral. Instead of signaling a jest by zooming in, he kept the actors in two-shot, encapsulating both action and reaction. "More than anything, this is great satire," claims Sonnenfeld, "which only works if you have the self-confidence to chance failure. With *Strangelove*, Kubrick wasn't interested in making something mildly amusing—it was either going to work or fail."[48]

Satire, while not always endurable for an audience, has without question always endured. Coined by Latin poet Gaius Lucilius, the word comes from "satura," a crude mockery of Roman customs and manners. The literary form, with its specific rules and regulations, was fine-tuned by Horace, Persius, and Juvenal. In 1704, Jonathan Swift wrote, "Satire is a sort of glass, wherein beholders do generally discover everybody's face but their own."[49] Common usage of "satire," however, now includes any work in which vices, follies, or abuses are held up to ridicule and contempt. According to Northrop Frye, essential ingredients are (1) humor based on a sense of the absurd and (2) an object of attack.[50] Kubrick found both in the possibility of atomic devastation. According to biographer Alexander Walker, "Ultimately the most critical decision [Kubrick] made in approaching the subject of nuclear destruction came from his perceiving how comedy can infiltrate the mind's defense mechanism and take it by surprise."[51]

Satire, which usually skewers topical subjects, doesn't, as a rule, age well. While it is possible to experience what Steve Allen calls "retrospective laughter," satire is usually current.[52] Critic Jeff Simon, writing in 1994, asks, "Is [*Dr. Strangelove*] out of date? Of course it is. . . . [N]one of us goes to sleep worrying about a nuclear payload landing in our left ear."[53] In 2003, audiences, heads full of headlines, purchase Sominex in the large economy size. Take a gander at North Korea—firing up plutonium-producing breeder reactors, stockpiling missiles capable of hitting Anchorage, kicking out UN nuclear weapons inspectors, and pulling out of the Nuclear Nonproliferation Treaty. Terrorists, in addition, are always hoping to join the nuclear club and although Saddam didn't have nukes squirreled away somewhere in Iraq, he could have sold them to Bin Laden's boys.

Another problem with offering up satire is that the material just might be "too hip for the room." Parody, which is closely related to satire, deliberately copies a well-known work in a comic manner. A parodist, for example, might spoof the PBS hit *Antique Road Show* by inviting viewers to bring in their "oldest" frozen food items for appraisal. In *Dr. Strangelove*, the military relies on research from the Bland Corporation, a takeoff on the top secret, government-funded Cold War think tank. The audience so identified Rand Corporation with nuclear planning that everybody got the joke. Meanwhile, the *Leper Colony*'s primary bombing target in Russia is Laputa.[54] Those who read *Gulliver's Travels* are aware that Laputa is an imaginary flying island populated by pseudoscientists, so self-absorbed that they must be brought back to reality by being hit on the head. For those who have successfully avoided the classics, however, knowing the derivation of Laputa is not essential to grasping the plot—the literary reference merely enriches the cinematic experience.

Kubrick et al.'s main targets (Curtis LeMay, Nikita Khrushchev, and Wernher Von Braun) were recognizable public figures in 1964. It is interesting to note that only those critics writing after 1968 insist that the title character is modeled after Dr. Henry Kissinger, who in 1964 toiled in obscurity at Harvard. Screenwriter Terry Southern offers the definitive word; he claims Dr. Strangelove was modeled after Wernher Von Braun.[55]

"The best satires," according to Steve Allen, "are those which make use of a great many components of the target's overall makeup, rather than just picking up a particular aspect or two of that totality."[56] Take the character of Group Captain Lionel Mandrake, who is not just another stereotypically unflappable Limey. While Richard Corliss sees in Mandrake "a gentle exaggeration of Trevor Howard's wartime persona,"[57] Mandrake is also a damn good shrink, the best of whom are empathetic and especially adroit at inhabiting the worlds of their patients. Mandrake, in fact, becomes so nimble at getting inside Ripper's head that he is able to figure out from Ripper's doodles the code that would recall the bombers.

Satirists also run the risk of going too far. There's a slippery slope that descends from clever send-up to clumsy slapstick. *Saturday Review* reproved Kubrick for plunging "to such low farce as to have a Coca Cola machine squirting itself in the face of a colonel."[58] Andrew Sarris also notes that the sign "Peace is our Profession" was funny the first time—after that, the joke got really old.[59]

Kubrick intended *Dr. Strangelove* to end with a custard pie fight between the Russians and the Americans in the War Room. According to
Ken Adam, "It was quite brilliant, like *Hellzapoppin.* You had George C.
Scott swinging from the lighting and Peter Sellers (as the president) sitting in the middle of the room making custard 'sandcastles' with the Russian ambassador. After [five] days of filming, the room was ankle-deep in
pie."[60] This sensationally funny footage, however, ended up on the cutting room floor. Upon reflection, Kubrick considered the material too far-
cical and replaced it with a montage of mushroom clouds.[61] Peter Bull,
who portrayed the Russian ambassador, recalls that the fight "took nearly
a fortnight to complete and must have cost thousands and thousands of
dollars."

As a dove, Kubrick couldn't have allowed a Three Stooges–like ending to trivialize his antinuke argument. After all, if the hawks really had
their way, the world wouldn't be covered in whipped cream, but nuclear
winter. Southern concurred with Kubrick's decision: "What was happening in the pie fight is that people are laughing. It's supposed to be
deadly serious."[62]

In addition, Geoffrey Shurlock, who doled out Motion Picture Association of America Code seals, objected to involving the Leader of the Free
World in a silly slapstick sequence. Kubrick, dodging Shurlock's concerns,
countered "because the film took place in the indefinite future, it avoided
ethical problems as they related to the current administration."[63] In addition, at one point, a pie knocks President Muffley off his feet, prompting
General Turgidson to cry out, "Gentlemen! Our gallant young president
has just been struck down in his prime!" Although Kubrick had already
decided to edit out the pie fight before President Kennedy's assassination,
this line (or possibly even the entire sequence) would have been eliminated with the JFK tragedy.

According to Calvin Trillin, "In modern America, anyone who attempts
to write satirically about the events of the day finds it difficult to concoct a
situation so bizarre that it may not actually come to pass while his article
is still on the presses."[64] A 1948 Newburgh, New York, study, coupled with
some heavy-duty lobbying by dentists, convinced most Americans that
they should fluoridate their water.[65] Yet, there were a number of holdouts,
especially in rural areas, who were not only opposed to any sort of collective (read Communist) government action but who were also concerned
about fluoride as a health threat, since it was already present in hundreds
of food products. Ripper wasn't exaggerating their views when he said, "A
foreign substance is introduced into our precious bodily fluids without the
knowledge of the individual. Certainly without any choice." Further, little
did Kubrick realize that, forty years later, patients would be diagnosed
with the "Dr. Strangelove syndrome." The previously unrecognized condition leaves victims with an appendage that refuses to behave. According

to the London *Times,* "The sufferers find that, despite their best intentions, the hand will pick up objects such as scalding cups of coffee or steal ice creams and other food from friends."[66]

James D. Harris was positive Kubrick was making a big mistake.[67] Even if his partner could successfully translate Peter George's somber treatise, *Red Alert,* into a spoof of Cold War hawkism, according to Tinsel Town conventional wisdom, "Satire closes on Saturday night. Political satire starts dead." Kubrick, however, kept insisting that he couldn't play it straight—"the only way this thing really works for me is as a satire. It's the same point, but it's a better way of making the point."[68]

Fortunately for Kubrick, satire, in reaction to the middle-class square-ness of postwar America, had reached a mid-'60s peak. Americans sub-scribed to *Mad* magazine and played Tom Lehrer, Mort Sahl, and Lenny Bruce comedy albums on their record players. *Beyond the Fringe,* a 1960 English college-revue show spin-off featuring Peter Cook, Dudley Moore, Jonathan Miller, and Alan Bennett, ushered in such radical television fare as *That Was the Week That Was (TW³),* a 1964 Saturday late-night hit that anticipated *Saturday Night Live* by more than a decade.[69] The volatile po-litical climate (coupled with the young liberal demographic represented by baby boomers) caused network programming executives to demand topical satire. *TW³* regularly entertained hip '60s audiences with sketches about racism, alienated youth, suppression of dissent and, of course, nu-clear war.

Satire may have made moguls break out in a rash, but their autonomy eroded in direct proportion to the impact of television. In addition, with the studio system circling the drain, Hollywood's traditional contacts with the military followed suit.[70]

The Devil's in the Details

By the early '60s, Kubrick was obsessed by the subject of thermonuclear war.[71] According to his biographer, Vincent LoBrutto, "The idea of an im-pending nuclear holocaust often crept into his already dark and pes-simistic vision of the world."[72] In fact, when he lived on New York's East Tenth St. he considered moving to Australia—a country well out of the central nuclear bomb target range.[73] Apparently, Kubrick had missed *On the Beach.*

You can't say Kubrick didn't do his research. Ken Adam, the film de-signer on *Dr. Strangelove,* found Kubrick "so steeped in his material that when we first met to discuss it, his conversation was full of fail-safe points, mega-deaths, gyro-headings, strobe markings, and CRM-114s. I didn't know what he was talking about."[74] Kubrick waded through some seventy heavy-duty academic tomes;[75] devoured the writings of such nu-clear strategists as Herman Kahn, Thomas Schelling, and Edward Teller;

and kept up an ever-expanding file of newspaper and magazine articles on lost or damaged nuclear devices, or "broken arrows." During the '50s, there were nineteen crashes of planes involving nuclear weapons. While none of the weapons exploded, several disseminated radioactive material at the crash site. During the '60s, twelve more mishaps were mentioned in unclassified literature.[76]

Kubrick was introduced to Peter George's *Red Alert* by Alistair Buchan, director of the Institute for Strategic Studies in London, who pronounced it "the only feasible, factually accurate fictionalization of the way in which an H-bomb could start without any sane cause or prompting."[77] In a handwritten letter introducing himself to George, Kubrick gushed, "I found your book to be the only nuclear fiction I'd come across that smacked of knowledge." He did, however, express some reservations about the plot, questioning George's curb on "a U.S. president . . . making an all-out attack in these circumstances."[78]

Polaris Productions bought the screen rights for $3,500.[79] Kubrick, Harris, and George began adapting the novel in Kubrick's apartment.[80] According to Harris, "We were working on the script as a serious piece," but apparently Kubrick had been at war with himself.[81] As he attempted to visualize the manner in which events might transpire or dialogue evolve, he found himself discarding any material that provoked laughter. Yet, according to Kubrick, after a month or so, he began to realize "that all the things I was throwing out were the things which were most truthful," so he decided that the only way to tell the story was as "a nightmare comedy where the things you laugh at most are really the heart of the paradoxical postures that make nuclear war possible."[82]

In fact, the film proclaims its satiric intent with the opening sequence—a bomber refueling in midair, juxtaposed against a romantic orchestral interpretation of the 1932 standard, "Try a Little Tenderness." Most of the humor in *Strangelove* arises from ordinary, even mundane behavior carried out within a context of insanity. Take the Bob Newhartesque telephone conversation with the vodka-swilling Premier Kissof—the audience can't help but picture a red-in-the-face, tantrum-throwing Khrushchev on the other end of the line. As Kubrick once wryly observed, "Confront a man in his office with a nuclear alarm, and you have a documentary. If it catches him in the living room, you have a drama. In the lavatory, you have a comedy."[83]

After Kubrick decided to turn *Red Alert* into a satire, he needed some sort of anarchist writer who could tap into the anger and angst of the '60s to help him out. According to biographer Michael Herr, Kubrick's "view and his temperament were much closer to Lenny Bruce's than to any other director." Terry Southern, recommended by both Peter Sellers and long-time Harris associate James Gaffney, seemed to fit the bill.[84] Not only was he a proven collaborator, but also he was hip enough to later become the only guy on the *Sgt. Pepper* album cover wearing sunglasses. Southern spelled out his artistic credo in an interview in 1964: "The important thing in writing," he said, "is the capacity to astonish. Not shock—shock is a worn-out word—but astonish. The world has no grounds whatever for complacency. The Titanic couldn't sink, but it did. Where you find smugness, you find something worth blasting. I want to blast it."[85]

The fantasy sketch was central to Southern's subversive comic technique. In his novel *Flash and Filigree,* the popular '50s TV show *What's My Line?* becomes *What's My Disease?* with suffering contestants hoping to stump a panel of notables with their peculiar infirmities. In the picaresque *The Magic Christian,* copies of which Peter Sellers doled out as Christmas presents, Guy Grand prepares elaborate and expensive practical jokes. According to biographer Lee Hill, "If there was one thing Terry was a master of, it was black comedy. Through influences like Kafka, Celine, and especially Henry Green, Southern understood that the most banal situations and statements could be charged with multiple meanings."[86]

It seems unlikely that George came up with much of the funny stuff in *Dr. Strangelove.*[87] *Red Alert* is an unsmiling thriller, replete with wonkish details. The message, a caveat against the dangers of hair-trigger nuclear retaliation systems, does, however, wrap up with an optimistic ending—a dud bomb averts catastrophe and Russia is persuaded by the American president to opt for peace. George, a former Royal Air Force lieutenant and active member of the Campaign for Nuclear Disarmament, wrote the novel to articulate his anxiety about the nuclear arms race. He was, according to Hill, "an odd duck—a hack with pretensions."[88] In his introduction to the 1979 edition of the *Dr. Strangelove* screenplay, Richard Gid Powers contends that Kubrick and Southern's screenplay altered George's original work not only beyond what George had envisioned, but beyond his talent as well.[89]

According to Tobias Gray, "Kubrick was, despite various other qualities, about as funny as a heart attack."[90] The shooting script, at least to major critics, seemed to have Southern's fingerprints all over it. According to Richard Corliss, Southern was probably responsible for the Major Kong character, Colonel Bat Guano's memorable "deviated pervert" speech, and Ripper's monologue on "precious bodily fluids."[91] Kubrick, however, told the *New York Times* that Southern contributed to an "already completed" screenplay, merely adding more "icing on the cake."[92]

When the reviews for *Dr. Strangelove* came in, the press, especially *Life* and the *New York Times,* were quite generous in praise of Southern. He received the lion's share of credit for the satire's hilarity, which is probably the single most important ingredient. Andrew Sarris suspects "that most of the clever touches in the script can be credited to Terry Southern."[93]

Seeing Southern showered with accolades, however, didn't sit well with Kubrick. He, like his role models (Orson Welles, Charlie Chaplin,

Sergei Eisenstein, and Max Ophuls) was not only a swaggering icono-
clast but also a supreme egotist. According to Southern, "Stanley's obsession with the auteur theory—that his films are by Stanley Kubrick—
overrides any other credit at all."[94] According to biographer John Baxter,
Kubrick viewed the script as a necessary evil and tended to make films
in which the dialogue is not only pared down more than necessary but
also dehumanized, such as is the case with the army slang and various
kinds of jargon employed in *Strangelove*.[95] Perhaps Steve Allen can also
shed some light here. "We will take almost any kind of criticism," says
the comedian extraordinaire, "except the observation that we have no
sense of humor."[96]

When MGM promoted *The Loved One* in *Variety* with "by the writer of
Dr. Strangelove," an apoplectic Kubrick insisted, "Mr. Southern was employed from 16 November to December 28, 1962 [and] had no further part
to play in the production, either as writer or consultant."[97] "I guess," explained a rather disingenuous Kubrick, "I was being generous when I
gave him the third writer's credit on [*Dr. Strangelove*] but I thought it
might help him get more work, if he wanted it."[98]

In letters between Kubrick and George (dated April 1963), Kubrick talks
about changes made while Southern was on board, specifically mention-
ing Major King Kong, who "rides out on the bomb," the pie-throwing
fight, and Strangelove's "psychosomatic reflex of the right arm."[99] But a
screenplay draft dated August 1962, before Southern was employed, did
not contain the Dr. Strangelove character, but did include a scientist
named Von Klutz and a General Buck O'Connor (not Turgidson).[100]

Southern, however, would be the first to point out the considerable in-
put of Peter Sellers, who ad-libbed speeches as all three characters he
played—President Merkin Muffley, Dr. Strangelove, and Group Captain
Lionel Mandrake.[101] In a post-Freudian era, a single actor playing roles
representing the ego, id, and superego makes perfect sense and tends to
unify the cinematic point of view. As Mandrake, Sellers depicts someone
a little too in touch with his feminine side to fit in with the rest of the ma-
cho-to-the-max military, but provides, at just the right moment, the voice
of reason. As Muffley, Sellers reveals a president, despite the title commander in chief, unable to wrest control from the military–industrial complex. In Strangelove, Sellers exposes the dark side of a superior intellect as
well as the deification of science and technology in an anxious age. According to Joseph Adamson, *Dr. Strangelove* embodies "in a single concept, elements that have always been considered diametrically opposed."[102]

Sellers admitted coming up with "Gentlemen, you can't fight in here,
this is the War Room," a "Say, what?" statement that might escape the lips
of our current president. Sellers played Mandrake mostly as written, but
in reference to a game leg he did come up with "My string's gone, I'm

afraid." And who can forget "Do I look all rancid and clotted?" in response to Ripper's lengthy treatise on bodily fluids? Southern especially
remembers, "Good idea, General, splash a bit of cold water on the back of
the neck" as marvelously British. In the sequence in which the president
talks to the Russian premier, Sellers supplied a memorable monologue
about feelings. According to Kubrick, "Peter took the most incredible
chances with characterization."[103]

Why *Dr. Strangelove* Worked

Despite Kubrick's about-face, credit-wise, Southern summed up his collaboration with Kubrick as "We shared the vision." He found the dialogue
in earlier Kubrick–George drafts simply not funny—straining for smiles
and reading like high school parody. The Kubrick–Southern version, however, raised the bar for black comedy. First, the script was stunningly simple, crosscut among only three extremely realistic-looking locales: the air
force base, the B-52 bomber, and the War Room. When the military refused to provide technical assistance, Kubrick based Burpelson on old air
force movies, the B-52 cockpit on a British flight magazine photograph,
and the War Room's 380 square-foot circular desk, halo of lights, back-
projected maps, and darkness on art director Ken Adam's fertile imagination.[104] Adam's bomb shelter–like underground crisis center was a remarkable achievement—the Pentagon hadn't even acknowledged the
existence of such a chamber, much less released pictures of it. "If the end
result bore little resemblance to actual Air Force procedures or equipment," claims Lawrence H. Suid. "most people accepted it as reality in
spite of the film's comic motif."[105] According to *Newsweek*'s Jack Kroll, no
living film director "matches Kubrick in his ability to create a physical
world that transmits a film's emotional frequency."[106]

Second, the satire was anchored in highly detailed realism—all the di-
rector's research paid off. Kubrick claimed he pulled the death statistic for
General "Buck" Turgidson's claim, "no more than ten to twenty million
killed, tops, uh, depending on the breaks" from an actual military journal.
Southern supplied characters with "all the jargon, vernacular, and vocab-
ulary that are specific, peculiar, and particular to their skills and positions.
There is something so utterly pompous about the phrases themselves. . . .
[They] become funny."[107]

Third, the vaguely familiar major characters, although inspired by real-
life personalities, aren't merely humdrum, one-trick pony caricatures.
Major T. J. "King" Kong may seem like a straightforward cowboy who is
just following orders, but he doesn't take Wing Attack Plan R at face
value. Once the message and code are confirmed, however, he delivers a
gung ho patriotic speech over a heavy snare drum–accented "When
Johnny Comes Marching Home" that acknowledges the ambiguous emo-

tions of his men. Finally, the dogged ingenuity that permits him to carry out his mission (despite all manner of obstacles) also allows him to relish the ride of his life. This is no stereotypical Texan.

Fourth, satirists often signal that a work is tongue-in-cheek by supplying parodied names for the characters. Kubrick and Southern, heavily influenced by *Gulliver's Travels,* called on their sexual and scatological expertise with monikers that provoke chuckles of appreciation decades later.[108] In fact, the names of General Buck Turgidson, Group Captain Lionel Mandrake, Colonel "Bat" Guano, and Merkin Muffley sent an entire generation scurrying to the *Oxford English Dictionary.*[109]

Fifth, Kubrick made satiric points by matching visual images with seemingly incongruous musical themes. For example, he uses "Try a Little Tenderness" as two airplanes hook up for midflight refueling,[110] a delicate operation that, if the B-52 (bearing nuclear weapons) even taps the tanker, could end the movie before it begins.[111] In addition, for Kubrick, music is not just background accompaniment, but an actual character. Take the brassy version of "We'll Meet Again" that Vera Lynn croons against a montage of mushroom clouds.[112] The sappily sentimental World War II song was written to boost morale during the fight against fascism. The Cold War, however, was turning out to be an entirely different matter. "We'll Meet Again" promises a reunion "some sunny day," but "sunny day" takes on a whole new meaning when it's illuminated by a hundred exploding bombs.[113]

Deconstructionists, in all academic seriousness, had a ball exploring the relationship between sex and death in the first "make love, not war" film of the '60s. George W. Linden, who wrote extensively on "the American pornography of power," delineated the film as an attack on our propensity to substitute violence for love.[114] Robert Kolker adds that the sexuality in the film "turned to necrophilia, which in turn is part of a greater mechanism of destruction over which the individuals in the films are powerless."[115] Instead of teasing out a connection between sex and death, anarchist Southern probably just wanted to blast away at the cinematic taboo that the production code had made out of intercourse. Further, for the ordinary Joes at the Bijou, sexual references are knee-slappingly funny.[116] As to sexual imagery, the average viewer probably doesn't grasp half of the phallic symbols (from Ripper's cigar, microphone, and pistol to the sleek nose of the B-52 *Leper Colony* to the nuclear bomb nicknamed "Hi There"[117] that Major Kong straddles and rides, rodeo-style, down to earth), but he probably laughs out loud at Ripper's Communist conspiracy explanation for postcoital fatigue; at Strangelove, in the dark, womblike War Room, giving scientific credence to supplying a surplus of sexual partners to government officials; and at Colonel "Bat" Guano suspecting the rather fussy Group Captain Lionel Mandrake of being "some kind of deviated prevert." Phillip L. Gianos points out that "it is difficult to watch the reborn Strangelove arise and not hear "mineshaft" as 'mein shaft.' It is the ultimate phallic reference."[118]

Dr. Strangelove invited moviegoers to eavesdrop on an archetypal locker room conversation. In fact, the "no girls allowed" environment of the War Room is underscored by the hypermasculine Turgidson talking in hushed tones to his sex object "secretary"—"Of course, I deeply respect you as a human being." With all the unabashed sexual innuendo going on in the movie, it seems remarkable that only three issues concerned MPAA censor Geoffrey Shurlock: the phrase "rotten sons of bitches"; the survival kit prophylactics that prompt Kong to say, "Shoot, a fella could have a pretty good weekend in Vegas with all that stuff"; and the coverage area of Miss Scott's teeny, weeny bikini.[119]

Had Shurlock been a feminist, he would have been even more concerned with the objectification of female sexuality and the linking of women with atomic weaponry. In an exchange with Scott (the only female in the film) as he leaves to go to the War Room, Turgidson says, "You just start your countdown, and old Bucky'll be back here before you can say . . . Blast Off!" Yet, according to historian Elaine Tyler May, "You could find this [phenomenon] everywhere from the popular culture—if you opened up a magazine, you could see the picture of a bathing beauty [in a bikini] . . . labeled 'the anatomic bomb.'"[120] According to Anthony Macklin, "the film ends with mushroom clouds of orgiastic world destruction."[121] Tim Dirks also interprets the multiple explosion finale as an endless orgasm.[122] Just think, before Kubrick, literary types used to refer to sexual release as "the *little* death."

Ready, Aim, Fire—A Dove Mocks the Hawks

When *Dr. Strangelove* was released in 1964, White House officials and Pentagon generals alike protested that no nuclear attack could be launched without "civilian authority," or the finger of the president on the red button. In fact, the Department of Defense insisted on a proviso that read "It is the stated position of the U.S. Air Force that their safeguards would prevent the occurrence of such events as depicted in the film." The military maintained that fail-safe procedures, spelled out in the Positive Control Safeguards, could not be subverted as the movie had depicted. Documents declassified in September 1998, however, proved that, in fact, authority to approve a nuclear launch had been "pre-delegated" by the president to the military from the time of Eisenhower.

A plan eerily like Plan R was in full force at the time the film debuted. According to Bill Burr of the Washington-based National Security Archive, declassified documents disclosed "top military commanders had presidentially-authorized instructions providing advance authority to use nuclear weapons under specified emergency conditions."[123] Bruce G.

Blair, author of *The Logic of Accidental Nuclear War,* claimed, "The assumptions of the movie were very valid in that it was quite possible for a lower-
level officer in [the Strategic Air Command (SAC)] to start World War
III."[124] In addition, Jacqueline Kennedy underscored America's deepening
anxiety when she wrote Khrushchev, "The danger which troubled my
husband was that war might be started not so much by the big men as by
the little ones."[125]

Curtis Le May

Until he died, Kubrick was not entirely assured "that somewhere in the
Pentagon or Red Army upper echelon there does not exist the real-life
prototype of Gen Jack D. Ripper."[126] The unsmiling, cigar-chomping Curtis LeMay was an ardent anti-Communist and all business when it came
to matters military. Unlike Ripper, whose lack of emotion was due to obsessive paranoia, LeMay couldn't help appearing cold-blooded. While
leading the 305th to Europe, he was struck by Bell's Palsy, which left his
face frozen for life.

In 1948, LeMay took charge of the Strategic Air Command. During an
early simulation, he was appalled that most long-range bombers missed
their targets by miles. After years of rigorous training, however, "Old Iron
Ass" transformed SAC into an elite unit and the most compelling nuclear
offensive force on the planet. By 1953, SAC was capable of delivering
LeMay's all-out "Sunday punch" anywhere in the world. Like General
Jack D. Ripper, LeMay pushed the world within hairsbreadth of nuclear
oblivion. Unlike General Jack D. Ripper, LeMay did it twice.

LeMay not only ordered a series of what could have been considered
"provocative flights" on spy missions over the Soviet Union without the
permission of President Eisenhower, but he also brought the world to the
brink of nuclear war during the Cuban Missile Crisis.[127] As chief of the air
force, he pushed for a preemptive air strike followed by an invasion, the
most extreme of hawk positions. Convinced by unreliable CIA intelligence that America held overwhelming strategic capability, he asserted
that overrunning the island would get missiles as well as Communists out
of Cuba. "The Russian bear has always been eager to stick his paw in
Latin American waters," he observed. "Now we have got him in a trap,
let's take his leg off right up to his testicles. On second thought, let's take
off his testicles, too."[128] LeMay would have been sorry. In *Khrushchev Remembers,* the Soviet leader recalls, "We had installed enough missiles already to destroy New York, Chicago and the other industrial cities, not to
mention a little village like Washington."[129]

Did LeMay, like the psychotic General Ripper, intend to provoke nuclear
war with the Soviet Union? At Fairford Air Force Base in Britain on May 8,
1954, an RB-47 "Stratojet" from the Ninety-First Strategic Reconnaissance

Wing cruised deep into Soviet airspace under LeMay's orders. Following their mission, Hal Austin and his crew were summoned back to the United States—LeMay wanted to decorate them for bravery. According to Austin, General LeMay quipped, "Well, maybe if we do this overflight right, we can get World War III started."[130] Austin couldn't tell if LeMay's comment was meant to amuse General Thomas Powers or if he was deadly serious.[131] Austin crossed paths with LeMay again in the late '80s, at a retirement community in Riverside, California. "I brought up the subject of the mission we had flown," Austin recalled, "and he apparently remembered it like it was yesterday. His comment again was 'Well, we'd have been a hell of a lot better off if we'd got World War III started in those days.'"[132]

Like General Turgidson, LeMay had been an outspoken proponent of "preventative war," which proposed forcing the Soviets into a confrontation before they could acquire nuclear forces superior to those of the United States. Robert Sprague, a top civilian defense adviser to Eisenhower, remembers inquiring about SAC's state of readiness. LeMay's response to Sprague was quite graphic: "If I see that the Russians are amassing their planes for an attack, I'm going to knock the [expletive] out of them before they take off the ground."[133]

During a 1981 interview with Michael Sherry, "there was a hint that [LeMay] wouldn't have minded if such over-flights had provoked an escalating series of incidents between the U.S. and Russia that would allow that kind of preventative attack to take place." Early in his career, LeMay argued that if one is going to use military force, then one ought to use overwhelming military force. The point was to save lives—both one's own troops as well as the enemy's. You can hear echoes of LeMay's philosophy when Turgidson, rifling through a binder entitled *World Targets in Megadeaths,* offers the president a choice between 10 million and 150 million people killed.

Muffley, representing the dove point of view, refuses to buy the idea of a "winnable" nuclear war or "acceptable" civilian casualty numbers, insisting, "I don't intend to go down in history as the greatest mass murderer since Adolf Hitler." With this scene, Bosley Crowther applauds Kubrick for cutting "right to the soft pulp of the kind of military mind that is lost from all sense of reality in a maze of technical talk, and it shows up this type of mentality for the foolish and frightening thing it is."[134]

Yet in a sense, Muffley, also a target of Kubrick's satire, blunts the dove message. Although Kubrick maintained the film was placed in the indefinite future, most analysts believe Muffley was modeled after the balding, liberal two-time Democratic presidential loser, Adlai Stevenson. Seller did interpret Muffley as prissy and somewhat effeminate, without the nuances of the film's hawk foils. Employing a flat Midwestern accent, Sellers portrays Muffley as a somewhat limp-wristed milquetoast. In contrast, George's president is much more forceful and competent. "Nuclear war is a serious business," claims Thomas Allen Nelson, "one that demands a naturalistic film treatment, with primary characters who impress the audience with their humanity and sense of responsibility; for, after all, it is a problem we all must share and for which we all must be held accountable."[135] At the close of *Dr. Strangelove,* the president, as impotent as Turgidson and Ripper, fails to save the day. Peacenik audience members must have been sorely disappointed in the apocalyptic ending. According to Stanley Kauffmann "This is not a film to please Peace Marchers or Nuclear Disarmers. It does not tell us what we must do to be saved. This film says, 'Ban the bomb' and they'll find another way."[136]

Nikita Khrushchev

On October 5, 1957, as the last vestiges of sunlight disappeared into dusk, Americans squinted at the darkening heavens, trying to distinguish a satellite—the first—from the countless stars blinking awake in the night sky. Hurtling around the planet at eighteen thousand miles per hour, the 184-pound polished metal ball, equipped with a rudimentary radio transmitter, chirped its presence to ham radio operators. Americans, who could only catch a glimpse of the satellite for a few minutes morning and evening, were heady with excitement. After a closer look, however, they grew anxious and angry—the name on the satellite was Russian.[137] President Eisenhower, endeavoring to shrug off the accomplishment, barked, "They put one small ball in the air,"[138] yet the question on everyone's lips was "are the Russians really that smart?" Those who had encountered Nikita Khrushchev, the barely educated peasant and protégé of Stalin at the pinnacle of the Communist Party structure, remained unconvinced.

Still reeling from the shock of the Russians exploding their own bomb in 1949, in-denial Americans tried to write off the circling spacecraft as a hoax, much like General Turgidson's knee-jerk response to the doomsday machine as "a load of Commie bull" and "an obvious Commie trick." *Sputnik II,* loaded with the first space traveler (a dog named Laika) a month later, erased all doubt. The USSR was undeniably capable of accelerating a rocket to seventeen thousand miles per hour, putting six tons in orbit, and operating a life-support system in space. Nuclear scientist Edward Teller called the achievement a technological Pearl Harbor. The United States had always been first, as with the Wright Brothers' *Kitty Hawk,* and best, as with Operation Paperclip, which lured Germany's leading rocket scientists to this country after World War II. Yet, Americans were beginning to wonder if Russia's German scientists might be better than America's German scientists.

In the aftermath of *Sputnik,* Sino–Soviet relations began to sour when Khrushchev wouldn't help China construct nuclear weapons, released Stalin's victims from prison, ended the threat of police terror, and loosened government control over artistic and intellectual expression.[139] Described at the Twentieth Party Congress, Khrushchev's vision of a new Soviet foreign policy included peaceful coexistence between East and West, the avoidability of war, and the recognition that a plurality of paths (one size does not fit all) led to socialism. The most odious remark, made to Mao Zedong, was Khrushchev's prediction that communism would triumph over capitalism via economic, rather than military strength. Kubrick and Southern were thinking of Khrushchev's speech as they framed the Soviet motivation for the doomsday machine as a simple economic strategy.

The Cuban Missile Crisis was followed by a new surge in Soviet–American cooperation. The arms race was curtailed by a 1963 ban on atmospheric nuclear testing and the Soviet Union began to import food from the United States. According to Sergei N. Khrushchev, the son of the former Soviet leader, had his father not been ousted, the Cold War would have ended in the late '60s and the first lunar mission might have been a joint Soviet–American undertaking.[140] With the increasing need for agricultural workers and seeing future warfare, just as Eisenhower had, in strictly nuclear terms, Khrushchev had fully intended to chop the Soviet military—leaving just border and submarine defenses.[141] The Soviet leader confided in his memoirs that, in an effort to avoid nuclear annihilation, he did in fact commit political suicide by opting to trust Eisenhower during the U-2 incident and backing down during the Cuban Missile Crisis.[142]

Unable to reach Dmitri Kissof by telephone (the Soviet premier was "unavailable") the president invites the Russian ambassador into the War Room. Decked out in a prissy frock coat, Ambassador Alexei de Sadesky trolls an elaborate buffet table groaning with an array of meats, breads, and pies.[143] The overweight Nikita Khrushchev was the real-life epitome of the sensual yet shrewd Russian oaf. With his typical barnyard humor, Khrushchev once patted the stomach of a 240-pound Iowa farmer and remarked that the grower made "a good advertisement for America." Singling out two big, healthy-looking blond women in the next breath he growled, "I vant to meet these slaves of capitalism."[144] Although, according to Slavic expert Harlow Robinson, he was "offensive and crude—[there was] something appealingly human and spirited—in Khrushchev's personality that Americans could understand and appreciate."[145]

After stocking up on poached eggs and Havana cigars, de Sadesky provides an unlisted phone number (B-86543) for the president to reach Kissof. The Communist leader, he confides, "is a man of the people, but he is also a man, *if you follow my meaning.*" There is no evidence, however, that Khrushchev was some sort randy Rooskie who might frequent a Moscow brothel. During their 1959 tour, Americans especially took to Nina, Khrushchev's positive and maternal wife. Her unswerving devotion to her husband was exemplified at Blair House, when she calmly interrupted a news conference to bid *dos vedanya* as hubby set out for Camp David. Later, at a Hollywood gala, the Khrushchevs exchanged "lingering glances" while Frank Sinatra warbled a love song.[146]

When Muffley finally gets Kissof on the horn, the premier is pickled. In fact, he is so inebriated he can't remember the phone number of the People's Central Air Defense Headquarters, suggesting that Muffley try Omsk Information. Khrushchev, likewise, didn't mind overtippling on occasion. During the '50s, the Communist Party first secretary got sloshed on a regular basis. On a visit to Belgrade, he even took Tito aback by getting so plastered he had to be carried back to the Soviet embassy. According to Paul Boyer, during the Cuban Missile Crisis, the White House received a long, almost incoherent message from Nikita Khrushchev, prompting Kennedy's top decision makers to wonder whether the Soviet leader had been drunk.[147] According to Khrushchev's butler, while he could have sampled the finest wines, the premier preferred homemade vodka. In fact, Khrushchev's peasant palate was delighted when, on a hunting trip with Cuba's Fidel Castro, he was offered some local, decidedly rotgut, *samogon*. "Get the recipe," he ordered, "I want this drink on my dining table."[148]

As the ambassador explains, the doomsday machine was to be announced at the upcoming Party Congress. "As you know," he adds, "the Premier *loves* surprises," a remark that harkens back to the most dramatic moment in Nikita Khrushchev's political career. At the 1956 Communist Party Congress, he staggered those assembled with a scathing eight-hour discourse assailing Stalin's murder of innocent Communists, trust in Hitler, and cultivation of "a cult of personality" to enhance his own deification. Not realizing the true extent to which Stalin had ordered arrests, executions, imprisonment, and torture and bankrupted lives, "they listened in shocked silence, only occasionally interrupting the speaker with exclamations of amazement and indignation," according to dissident Soviet historian Roy Medvedev.[149]

The second time the president has to repeat "let me finish, Dmitri," he has run out of patience—and time. Hopping-mad Kissof will just have to wait until the world is saved before he can blow his top. Khrushchev's hair-trigger temper was also legend. His prickly pride would prompt him to fly off the handle at perceived slights or insults. During the 1960 UN meetings in New York, he actually took off his shoe and banged it on the table, he was so enraged by a Western delegate's speech. The Soviet Union was fined ten thousand dollars for his boorish breach of protocol.

When John F. Kennedy met with Nikita Khrushchev in June 1961, he noticed a medal hanging around the Soviet premier's neck. It was the Lenin Peace Prize. With a smile, Kennedy quipped, "I hope you'll keep it."[150] President Kennedy especially relished bantering with the Soviet leader, although Khrushchev didn't always accept kidding in the spirit

JFK intended. When lighting a cigar, Kennedy dropped the match behind Khrushchev's chair. Khrushchev, not entirely sure of the American president's intent, accused, "Are you trying to set me on fire?" Kennedy, however, just grinned and then added with characteristic wit, "Ah, [as] a capitalist, not [as] an incendiary."[151]

Dr. Strangelove, however, features the two leaders taking time to share feelings as well as information in a disjointed conversation that culminates in a seemingly endless series of apologies—"I'm sorry too, Dmitri. I'm very sorry. All right! You're sorrier than I am! But I am sorry as well. I am as sorry as you are Dmitri. Don't say that you are more sorry than I am, because I am capable of being just as sorry as you are. So we're both sorry, all right? All right?" Interestingly enough, when closely scrutinized, the sorry "sorry" argument between Kissof and Muffley also juxtaposes the hawkish "we can't let the Reds get ahead" viewpoint against the typical dove contention that "we are all human beings with the same thoughts, feelings, and dreams." As that distinguished philosopher Eric Segal once wrote, "love means never having to say you're sorry." Sorry.

Wernher Von Braun

As far as Terry Southern was concerned, Strangelove was a combination of "the great crazy German scientists of the period and Wernher Von Braun [as well as] Peter Sellers presenting [the type] as madman."[152] Sellers, whose gift/curse was to be totally possessed by his character, couldn't wait to wrap his mind around Strangelove.[153] A veritable chameleon, Sellers could immerse himself in any emotional state, including insanity. In fact, as various biographers contend, psychosis wasn't much of a stretch for him. "There used to be a real me," Sellers once quipped, "but I had it surgically removed."[154]

As an actor, Peter Sellers always worked on a character's voice first. Kubrick speculated that Strangelove's intonation "was probably inspired by the physicist Edward Teller who became known as the Father of the H-Bomb." It's unlikely, however, that Sellers took Teller as a model, since most moviegoers are sophisticated enough to distinguish between a Hungarian and a German accent. Kubrick eventually admitted that Seller's interpretation of Strangelove wasn't at all close to Teller.[155] Actually, Sellers claimed he based Strangelove's strangled accent on Weegee, the famous German-born crime photographer of the 1950s. New York's Finest gave Arthur Fellig the homophonic nickname "Weegee" because of his uncanny ability to show up at murder scenes even before the cops did—as if he had consulted a Ouija Board. Actually, Sellers met Fellig (an early influence on the fledgling photographer Stanley Kubrick) during an on-set visit.[156]

Next, after working with costumes and makeup, Sellers usually practiced the character's walk. The problem was Strangelove, unlike the athletic Von

Braun (who enjoyed scuba diving, fishing, hunting, sailing, and flying), was confined to a wheelchair.[157] While critics have surmised that the conveyance was necessitated by Sellers' injured ankle, in reality Kubrick and Sellers were looking for a prop to illustrate their notion that "politically powerful figures are impotent in some way."[158]

When Sellers initially focused on Strangelove's black-gloved hand (Kubrick's "homage" to the Rotwang character in *Metropolis*),[159] he unexpectedly realized, "Hey that's a storm-trooper's arm." So instead of allowing the upper limb to hang limply, "looking malignant," he decided to give the appendage a life of its own. "That arm hated the rest of the body for having made a compromise," explained Sellers. "That arm was [still] a Nazi."[160] Kubrick always gave the highly imaginative Sellers complete freedom to express himself. In fact, the director planted cameras all over the set to capture any megamagic that evolved as a frenzied Sellers improvised. According to LoBrutto, "During one of his hysterical tirades for the conclusion of the film, Sellers, as the maniacal doctor, who has little control over his body, threw his arm into a Nazi salute and screamed, 'Heil Hitler.'" As Kubrick and Sellers refined the scene during a protracted series of takes, Kubrick asked Sellers to work in that particular piece of business. Sellers was more than happy to oblige.[161] Kubrick's wife, Christiane, who often sketched on the set, readily recollected Sellers's hyperactive creativity and the way the crew had to choke down giggles as Sellers employed Strangelove's mechanical hand to deliver obscene gestures.[162]

To find out more about the doomsday machine, President Merkin Muffley consults with the movie's title character, a blond, blue-eyed scientist who serves as director of weapons research and development. In fact, Strangelove looks exactly like Wernher Von Braun, a television celebrity, a national hero, and the most famous rocket scientist of his time.

Dr. Strangelove's "Heil Hitler" salute and references to President Muffley as "Mein Führer" allude to his Nazi heritage. Von Braun not only joined the Nazi Party in 1937, but also enlisted in the SS, the elite group that controlled military police activities, Nazi intelligence, and the administration of death camps. Von Braun later claimed that, without doing so, he could have kissed off a career in rocketry.[163] He admitted, however, being fully aware that three thousand of his rockets were aimed at London, Antwerp, and Brussels during the closing stages of the war. Although 2,774 people were killed in Britain alone, V-2s failed to alter the course of the war as Hitler hoped.[164] When the first rocket hit London, in fact, Von Braun recalled thinking the V-2 is "a success but it has landed on the wrong planet."[165]

Von Braun skirted the moral aspects of his Nazi Party membership by claiming he intended his rockets to be used for space travel instead of weaponry. In fact, a girlfriend turned him in for saying so and Heinrich

Himmler himself arrested Von Braun for sabotage and intent to defect. Von Braun spent two weeks in jail before Minister of Armaments Albert Speer, anxious to get his top rocket scientist back, arranged for his release. Yet, in 1995 *Nature* magazine disclosed that, as a senior SS officer, Von Braun had ordered executions and didn't object to the use of concentration camp inmates and POWs on the V-2 production line. Von Braun was cognizant of the fact that at Mittelwerk, approximately six thousand rockets were manufactured using forced labor. At Nordhausen, after completing an inspection of the factory, Von Braun supposedly uncovered evidence of sabotage and twelve men were hanged.[166]

Kubrick et al. were not the first to ridicule Von Braun. During the '60s, political satirist Tom Lehrer (who claimed "political satire is dead" when Henry Kissinger was awarded the Nobel Peace Prize) wrote, "When the rockets are up, who cares where they come down. 'That's not my department,' says Wernher Von Braun." In another vein, Von Braun "aimed for the stars," Mort Sahl liked to muse, "but sometimes he hit England."

When the cinematic Strangelove became a U.S. citizen, he Americanized Merkwuerdigliebe to its literal German meaning, namely "Strangelove." On April 15, 1955, Von Braun and forty of his associates became naturalized citizens, prompting a question government officials have avoided since World War II, namely, "How ethical was it to put Nazi scientists to work for the United States?" In *Secret Agenda,* Linda Hunt writes "Dazzled by German technology that was in some cases years ahead of our own," the powers that be "simply ignored its evil foundation . . . and pursued Nazi scientific knowledge like a forbidden fruit."[167] One justification for "importing" Von Braun and 115 German scientists to build rockets for Uncle Sam was that if we didn't use them the Russians would. Americans had been scouring Germany for scientific talent and under the terms of the 1945 Yalta Agreement the German region where V-2 production factories were located would fall under Russian control. To preempt the Reds from grabbing valuable personnel and equipment, American government officials shuffled them through organizations with names such as Joint Intelligence Objectives Agency, National Interest, Washington Liaison Group, Combined Intelligence Objectives Subcommittee, and the Inter-American Defense Board. Investigative journalists have since uncovered evidence that Operation Paperclip administrators, to keep the Germans in this country and to protect them from outraged Americans, stonewalled, committed perjury, obstructed justice, destroyed/altered records, and contravened the president's explicit orders to close U.S. borders to Nazis, arguing the ends justified the means.[168]

In the movie, President Muffley poses the question, "Could Russia really have a Doomsday Machine?" The short answer, according to Strangelove, is "yes." According to Bruce G. Blair, U.S. intelligence in 1984 actually detected a Russian doomsday device, programmed to automatically fire its nuclear missiles in the event the country's military hierarchy is killed or unable to push the button.[169] The secret system, which Russia dubbed "the dead hand," was developed by Soviet scientists during the 1970s and was still operative as of 1993.[170]

The real Von Braun possessed an energetic personality and the remarkable ability to express complicated ideas succinctly and clearly. "He was a man of irresistible charm coupled with almost magic powers of persuasion," according to associate Ernst Stuhlinger. Strangelove is as animated and credible as he outlines the history of the doomsday project in America. After reviewing the Bland Report, Strangelove recommended a "no go"—"My conclusion was that this idea was not a *practical* deterrent, for reasons which, at this moment, must be all too obvious." To Strangelove, the automatically triggered doomsday machine, while certainly terrifying (and therefore, the epitome of deterrence), was unfortunately, also highly impractical, with no way to "unplug" the machine. Herman Kahn, a real-life Rand think-tank physicist, also rejected automated response systems as nuclear deterrents.[171] He additionally argued in *On Thermonuclear War* (1960) and *Thinking about the Unthinkable* (1962) that while the probability of accidental war was higher than most hawks wanted to admit, there was little evidence to validate the dove prediction that no life would survive a nuclear explosion. Kahn summarily rejected MAD (mutually assured destruction) and maintained that with proper planning (there was a fallout shelter in his residence) not only could an acceptable number of humans survive a nuclear conflict but also a prewar standard of living could be restored within a relatively short period of time.

In the film, Strangelove swings around in his wheelchair to predict, even with the doomsday machine activated, that all is not lost. After making rapid calculations on a circular slide rule, he proposes a one hundred-year plan for survival in radiation-proof mineshafts equipped with nuclear reactors, greenhouses, and barnyard animals. Von Braun, who also held out hope for the future, would have looked to the sky rather under the earth's surface for the answers.[172]

When, in regard to the mineshaft survival plan, President Merkin Muffley admits discomfort at the idea of having to decide who would stay and who would go, Strangelove clucks, "Well, that would not be necessary. It could easily be accomplished with a computer." He goes on to explain, his excitement growing with each detail, that selective sexual breeding would hasten the repopulation of the earth. He makes a quick estimate, figuring a ratio of ten females to one male, saying "I would guess that they could then work their way to the present gross national product within say, twenty years."[173] Kahn would have been proud.

Strangelove truly lived up to his name. Do not forget that the philosophical roots of Nazism, which allowed Germans to subjugate others without qualm, held that there is nothing unique about the individual, nor universal about humanity. His strictly scientific version of "go forth and multiply," however, an involuntary and impersonal twist on what should be an inspired and intimate act, is "strange love," indeed.

Von Braun once observed, "We are all on a spaceship and that spaceship is earth. Four billion passengers—and no skipper."[174] Perhaps Strangelove's aspiration, to rule the world, has been halted by wheeling and dealing politicians or generals. In addition, an ex-Nazi in a wheel-chair could symbolize the crippled state of fascism. Finally, Strangelove, scrunched down in the metal-framed transport, seems to appear only child-sized, but then any man wrapped up totally in himself makes for a very small package.

According to Anthony Macklin, the impotent Strangelove "is [a] prod-uct of German science, talking in a measured, clipped accent, his arm snapping at his throat and his crotch in an uncontrollable attack."[175] How-ever, as he starts to lay out his mineshaft "survival of the fittest" scheme, with *himself in charge,* he feels his virility stirring. When Strangelove cries out, "Mein Führer, I can walk," the power of fascism, once restricted to a prosthesis, can now somewhat miraculously direct his entire, *erect* body into a full-on, self-worshipping goosestep. As the earth dies, he is born again as the Hitlerian savior of humanity.[176]

In the excised ending, according to Seller's biographer, Roger Lewis, "Suddenly, you see a heaving mess (of custard muck) drag himself out and it's Strangelove. He gets a gun and fires it in the air and says: 'Gen-tlemen, gentlemen, don't you realize what will happen to us all in a mo-ment? This pie is non-protective! We must go down to the shelter as quickly as possible. Don't worry about showers [He couldn't mean cyanide-dispensing showers, could he?] we have plenty down there. Through the mine shaft!'"[177] With Strangelove, fascism wouldn't die with Hitler. According to biographer Daniel De Vries, "The Kubrick world . . . is marked by belief in the badness of human nature, and the suggestion that there is at work in the universe some malevolent force, whose chief aim is to destroy human beings and their expectations."[178]

The sinister Strangelove is not a likable guy. In fact, Kubrick hid him be-hind dark glasses and only brought him out of the shadows at the end to pontificate. Further, Kubrick used Strangelove to play "What If," asking the audience to imagine what horrors would have befallen the world if the Nazis, instead of the United States, had developed the bomb. Not con-tent to remain merely a high priest worshipping at the altar of science, Strangelove yearns to be worshipped himself—and he sees that happen-ing deep in the bowels of the earth, where some contend Satan resides.

While Von Braun detractors also considered him the devil incarnate, the ex-Nazi's profound spirituality and life-long belief in God remains a dra-matic contrast to Strangelove's plot to build the perfect race. "We should remember that science exists only because there are people," warned Von

Braun, "and its concepts exist only in the minds of men. Behind these concepts lies the reality which is being revealed to us." He paused to add, "but only by the grace of God."[179]

THE AUDIENCE RESPONDS

Although postproduction was wrapped before the assassination of President John F. Kennedy, the film's premiere was "not considered suitable for the present moment" and was delayed until January.[180] Coincidentally, the president, before his untimely demise, had settled back into a more dovish position, affirming "that the chance of annihilation through accident, miscalculation or madness [was] far greater than the possibility of nuclear war being started deliberately by either side."[181]

According to John Massengale, "One way you know for sure that things are about to change is when the status quo becomes the absurd."[182] The status quo, namely, a policy of mutually assured destruction, had gotten pretty absurd, but things were about to change. *Dr. Strangelove* reverberated through the emerging American counterculture in much the same way as nuclear explosions do in the closing scene. *Dr. Strangelove* started a dialogue about not only the possibility of accidental nuclear war but also the morality of tackling such a subject as a cinematic comedy.[183] Radical criticism of America's nuclear policy started to fill opinion pages domestically and abroad. The word "Strangelove," defined as a prophetic look at the insanity of superpower politics, started appearing in modern political discourse.

"Not that [it was] entirely a case of *post hoc, ergo propter hoc*," argues Alexander Walker, "for the film's release coincided with the eruption of many forms of vocal and active protest by a new generation."[184] Stanley Kramer, whose similarly plotted *Fail-Safe* was released within months of *Dr. Strangelove*, would agree: "I'm convinced that you can't change anyone's mind with a movie."[185] Even though nothing could be done to prevent France and China from joining the nuclear club in 1968, the next year did see the U.S. Senate ratify the Nuclear Non-Proliferation Treaty. In four more years, the United States and the Soviet Union would initial both the first Strategic Arms Limitation Treaty as well as the Anti–Ballistic Missile Treaty.

The film industry was also changing. *Strangelove*'s unexpected success convinced movie studios that antiestablishment, counterculture films held mainstream appeal.[186] In fact, Seth Cagin and Philip Dray further contend that Kubrick fathered the American independent film movement, established the notion of director as superstar, and inspired peers Sidney Lumet, Francis Coppola, Hal Ashby, the late Alan Pakula, Mike Nichols, Robert Altman, Arthur Penn, and Martin Scorsese to make important political films during the next ten years.[187]

Kubrick did contribute several of the silver screen's most indelible screen images—Slim Pickens bronco riding a bomb to global annihilation, the German expressionist "You can't fight here" War Room, and the manic General Jack D. Ripper staving off American troops with a "Peace is our Profession" plaque looming in the background. According to James Verniere, "Kubrick not only raised the art of filmmaking to new levels [but] helped to turn film criticism into a more challenging and respectable profession."[188]

Kubrick wasn't so sure about the latter—he attributes hostility toward his movies to "critics coming to my films expecting to see the last film."[189] He seemed to be rather proud that none of his movies received unanimously positive reviews or did a blockbuster business. Popularity has never meant quality in The Biz.

Dr. Strangelove certainly had its detractors. Establishment critics such as Hedda Hopper,[190] Penelope Gilliatt, and Bosley Crowther considered the topic unfunny, the treatment subversive, and Kubrick anti-American. Their negative reactions underscored the growing gap between American youth and their elders, with Kubrick's baby-boomer fans cheering from the counterculture wings. "Loving" *Dr. Strangelove* was considered a protest against the futility of nuclear brinkmanship. *Life's* Loudon Wainwright provided a response to those who contended that Kubrick had actually betrayed his country with such an irreverent spoof: "As a satirist, he is involved in revealing the human folly through burlesque. I don't see why an artist has to do any more than produce an artistic experience that reflects his thinking."[191]

In fact, earning Hopper's disapproval was considered a plus. As to Gilliatt of the British *Observer*, although she considered the film "as specific as the wound of a stiletto and so close to the facts that it makes you feel ill," she also allowed that "only an American would have the guts to do it."[192] Crowther of the *New York Times* found himself divided "because there is so much about it that is grand," but he was particularly "troubled by the feeling, which runs all through the film, of discredit and even contempt for our whole defense establishment, up to and even including the hypothetical Commander in Chief."[193] Later that year, however, Crowther ended up including *Strangelove* on his "Ten Best" list, which prompted Arthur C. Clarke to christen him "The Critic Who Came in from the Cold."[194]

Another difficulty, according to George Linden, was the inability of critics or audiences to classify the film. "Is *Dr. Strangelove* a comic *On the Beach*, a sardonic *Fail-Safe*, or an insane *Seven Days in May*? Linden considered *Strangelove* the work of a committee.[195]

The film brought in a respectable $5 million on a $1.5 million investment and became the fourteenth highest grossing picture of 1964.[196] *Dr. Strangelove* broke opening day records in New York as well as London.[197]

The film did exceptionally well in Europe, drawing a strong box office in Scandinavia, Italy, and France.[198] Columbia executives, alarmed that JFK's assassination might have tainted the public's taste for topical comedy, did cartwheels when box office receipts arrived.

The film was showered with honors—the Academy of Motion Picture Arts and Sciences nominated the film, Kubrick, Sellers, and the screenplay for Oscars. The Society of Film and Television Arts bestowed a best film award on *Dr. Strangelove,* the New York Film Critics named Kubrick best director, and the screenplay won the Writer's Guild award for best written American comedy and a Hugo for best science fiction. The picture made the 1964 ten best lists of the *New York Herald Tribune* and the *New York Times, Time* magazine's "Top Ten of the 60s," and *American Movie Line's* "Top 100," and it nabbed the twenty-sixth spot on the American Film Institute's "Top 100 films in 100 Years."

Critics who loved satire couldn't get enough of *Dr. Strangelove.* According to Phil Hardy, "The resulting film with its delicious mix of polished realism and bleak, despairing satire, remains the funniest work about nuclear war."[199] *Time* applauded Kubrick for his "dash, boldness, and Swiftian spirit," noting "that the message never quells the madness. His film definitely thumbs its nose at the fate all men fear."[200] *Newsweek* concurred: "The use of comedy to convey the message made his observation all the sharper, all the clearer, and that much better a film."[201]

A number of reviewers, however, shivered behind the snickers. Tom Milne was impressed with "a style that allows [Kubrick] to range with perfect freedom from utter seriousness to the wildest slapstick, without ever loosening the film's claw-like grip on the audience."[202] According to Joseph Adamson III, the viewer "is shocked into laughing at the horror of the threat of nuclear destruction rather than in spite of it."[203] In the *New York Review of Books,* Robert Brustein argued that *Dr. Strangelove* possesses "a great many distinctions as a work of the imagination . . . [and that it] is a plague experienced in the nerves and the funny bone—a delirium, a conflagration, a social disaster."[204] According to *Variety,* "while there are times when it hurts to laugh because somehow there is a feeling that the mad events in *Strangelove* could happen, it emerges as a most unusual combination of comedy and suspense."[205] Years later, Joe Holleman claimed Kubrick set "new heights in black-and-white filmmaking, pushing all borders of dark comedy and crafting a film that still stands as the funniest horror movie—or the scariest comedy—ever made."[206] Lastly, contemporary critic Judith Crist weighed in saying "behind the flashing needles and knives Kubrick wields against the sacred cows there is a gripping suspense thriller, sharply unfolded, tightly told, neatly cut from climax to climax."[207]

Dr. Strangelove encapsulates a moment in American history when wariness and worry informed both government policy and popular culture.

Four decades later, Kubrick's film remains a cautionary tale and a persuasive reminder that somewhere in the human spirit lurks the insane impulse—and the means—to blow up the world.

. . . Just when you thought it was safe to go back in the War Room.

NOTES

1. Quoted in Kim Newman, *Apocalypse Movies: End of the World Cinema* (New York: St. Martin's, Griffin, 1999), 7.

2. Joseph S. Nye Jr., *Understanding International Conflicts: An Introduction to Theory and History,* 3rd ed. (New York: Longman, 2000), 132.

3. Quoted in Anne McElvoy, "The Doves Are Wrong, We Are Morally Right to Fight for Peace," *Independent* (London), November 4, 2001, 27.

4. Easy-to-assemble shelters, ranging in price from $1,795 to $3,895, were advertised in *Life* magazine.

5. In fact, nuclear fear would be blamed for everything from declining SAT scores to rising suicide rates.

6. Stephen E. Ambrose, *Eisenhower* (New York: Simon & Schuster, 1983), 184.

7. Paul Lashmar, "Portrait: The Real Dr. Strangelove," *Guardian,* October 8, 1996, T8.

8. Lashmar, "Portrait."

9. The United States insisted on the time lag so the world would not consider the deal a quid pro quo.

10. Quoted in Todd Gitlin, *The Sixties: Years of Hope, Days of Rage* (New York: Bantam, 1993), 86.

11. Pier M. Wood, "Selected Quotations," *Center for Defense Information,* www.cdi.org.

12. David Halberstam, *The Fifties* (New York: Fawcett Columbine, 1993), 29.

13. Public Broadcasting Service, *The American Experience,* "Interview with Martha Smith,"www.pbs.org/wgbh/amex/bomb/filmmore/reference/interview/marthasmith01.html.

14. Gitlin, *Sixties,* 94.

15. Nye, *Understanding International Conflicts,* 134.

16. Quoted in Halberstam, *Fifties,* 28.

17. Keith Robbins, *The World Since 1945: A Concise History* (Oxford: Oxford University Press, 1998), 99.

18. In 1982, John McMahon, deputy director of the CIA, testified before Congress that the USSR had channeled $100 million annually to the Western disarmament movement, enabling it to grow beyond its inherent capabilities.

19. See C. Cull, A. Erskine, U. Haug, A. Roper–Hall, and J. Thompson, "Human Fallibility in the Control of Nuclear Weapons," in *The Human Cost of Nuclear War,* edited by S. Farrow and A. Chown (Cardiff, Wales: Medical Campaign against Nuclear Weapons/Titan Press, 1983).

20. See Office of Technology Assessment, Congress of the United States, *MX Missile Basing* (Washington, D.C.: U.S. Government Printing Office, 1981).

21. See Scott D. Sagan, *At the Limits of Safety* (Princeton, N.J.: Princeton University Press, 1993).

22. The intruder turned out to be a bear.

23. The potential for a serious false alarm was realized with this event, and orders were given that radar warning sites must be notified in advance of test launches.

24. Paul Lashmar, "Dr. Strangelove's Secrets," *Independent* (London), September 8, 1998, 8.

25. Michael Haederle, "Unmasking the Myth," *Los Angeles Times,* August 9, 1994, E1.

26. See Dwight D. Eisenhower, *Mandate for Change, 1953–1956: The White House Years* (Garden City, N.Y.: Doubleday, 1963), and *Waging Peace, 1956–1961: The White House Years* (Garden City, N.Y.: Doubleday, 1965).

27. Richard Gid Powers, *Not without Honor: The History of American Anticommunism* (New York: Free Press, 1995), 311.

28. Public Broadcasting Service, *The American Experience*, "Interview with John Lewis Gaddis," www.pbs.org/wgbh/amex/bomb/filmmore/reference/interview/gaddis7.html. Gladdis entitled his 1986 bestseller *The Long Peace.*

29. Nitze was obsessed with civil defense and believed that, with enough shelters, civilians could survive a nuclear war.

30. Nye, *Understanding International Conflicts,* 138.

31. Public Broadcasting Service, *The American Experience*, "Interview with General Andrew Goodpaster," www.pbs.org/wgbh/amex/bomb/filmmore/reference/interview/goodpaster01.html.

32. Public Broadcasting Service, *The American Experience*, "Race for the Superbomb: Nikita Khrushchev," www.pbs.org/wgbh/amex/bomb/filmmore/trascript/html.

33. Public Broadcasting Service, *The American Experience*, "Interview with Cargill Hall,"www.pbs.org/wgbh/amex/bomb/filmmore/reference/interview/hall4.html.

34. Early biographer Marquis W. Childs *(Eisenhower, Captive Hero: A Critical Study of the General and the President)* portrayed Eisenhower as a do-nothing incompetent, and a 1962 poll of historians ranked the president twenty-second (out of thirty-one). More recently, however, scholars have considered the thirty-fourth president a shrewd, moderate peacemaker and have subsequently reranked him in the top ten.

35. See John Lewis Gaddis, *We Now Know: Rethinking Cold War History* (Oxford: Oxford University Press, 1997).

36. As leader of the free world, Kennedy had felt it was his responsibility to preempt Communist advances wherever they might occur—for example, in the Bay of Pigs, his escalation of the Vietnam War, and the Cuban Missile Crisis.

37. See *Dictionary of American Biography, Supplement 7: 1961–1965* (New York: American Council of Learned Societies, 1981).

38. Some references show the date of this film as 1963. Its world premiere was scheduled for December 12, 1963, but John F. Kennedy's assassination on November 22 moved the debut up to January 1964.

39. *Leper Colony* was the name of a plane of misfits in *Twelve O'clock High* (1949).

40. Robert Kolker, *A Cinema of Loneliness*, 3rd ed. (Oxford: Oxford University Press, 2000), 126.

41. Bosley Crowther, *"Dr. Strangelove or How I Learned to Stop Worrying and Love the Bomb," The New York Times Film Reviews: 1913–1970* (New York: Arno, 1971), 374.

42. Mutually assured destruction, the nuclear strategy propelling the arms race, was based on the notion that knowledge that the use of nukes would also wipe out the aggressor would deter either side from launching a first strike.

43. Quoted in William L. O'Neill, *Coming Apart* (New York: Quadrangle, 1971), 214–15.

44. Roger Ebert, *"Dr. Strangelove," Chicago Sun-Times*, July 11, 1999, 5.

45. *Get Shorty* (1995), *The Addams Family* (1991), *Addams Family Values* (1993), *Men in Black* (1997), and *Men in Black II* (2002).

46. Sarah Donaldson, "Filmmakers on Film," *Daily Telegraph*, July 27, 2002, 10.

47. Ebert, *"Dr. Strangelove,"* 5.

48. Ebert, *"Dr. Strangelove,"* 5.

49. Jonathan Swift, *The Battle of the Books* (1704), quoted in Wesley D. Camp, *World Lover's Book for Unfamiliar Quotations* (Paramus, N.J.: Prentice–Hall, 1990), 321.

50. Northrop Frye, *Anatomy of Criticism* (Princeton, N.J.: Princeton University Press, 1957),

51. Alexander Walker, *Stanley Kubrick Directs* (New York: Harcourt Brace Jovanovich, 1971), 158.

52. Steve Allen with Jane Wollman, *How to Be Funny: Discovering the Comic You* (New York: McGraw–Hill, 1987), 157.

53. Jeff Simon, "Strange Magic," *Buffalo News*, December 1, 1994, 1.

54. *La puta* is also Spanish for "prostitute" or a crude term for female private parts.

55. Lee Hill, *A Grand Guy: The Art and Life of Terry Southern* (New York: Harper-Collins, 2001), 118.

56. Allen, *How to Be Funny*, 157.

57. Richard Corliss, *Talking Pictures: Screenwriters in the American Cinema 1927–73* (New York: Penguin, 1974), 349.

58. Hollis Alpert, "Dr. Strangelove," *Saturday Review*, January 25, 1964.

59. Andrew Sarris, *Confessions of a Cultist: On the Cinema, 1955/1969* (New York: Touchstone, 1971), 121.

60. Nigel Andrews, "Designer of the Kubrick Era," *Financial Times* (London), March 13, 1999, 7.

61. Images were taken from unclassified 1963 newsreel footage, the original 1945 Trinity test, other atmospheric explosions, and the Bikini Island blast.

62. Hill, *Grand Guy*, 120.

63. Vincent LoBrutto, *Stanley Kubrick: A Biography* (New York: Da Capo Press, 1997), 232.

64. Calvin Trillin, Introduction to *Uncivil Liberties* (1982), quoted in Leonard Roy Frank, *Quotationary* (New York: Random House, 1999), 750.

65. The study, which in hindsight should have included socioeconomic variables, overwhelming demonstrated that the easiest/cheapest way to prevent cavities was fluoridating the water.

66. "Strangelove Syndrome Gives Hands a Life of Their Own," *Times* (London), September 8, 2000.

67. The partnership of Harris–Kubrick had produced *The Killing, Paths of Glory*, and *Lolita*.

68. LoBrutto, *Stanley Kubrick*, 229.

69. *TW3* later ran in prime time.

70. Lawrence Suid, "The Pentagon and Hollywood: *Dr. Strangelove,*" in *American History/American Film: Interpreting the Hollywood Image,* edited by John E. O'Connor and Marilyn A. Jackson (New York: Continuum, 1988), 223.

71. Having made one major antiwar statement in *Paths of Glory* (1957), he was drawn to the premise of nuclear war started by accident or madness.

72. LoBrutto, *Stanley Kubrick,* 227.

73. LoBrutto, *Stanley Kubrick,* 227.

74. LoBrutto, *Stanley Kubrick,* 231.

75. *The Effects of Nuclear Weapons, Soviet Military Strategy, Man's Means to His End, The Causes of WW III,* and *Nuclear Tactics.*

76. Helen Caldicott, *Missile Envy: The Arms Race and Nuclear War* (New York: Morrow, 1984), 44.

77. James Howard, *Stanley Kubrick Companion* (London: Batsford, 1999), 91. The book had been previously published under the pseudonym Peter Bryant as *Two Hours to Doom.* The idea for *Red Alert* came to George when he was buzzed by a Vulcan bomber near Bristol.

78. Louise Jury, "Unique Kubrick Archive for Sale," *Independent* (London), July 9, 2000), 10.

79. Some sources say $3,000.

80. LoBrutto, *Stanley Kubrick,* 228.

81. Howard, *Stanley Kubrick,* 91.

82. LoBrutto, *Stanley Kubrick,* 230.

83. Quoted in Walker, *Stanley Kubrick,* 176.

84. Peter Sellers's contract supposedly stipulated that Terry Southern write the screenplay.

85. Eric Pace, "Terry Southern, Screenwriter, Is Dead at 71," *New York Times,* October 31, 1995, A25.

86. Hill, *Grand Guy,* 114.

87. Forty-two-year-old Peter George, ravaged by alcoholism, killed himself in June 1966.

88. Hill, *Grand Guy,* 111.

89. See Stanley Kubrick, Peter George, and Terry Southern, *Dr. Strangelove* (New York: Gregg, 1979).

90. Tobias Grey, "All up for the Quality Lit Game," *Financial Times* (London), July 7, 2001, 5.

91. Corliss, *Talking Pictures,* 349.

92. Hill, Grand Guy, 114.

93. Sarris, *Confessions,* 120.

94. Hill, *Grand Guy,* 125.

95. Robin Buss, "Paths of Glory and a Clockwork Ego," *Independent* (London), September 28, 1997, 30.

96. Allen, *How to Be Funny,* 9.

97. Howard, *Stanley Kubrick,* 93.

98. Howard, *Stanley Kubrick,* 93.

99. William Russell, "A Rare Glimpse into the World," *Glasgow Herald,* July 13, 2000, 6.

100. Louise Jury, "Unique Kubrick Archive for Sale," *Independent* (London), July 9, 2000, 10.

101. Kubrick wanted Sellers to play what he called "the lead and the lead and the lead." As to Sellers "conveniently" spraining his ankle because he was unable to pull off a Texas accent for Major Kong (the fourth character Kubrick wanted him to play), Southern, who likewise possessed a talent for mimicry, testified that the actor mastered the accent in about ten minutes.

102. "Stanley Kubrick," *Contemporary Authors Online* (Gale Group, 2000). Reproduced in Biography Resource Center (Farmington Hills, Mich.: Gale Group, 2001), www.galenet.com/servlet/BioRC.

103. LoBrutto, *Stanley Kubrick*, 239.

104. Andrews, "Designer of the Kubrick Era," 7. Unsure about the cockpit's CRM (fail-safe device), Ken Adam claimed he "just made it up." After a couple of air force personnel blanched upon viewing Adam's "invention," he realized he had come close. As for the War Room's large, circular conference table, Kubrick insisted on a poker table–like green felt, while the animated wall maps were achieved with light bulbs behind black Plexiglas.

105. Lawrence H. Suit, *Guts and Glory—Great American War Movies* (Reading, Mass: Addison–Wesley, 1978), 195.

106. Jack Kroll, "1968: Kubrick's Vietnam Odyssey," *Newsweek*, June 29, 1987, 64–65.

107. Quoted in Hill, *Grand Guy*, 117.

108. Jonathan Swift invented the name "Master Bates" for a *Gulliver's Travels* character.

109. Buck Turgidson's first name essentially means "virile man," while his last name means "swollen son"; the name "Mandrake" alludes to a forked root that resembles an erect male member; bird or bat excrement is called "guano"; and the president's names refer to a pubic hairpiece ("merkin") and the real thing ("muff").

110. The concept of two planes gently rocking together in simulated sex was Kubrick's, although he recalls a nuclear scientist was reminded of a mother suckling her infant.

111. On January 17, 1966, two years after the release of *Dr. Strangelove*, a B-52 and KC-135 collided over Palomares, Spain, during a routine high-altitude refueling operation. Uproar over the accident led to various European nations rescinding permission for SAC to occupy their airspace.

112. Vera Lynn's most famous song, written by Ross Parker and Hughie Charles in 1939, was first sung in 1939.

113. Kubrick considered running the lyrics over the mushroom cloud footage with a "bouncing ball" invitation for the audience to join in. The idea, fortunately, was discarded.

114. George W. Linden, "Dr. Strangelove," *Nuclear War Films*, edited by Jack G. Shaheen (Carbondale: Southern Illinois University Press, 1978), 58–67.

115. Kolker, *Cinema*, 125.

116. Howard Stern enjoys millions of listeners.

117. A sexual salutation, usually used as a homosexual advance. The second bomb was "Dear John" in the film and "Lolita" in George's novel.

118. Phillip L. Gianos, *Politics and Politicians in American Film* (Westport, Conn.: Praeger, 1998), 145.

119. Originally, Kong referred to Dallas rather than Las Vegas, but the city name was overdubbed after President Kennedy's assassination. Miss Scott is also the *Playboy* centerfold "Miss Foreign Affairs."

120. Public Broadcasting Service, *The American Experience*, "Interview with Elaine Tyler May," www.pbs.org/wgbh/amex/bomb/filmmore/reference/interview/tylermay3.html. The bikini was named for an atomic test site.

121. F. Anthony Macklin, "Sex and *Dr. Strangelove*," *Film Comment* 3 (Summer 1965): 55.

122. "Dr. Strangelove, Or: How I Learned to Stop Worrying and Love the Bomb (1964)," www.filmsite.org/drst.html.

123. Paul Lashmar, "Dr Strangelove's Secrets," *Independent*, September 8, 1998, 8.

124. Eric Lefcowitz, "*Dr. Strangelove* Turns 30. Can It Still Be Trusted?" *New York Times*, January 30, 1994.

125. Stephen Kurkjian, "Retracing Steps in 'The Crisis Years'," *Boston Globe*, July 15, 1991, 33.

126. Gene D. Phillips, *Stanley Kubrick: A Film Odyssey* (New York: Popular Library, 1975), 114.

127. The U-2 Crisis, which occurred on May 1, 1960, did not occur on LeMay's watch. He left SAC in 1957.

128. "Curtis LeMay, Chief of Staff of the United States Air Force, 1961–1965," *The Cold War, 1945-1991*, 3 vols., edited by Benjamin Frankel (Gale Research, 1992). Reproduced in Biography Resource Center (Farmington Hills, Mich.: Gale Group, 2002), www.galenet.com/servlet/BioRC.

129. "Nikita Sergeyevich Khrushchev, 1894–1971," *Contemporary Authors Online* (Gale Group, 2002). Reproduced in Biography Resource Center (Farmington Hills, Mich.: Gale Group, 2002), www.galenet.com/servlet/BioRC.

130. Paul Lashmar, "Stranger than 'Strangelove': A General's Forays into the Nuclear Zone," *Washington Post*, July 3, 1994), C9.

131. General Thomas Power's own officers considered their superior even more hawkish and mentally unstable than General Curtis LeMay.

132. Lashmar, "Stranger than 'Strangelove,'" C9.

133. Lashmar, "Stranger than 'Strangelove,'" C9.

134. Crowther, "*Dr. Strangelove*," 375.

135. Thomas Allen Nelson, *Kubrick: Inside a Film Artist's Maze* (Bloomington: Indiana University Press, 1982), 82.

136. Stanley Kauffman, *New Republic* (January 1, 1964).

137. *Sputnik* meant "fellow traveler."

138. Tim Radford, "Countdown: Space Racers," *Guardian*, June 30, 1994, S10.

139. One of the innocent Soviet citizens, sentenced to hard labor in a Siberian concentration camp, was Khrushchev's own daughter-in-law.

140. Khrushchev relished the fact that his political enemies, post–de-Stalinization, had gotten rid of him via the ballot box instead of assassination.

141. Mark A. Brunelli, "Cold War Revisited at Northeastern," *Boston Globe*, January 24, 1998, B3.

142. See Nikita Sergeyevich Khrushchev, *Khrushchev Remembers*, translated by Strobe Talbott, introduction by Edward Crankshaw (New York: Little, Brown, 1970).

143. The ambassador is named for the Marquis de Sade, the father of sadomasochism.

144. Robert Pear, "Summit in Washington," *New York Times,* June 3, 1990, 1:12.

145. Harlow Robinson, "A Dissident Soviet Historian's View," *Christian Science Monitor,* May 13, 1983, B1.

146. Albin Krebs, "Nina Khrushchev Is Dead at 84," *New York Times,* August 22, 1984, 23.

147. Mark C. Carnes, ed., *Past Imperfect: History According to the Movies* (New York: Holt, 1995), 266.

148. Alan Philips, "Butler Spills the Beans on Khrushchev's Table Manners," *Daily Telegraph,* February 19, 1998, A9.

149. Quoted in Robinson, "Dissident," B1.

150. Theodore C. Sorensen, *Kennedy* (New York: Bantam, 1966), 612.

151. Sorensen, *Kennedy,* 612.

152. Hill, *Grand Guy,* 118.

153. According to Roger Lewis *(The Life and Death of Peter Sellers)* and Ed Sikov *(Mr. Strangelove),* Sellers was an antisocial, drug-addicted, sadomasochistic, megalomaniacal psychopath comparable to both Hitler and the devil himself.

154. Alison Kerr, "Sourpuss behind the Pink Panther," *Herald* (Glasgow), July 24, 2000, 13.

155. LoBrutto, *Stanley Kubrick,* 230.

156. LoBrutto, *Stanley Kubrick,* 12.

157. John von Neumann (1903–1957), best known for his work on the Manhattan Project, attended Atomic Energy Commission meetings in a wheelchair.

158. LoBrutto, *Stanley Kubrick,* 239.

159. Gene D. Phillips, "On the Golem and the Future," *New York Times,* September 2, 1984, 2: 9.

160. Howard, *Stanley Kubrick,* 93.

161. LoBrutto, *Stanley Kubrick,* 242.

162. Hill, *Grand Guy,* 119.

163. Michael Evans, "Genius of V-2 Who Put Americans on the Moon First," *Times* (London), May 2, 1995.

164. Tony Patterson, "Germans at Last Learn Truth about von Braun's 'Space Research' Base," *London Telegraph,* June 10, 2001, 30.

165. Evans, "Genius of V-2."

166. Evans, "Genius of V-2."

167. Peter A. Masley, "The Paperclip File; America's Secret Agenda to Import Nazi Intelligence," *Washington Post,* August 16, 1991, D3.

168. Masley, "Paperclip File."

169. Editorial, "Doomsday Machine," *Houston Chronicle,* October 14, 1993, B18.

170. Wolfgang Munchau, "Russia Holds Strangelove Key to Global Obliteration," *Times* (London), October 9, 1993.

171. In *The Year 2000* (1967), Kahn envisioned a world in which the Soviet Union had collapsed because of its own economic shortcomings.

172. J. Y. Smith, "Dr. Wernher von Braun, 65, Dies," *Washington Post,* June 18, 1977, A7.

173. "Thirteen Women and Only One Man" was Bill Haley and the Comets' double entendre-filled flipside to their 1954 hit "Rock Around the Clock."

174. Smith, "Dr. Wernher von Braun," A7.

175. Macklin, "Sex," 57.

176. Hitler's favorite portrait of himself featured der Führer on a white horse and in Wagnerian garb.

177. Donald Newlove, "Sellers' Bio a Riveting Tale of Evil, Obsession," *Denver Rocky Mountain News,* December 17, 1996, 15D.

178. Daniel DeVries, *The Films of Stanley Kubrick* (Grand Rapids, Mich.: Eerdmans, 1973), 5–6.

179. Ron Davis, "Wernher von Braun Is Eulogized; Astronaut Lauds Rocket Scientist," *Washington Post,* June 23, 1977, C11.

180. Howard, *Stanley Kubrick,* 95.

181. Howard, *Stanley Kubrick,* 95.

182. John Massengale, "Response to Alan Plattus," *New Urban Post* (September 2002), 1.

183. LoBrutto, *Stanley Kubrick,* 248.

184. Walker, *Stanley Kubrick,* 212.

185. Gene D. Phillips, *Stanley Kubrick: A Film Odyssey* (New York Popular Library, 1975), 126.

186. Douglas Brode, *The Films of the Sixties* (Secaucus, N.J.: Citadel, 1980), 132–33.

187. Seth Cagin and Philip Dray, *Hollywood Films of the Seventies* (New York: Harper and Row, 1984), 1–2. The "film director as superstar" notion, in fact, which comes from a book title by Joseph Gelmis, was not new—think Orson Welles.

188. James Verniere, "Director's Influence Led Many Critics to Their Craft," *Boston Herald,* March 8, 1999, 017.

189. Howard, *Stanley Kubrick,* 20.

190. Howard, *Stanley Kubrick,* 97.

191. Howard, *Stanley Kubrick,* 98.

192. Howard, *Stanley Kubrick,* 97.

193. Crowther, "*Dr. Strangelove,*" 375.

194. Howard, *Stanley Kubrick,* 97.

195. Linden, "Dr. Strangelove," 67.

196. Rob Edelman, *Magill's Survey of Cinema,* edited by Frank N. Magill, First Series (Englewood Cliffs, N.J.: Salem, 1980), 466.

197. Howard, *Stanley Kubrick,* 97.

198. LoBrutto, *Stanley Kubrick,* 248.

199. Phil Hardy, *Science Fiction* (London: Aurum, 1991), 229.

200. "*Dr. Strangelove; Or, How I Learned to Stop Worrying and Love the Bomb,*" *FilmFacts* 2, no. 8 (March 26, 1964): 35.

201. *Newsweek,* February 3, 1964, 79.

202. Tom Milne, "How I Learned to Stop Worrying and Love Stanley Kubrick," *Sight and Sound* (Spring 1964): 64–72.

203. Joseph Adamson III, "Stanley Kubrick," *Dictionary of Literary Biography, American Screenwriters* 26(Gale, 1984): 191–98.

204. Robert Brustein, "Out of This World," *New York Review of Books,* February 6, 1964, 3–4.

205. "*Dr. Strangelove,*" *FilmFacts,* 35.

206. Joe Holleman, "Kubrick: The Eye-Opener," *St. Louis Post–Dispatch,* July 18, 1999, C1.

207. Judith Crist, *New York Herald Tribune,* January 30, 1964.

John Wayne's interventionist message comes through loud and clear in The Green Berets. *Courtesy of Batjac Productions and the Academy of Motion Picture Arts and Sciences.*

10

☆

Conclusion: Myth, Megaphone, Metaphor, Mirror, Microscope, and Magic Carpet

What product or service do we purchase when we slap down $7.50 (popcorn extra) in exchange for a movie ticket? Apparently, what we have bought and paid for, in addition to the torn stub offered by the guy in a pseudomilitary uniform, is a story—but something a little more absorbing than the "How was your day?" tales our friends and family recount. As Alfred Hitchcock was fond of saying, "cinema is life with the boring bits cut out." We tend to evaluate our experience with "cinematic narrative" (that's the technical term, film studies–wise) on a strictly individual basis. Sometimes we employ the question, "did I get my money's worth?" Sometimes we use the criteria established by critic Charles Champlin. "The essential function of the movies," he insists, "is still to engross us, to make the screen dissolve and the camera disappear, and to thrust us into the consciousnesses of people who are not ourselves."[1]

A politico who might have spent a little too much time at his friendly neighborhood theater was Ronald Reagan. Not only did he slip pithy Clint Eastwood lines into his campaign addresses, but also, when President-elect Reagan toured the White House in 1980, he was sorely disappointed to discover that the War Room from *Dr. Strangelove* was nowhere to be seen. He shook his head, trying to take in the fact that the striking secret chamber and the twinkling light-tracked Big Board were merely ingenious inventions of scenic designer Ken Adam.

Cinema, according to Jean-Luc Godard, exists in the space between the audience and the screen. Allowing the camera to frame a scene from a certain perspective can generate an ideological message, distinct from either dialogue or action. "Thanks to the mobility of the camera, to the multiplicity of shots," claims Jean Mitry, "I am everywhere at once. I am both in the action and outside it."[2]

283

On occasion, film images, if startling enough, indelibly imprint them-selves upon our minds and memories. The front yard full of yapping pooches resulting from Lonesome Rhodes's suggestion that Big Jeff was probably better suited to dogcatcher than mayor, testifies to Rhodes's power as a populist demagogue. The Greenwich Village bar seemingly populated by gender-ambiguous men in *Advise and Consent* is a cinematic walk on the wild side. Few have forgotten Major "King" Kong, nuclear missile between his thighs, cowboy hat cum riding crop in hand as he hurtles to an explosive finish. For those who respond more readily to an audio cue, there's always the jangling Skeffington jingle that burrows its way inside one's noggin and threatens to remain forever. Sometimes the musical accompaniment can actually eclipse the film itself. Vietnam vet Hal Moore supposes, "If you were to ask me, what did I think of *The Green Berets*, I'd say, 'Well that's a hell of a song.'"[3]

MOVIES AS MYTH

"If Hollywood," contends Ian Scott, "has constructed a pattern of mythi-cal and abstract thinking that is able to instruct our analysis of the real po-litical world through imagery and perception, then it is also critical to our understanding of the medium's influence to recognize its contribution to the representation of political ideas; ideas that have long been an intrinsic part of American society."[4] One cinematic shortcut moviemakers employ to plug into prevalent political thinking is the fantasy theme. "The Land of Opportunity" finds its roots in the Horatio Alger rags-to-riches story. Immigrants came to America with the idea that hard work would lead to endless wealth. Political bosses such as Skeffington in *The Last Hurrah* as-sisted the assimilation of émigrés by offering whatever was needed— whether it be a job with the city or a small business loan—in exchange for an "X" next to the candidate's name on election day. Seabright Cooley, born thirteenth in an impoverished Southern family, has worked his way up to membership in "the most exclusive club in the world." The senator can waltz into any government office and walk out with confidential records; he is privy to the news before it is printed in the *Washington Post*; and he is considered a legend in a town overflowing with legends. On a similar upward trajectory, the synthetic "just folks" Lonesome Rhodes manages to leverage his homespun charm and his persuasive gifts not only into network stardom but also into a consultant's gig for a presiden-tial candidate.

Even the most economically challenged in the audience is provided with an alternative method of determining "real wealth" with the "no man is poor who has friends" fantasy theme. Lonesome Rhodes stumbles over Mrs. Cooley among the homeless in Handy and invites the black woman to appear on his show. He begs his friends the viewers to provide her and her seven kids with a decent house. "Please nobody send in more than four bits, " he cautions, "cuz you may not be able to spare it yourself." Quarters arrive by wheelbarrow. Grizzly Sergeant Zack exposes his heart to the steadfastly loyal South Korean orphan, despite Zack's belief that only loners survive during war. In *The Last Hurrah*, Ford affords Skeffington, by no means a rich man, life's ultimate achievement by allowing the mayor to shake hands with the Grim Reaper while surrounded by a cadre of cronies.

The "knowledge is power" fantasy theme is derived from the wisdom of Francis Bacon. In *Advise and Consent*, the fictional president denies Harley M. Hudson any information about his plans in order to keep Hudson weak and ineffective—in the same way the real-life FDR left Vice President Truman completely out of the loop during his administration. It is Dr. Strangelove's special knowledge concerning radiation-free underground caverns, fruitful male–female ratios, and nuclear-powered greenhouses that puts him in charge of the mineshaft survivors. The entire world may have been slumbering while fascism reared its ugly head, but in *Seven Days in May*, Jiggs Casey fits together a puzzle of innocuous-appearing clues, just in time to interrupt General Scott's military coup.

"Power is the greatest aphrodisiac," claimed Henry Kissinger. From Benjamin Franklin to William Clinton, women have found political powerhouses particularly irresistible. In *Advise and Consent*, bachelor senators such as Lafe Smith and Robert Munson aren't above procuring pulchritude with political power. In *The Green Berets*, the key to kidnapping a prominent North Vietnamese officer is convincing the victim that he is absolutely irresistible to a stunning Vietnamese model. Lonesome Rhodes doesn't marry a smart gal who might help him realize his potential; he instead elopes with a seventeen-year-old baton twirler, who gushes "You're my idol." As Dr. Strangelove realizes he will finally get to order generals and presidents around, he feels his own vigor swelling.

For the political candidate, the professional athlete, and the American businessman, "winning isn't everything, it's the only thing." Joey de Palma has the next Lonesome Rhodes waiting in the wings when the fickle American public finds the fascist a fraud. When Marco recognizes Chunjin as the translator who led this platoon into an ambush, he plans to fight the North Korean to the death. The Oval Office can house only one president—either Jordan Lyman or General James Matoon Scott. The other movies discussed in this book, however, better exhibit the flipside to this fantasy theme—"victory in defeat." Skeffington is still the best man, even though he doesn't win the election. In *Advise and Consent*, the scheming and conniving senator from Georgia doesn't impress us; it's the contrite Cooley who steals our hearts with his release of pledged votes and his unexpected apology. Before committing suicide, Raymond Shaw pauses briefly to don the Congressional Medal of Honor. While the award may have been undeserved before he stopped the Iselins from defiling the White House, his final act of courage truly amends the record.

MOVIES AS MEGAPHONE

During the '50s, according to Peter Biskind, "A conservative director may work with a liberal writer, or vice versa, and both, even if they are trying to impose their politics on the films (which often they're not) may be over-ruled by the producer who is only trying to make a buck."[5] For the most part, smart studio heads held that political subjects were largely to be avoided. In steering clear of explicitly political themes, however, films were actually dispatching the message that politics is neither interesting nor important. The reality, however, was just the opposite. In light of the HUAC hearing brouhaha, politics, as a cinematic focus, proved too inter-esting and too important.

The House Un-American Activities Committee never proved that Com-munist Party members ever put out a single subversive movie. As to al-leged leftist images and seditious dialogue in American films, no credible claims ever turned up in that regard either. To be filed under "reality, what a concept," the Hollywood studio system was based on a strict hands-on control by the moguls, who en masse had adopted Sam Gold-wyn's "If you want to send a message, use Western Union" as their mantra. They didn't make ideological films because ideological films didn't make money.

Tinsel Town bosses, who rarely harbored furtive cravings to serve as social revolutionaries, understood that only a narrow window for signif-icant cultural change ever exists. While some industry heads buckled un-der and churned out profitless anti-Communist cant, they really knew better—it was the movie-going public who determined content by voting with their feet. If Jane and John Q. Public purchased the commodity known as entertainment, then it was up to the dream factory to give them exactly what they wanted. In fact, Hollywood's task was to ascertain the longings and ambitions of the audience, reduce same to a formula, and then repeat the formula in picture after picture, a lesson Hollywood's more prodigious stepchild, television, took to her ample bosom.

In an interview with *Movie*, Otto Preminger admitted, "I always like to project my viewpoint on the audience, but without them knowing it."[6] In *Advise and Consent*, Preminger's message isn't as subtle as he might have hoped. *Advise and Consent* created an unmitigated furor, including ex-tended picketing by the American Legion, the threat of a bill preventing Columbia from distributing the picture outside the United States, and strenuous objections from Edward R. Murrow.

Kubrick, for his part, must have taken a lesson from Darryl F. Zanuck. "If you have something worthwhile to say," counseled Zanuck in 1943, "dress it in the glittering robes of entertainment, and you will find a ready market. . . . [W]ithout entertainment, no propaganda film is worth a dime."[7] Kubrick was taking a big chance by attempting a satire—they usually close on Saturday night. When the Motion Picture Academy and the usual film industry suspects showered *Dr. Strangelove* in prestigious honors, Hollywood wasn't surprised. When ticket buyers plunked down $5 million to see the picture, they were impressed. But nobody was interested in a dark and chilling suspense story like *The Manchurian Candidate* at a time when the economy was in overdrive, the middle class was getting fat, and the future looked rosy. Frankenheimer's "masterpiece" was one Cuban Missile Crisis ahead of its time. Further, Frankenheimer's ploy to get laughs, a parody of McCarthy, doesn't add the right entertainment value—in fact, it distracts from the thriller intent. Budd Schulberg and Elia Kazan shared a similar problem with *A Face in the Crowd.* Not only did their overarching political bias drive them to caricature characters such as Rhodes and Fuller (fascists who represented everything the two former Communists reviled) but they also used the weak and ineffectual Mel Miller as the primary spokesperson for their political message.

If there was one political message, however, that did come through '50s and '60s movie megaphones loud and clear, it was the film industry's blatant antitelevision bias. While it's never a good idea to underestimate an adversary, it's even more reckless to ignore one's competition in the hopes that it will just disappear. Writing in the *New York Times* in 1948, Samuel Goldwyn observed, "Even the most backward-looking of the topmost tycoons of our industry cannot now help seeing just around the corner, a titanic struggle to retain audiences. . . . It is a certainty that people will be unwilling to pay to see poor pictures when they can stay home and see something which is, at least, no worse."[8] It was ironic that, as movies were being touted as the true American art form, film attendance was plummeting. In the decade between 1946 and 1956, ticket buying dropped by more than half. In fact, 25 percent of the nineteen thousand movie theaters in the United States closed their doors between 1946 and 1953.[9] Average weekly box office receipts during the '60s came in at less than half the numbers seen during the '50s. Only 121 feature films, an unprecedented low, came out during 1960.[10]

Hollywood had good reason to loathe Philo T. Farnsworth's magic box—TV had almost bankrupted the film industry. Yet, moviemakers, who had seriously underestimated the boob tube, didn't want to be seen as taking a sour grapes attitude. Films such as *The Last Hurrah* and *A Face in the Crowd* made the case that the unsuspecting boobs in TV Land were being sold everything from soap to political candidates. In actuality, television was just another spinner of illusions—only this medium made its home in your very own living room. Frankenheimer puts a fine point on television's ability to distort with his ingenious Committee Hearing Room scene in *The Manchurian Candidate*. We see a manipulative Mrs. Iselin, the puppet master, doing her thing in the foreground while Senator Iselin, the puppet, spews venom in the background and the secretary of defense, the target of Iselin's attacks, is trying to be heard over the brouhaha. They share the same *mise en scène* in reality, but that's not the reality the television audience is being fed. The monitor documents what is going out over the airwaves—namely, an out-of-control secretary of defense who appears to be guilty of something. *Seven Days in May*, also the brainchild of the TV-savvy Frankenheimer, is likewise crammed with television screens. Frankenheimer's message is simple. He reminds politicos that just as the boob tube provided the nation with a window into McCarthy's world (and proved the camera-keen demagogue's undoing), television can make or break them as well. When the president asks Scott to resign, Scott decides, Nixon-like, to take his case directly to the people. In fact, he plans on using ECOMCON to black out President Lyman's scheduled news conference. In a sense, Scott attempts to employ television to destroy the Constitution. When Scott is forced, however, to back off once his support group, the Joint Chiefs, falls away, fascism is foiled again. Interestingly enough, John Wayne should have made the journalist in *The Green Berets* a TV reporter. After all, television brought body counts and battles into American homes every evening. More important, images of napalmed children and burning villages did a great deal more than the printed word to undermine popular support for the war. Don't political communication experts customarily advise candidates who are being smeared to respond in the same medium as their accusers?

MOVIES AS METAPHOR

The silver screen isn't really silver, but it is certainly larger than life. Its sheer size permits the viewer to pay attention to specificity on a level that is simply not possible with television or any other electronic medium. Movies, according to Stanley Kauffman, manage to "make poetry out of doorknobs, breakfasts, furniture. Trivial detail, of which everyone's universe is made, can once again be transmuted into metaphor, contributing to imaginative art."[11]

Every viewer sees a different movie. According to Philip Taylor, "Too little do historians recognize when they are deconstructing film as texts, that the medium of film can play upon audience emotions, which tell us more about ourselves than the film ever can."[12] David Selznik used to talk about "the icebox element." He contended that a really good film ought to provoke a conversation so animated that the participants feel compelled to grab a midnight snack in order to continue the discussion. The ability to inspire a number of interpretations also defined excellence in filmmaking for Stanley Kubrick, although with 2001 his ambiguity was so over the top that folks scratched their heads and thought about asking for a refund.

Actually, movies provide a circular cultural flow. Viewers are influenced by the story, at the same time screenwriters respond not only to what is going on in the zeitgeist but also to the realization they cannot capsize prevailing social consensus—not if they wish to become richly compensated. According to Andrew Sarris, who has been reviewing films since 1955, "every movie I have ever seen keeps swirling and shifting in ever changing contexts. What is particularly fascinating is how the same movie can keep changing its ideological coloration over the years."[13] While Sarris is thinking of shop girl romances now being touted as feminist parable, he could be talking about *The Last Hurrah*. Ford saw nothing wrong with reaching back to recycle what had previously worked for him. Today we find his gags tired, his imagery hackneyed, and his cinematic shorthand for character types decidedly distasteful, especially the stereotyped Irish Catholic hag and the developmentally disabled Norman Cass Jr., whom Ford further saddled with a lisp.

Film also provides an indirect route to the emotions. As interpersonal communication tools, John Trent and Gary Smalley employ emotional word pictures or metaphorical stories to represent feelings in order to move a relationship to a deeper level of intimacy.[14] Emotional word pictures allow practitioners to access the inaccessible just as a filmmaker decides to move the focal point of a shot from the well-lit center to the foggy-yet-consequential periphery. With *Dr. Strangelove*, Kubrick never loses sight of his obligation to entertain. He serves up his pacifist ideology with a dollop of drollery. By taking the roundabout route, he also avoids creating the cognitive dissonance that would force the viewer to choose between competing values such as patriotism and survival. In *Steel Helmet*, the mute soldier who speaks up only when knifed in the back reflects America's confusion and alienation with Korea, demonstrating exactly why the "Forgotten War" never proved a popular subject for Hollywood filmmakers.

Like a clever Don Juan, Hollywood takes the circuitous route to seduce us. In the darkened theater, we are encouraged to accept film fantasies as substitutes for "what is humdrum, confining, discouraging, and unpleasant in our ordinary lives."[15] From their entry into the glittery entrance lobby to the dimming of the lights, the whole idea is to cut viewers off from reality and propel them into the alternative world on the screen.

MOVIES AS MIRROR

According to Stewart Samuels, films "reflect, embody, reveal, mirror, and symbolize existing ideologies by reproducing (consciously or unconsciously) the myths, ideas, concepts, beliefs, images of an historical period in both the film content and film form."[16] If art reflects life, one might hypothesize, it does so with funhouse mirrors. Sam Fuller, writing in 1994, was convinced that in only a decade or two movies would be available to suit "each person's exact emotions and needs, whatever he wants available at that moment, instantly created—stories, biographies, pornography."[17] *The Manchurian Candidate* fulfilled its definitional obligations as a thriller: Frankenheimer told a rivetingly good story that mirrored real fears about brainwashing in Korea. In *Dr. Strangelove,* you can hear echoes of Curtis LeMay's philosophy in General Buck Turgidson's eleventh-hour analysis. John Wayne was considered the quintessential American—at least by millions of fans who have been taught how to stand tall, snatch a kiss, or take a fist on the chin by the actor. While he didn't always achieve the ideal (anymore than we do), his patriotism, bravery, honesty, principals, decency, and strength symbolized our own best selves.

As Jacques Barzun reminds us in *God's Country and Mine,* "Whoever wants to know the heart and mind of America had better learn baseball, the rules and realities of the game—and do it by watching first some high school or small-town teams."[18] Our nation's pastime provides the consummate metaphor for a country in which each player must succeed as an individual for the team to prevail. Baseball rewards personal achievement with a champion's laurel while sometimes entreating a sacrificial offering allowing someone else to be commended for the winning score. The objective remains, in the long run, to return home.

The dicey dichotomy between singular and collective persists in our technology-driven, globalized, postindustrial society for good reason. Oppositional points of view, which actually enhance the pluralistic goal of democracy, will continue to compete in the public square just as they did between 1950 and 1969. At the present time, the *e pluribus unum* folk at one end of the political spectrum mourn the tragedy of educators no longer inculcating American values, while at the other, multiculturalists, arguing for empowerment, celebrate salad bowl individualism.

Take the founding fathers—the Federalists and the Antifederalists really mixed it up. Joseph Ellis reports, "Both sides in the debate have legitimate claims on historical truth and both sides speak for the deepest impulses of the American Revolution. Different factions came together in common cause to overthrow the reigning regime, then discovered in the aftermath of their triumph, that they had fundamentally different and politically incompatible notions of what they intended. . . . Taking sides in this debate is like choosing between the words and the music of the American Revolution."[19]

Ford's work, especially in *The Last Hurrah,* examines the community–individual duality that is uniquely American. On one hand, Skeffington exhibits the propensity to identify totally with his ethnic origins. He is being, according to the Anglican bishop, "a little too Irish" as he confronts the Brahmins in the Plymouth Club, "their musty shrine to their blue-nosed ancestors." On the other hand, he is also obsessed with his role as heroic loner. He suffers the inattentions of his son, takes the time and energy to listen to every supplicant who lines up outside his door, and trudges home alone after his electoral defeat. Van Ackerman, in *Advise and Consent*, is another case in point. Surrounding himself with an entourage of sycophants (his "brain trust"), he just can't understand why Brig Anderson is "in the club" and he's not.

MOVIES AS MICROSCOPE

"I also learned," recounts Elia Kazan, "that the camera is not only a recording device but a penetrating instrument. It looks *into* a face, not *at* a face. A camera can . . . linger, enlarge, analyze, study. It is a very subtle instrument, can make any face heavier, leaner, drawn, flushed, pale, jolly, depraved, [or] saintly."[20]

Ideology is like the staining agent that lab technicians employ to make cells (both good and bad) pop into view under the microscope. Sometimes it is impossible to see the political point of a movie without an ideology to connect the dots. Unless a *Dr. Strangelove* fan realizes that Kubrick is pushing an antinuke agenda, he or she might get caught up in the chuckles and miss the message. Had Kubrick kept the pie-throwing, slaphappy ending, the audience might have failed to spot the satire altogether.

Nobody in Hollywood, except Walter Wanger and William Randolph Hearst, ever made a profascist movie—and even that was disguised as a heavenly fantasy in which a benign Angel Gabriel gets depression-era America back on track. When, however, one applies the fascist coloring agent, the cancer underlying this supposed instance of divine intervention snaps into focus. The unilateral dismissal of Congress, the illegal seizure of emergency powers, and the shredding of constitutionally guaranteed rights (the Bills of Rights also protects gangsters) is concealed beneath the laudable goal of "cutting through red tape to get back to first principles." Further, without understanding the preconditions for a fascist coup d'etat, President Lyman's soliloquy in *Seven Days in May* makes no sense. What man on a white horse is he talking about?

Not all countries have the freedom to tackle topics as critical of government as we do in the United States. With all the zeal of a naturalized citizen, Otto Preminger banged out a portrait of the Senate several notches below the idealism of Frank Capra's *Mr. Smith Goes to Washington*. He argued, beneath all the bedroom intrigue and dog-eat-dog competition, that no single individual in a democratic republic holds enough power to overtake the entire government. According to Andrew Sarris, "The cinema as I understand it depends for its survival upon a civilization that possesses the largeness of spirit to preserve its past, warts and all."[21] John Frankenheimer, who brought the military–industrial complex as well as McCarthyism under his microscope, allowed, "I've always believed there is no other nation in the world which makes films as provocative, self-critical, as socially revealing, as those of American directors. Russian critics give learned discussion on the 'lack of realism' in certain American films, yet their directors, and many in other countries, could never make the films we do in the United States, because of their lack of freedom."[22]

"Film itself," writes Sarris, "can best be understood in terms of its unresolved dialectics.[23] One of the pluses of this book, and of its precursor, *Reelpolitik: Political Ideologies in '30s and '40s Films*, is that the political ideologies are organized into opposing pairs—thus affording a built-in impetus for discussion and, more important, allowing folks to find truth, which is said to lie, quite tantalizingly, somewhere in between. Hollywood has this bad habit of producing polarizing films—there's usually little subtlety or balance when moviemakers espouse political messages. According to veteran director Rod Lurie, "Hollywood is an area of extremes. In terms of their politics, [it's] Good versus Evil."[24]

During the '50s and '60s, a coalition of elites known as the military–industrial complex collected and kept all the marbles. At the same time, populism bubbled up in the early '50s as traditional resistance to big government evaporated, TV changed voting habits, and the political machine opened up urban areas. Populism cycled back again during the '60s, when the nation underwent a heightened period of unrest in response to the Vietnam War, the arms race, and civil rights issues. Fascism under McCarthy and HUAC lasted only four years, but it was a very long four years. Essentially a reactive force, post–World War II antifascism slumbered until 1960, when antiestablishment advocates ushered in a veritable cultural revolution, not only opposing the nationalism and militarism fueling Vietnam and the Cold War, but also going up against entrenched racism and, later, sexism. Interventionists promoted America as the peacemaker to the world—first, with the Marshall Plan and then with Korea and Vietnam. Isolationists, used to calling the foreign policy shots during the past two centuries, couldn't understand why America was sticking her nose in the business of sovereign nations. Antiwar protestors joined them during the turbulent '60s. The Cold War prompted anti-Communists to choose up sides depending on whether you favored a "let's catch the Reds with their pants down" or a "sit back and see" approach. The hawks held sway during the '50s, while the doves ascended after the Cuban Missile Crisis.

Although Americans will continue to dispute *who* they are, the advent of film permitted Americans to visualize *what* they are. This medium was the first to translate, however loosely, a transcendent and homogeneous collective unconscious, which has been sporadically characterized as the

American "can do" attitude. In other words, no obstacle was considered too immense, no challenge too vast, no goal too distant, and no sacrifice too weighty for the "I'll make it work" U.S. citizen.

Most Americans, in addition, pride themselves on common sense and thinking for themselves. Like the Swede in 1930's *Our Daily Bread* who admits, "I don't even know what those [isms] mean," many Americans refuse to encumber themselves with political labels and are content to remain simultaneously fragmented yet somehow united by a fundamental essence that, like obscenity, they can't quite define but readily recognize.

"Ideology obscures the real conditions of existence by presenting partial truths," according to Catherine Belsey. "It is a set of omissions, gaps rather than lies, smoothing over contradictions, appearing to provide answers to questions which in reality it evades, and masquerading as coherence."[25] Daniel Bell agrees. "Ideology," he contends, "makes it unnecessary for people to confront individual issues on their individual merits. One simply turns to the ideological vending machine, and out comes the prepared formula. And when these beliefs are suffused with sufficient fervor, ideas become weapons, and with dreadful results."[26] How true—our ideological windowpanes are sticky with the fingerprints of folks who would seek to hard-sell their one-size-fits-all utopian view of the world.

In his revisionist biography, *Frank Capra: The Catastrophe of Success,* Joseph McBride asserts that Capra espoused communism, fascism, Marxism, populism, conservatism, McCarthyism, New Dealism, jingoism, socialism, and capitalism at various points in his film career.[27] Attributing this tangle of ideologies to a clash between Capra's rigid conservatism and his liberal screenwriters, as McBride contends, just isn't credible. Capra, in the manner of most Americans, may have momentarily entertained all sorts of political notions, especially after the psychic upheaval of the depression, but both he and they generally returned to a "land of the free" consciousness when economic conditions returned to normal.

MOVIES AS MAGIC CARPET

"When we saturate ourselves in old films," says Nora Sayre, "we can employ them as hidden memories of a decade—directly or indirectly, they summon up the nightmares and daydreams that drifted through segments of our society—and exploring them from a distance unearths many of the obsessions of the past."[28]

Eight films took us on a magic carpet ride back to the '50s and '60s. We learned that the more America tried to stop Communist expansion abroad, the more repressive the climate became at home. In a four-year circus sideshow, HUAC red hunters and Senator Joseph McCarthy submitted the federal government, academia, the army, and mass media to unqualified violations of their First and Fifth Amendment rights, vague and sweeping accusations, the assumption of guilt by association, and massive intimidation.

Postwar capitalism succeeded beyond anyone's wildest dreams. While World War II had recharged the American economy, the Cold War extended the boom, thanks to a quasi-permanent military–industrial complex, two decades into peacetime, with nuclear weapons production serving as America's new growth industry.

Not everyone, however, agreed that an expanding economy was the best measure of human happiness—a disquieting psychological shift was also taking place. Corporate workers were compelled to squelch individual needs in return for six-figure incomes and a gold watch at the end of thirty years. Unlike the pioneers, inventors, entrepreneurs, and artists who came before, Americans grew more concerned with blending in than standing out. The country also shivered in a culture of fear. The recently prosperous riddled their new digs with burglar alarms, the government became obsessed with national security, both Republicans and Democrats agreed that the Soviets endangered the American way of life, and everybody felt menaced by the bomb.

Korea was the first hot flash in the Cold War. President Harry Truman and the United Nations were as grittily determined to freeze the Communists at the Thirty-eighth Parallel as they were resolved to thwart any threat of World War III. When the war ended in July 1953, however, no real estate changed hands, and the people of the United States bitterly resented paying for a "police action" with the lives of 36,516 Americans.

Vietnam was fought in America's living rooms, live and in color. Despite U.S. technical advice and assistance to South Vietnam, the enemy was overrunning the country. President Eisenhower propped up the sagging Saigon regime with military advisers, hefty financial backing, and American-made arms. In 1961, President Kennedy upped the ante in an agreement that included American support troops and the formation of the U.S. Military Assistance Command. The next year, four thousand troops were stationed in Vietnam and body bags started coming home. Presidents from Eisenhower to Nixon took the position that if America didn't fill the vacuum left by the French pullout, then the Communists would. Further, they maintained, if Communist expansion was not curbed in South Vietnam, the remaining Asian states would also buckle.

The decade of the '60s, however, with its sickening parade of assassinations, race riots, and campus unrest, was an even worse period of panic-inducing upheaval, during which the nation cleaved between those who backed and those who opposed the war. Most Americans counted themselves as members of the "silent majority." Largely law-abiding, they were incensed by the unruly and disruptive protests occurring on college campuses as well as in inner cities. Tom Brokaw's "Greatest Generation" had carried on during the depression, had served and sacrificed during World War II, and were now staking out a personal claim to the American Dream. They were decidedly disgusted when their own offspring ridiculed their values by burning flags, bras, and draft cards.

Does a glance behind, with respect to old movies, allow us to spy ahead?

September 11, 2001, did not just jar the smug self-confidence of the American people, but it also brought on the same sort of fascist reaction that swirled around the edges of the American psyche during the depths of the depression and then again under McCarthy and HUAC. The USA Patriot Act and government directives gnawing away at individual freedoms in the name of security are beginning to look a lot like unprecedented police powers. Furthermore, the American public is simply fed up with the unfettered greed of corporations, troubled by the lack of morality in a post-Enron world, worried about a sluggish economy, uneasy that weapons of mass destruction were never found in Iraq, reluctant to travel when terrorists are poised to strike anywhere, anytime, and deeply concerned that our elected officials are headed in precisely the wrong direction. They yearn to spend more time with their families, are increasingly convinced that spiritual strength can cure what ails us, and despite the fact that de Tocqueville never said it, burn to believe, with all their hearts, that this country is great because this country is good. They have come to realize that the political process is currently hog-tied by a dependence on special interest capital and that any real reform remains merely a pipedream—in fact, a pipedream rivaling Hollywood's best efforts.

William Strauss and Neil Howe, best-selling authors of *Generations* and *13th-GEN*, predict that by 2005 American history will be repeating itself, in fact, paralleling the events that unfolded as John Ford, Otto Preminger, Elia Kazan, John Frankenheimer, John Wayne, Sam Fuller, and Stanley Kubrick released the films that are reviewed in this book.[29] As they peer into their well-worn crystal ball, Strauss and Howe foresee America poised on a "fourth turning" that could play out in any number of surrealistic scenarios—all bad. Take your pick among terrorists armed with portable nuclear weapons, a fascist in the Oval Office, or an interventionist war that never ends.[30]

Sound familiar? Just remember you've already taken a magic carpet excursion, "back to the future" through eight '50s and '60s flicks. As George Santayana reminds us, "those who cannot remember the past are condemned to repeat it." The problem with the future is that we can't elude it, the problem with the present is that we can't preserve it, and the problem with the past is that we can't agree about it—but with cinematic images, perhaps we can find common ground or at least a language to think about politics, American style.

Who says academic inquiry has to be arduous and agonizing? Pass the popcorn.

NOTES

1. Charles Champlin, *The Flicks: Or Whatever Became of Andy Hardy?* (Pasadena, Calif.: Ward Ritchie, 1977), 11.

2. Quoted in Charles Affron, *Cinema and Sentiment* (Chicago: University of Chicago, 1982), 7.

3. John Moore, "Vietnam: The Movies and Its Critics," *Cleveland Plain Dealer*, March 19, 2001.

4. Ian Scott, *American Politics in Hollywood Film* (Chicago: Fitzroy Dearborn, 2000), 16.

5. Peter Biskind, *Seeing Is Believing: How Hollywood Taught Us to Stop Worrying and Love the Fifties* (New York: Pantheon, 1983), 5.

6. "Interview with Otto Preminger," *Movie* 4 (November 1962): 18–20.

7. Quoted in Roger Manvello, *Films and the Second World War* (New York: Dell, 1974), 20.

8. Quoted in Champlin, *Flicks,* 46.

9. Champlin, *Flicks,* 31.

10. Robert Sclar, *Film: An International History of the Medium* (New York: Abrams, 1993), 416.

11. Stanley Kauffman, *A World on Film: Criticism and Comment* (New York: Harper and Row, 1966), 417.

12. Philip Taylor, "The Green Berets," *History Today* 45, no. 3 (March 1995): 21.

13. Andrew Sarris, *Politics and Cinema* (New York: Columbia University Press, 1978), 3–4.

14. See Gary Smalley and John Trent, *The Language of Love* (Pomona, Calif.: Focus on the Family, 1988).

15. Champlin, *Flicks,* 11.

16. Quoted in Steven Mintz and Randy Roberts, *Hollywood's America: United States History Through Its Films* (St. James, N.Y.: Brandywine, 1993), 221.

17. Quoted in Lee Server, *Sam Fuller: Film Is a Battleground* (Jefferson, N.C.: McFarland, 1994), 58.

18. Jacques Barzun, *God's Country and Mine: A Declaration of Love Spiced with a Few Harsh Words* (1954), quoted in Leonary Roy Frank, *Quotationary,* (New York: Random House, 1999), 55. Interestingly enough, the AFI "Top 100 Films in 100 Years" list does not include a single baseball movie.

19. Joseph J. Ellis, *Founding Brothers: The Revolutionary Generation* (New York: Knopf, 2001), 15.

20. Elia Kazan, *Kazan on Kazan* (New York: Anchor, 1989), 381.

21. Kazan, *Kazan on Kazan,* 8.

22. Gerald Pratley, *The Cinema of John Frankenheimer* (London: Zwemmer, 1969), 236.

23. Andrew Sarris, *Politics and Cinema* (New York: Columbia University Press, 1978), 6.

24. Quoted in Jeff Dawson, "All the President's Mien," *Times* (London), March 9, 1998, 20.

25. Catherine Belsey, *Critical Practice* (London: Methuen, 1980), 57,

26. Daniel Bell, *The End of Ideology* (New York: Collier, 1960), 373.

27. See Joseph McBride, *Frank Capra: The Catastrophe of Success* (New York: Simon and Schuster, 1993).

28. Nora Sayre, *Running Time: Films of the Cold War* (New York: Dial, 1982), 25–26.

29. See William Strauss and Neil Howe, *The Fourth Turning: An American Prophecy* (New York: Broadway, 1997). This book promotes the thesis that modern history moves in eighty-year cycles composed of a period of confident expansion as a new order takes root, followed by a spiritual awakening against the established organization, an unraveling in which individualism triumphs over crumbling institutions, and a history-changing crisis or fourth turning.

30. Strauss and Howe, *Fourth Turning*, 272–79. See also William Knoke, *Bold New World: The Essential Road Map to the Twenty-first Century* (New York: Kodansha International, 1996).

Ideological Filmography

POPULISM

The Crowd (1928), *Washington Merry-Go-Round* (1932), *The Dark Horse* (1932), *Our Daily Bread* (1934), *Judge Priest* (1934), *Gorgeous Hussy* (1936), *Mr. Deeds Comes to Town* (1936), *Young Mr. Lincoln* (1939), *Mr. Smith Goes to Washington* (1939), *Abe Lincoln in Illinois* (1940), *The Great McGinty* (1940), *Meet John Doe* (1941), *Hail the Conquering Hero* (1944), *The Farmer's Daughter* (1947), *The Senator Was Indiscreet* (1947), *State of the Union* (1948), *All the King's Men* (1949), *A Lion in the Streets* (1953), *The President's Lady* (1953), *The Last Hurrah* (1958), *Inherit the Wind* (1960), *Medium Cool* (1969), *Putney Swope* (1969), *Alice's Restaurant* (1969), *Give 'Em Hell, Harry!* (1975), *Nashville* (1975), *Bound for Glory* (1976), *Rocky* (1976), *Being There* (1979), *Protocol* (1984), *True Believer* (1989), *Dave* (1993), *Primary Colors* (1998), *Bulworth* (1998), *Seabiscuit* (2003).

ELITISM

The Gold Rush (1925), *Alice Adams* (1935), *My Man Godfrey* (1936), *Dodsworth* (1936), *Kitty Foyle* (1940), *Wilson* (1944), *The Late George Apley* (1947), *The Magnificent Ambersons* (1948), *State of the Union* (1948), *The Man in the Gray Flannel Suit* (1956), *The Best of Everything* (1959), *Advise and Consent* (1962), *The Best Man* (1964), *The Graduate* (1967), *The Candidate* (1972), *The Seduction of Joe Tynan* (1979), *Wall Street* (1987), *The Firm* (1993), *Executive Power* (1997), *Tucker* (1998), *You've Got Mail* (1998), *Antitrust* (2001).

FASCISM

Little Caesar (1930), *Scarface* (1932), *This Day and Age* (1933), *Gabriel Over the White House* (1933), *The Cat's Paw* (1934), *The President Vanishes* (1934), *Citizen Kane* (1941), *Keeper of the Flame* (1943), *Flamingo Road* (1949), *A Face in the Crowd* (1957), *Al Capone* (1959), *The Man Who Shot Liberty Valance* (1962), *Wild in the Streets* (1968), *The Godfather* (1972), *The Godfather, Part II* (1974), *The Man Who Would Be King* (1975), *Dog Day Afternoon* (1975), *The Boys from Brazil* (1978), *The Great Santini* (1979), *The Untouchables* (1987), *The Godfather, Part III* (1990), *Goodfellas* (1990), *Bugsy* (1991), *Bob Roberts* (1992), *Nixon* (1995), *Escape from LA* (1996).

ANTIFASCISM

Duck Soup (1933), *Confessions of a Nazi Spy* (1939), *Foreign Correspondent* (1940), *The Great Dictator* (1940), *To Be or Not to Be* (1942), *The Hangman Also Dies* (1943), *Hitler's Children* (1943), *Lifeboat* (1944), *Hotel Berlin* (1945), *The Senator Was Indiscreet* (1947), *Crossfire* (1947), *Broken Arrow* (1950), *The Thing* (1951), *Goodbye, My Fancy* (1951), *High Noon* (1952), *Deadline USA* (1952), *Johnny Guitar* (1954), *Invasion of the Body Snatchers* (1956), *Storm Center* (1956), *The Blob* (1958), *The Diary of Anne Frank* (1959), *Bad Day at Black Rock* (1955), *Seven Days in May* (1964), *Fahrenheit 451* (1966), *The Way We Were* (1973), *Star Wars* (1977), *The Empire Strikes Back* (1980), *Return of the Jedi* (1983), *Schindler's List* (1993), *Carlito's Way* (1993), *Tea with Mussolini* (1999).

INTERVENTIONISM

Hearts of the World (1918), *Blockade* (1938), *The Invaders* (1941), *Sergeant York* (1941), *Wake Island* (1942), *Casablanca* (1942), *Flying Tigers* (1942), *Mrs. Miniver* (1942), *One of Our Aircraft Is Missing* (1942), *I Want You* (1951), *Mr. Walkie Talkie* (1952), *One Minute to Zero* (1952), *Retreat, Hell!* (1952), *Year of the Tiger* (1964), *Commandos in Vietnam* (1965), *The Green Berets* (1968), *Patton* (1970), *Heartbreak Ridge* (1986), *The Siege of Firebase Gloria* (1989), *The Three Kings* (1999).

ISOLATIONISM

Civilization (1916), *Intolerance* (1916), *The Four Horsemen of the Apocalypse* (1921), *The Big Parade* (1925), *What Price Glory* (1926), *All Quiet on the Western*

Front (1930), *The Steel Helmet* (1950), *The Bridge on the River Kwai* (1957), *Paths of Glory* (1957), *The Americanization of Emily* (1964), *M*A*S*H* (1970), *Catch-22* (1970), *A Bridge Too Far* (1977), *Go Tell the Spartans* (1978), *The Boys in Company C* (1977), *Coming Home* (1978), *The Deer Hunter* (1978), *Apocalypse Now* (1978), *Rambo: First Blood Part II* (1985), *Platoon* (1986), *Full Metal Jacket* (1987), *Good Morning, Vietnam* (1987), *Gardens of Stone* (1987), *Casualties of War* (1989), *Born on the Fourth of July* (1989), *A Midnight Clear* (1992), *Wag the Dog* (1997), *A Bright and Shining Lie* (1998).

COLD WAR HAWKISM

Walk a Crooked Mile (1948), *The Iron Curtain* (1948), *The Red Menace* (1949), *The Fountainhead* (1949), *I Married a Communist* (1950), *The Red Danube* (1950), *I Was a Communist for the FBI* (1951), *Diplomatic Courier* (1952), *Invasion, USA* (1952), *Walk East on Beacon* (1952), *My Son John* (1952), *The Thief* (1952), *Big Jim McClain* (1952), *Shane* (1953), *The Wild One* (1953), *Pickup on South Street* (1953), *Them!* (1954), *Night People* (1954), *Strategic Air Command* (1955), *Trial* (1955), *The Tin Star* (1957), *The Red Nightmare* (1957), *The Fearmakers* (1958), *Rio Bravo* (1959), *Dr. No* (1962), *The Prize* (1962), *The Manchurian Candidate* (1962), *The Spy Who Came in from the Cold* (1965), *Topaz* (1969), *Missiles of October* (1974), *Firefox* (1982), *Red Dawn* (1984), *The Falcon and the Snowman* (1985), *Independence Day* (1996).

COLD WAR DOVISM

The North Star (1943), *Mission to Moscow* (1943), *So Proudly We Hail* (1943), *Song of Russia* (1944), *The Day the Earth Stood Still* (1951), *War of the Worlds* (1953), *The Story of Mankind* (1957), *On the Beach* (1959), *Fail-Safe* (1964), *Dr. Strangelove* (1964), *Twilight's Last Gleaming* (1977), *Reds* (1981), *The Atomic Cafe* (1982), *War Games* (1983), *Superman IV: The Quest for Peace* (1987), *Amazing Grace and Chuck* (1987), *Fat Man and Little Boy* (1989), *The Hunt for Red October* (1990).

Selected Bibliography

Adair, Gilbert. *Vietnam on Film: From the Green Berets to Apocalypse Now.* New York: Proteus, 1981.

Adams, John. *Discourses on Davila.* Boston: Russell and Cutler, 1895.

Affron, Charles. *Cinema and Sentiment.* Chicago: University of Chicago Press, 1982.

Alexander, Robert J. *Juan Domingo Perón: A History.* Boulder, Colo.: Westview, 1979.

Anderson, Lindsay. *About John Ford.* London: Plexus, 1981.

Auster, Albert, and Leonard Quart. *How the War Was Remembered: Hollywood and Vietnam.* New York: Praeger, 1988.

Bachrach, Peter. *The Theory of Democratic Elitism: A Critique.* Boston: Little, Brown, 1967.

Baldwin, James. *The Price of the Ticket: Collected Nonfiction, 1948–1985.* New York: St. Martin's, Marek, 1985.

Beard, Charles A., and Mary R. Beard. *America in Midpassage.* Vol. 2. New York: Macmillan, 1939.

Bell, Daniel. *The End of Ideology.* New York: Collier, 1960.

Bell, Jeffrey. *Populism and Elitism: Politics in the Age of Equality.* Washington, D.C.: Regnery, 1992.

Belsey, Catherine. *Critical Practice.* London: Methuen, 1980.

Belton, John. *American Cinema/American Culture.* New York: McGraw–Hill, 1994.

Biderman, Albert. *March to Calumny: The Story of the American POWs in the Korean War.* New York: Macmillan, 1963.

Biskind, Peter. *Seeing Is Believing: How Hollywood Taught Us to Stop Worrying and Love the Fifties.* New York: Pantheon, 1983.

Bloom, Harold, ed. *Sophocles' Oedipus Rex.* New York: Chelsea House, 1988.

Blum, John Morton. *Years of Discord: American Politics and Society, 1961–1974.* New York: Norton, 1991.

Bogdanovich, Peter. *Who the Devil Made It?* New York: Knopf, 1997.

Brackman, Arnold C. *The Other Nuremberg: The Untold Story of the Tokyo War Crime Trials.* New York: Morrow, 1987.

Bradlee, Benjamin C. *A Good Life: Newspapers and Other Adventures.* New York: Simon and Schuster, 1995.

Brode, Douglas. *The Films of the Fifties: Sunset Boulevard to On the Beach.* Secaucus, N.J.: Citadel, 1976.

Browne, Courtney. *Tojo: The Last Banzai.* New York: Holt, 1967.

Brownstein, Ronald. *The Power and the Glitter: The Hollywood–Washington Connection.* New York: Vintage, 1990.

Buford, Kate. *Burt Lancaster: An American Life.* New York: Knopf, 2000.

Buhle, Mari Jo, Paul Buhle, and Dan Georgakas, eds. *Encyclopedia of the American Left.* New York: Oxford University Press, 1998.

Bullock, Alan. *Hitler: A Study in Tyranny.* New York: HarperCollins, 1964.

Bunch, Lonnie G., Spencer R. Crew, Mark G. Hirsch, and Harry R. Rubenstein. *The American Presidency: A Glorious Burden.* Washington, D.C.: Smithsonian Institution Press, 2000.

Butler, Ivan. *The War Film.* New York: Barnes, 1974.

Butow, Robert J. C. *Tojo and the Coming of the War.* Princeton, N.J.: Princeton University Press, 1961.

Cagin, Seth, and Philip Dray. *Hollywood Films of the Seventies.* New York: Harper and Row, 1984.

Campbell, Angus, Phillip E. Converge, Warren E. Miller, and Donald E. Stokes. *The American Voter.* New York: Wiley, 1960.

Canovan, Margaret. *Populism.* London: Junction, 1981.

Carlson, Lewis H. *Remembered Prisoners of a Forgotten War.* New York: St. Martin's, 2002.

Chambers, Whittaker. *Witness.* New York: Random House, 1952.

Champlin, Charles. *The Flicks: Or Whatever Became of Andy Hardy?* Pasadena, Calif.: Ward Ritchie, 1977.

Ciment, Michel. *Kazan on Kazan.* New York: Viking, 1974.

Clausewitz, Carl von. *On War.* Edited and translated by Michael Howard and Peter Paret. Princeton, N.J.: Princeton University Press, 1984.

Coffin, Tristram. *Senator Fulbright: Portrait of a Public Philosopher.* New York: Dutton, 1966.

Coles, S. F. A. *Franco of Spain.* London: Neville Spearman, 1955.

Cragan, John, and Don Shields. *Applied Communication Research.* Prospect Heights, Ill.: Waveland, 1981.

Crassweller, Robert D. *Perón and the Enigmas of Argentina.* New York: Norton, 1987.

Crowther, Bosley. *Hollywood Rajah.* New York: Henry Holt, 1960.

Crozier, Brian. *Franco: A Biographical History.* London: Eyre and Spottiswoode, 1967.

Curtis, Michael. *The Great Political Theories.* Vol. 2. New York: Avon, 1981.

Dallek, Robert. *Flawed Giant: Lyndon Johnson and His Times 1961–1973.* Oxford: Oxford University Press, 1998.

Davis, Ronald L. *John Ford: Hollywood's Old Master.* Norman: University of Oklahoma Press, 1995.

Devine, Jeremy M. *Vietnam at 24 Frames a Second: A Critical and Thematic Analysis of over 400 Films about the Vietnam War.* Jefferson, N.C.: McFarland, 1995.

DeVries, Daniel. *The Films of Stanley Kubrick.* Grand Rapids, Mich.: Eerdmans, 1973.

Diggins, John P. *Mussolini and Fascism: The View from America.* Princeton, N.J.: Princeton University Press, 1972.

Dittmar, Linda, and Gene Michaud. *From Hanoi to Hollywood: The Vietnam War in American Film.* New Brunswick, N.J.: Rutgers University Press, 1990.

Dixon, Wheeler W. *The B Directors: A Biographical Directory.* Metuchen, N.J.: Scarecrow, 1985.

Domhoff, G. William. *The Power Elite and the State: How Policy Is Made in America.* New York: De Gruyter, 1990.

——. *The Powers That Be: Processes of Ruling Class Dominion in America.* New York: Vintage, 1979.

——. *Who Rules America Now? A View for the '80s.* Englewood Cliffs, N.J.: Prentice–Hall, 1983.

Dowd, Nancy, and David Shepherd. *King Vidor, Directors Guild of America Oral History.* Metuchen, N.J.: Scarecrow, 1988.

Durgnat, Raymond, and Scott Simmon. *King Vidor, American.* Berkeley: University of California Press, 1988.

Dye, Thomas R. *Who's Running America? Institutional Leadership in the United States.* Englewood Cliffs, N.J.: Prentice-Hall, 1976.

Dye, Thomas R., and L. Harmon Zeigler. *The Irony of Democracy: An Uncommon Introduction to American Politics.* 5th ed. Monterey, Calif.: Duxbury, 1981.

Ebenstein, William, and Edwin Fogelman. *Today's Isms.* 9th ed. Englewood Cliffs, N.J.: Prentice-Hall, 1985.

Ebert, Roger. *The Great Movies.* New York: Broadway, 2002.

Edwards, Paul M. *A Guide to Films on the Korean War.* Westport, Conn.: Greenwood, 1997.

Ellis, Joseph. *Founding Brothers: The Revolutionary Generation.* New York: Knopf, 2001.

Eyles, Allen. *John Wayne.* New York: Barnes, 1979.

Eyman, Scott. *Print the Legend: The Life and Times of John Ford.* New York: Simon and Schuster, 1999.

Fehrenbach, T. R. *This Kind of War.* Washington, D.C.: Brassey's, 1998.

Fermi, Laura. *Mussolini.* Chicago: University of Chicago Press, 1961.

Fleming, Donald. *The Cold War and Its Origins.* New York: Doubleday, 1961.

Fox, Stephen. *The Mirror Makers: A History of American Advertising and Its Creators.* New York: Morrow, 1984.

Freud, Sigmund. *A General Introduction to Psychoanalysis.* New York: Pocket Books, 1924.

Frischauer, Willi. *Behind the Scenes of Otto Preminger.* New York: Morrow, 1974.

Fuller, Samuel, with Christa Lang Fuller and Jerome Henry Rudes. *A Third Face: My Tale of Writing, Fighting, and Filmmaking.* New York: Knopf, 2002.

Furhammar, Leif, and Folke Isaksson. *Politics and Film.* Translated by Kersti French. Westport, Conn.: Praeger, 1971.

Gabler, Neal. *An Empire of Their Own: How the Jews Invented Hollywood.* New York: Doubleday/Anchor, 1989.

Galbraith, John Kenneth. *American Capitalism: The Concept of Countervailing Power.* Boston: Houghton Mifflin, 1956.

Gallagher, Tag. *John Ford: The Man and His Films.* Berkeley: University of California Press, 1986.

Garnham, Nicholas. *Sam Fuller.* New York: Viking, 1971.

Gianos, Phillip L. *Politics and Politicians in American Film.* Westport, Conn.: Praeger, 1998.

Gilbert, Martin. *The Holocaust: A History of Jews of Europe During the Second World War.* New York: Henry Holt, 1985.

Gitlin, Todd. *The Sixties: Years of Hope, Days of Rage.* New York: Bantam, 1993.

Goodwin, Doris Kearns. *Lyndon Johnson and the American Dream.* New York: Harper and Row, 1976.

Goodwyn, Lawrence. *Democratic Promise: The Populist Movement in America.* New York: Oxford University Press, 1976.

Greider, William. *Who Will Tell the People: The Betrayal of American Democracy.* New York: Simon and Schuster, 1992.

Gross, Bertram. *Friendly Fascism: The New Face of Power in America.* New York: Evans, 1980.

Halberstam, David. *The Fifties.* New York: Fawcett Columbine, 1993.

Hardy, Phil. *Samuel Fuller.* Westport, Conn.: Praeger, 1970.

Harris, Fred. *The New Populism.* Berkeley, Calif.: Thorpe Springs, 1973.

Hayward, Jack, ed. *Elitism, Populism and European Politics.* Oxford: Clarendon, 1996.

Henriksen, Margot. *Dr. Strangelove's America: Society and Culture in the Atomic Age.* Berkeley: University of California Press, 1997.

Henry, William A., III. *In Defense of Elitism.* New York: Doubleday, 1994.

Hermes, Walter. *United States Army in the Korean War: Truce Tent and Fighting Front.* Washington, D.C.: U.S. Government Printing Office, 1966.

Hicks, John D. *The Populist Revolt.* Lincoln: University of Nebraska Press, 1961.

Higham, Charles, and Joel Greenfield, eds. *The Celluloid Muse.* London: Angus and Robertson, 1969.

Hitler, Adolf. *Mein Kampf.* Translated by Ralph Manheim. Boston: Houghton Mifflin, 1971.

———. *The Speeches of Adolf Hitler, April 1922–August 1939.* Edited by Norman H. Baynes. New York: Gordon, 1942.

Hollinger, Robert. *The Dark Side of Liberalism: Elitism vs. Democracy.* Westport, Conn.: Praeger, 1996.

Howard, James. *Stanley Kubrick Companion.* London: Batsford, 1999.

Isserman, Maurice, and Michael Kazin. *America Divided: The Civil War of the 1960s.* Oxford: Oxford University Press, 2000.

Jefferson, Thomas. *Writings.* Edited by Merrill D. Peterson. New York: Library of America, 1984.

Kauffman, Stanley. *A World on Film: Criticism and Comment.* New York: Harper and Row, 1966.

Kazan, Elia. *A Life.* New York: Doubleday, 1989.

———. *Kazan on Kazan.* New York: Anchor, 1989.

Kazin, Michael. *The Populist Persuasion.* New York: HarperCollins, 1995.

Keller, Suzanne. *Beyond the Ruling Class.* New York: Ayer, 1963.

Kelley, Beverly Merrill. "The Impact of John Dean's Credibility Before the Senate Select Committee on Presidential Campaign Practices." Ph.D. diss., University of California at Los Angeles, 1977.

———. *Reelpolitik: Political Ideologies in '30s and '40s Films*. Westport, Conn.: Praeger, 1998.

Kennan, George F. *Russia and the West*. New York: New American Library, 1960.

Kershaw, Ian. *The Hitler Myth: Image and Reality in the Third Reich*. Oxford: Oxford University Press, 1987.

Kirkpatrick, Ivone. *Mussolini: Study of a Demagogue*. London: Oldhams, 1964.

Knoke, William. *Bold New World: The Essential Road Map to the Twenty-First Century*. New York: Kodansha International, 1996.

Knox, MacGregor. *Mussolini Unleashed, 1939–41: Politics and Strategy in Fascist Italy's Last War*. Cambridge: Cambridge University Press, 1982.

Kornhauser, Arthur, ed. *Problems of Power in American Society*. Detroit: Wayne State University Press, 1957.

Kovic, Ron. *Born on the Fourth of July*. New York: McGraw–Hill, 1976.

Langman, Larry, and Ed Borg. *Encyclopedia of American War Films*. New York: Garland, 1989.

Lanning, Michael Lee. *Vietnam at the Movies*. New York: Fawcett Columbine, 1994.

Lash, Joseph P. *Eleanor and Franklin*. New York: New American Library, 1971.

———. *From the Diaries of Felix Frankfurter*. New York: Norton, 1975.

Lasswell, Harold, and Daniel Lerner. *The Comparative Study of Elites*. Palo Alto, Calif.: Stanford University Press, 1952.

Lazarsfeld, Paul, Bernard Berelson, and Hazel Gudet. *The People's Choice*. New York: Columbia University Press, 1968.

Lech, Raymond B. *Broken Soldiers*. Urbana: University of Illinois Press, 2000.

Lewy, Guenter. *The Catholic Church and Nazi Germany*. New York: McGraw–Hill, 1964.

Lindbergh, Anne Morrow. *The Wave of the Future: A Confession of Faith*. New York: Harcourt Brace, 1940.

LoBrutto, Vincent. *Stanley Kubrick: A Biography*. New York: Da Capo, 1997.

Lordeaux, Lee. *Italian and Irish Filmmakers in America: Ford, Capra, Coppola, and Scorsese*. Philadelphia: Temple University Press, 1990.

Lundberg, Ferdinand. *The Rich and the Super-Rich*. Secaucus, N.J.: Carol, 1968.

MacDonald, J. Fred. *One Nation under Television: The Rise and Decline of Network TV*. Chicago: Nelson–Hall, 1994.

Malo, Jean-Jacques, and Tony William. *Vietnam War Films*. Jefferson, N.C.: McFarland, 1994.

Maltby, Richard, and Ian Craven. *Hollywood Cinema*. Oxford: Blackwell, 1995.

Marshall, S. L. A. *Pork Chop Hill: The American Fighting Man in Korea*. Nashville: Battery, 1986.

———. *The River and the Gauntlet*. Westport, Conn.: Greenwood, 1953.

Mast, Gerald. *A Short History of the Movies*. 3rd ed. Indianapolis: Bobbs–Merrill Educational, 1981.

Matthews, Donald R. *The Social Background of Political Decision-Makers*. New York: Doubleday, 1954.

McBride, Joseph. *Frank Capra: The Catastrophe of Success*. New York: Simon and Schuster, 1993.

McGilligan, Patrick, and Paul Buhle. *Tender Comrades: A Backstory of the Hollywood Blacklist*. New York: St. Martin's, 1997.

McKenna, George. *American Populism*. New York: Putnam & Sons, 1966.

Michels, Robert. *Political Parties: A Sociological Study of the Oligarchical Tendencies of Modern Democracy*, translated by Eden Paul and Cedar Paul. Glencoe, Ill: Free Press, 1958 and 1962.

Miller, Douglas, and Marion Nowak. *The Fifties: The Way We Really Were*. New York: Doubleday, 1977.

Mills, C. Wright. *The Power Elite*. New York: Oxford University Press, 1956.

Mintz, Steven, and Randy Roberts. *Hollywood's America: United States History through Its Films*. St. James, N.Y.: Brandywine, 1993.

Mosca, Gaetano. *The Ruling Class*. New York: McGraw-Hill, 1939.

Mosse, George L. *Masses and Man: Nationalist and Fascist Perceptions of Reality*. New York: Howard Fertig, 1980.

Mulvey, Laura. *Citizen Kane*. London: BFI, 1994.

Muse, Eben J. *The Land of Nam: The Vietnam War in American Film*. Lanham, Md.: Scarecrow, 1995.

Neve, Brian. *Film and Politics in America: A Social Tradition*. London: Routledge, 1992.

Nimmo, Dan, and James Combs. *Mediated Political Realities*. New York: Longman, 1983.

Nuechterlein, Donald E. *A Cold War Odyssey*. Lexington, Ky.: University Press of Kentucky, 1997.

Nye, Joseph S., Jr. *Understanding International Conflicts: An Introduction to Theory and History*. 3rd ed. New York: Longman, 2000.

O'Neill, Tip, with Gary Hymel. *All Politics Is Local*. Holbrook, Mass.: Bob Adams, 1994.

O'Neill, William. *Coming Apart: An Informal History of America in the 1960's*. Chicago: Quadrangle, 1971.

Owen, Frank. *Perón: His Rise and Fall*. London: Cresset, 1957.

Packard, Frederick C., Jr., ed. *Great Americans Speak*. New York: Scribner's, 1951.

Page, Joseph A. *Perón: A Biography*. New York: Random House, 1983.

Pareto, Vilfredo. *Mind and Society*. New York: Harcourt, Brace, 1935.

Pauly, Thomas H. *An American Odyssey: Elia Kazan and American Culture*. Philadelphia: Temple University Press, 1983.

Payne, Stanley G. *The 1936–1975 Franco Regime*. Madison: University of Wisconsin Press, 1987.

Phillips, Gene D. *Stanley Kubrick: A Film Odyssey*. New York: Popular Library, 1975.

Phillips, Gene D., and Rodney Hall. *The Encyclopedia of Stanley Kubrick*. New York: Checkmark, 2002.

Pinkerton, James P. *What Comes Next: The End of Big Government and the New Paradigm Ahead*. New York: Hyperion, 1995.

Powers, Richard Gid. *Not Without Honor: The History of American Anticommunism*. New York: Free Press, 1995.

Pratley, Gerald. *The Cinema of John Frankenheimer*. London: Zwemmer, 1969.

Preminger, Otto. *Preminger: An Autobiography*. Garden City, N.Y.: Doubleday, 1977.

Rauschning, Hermann. *The Revolution of Nihilism*. New York: Longmans, Green, 1930.

Rees, David. *Korea: The Limited War*. New York: St. Martin's, 1964.

———. *The Korean War: History and Tactics*. New York: Crescent, 1984.

Riesman, David. *The Lonely Crowd: A Study of the Changing American Character.* New Haven: Yale University Press, 1973.

Roberts, Randy, and James S. Olson. *John Wayne: American.* New York: Free Press, 1995.

Roder, Thomas, Volker Kubillus, and Anthony Burwell. *Psychiatrists: The Men Behind Hitler.* Los Angeles: Freedom, 1995.

Rosenthal, Paul Irwin. "Ethos in the Presidential Campaign of 1960: A Study of the Basic Persuasive Process of the Kennedy–Nixon Television Debates." Ph.D. diss., University of California at Los Angeles, 1963.

Rostow, W. W. *The Stages of Economic Growth: A Non-Communist Manifesto.* Cambridge: Cambridge University Press, 1960.

Rousseau, Jean-Jacques. *The Social Contract and Discourse.* Book III, chapter 4. London: Dent, 1973.

Russo, Vito. *The Celluloid Closet: Homosexuality in the Movies.* New York: Harper & Row, 1987.

Sarris, Andrew. *Politics and Cinema.* New York: Columbia University Press, 1978.

Sayre, Nora. *Running Time: Films of the Cold War.* New York: Dial, 1982.

Schlesinger, Arthur M., Jr. *The Vital Center: The Politics of Freedom.* Boston: Houghton Mifflin, 1949.

Sclar, Robert. *Film: An International History of the Medium.* New York: Abrams, 1993.

Scott, Ian. *American Politics in Hollywood Film.* Chicago: Fitzroy Dearborn, 2000.

Sebald, Hans. *Momism: The Silent Disease of America.* Chicago: Burnham, 1976.

Server, Lee. *Sam Fuller: Film Is a Battleground.* Jefferson, N.C.: McFarland, 1994.

Sherman, Eric, and Martin Rubin. *The Director's Event: Interviews with Five American Film-makers.* New York: Atheneum, 1970.

Shils, Edward A. *The Torment of Secrecy.* London: Heinemann, 1956.

Silk, Leonard, and Mark Silk. *The American Establishment.* New York: Basic, 1980.

Skidmore, Max J. *Ideologies: Politics in Action.* San Diego: Harcourt Brace Jovanovich, 1989.

Smith, Adam. *The Theory of Moral Sentiments.* Indianapolis: Liberty Fund, 1982.

Smith, Craig R. *Silencing the Opposition: Government Strategies of Suppression of Freedom of Expression.* Albany: State University of New York Press, 1996.

Smith, Denis Mack. *Mussolini.* New York: Vintage, 1982.

Sophocles. *Antigone, Oedipus the King, Electra.* Translated by H. D. F. Kitto. Oxford: Oxford University Press, 1994.

Sorensen, Theodore C. *Kennedy.* New York: Bantam, 1966.

Stark, Steven D. *Glued to the Set: The 60 Television Shows and Events That Made Us Who We Are Today.* New York: Free Press, 1997.

Stott, William. *Documentary Expression in America.* London: Oxford University Press, 1973.

Strauss, William, and Neil Howe. *The Fourth Turning: An American Prophecy.* New York: Broadway, 1997.

Strecker, Edward. *Their Mother's Sons.* New York: Lippincott, 1951.

Suid, Lawrence H. "The Film Industry and the Vietnam War." Ph.D. diss., Case Western Reserve University, 1980.

———. *Guts & Glory: Great American War Movies.* Reading Mass.: Addison-Wesley, 1978.

310 Selected Bibliography

Swing, Raymond Gram. *Forerunners of American Fascism.* Freeport, N.Y.: Books for Libraries, 1969.

Tierney, Gene, with Mickey Herskowitz. *Self-Portrait.* New York: Berkley, 1980.

Toland, John. *Adolf Hitler.* New York: Doubleday, 1976.

———. *In Mortal Combat: Korea, 1950–1953.* New York: Morrow, 1991.

Truffaut, François. *The Films in My Life.* Translated by Leonard Mayhew. New York: Simon and Schuster, 1975.

Truman, Harry. *Memoirs: Years of Trial and Hope.* Garden City, N.Y.: Doubleday, 1955.

Warren, Bill, ed. *The Middle of the Country: The Events of May 4th as Seen by Students and Faculty at Kent State University.* New York: Avon, 1970.

Washington, George. "Farewell Address." In *The World's Famous Orations,* edited by William Jennings Bryan, Vol. 7. New York: Funk and Wagnalls, 1906.

Weigley, Russell. *History of the U.S. Army.* New York: Macmillan, 1967.

Weintraub, Stanley. *MacArthur's War: Korea and the Undoing of an American Hero.* New York: Touchstone, 2000.

Wetta, Frank J., and Stephen J. Curley. *Celluloid Wars: A Guide to Film and the American Experience of War.* New York: Greenwood, 1992.

Williams, William A. *The Tragedy of American Diplomacy.* Cleveland: World, 1959.

Wills, Garry. *John Wayne's America.* New York: Touchstone, 1997.

Wills, Morris R. *Turncoat: An American's 23 Years in Communist China: The Story of Morris R. Wills as Told to J. Robert Moskin.* Englewood Cliffs, N.J.: Prentice-Hall, 1968.

Wood, Michael. *America in the Movies: Or, "Santa Maria," It Had Slipped My Mind.* New York: Basic, 1975.

Woolf, S. J. ed. *Fascism in Europe.* London: Methuen, 1981.

Wylie, Philip. *Generation of Vipers.* New York: Rhinehart, 1942.

Young, Jeff. *Kazan: The Master Director Discusses His Films.* New York: New Market, 1999.

Zinn, Howard. *A People's History of the United States: 1492–Present.* Revised ed. New York: HarperPerennial, 1995.

Index

Abe Lincoln in Illinois, 299

accomodationist, 59, 73. *See*
appeasement

Acheson, Dean, 90, 182, 200n15, 207

ACLU. *See* American Civil Liberties
Union

Adair, Gilbert, 169

Adam, Ken, 253–54, 258, 278n104, 283

Adams, Eddie, 143–44

Adams, Henry Brooks, 56

Adams, Joe, 221

Adams, John, 43, 45, 52, 63

Adamson, Joseph, 257

The Addams Family, 276n45

Addams Family Values, 276n45

Adler, Renata, 169

Advise and Consent, 4, 284–85, 291, 299;
analysis, 50–73; audience response,
72–73; homosexuality, 70–71; plot,
50–51

African Americans. *See* blacks

The Alamo, 161

Alexie, Sherman, 162

Alice Adams, 299

Alice's Restaurant, 299

Allen, Fred, 92

Allen, Gracie, 54

Allen, Steve, 7, 251–52, 257

All Fall Down, 134

All Quiet on the Western Front, 5,
177–78, 198, 300–301

All the King's Men, 299

ally/adversary confusion: and Korea,
186, 188; and Vietnam, 149

Alpert, Hollis, 157

Alter, Jonathan, 205

Amazing Grace and Chuck, 301

American Civil Liberties Union
(ACLU), 120, 122, 229

American Communist Party, 120,
234n3, 286

The Americanization of Emily, 301

American Legion, 73, 130, 222, 286

American Revolution, 9, 44, 178

Anatomy of a Murder, 69

Anderson, Clinton P., 73, 155

Anderson, Lindsay, 11, 22, 36

Anderson, Richard, 129

Andrews, Nigel, 164

Anti-Ballistic Missile Treaty (1972),
271

anticommunism, 4, 6, 206, 224, 229,
244, 286, 292

antifascism, 4, 113–23; Communists,
114–15; definition, 113;
democracies, 118–19; and the
fifties, 119–23, 292; and internal
resistance, 113–14; and labor,

115–16; and religious resistance, 116–18

antifederalists, 42–43

anti-intellectualism, 20–23

antimaterialism, 18–20

antimedia, 23–27

antinuclear movement, 243, 274n18

Antitrust, 299

Apocalypse Now, 157, 301

appeasement, 59, 73, 118, 147, 207, 246, 249; opposition to, 73

Aristotle, 42

Arlen, Richard, 86

arms race, 216, 245–46, 249, 292

Army of the Republic of Vietnam (ARVN), 144–45, 244

Arnold, Gary, 164

ARVN. *See* Army of the Republic of Vietnam

Ashby, Hal, 271

Askew, Luke, 150

The Asphalt Jungle, 88

Atmospheric Nuclear Weapons Test Ban Treaty (1963), 136, 248–49, 264

atomic bomb, 63, 76n61, 180, 184, 207, 209, 241, 294

The Atomic Café, 301

Audubon, John James, 229

Auster, Albert, 160

Austin, Hal, 262

auteur theory, 30, 257

Axelrod, 218–19, 232–34, 239n110

Ayers, Lew, 62, 178

Bacall, Lauren, 86, 228

Back to Bataan, 159

Bacon, Francis, 62

Bad Day at Black Rock, 300

Bailey, Charles W., 5

Baker, Carroll, 103

Baldwin, James, 121

Ball, George, 94

Ball, Lucille, 236n44

"Ballad of the Green Berets," 153

Balsam, Martin, 88, 127

Ban the Bomb. *See* antinuclear movement

Bank, Aaron, 151

Barbarian and the Geisha, 162

Barnum, P. T., 5

Barrett, James Lee, 153

Baruch, Bernard, 206

Baruch, Don, 153

Barzun, Jacques, 290

Baxter, John, 25, 257

Baxter, Leona, 2

Bay of Pigs, 131–32, 216

Beard, Charles and Mary, 42

Beatty, Warren, 2, 103

Beery, Wallace, 85

Being There, 299

Bell, Daniel, 293

Bell, Jeffrey, 41

Belsey, Catherine, 293

Bennett, Alan, 254

Benny, Jack, 83

Bentley, Eric, 5, 169

Berger, Thomas, 227

Berlin Crisis, 216, 248

Berlin Wall, 6, 216

Bessie, Alvah, 86, 106n33

The Best Man, 299

The Best of Everything, 299

Beyond the Fringe, 254

Biberman, Herbert, 86, 106n32

Biderman, Albert D., 212

Big Jim McClain, 301

The Big Parade, 300

The Big Red One, 194, 196–97

The Big Trail Magazine, 162, 174n82

Bill of Rights, 46–47

Bin Laden, Osama, 252

Birdman of Alcatraz, 134

Biskind, Peter, 286

Bissel, Whit, 128

blacklist,11, 86–88, 244. *See also* Hollywood Ten

blacks: and Korea, 192–93; and World War II, 192–93

Blair, Bruce G., 260–61, 268

blitzpogrom, 112, 138n5

The Blob, 300

Blockade, 300

Bloom, Harold, 224

Bob Roberts, 300

Bogart, Humphrey, 86–87, 228

Bogdanovich, Peter, 70
bomb shelter, 242, 269, 274n4, 275n29
Bond, Ward, 11, 167
Bonesteel, Charles, 200n13
Bonhoeffer, Dietrich, 117
Bonus Army, 130, 133
Born on the Fourth of July, 301
Bouchey, Willis, 17, 34
Bound for Glory, 299
Boyer, Paul, 265
The Boys from Brazil, 300
The Boys in Company C, 301
Bradlee, Ben, 131
Bradley, Omar, 180, 185
brainwashing, 6, 186, 205, 210–14; and
    Rosie the Riveter, 228;
and Shaw (sergeant), 226, 233;
    television, 231
Brando, Marlon, 103
Brasfield, Rod, 99
The Brave One, 106n33
Brecht, Bertolt, 86
Brent, George, 85
The Bridge on the River Kwai, 88, 301
Bridges, Lloyd, 87
Bridges, Styles, 200n16
A Bridge Too Far, 301
A Bright and Shining Lie, 301
Brode, Douglas, 158
Brodie, Steve, 187
Broken Arrow (film), 300
broken arrows, 255, 278n111
Bromberg, J. Edward, 88
Brooke, Edward W., 77n85
Brophy, Edward, 17
Browne, Malcolm, 159
Bruce, Lenny, 254–55
Bryan, William Jennings, 12
Buchan, Alistair, 255
Buchanan, Pt, 62
Buckman, Sidney, 87, 107n42
Bugsy, 300
Bull, Peter, 250, 253
Bulletin of the Atomic Scientist, 241, 248
Bulworth, 3, 299
Bundy, McGeorge, 148. *See also*
    Pentagon Papers
Burns, Bart, 129

Burr, Bill, 260
Burroughs, William, 227
Burrows, Abe, 87
Bush, George H. W., 41
Bush, George W., 1, 28, 41, 79, 205, 257
Bustein, Robert, 273
Butler, Ivan, 169
Butler, Smedley Darlington, 130

Cafritz, Gwendolyn, 66
Cagin, Seth, 271
Cagney, James, 31
Cahiers du Cinema, 68
The Caine Mutiny, 106n32
Cairo Declaration, 181
California Esquadrille. *See* Brent,
    George
California Light Horse Regiment. *See*
    McLaglen, Victor
Camelot, 168
Campbell, James T., 164
campaign financing, 54
Campaign for Nuclear Disarmament,
    256
The Candidate, 2, 299
Canovan, Margaret, 44
Cantril, Haley, 48
Canutt, Yakima, 166
capitalism, 44, 127, 206, 264, 266
Capone, Al, 300
Capra, Frank, 4, 10–11, 50, 54, 70,
    106n24, 291
Carlito's Way, 300
Carter, Jimmy, 3, 164
Carey, Harry, Jr., 166
Carlson, Lewis H., 212
Casablanca, 5, 300
Cassini, Oleg, 65–66
Castillo, Ramon, 80
Castro, Fidel, 265
Casualties of War, 301
Catch-22, 301
The Cat's Paw, 300
Central Intelligence Agency (CIA), 122
Central Treaty Organization (CETO),
    209
CFA. *See* Committee for the First
    Amendment

Chamberlin, Neville, 118
Chambers, Whittaker, 59–60, 88
Champlin, Charles, 283
Chaplin, Charlie, 83, 256
charisma, 83, 100, 125
checks and balances, 46
Chesterfield, Lord, 56
Chikami, Akira, 213
China Gate, 160, 173n68, 197
Chisum, 163
Chun, William, 187
Churchill, Winston, 68, 119, 235n7, 241
CIA. *See* Central Intelligence Agency
Citizen Kane, 5, 300
Civilization, 300
civil rights, 4, 139n37, 292–93
Civil Rights Act, 123
Civil War, 178
Clarke, Arthur C., 272
Cleopatra, 134
Cleveland, Grover, 64
Clinton, William J., 28, 41, 64, 68; and blacks, 192; and democracy, 17; and Hollywood, 1, 3
Cobb, Lee J., 87
Coffin, Tristram, 68, 76n73
Cohan, George M., 100
Cohn, Harry, 30, 85
Cold War, 4–6, 120–23, 127, 146, 159, 294, 181–82; *Dr. Strangelove*, 241, 251, 259; and Eisenhower, Dwight D., 246, 248–49; and history, 206–10, 213. *See also* dovism; hawkism; Korean War; National Security Council Document 68
Cole, Lester, 86, 106n33
Collins, Richard, 87
Coming Home, 301
Comintern, 115
Commandos in Vietnam, 300
Committee for the First Amendment (CFA), 86–87
Committee for Nonviolent Action, 244
communism, 4, 5, 80, 206, 264; and antifascism, 114–15; *Steel Helmet*, 193–94
Condin, Richard, 215, 218, 222, 225,

227–28, 232–33; and Hunt, Evelyn, 228
Confessions of a Nazi Spy, 300
Connecticut Compromise, 51
The Conqueror, 168
containment, 209. *See also* Kennan, George; Marshall Plan; NATO; Truman Doctrine
Cook, Peter, 254
Coolidge, Calvin, 99
Cooper, Gary, 85–86
Cooper, John Sherman, 155
Cooper, Merian, 36
Coppola, Francis Ford, 271
Corey, Jeff, 87
Corliss, Richard, 252, 256
corporate responsibility, 12
Corrigan, Lloyd, 215
Coughlin, Charles, 179
The Court Martial of Billy Mitchell, 69
credibility, 83
credibility gap, 144
The Crimson Kimono, 194
Crisp, Donald, 17, 34
Crist, Judith, 135, 273
Cronkite, Walter, 144, 190
Crosbie, Philip, 213
Crossfire, 106n31, 300
Crossley, Archibald, 48
The Crowd, 299
Crowther, Bosley, 137, 199, 219, 233, 250, 262, 272
Cuban Missile Crisis, 6, 123, 141n90, 216–17, 245–46, 249; and *Dr. Strangelove*, 264–65, 274n9; and Khrushchev, Nikita, 242–43, 261; and LeMay, Curtis, 242–43, 261; and *Manchurian Candidate*, 287
Cuomo, Mario, 28
Curley, James Michael: and jail, 36, 38n26; and Kennedy, John F., 25, 38n38; and *Last Hurrah*, 17–19, 38n47; and O'Connor, Edwin, 31, 38n25; and Truman, Harry S, 14–15, 38nn25–26
Curtis, Tony, 160, 238n94
Curtiz, Michael, 5

The Dark Horse, 299
Darwell, Jane, 32
DaSilva, Howard, 87
Dave, 299
Davies, Marion, 76n64
Davies, Joseph E., 66
Davis, Ronald, 11
The Day the Earth Stood Still, 301
dead hand, 268–69
Deadline USA, 300
Dean, James, 103
Dean, William F., 183, 201n51
death and sex, 259
Deer Hunter, 157, 301
Defense, Department of: and *Dr. Strangelove*, 260; funding, 126–27, 185; and *Green Berets*, 153–57; and *Seven Days*, 136; and *Steel Hemet*, 187–94; and Truman, Harry S, 209
democracy, 42–44, 47, 178–79
democratic elitism, 45–46
democratic republic, 42–45, 47
Democrats, 2, 53
Destination Tokyo, 106n31, 106n33
détente, 245
Devine, Jeremy, 156
DeVries, Daniel, 270
Dewey, Thomas E., 67
The Diary of Anne Frank, 300
Diem, Ngo Dinh, 148
Dies, Martin, 85, 90
Diplomatic Courier, 301
direct plebiscite. *See* democracy
Dirks, Tom, 260
Dirksen, Everett, 123
disarmament, 128
Disney, Walt, 86
District of Columbia. *See* Washington, D.C.
Dittmar, Linda, 160
divine right of kings, 44
Dmytryk, Edward, 86, 87, 106nn32–34, 138n11
DoD. *See* Defense, Department of
Dodds, E. R., 226
Dodsworth, 299
Dog Day Afternoon, 300
Doherty, Tomas, 209

Donovan, Wild Bill, 151
Douglas, Kirk, 7, 87, 123, 136
dovism, 4, 6, 153, 229, 241–49, 292; and *Dr. Strangelove*, 250–71
Down and Out in America, 88
Dray, Philip, 271
Dr. No, 301
Dr. Strangelove, 6, 241, 283–87, 289–91, 301; analysis, 250–21; audience response, 271–74; plot, 249–50; satire, 251–54
"Dr. Strangelove syndrome," 253–54
il Duce. *See* Mussolini, Benito
Duck Soup, 300
Duggan, Andrew, 128
Dulles, Allen, 211
Dulles, John Foster, 246
Dunne, Finley Peter, 63
Durgnat, Raymond, 11
Dury, Allen, 50–51, 55, 57–62, 64, 66–73

eagle, bald, 229, 238n109
Eastwood, Clint, 283
Eaves, Hillary, 51
Ebenstein, William, 125
Ebert, Roger, 257
Edwards, James, 187
Edwards, Paul M., 198
Edwards, Willard, 90
einsatzgruppen, 112
Einstein, Albert, 243
Eisenhower, Dwight D., 139n31, 275n34; as elitist, 15, 48, 50; as dove, 246–49; and Hollywood, 2; and Korea, 186, 246; and "The New Look," 247; as populist, 15; as "soldier of democracy," 126; and television, 50, 93; and Vietnam, 147. *See also* Khrushchev, Nikita; Nixon, Richard
Eisenhower, Ida, 247
Eisenstein, Sergei, 257
el Caudillo. *See* Franco, Francisco
elitism, 4; arguments in support of, 45–47; definition, 44; in the fifties and sixties, 47–50; history of, 41–47; and perfectionism, 59, 69–72

Ellis, Joseph, 290
Empey, Arthur Guy, 85
The Empire Strikes Back, 300
End Poverty in California (EPIC). *See* Sinclair, Upton
The Enemy Within, 139n45
Escape from LA, 300
Evans, Gene, 187–88, 196
Executive Order 9066. *See* Japanese relocation centers
Executive Power, 299
Exodus, 87
extended open debate. *See* filibuster
Eyman, Scott, 29, 32, 36

A Face in the Crowd, 4, 5, 87, 284–85, 287, 300; analysis, 95–105; audience response to, 104–5; origins of, 94–95; plot, 91–92
Fahrenheit 451, 300
Fail-Safe, 137, 271, 300
The Falcon and the Snowman, 301
fantasy themes: elitist, 62–68; populist, 27–29
farce, 253
The Farmer's Daughter, 299
Farnsworth, Philo T., 27, 287
fascism, 4–5, 79–91, 182, 189, 268–70, 287; and charismatic leadership, 82–84; definition, 80; and the fifties, 84–91, 292; and military spawning ground, 124; modus operandi, 81–82; and Nazi–Soviet Pact, 11; preconditions, 80–81
Fat Man and Little Boy, 301
Faulhaber, Cardinal, 117
The Fearmakers, 301
Federalists, 41–43
Fellig, Arthur "Weegee," 266
Ferrer, Jose, 104
Fifth Amendment, 85–86, 120, 294
fifties America, 119–22, 293–95
filibuster, 53
film: analysis, 7; versus television, 7, 133–34. *See also* television
Firefox, 301
The Firm, 299
First Amendment, 23, 80, 85–86, 120,

293
Fitzsimmons, Charles, 17, 25. *See* O'Hara, Maureen
Fixed Bayonets, 197
Flamingo Road, 300
Flanders, Ralph, 90–91
Fleming, Donald, 206
fluoridation, 250, 253, 276n65
Flying Tigers, 300
Fogelman, Edwin, 125
Fonda, Henry, 7, 50, 69, 167–68
Fong, Harold, 187
Force, Wallace, 26
Ford, Gerald, 64
Ford, Henry, 179
Ford, John, 4, 10–11, 197; and *Last Hurrah*, 17–20, 28, 30–36; and Wayne, John, 161, 166–67
Ford, Paul, 50
Foreign Correspondent, 232, 300
Foreman, Carl, 107n42
"Forgotten War." *See* Korean War
Foster, Dianne, 22
founding fathers, 44, 47, 178, 290
The Fountainhead, 6, 11, 301
The Four Horsemen of the Apocalypse, 300
Foxe, Fanne, 65
Foyle, Kitty, 299
Franciosa, Anthony, 97
Franco, Francisco, 80; as antidemocratic, 118; "New Man," 81; physical appearance of, 84; sitting out WWII, 82
Frank, Jerome D., 210
Frankenheimer, 5–6, 88, 292; biography of, 134; and *Manchurian Candidate* 219, 223, 231–34, 237nn67–68, 239n110, 239nn116–17; and *Seven Days* 135–38
Frankenstein, 101
Frankfurter, Felix, 60
Franklin, Benjamin, 44, 64, 71, 229
"free marketplace of ideas," 24
Freud, Sigmund, 220–21, 223–25
friendly fascism. *See* Gross, Bertram
Frost, Robert, 246

Frye, Northrop, 257
Führer. *See* Hitler, Adolf
Fulbright, J. William, 90, 155
Fuller, Sam, 5, 160, 187–90, 199–200, 290; biography of, 194–96
Full Metal Jacket, 157, 163

Gable, Clark, 167–68
Gabler, Neal, 85
Gabriel over the White House, 4, 291, 300
Gaddis, John Lewis, 247, 249
Gaffney, James, 255
Galbraith, John Kenneth, 243
Gallagher, Tag, 25
Gallup, George, 48
Gallup polls: March 1937, 82; March 1950, 210; August 1950, 210; September 1950, 182; 1951, 185, 201n20; January 1951, 206; March 1951, 180; December 1955, 206; June 1962, 217; November 1962, 217; February 1968, 145; March 1968, 145
Gardens of Stone, 301
Gardner, Ava, 123, 137
Garfield, James, 64, 126
Garfield, John, 87–88
Garner, John Nance, 63
Garnham, Nicholas, 188–89
Geer, Will, 50, 87
generation gap, 31–32
genius, 44. *See also* Jackson, Andrew
George, Peter, 6, 254–58, 262, 277n77, 277n87
Get Shorty, 276n45
Gianos, Phillip L., 259–60
Giap, Vo Nguyen, 144
Gilded Age, 12, 23
Gill, Brendan, 73
Gillette, Guy, 90
Gilliatt, Penelope, 272
Gingrich, Newt, 50, 162
Gitlin, Todd, 121–23, 145
Give 'Em Hell, Harry!, 299
Gleason, James, 17
Godard, Jean Luc, 169, 187, 283
The Godfather, 300

The Godfather, Part II, 300
The Godfather, Part III, 300
Godfrey, Arthur, 97, 108n89
Goebbels, Joseph, 178
The Gold Rush, 299
Goldwater, Barry, 11, 169
Goldwyn, Sam, 6, 68, 87, 286–87
Goodbye, My Fancy, 300
Goodfellas, 300
Good Morning Vietnam, 157, 301
Goodpaster, Andrew, 248
Gordon, Bennie, 191
Gorgeous Hussy, 299
Göring, Hermann, 113
Go Tell the Spartans, 301
Gottlieb, Sidney, 214, 219
The Graduate, 299
Grant, Lee, 88
Grant, Ulysses, 126
Grapes of Wrath, 11, 69
Gray, Tobias, 256
The Great Dictator, 83, 300
The Great McGinty, 299
Greatest Generation. *See* silent majority
The Great Man, 104
The Great Santini, 300
Greatest Story Ever Told, 153
Green Berets. *See* U.S. Army Special Forces
The Green Berets (film), 5, 188, 284–85 300; analysis of, 149–71; audience response to, 168–71; journalist character, 157–59; plot, 149–50; as a western, 159–162
Greer, John, 69
Gregory, James, 215
Griffith, Andy, 7, 91, 109n100
Grizzard, George, 57
Gross, Bertram, 85, 121
Gulf of Tonkin Resolution, 148, 172n24. *See* Johnson, Lyndon
Gwinnet, Button, 21

Hackett, Frank, 186
Hadyn, Sterling, 87, 249
"Hail, Hail, the Gang's All Here," 34
Hail the Conquering Hero, 299

Halberstam, David, 90, 121–22, 159,
183–84
Hamilton, Alexander, 41, 44, 46
Hammett, Dashiell, 87
The Hangman Also Dies, 300
Hardy, Phil, 190, 273
Harris, Billy Joe, 213
Harris, James D., 254, 55
Harris, Julie, 103
Harrison, William K., 126, 181
Harris polls: 1993, 162; 1994, 162; 1995,
162
Hart, Gary, 65
Harvey, Laurence, 205, 211, 215,
232–33, 237n72
hawkism, 4, 153, 242, 253, 292; history,
205–19; and Kennedy, John F.,
215–16; and *Manchurian Candidate*,
215–219, 227; and Truman, Harry S,
207
Hawks, Howard, 165–66
Hays, Wayne, 65
Hays, Will, 69, 228. *See also* Motion
Picture Production Code
Hayward, Susan, 175n121
Hearst, William Randolph, 20, 158,
179, 291
Heartbreak Ridge, 300
Hearts of the World, 300
Hell and High Water, 197
Heller, Joseph, 227
Hellman, Lillian, 87
Hellzapoppin, 253
Henderson, Don, 111
Henderson, Douglas, 227
Henricksen, Margot, 222
Henrickson, Robert C., 90
Henry, Mike, 150
Henry, William, 47
Hepburn, Katherine, 31
Herblock, 88, 184
Hercules, 134
Herr, Michael, 255
hierarchy, 10, 46, 48; military, 124, 128
High Noon, 30
Hill, Lee, 256
Himmler, Heinrich, 113–14, 267–68
Hinkle, Lawrence, 211–12

Hinson, Hal, 222, 229
Hiroshima, 206
Hiss, Alger, 59–60, 88, 90
Hitchcock, 137, 232, 283
Hitler, Adolf, 80; as anticommunist,
114–15; as antidemocratic, 118;
assassination attempts on, 115, 117;
and Catholic Church, 116;
Führerprinzip, 83, 115, 138n15; and
Jews, 106n196; and knight, 81,
281n176, 262, 267; and labor, 115;
and Law for Prevention of
Genetically Diseased Children, 113,
138n11; and *Mein Kampf*, 83, 113,
11; and National Labor Front, 115;
and Nazi-Soviet Pact, 111; and
Nuremberg Laws, 82, 118; and
Operation Mercy Killing, 113–16;
physical appearance of, 83;
propaganda, 83; rhetoric of, 83;
Soviet Union, invasion of
112
Hitler's Children, 138n11, 300
Holleman, Joe, 273
Hollinger, Robert, 47
Holly, Buddy, 162
Hollywood, and Washington, D.C.,
1–3
Hollywood Anti-Nazi League, 84
Hollywood Hussars. *See* Cooper, Gary
Hollywood Ten, 86, 87; film subject as,
106n31. *See also* Bessie, Alvah;
Biberman, Herbert; Dmytryk,
Edward; Lardner, Cole; Lawson,
John Howard; Maltz, Albert;
Ornitz, Samuel; Scott, Adrian;
Trumbo, Dalton
Holmes, Oliver Wendell, 60
holocaust, 112, 119
Hoover, Herbert, 1, 99, 130, 133
Hoover, J. Edgar, 122, 188
Hope, Bob, 230
Hopper, Hedda, 272
Horace, 251
Hotel Berlin, 106n31, 300
hotline, 246
Houseman, John, 125, 140n50
House of Bamboo, 194, 198

House Un-American Activities Committee (HUAC), 4–5, 11, 59, 90 188, 286; 1937, 85; 1947, 85–87, 244, 292; 1951, 85–87, 244, 292; Butler, 130; failure to evidence subversion, 85–86; McCarthyism, 91; modus operandi, 85–86, 120
Howard, Trevor, 252
Howe, Neil, 295
HUAC. *See* House on Un-American Activities Committee
Huggins, Roy, 87
Huitt, Ralph K., 56
humanitarian interventionism, 119
Humphrey, Hubert H., 17, 62
Hunt, Evelyn. *See* Condon, Richard
Hunt, Lester, 77n91
Hunt, Linda, 268
Hunter, Edward, 211
Hunter, Jeffrey, 17
Hunter, Kim, 88
The Hunters, 198
The Hunt for Red October, 301
Hussein, Saddam, 252, 86
Huston, John, 86
Hutton, Jim, 150, 160
Hutton, Robert, 187
Huxley, Aldous, 125
hydrogen bomb, 21, 242–43, 255, 266

Il-Sung, Kim, 182
I Married a Communist, 301
In Cold Blood, 168
Independence Day, 301
Indiana Jones and the Temple of Doom, 201n42
The Informer, 29, 197
Inherit the Wind, 12, 299
internationalism, 5, 179
interventionism, 4–5, 146–49, 292; in film, 150, 155–56, 197. *See also* Korean War; Marshall Plan; Vietnam
Intolerance, 300
The Invaders, 300
Invasion of the Body Snatchers, 219, 300
Invasion USA, 301
The Invisible Man Returns, 106n33

The Iron Curtain, 301
Iron Law of Oligarchy. *See* Michels, Robert
isolationism, 4–5, 82, 119, 145–46, 150; in the fifties, 180–86, 292; in U.S. history, 178–80
It Could Happen Here, 85
I Want You, 300
I Was a Communist for the FBI, 301
I Was a Teenage Werewolf, 134

Jackson, Andrew, 10, 44, 126, 164
Jaffe, Same, 88
Jakob the Liar, 138n5
Janssen, David, 149
Japanese fascism, 80; and General Mobilization Law, 116; and Great East Asia Co-Prosperity Sphere, 80; and Munitions Mobilization Law, 116; and Tojo, 84; and totalitarian thought control, 82
Japanese relocation centers, 191
Jarrico, Paul, 107n42
Jefferson, Thomas, 9–10, 41, 43–46; and McCarthy, Joseph, 111
Jessup, Philip C., 90
Jewish sanctuary, 117, 119
John XXIII (pope), 217
Johnny Guitar, 300
Johnson, Lyndon Baines, 64, 68, 105n3; and *Face in the Crowd*, 95; and *Green Berets*, 154; hawk, 246; as interventionist, 146–47; as populist, 15–16; and Vietnam, 143–44, 148, 244. *See also* Tet Offensive; Tonkin Gulf Resolution
Johnson, Nunnally, 36
Johnson, Samuel, 228
Jones, Robert, 214
Judge Priest, 299
Jue, Craig, 150
Jun, Chai Ung, 180
Jurow, Martin, 36
Juvenal (Decimus Junius Juvenalis), 251

Kahn, Herman, 254, 269, 280n171
Kai-shek, Chiang, 89

Kaltenborn, H. V., 89
Karloff, Boris, 101
Kauffman, Stanley, 135, 263, 288
Kaye, Danny, 86
Kazan, Elia, 87, 291; and AFI, 107n39;
    and *Face in the Crowd*, 5, 93,
    100–103; and family, 103–4,
    109n112; and fascism definition, 96;
    and Griffith, Andy, 109n100; and
    HUAC, 87; and Long, Huey, 96
Keeper of the Flame, 300
Kelley, Barry, 231
Kelly, Francis J., 152
Kelly, Gene, 86
Kelly, Tom, 72
Kennan, George, 179
Kennedy, Bobby and Ethel, 66
Kennedy, Jacqueline, 49, 65, 261
Kennedy, John F., 2–3, 31, 38n38, 51,
    64–68, 70, 161; and arms race, 6,
    127, 247; assassination of, 123, 138,
    215, 253, 271; and *Dr. Strangelove*,
    249; as elitist, 15, 48–52; and Green
    Berets, 152; hawk, 215–17, 246, 249,
    275n36; as interventionist, 146; and
    Khrushchev, Nikita, 216–17, 249,
    265–66; and *Manchurian Candidate*,
    215, 234, 236nn41–42; and *Seven
    Days*, 136; and Single Integrated
    Operational Plan, 249; and Test Ban
    Treaty, 243; and Vietnam, 147–48;
    and Walker, Edwin, 131. *See also*
    Bay of Pigs; Cuban Missile Crisis;
    Monroe, Marilyn; Tierney, Gene
Kennedy, Joseph P., 50, 65, 72, 89, 166
Kennedy, Robert, 164
Kent, James, 168
Kent State, 122
Kesey, Ken, 227
Khan, Aly, 66
Khrushchev, Nikita, 6, 242–43, 246,
    252, 279nn139–40; biography,
    263–66; and *Dr. Strangelove*, 255;
    and Eisenhower, Dwight D., 246,
    248; and Kennedy, John F., 216–17,
    249, 261, 265–66; and Sino-Soviet
    relations, 263; and Wayne, John,
    162. *See also* Cuban Missile Crisis

Khrushchev, Nina, 264–65
Khrushchev, Sergei N., 264
The Killing, 276
Kinder, Küche, und Kirche, 106n23
King, Charles, 191
King, Martin Luther, 69, 122
Kinkead, Eugene, 214
Kissinger, Henry, 64, 210, 242, 252, 268,
    285
Knebel, Fletcher, 5, 125
Knight, Arthur, 137
Knoke, William, 297
Kolker, Robert, 250, 259
Korean War, 4–5, 124–25, 146–47, 150,
    180–86, 289, 294; casualties, 181,
    183, 186, 200n20; and Cold War,
    210–11; and limited military
    conflict, 184; POWs, 6, 185–86,
    188–90, 205, 210–14, 218, 229; and
    Steel Helmet, 198–99
Korean War Monument, 177
Kovik, Ron, 162
Kramer, Stanley, 12, 271
Krauthammer, Charles, 55
Krim, Arthur, 233
Kristallnacht, 112
Kroll, Jack, 258
Kubrick, Christine, 267
Kubrick, Stanley, 250–74, 278n101,
    278n104

laissez-faire capitalism. *See* capitalism
Lamarr, Hedy, 76n70
Lancaster, Burt, 7, 123
Landon, Alf, 48
Langsdorf, Maryl, 241
Lanning, Michael, 171
Lansbury, Angela, 205, 215, 231,
    236n44, 237n72
La Pore, Richard, 218
Lardner, Ring, Jr., 86, 106n33
Larkin, John, 128
La Rosa, Julius, 97
The Last Hurrah, 4, 284–85, 287, 289–90,
    299; analysis, 117–36; audience
    response, 35–36; plot, 17–18
The Late George Apley, 299
Lattimore, Owen, 90

Laughton, Charles, 50, 62
Lawford, Peter, 57, 64
Lawrence, David, 148–49
Lawson, John Howard, 86, 106n33
Lawton, Charles, Jr., 35
Lazanfeld, Paul, 93
League of Nations, 179
Lebensraum, 113, 138n9
Lee, Anna, 35
Lee, Canada, 88
Lee, Henry, 9
Lee, Howard, 66
Lehman, Herbert H., 54
Lehrer, Tom, 254, 268
Leigh, Janet, 215, 228, 233, 238n94
LeMay, Curtis, 6, 148, 242–43, 252, 290;
    biography, 261–63, 279n127
Lemmon, Jack, 160
Lemnitzer, Lyman L., 131–32
L'Enfant, Pierre, 46
Lenin, Vladimir Ilyich, 245
Lennart, Isobel, 87
Lerner, Murray, 196
Lewis, Roger, 270
Lewis, Sinclair, 85
Lewy, Gunter, 116
Lichtenberg, Monsignor Bernard, 117
Lifeboat, 300
Limited Nuclear Test Ban Treaty. *See*
    Atmospheric Nuclear Weapons Test
    Ban Treaty
Lincoln, Abraham, 10, 20, 105n3;
    Gettysburg, 43; Grant, Ulysses, 126;
    Manchurian Candidate, 229–30
Lincoln Brigade, 114
Lindberg, Charles, 179
Linden, George W., 259, 272
A Lion in the Streets, 299
Little Caesar, 300
Loan, Nguyen Ngoc, 143–44, 171n2
LoBrutto, Vincent, 254, 267
Locke, John, 178–79
Lolita, 276n67
Lombardi, Vince, 66
Long, Huey, 94, 96–97, 108n87;
    Roosevelt, Franklin D., 133
The Longest Day, 154
Loo, Richard, 187

Lordeaux, Lee, 29
The Loved One, 257
Loveless, Jay, 185
Lowe, Rabbi Judah (The Maharal),
    101–2
Lowell, Tom, 218
LSD, 214
Luce, Henry, 183
Lucilius, Gaius, 251
Lueger, Karl, 83
Lumet, Sidney, 134, 137, 271
Lundberg, Ferdinand, 41
Lurie, Rod, 292
Lynn, Vera, 259, 278n112. *See also*
    "We'll Meet Again"

Macklin, Anthony, 260, 270
MacLeish, Roderick, 223
Macready, George, 129
Mad (magazine), 254
Madison, James, 43
Magill, Frank N., 223
The Magnificent Ambersons, 4, 299
Mailer, Norman, 227. Hi Norman!
majority rule. *See* democracy
Maltz, Albert, 86, 106n33, 107n42
The Man in the Gray Flannel Suit, 299
The Man Who Shot Liberty Valance, 300
Manchurian Candidate, 6, 134, 137,
    285–91, 301; analysis of, 214–30;
    audience response to, 233–34; plot,
    214–15
Manhattan Project, 241–42
Manoff, Arnold, 88
The Man Who Would Be King, 300
The Man with the Golden Arm, 69
March, Frederick, 123
Marlowe, Hugh, 128
Marshall, George C., 90, 184, 207–8. *See
    also* Marshall Plan
Marshall Plan, 146, 208
M*A*S*H, 106n33, 301
Maslin, Janet, 219, 231
Massengale, John, 271
The Master Race, 106n31
Matteotti, Giacomo, 113
Matthau, Walter, 92
Matthews, Chris, 61

Maxwell, Elsa, 66
May, Elaine Tyler, 260
Mayer, Louis B., 1, 86
Mayer, Rupert, 117
Mayer, William E., 210, 214
Mayes, Wendell, 69, 73
McArthur, Douglas, 89, 90, 124;
    farewell address of, 132, 141n78;
    and *Green Berets*, 151; and Korea,
    147, 149, 180, 182–84; and
    Manchurian Candidate, 226; and
    McCarthyism, 184; and *Seven Days*
    132; and Wayne, John, 167
McBride, Joseph, 10–11, 165, 293
McCain, John, 205
McCarran-Walter Immigration Act, 89,
    120
McCarthy, Eugene, 2, 145
McCarthy, Joseph, 94, 293; Army
    hearings for, 91; censure of, 91, 111,
    229; and China lobby, 89; and
    Drury, Allen, 68; and Eisenhower,
    Dwight D., 90; and *Manchurian
    Candidate*, 228–30; and media, 86,
    89–90; popularity of, 47, 88–89; and
    Seven Days, 131; and Truman, Harry
    S., 89, 90, 229; and Wheeling
    speech, 88, 90
McCarthyesque, 55, 57–59, 72
McCarthyism, 4, 120, 184, 188–89, 210,
    217, 222, 228–30, 244
McCloy, John J., 200n13
McCrea, Joel, 232
McCreign, Elaine, 130, 137
McGiver, John, 215
McGovern, George, 2
McHugh, Frank, 17, 28
McLaglen, Victor, 85
McLellan, Dennis, 168
McLuhan, Marshall, 7
McNamara, Robert S., 143, 249
McNamara-Rusk-Rostow rationale,
    150
Meader, Vaugn, 26
Medford, Kay, 103
media obligations, 23–24, 32
Medium Cool, 135, 299
Medvedev, Roy, 265

Meet John Doe, 299
Men in Black, 27n45
Men in Black II, 27n45
Mencken, H. L., 29, 55
Menjou, Adolphe, 86
merchants of defense. *See*
    military–industrial complex
Merriam, Frank, 2
Merrill's Marauders, 197
Mesmer, Franz, 220
Mesta, Perle, 65–66
Metropolis, 267
Mexican-American War, 178
Michaelis, John "Mike," 185
Michaud, Gene, 160
Michels, Robert, 45
A Midnight Clear, 301
mike forces, 152
Milestone, Lewis, 177, 197–98
military–industrial complex, 5, 48,
    125–26, 130, 292, 294
military and politics, 125, 129
Mill, John Stuart, 23
Miller, Arthur, 87
Miller, Jonathan, 254
Mills, Barry, 99
Mills, C. Wright, 55, 120–22
Mills, Wilbur, 65
Milne, Tom, 273
Mindszenty, Cardinal Josef, 211
Minh, Ho Chi, 157, 173n68
mise en scène, 288
missile gap, 6, 127, 247
Missiles of October, 301
Mission to Moscow, 5, 301
Mister Roberts, 160
Mitchum, Robert, 198
Mitry, Jean, 283
Mittelstand, 83
MK-ULTRA, 214
Mohr, Charles, 159
momism, 225
Monahan, Richard, 187
monarchy, 42–43
Monroe, Marilyn, 3
Monteau, Michele, 51
Montgomery, Robert, 86
The Moon Is Blue, 69

Moore, Dudley, 254
Moore, Hal, 284
Moore, Robin, 153, 179
Moorehead, Agnes, 175n121
Moos, Malcolm, 126
Morgan, Jerry, 185
Morly, Karen, 87
Morris, William, 92
Morrison, Marion Robert. *See* Wayne,
    John
Morton, George, 152
Moskin, J. Robert, 213
Mosse, George L., 125
Motion Picture Alliance for the
    Preservation of American Ideals,
    165
Motion Picture Association of
    America, 71
Motion Picture Democratic
    Committee, 85
Motion Picture Patents Co., 107n38
Motion Picture Production Code, 197,
    260. *See also* Hays, Will; Shurlock,
    Geoffrey
MPAA. *See* Motion Picture Association
    of America
MPPC. *See* Motion Picture Production
    Code
Mr. Deeds Comes to Town, 299
Mr. Lincoln, 69
"Mr. President," 43
Mrs. Miniver, 300
Mr. Smith Goes to Washington, 4, 11,
    50–51, 53–54, 72, 291, 299
Mr. Walkie Talkie, 300
Mullaney, Jack, 129
Mumford, Lewis, 251
Mundelein, George (cardinal), 113
Munich Pact, 118
Murphy, George, 155
Murray, Don, 51
Murrow, Edward R., 26, 73, 90–91, 286
Mussolini, Benito, 80, 113; as
    antidemocratic, 118; and black
    shirts, 81, 85; and Ethiopia, 82; and
    labor, 115; physical appearance of,
    83; and rhetoric, 84
Muste, A. J., 244

mutually assured destruction (MAD),
    251, 269, 271, 276n42
My Darling Clementine, 13
My Lai (Vietnam), 145
My Man Godfrey, 299
My Son John, 301
myth of presidency as elevating, 49, 63

Nam Il (lieutenant general), 181
Nashville, 299
National Committee for a SANE
    Nuclear Policy, 244
National Security Council Document,
    68, 209–10, 247
NATO. *See* North Atlantic Treaty
    Organization
natural aristocracy. *See* Jefferson,
    Thomas
Nazism. *See* fascism
Neal, Patricia, 91
Nellow, Ed, 90
Nelson, Tomas Allen, 263
Newman, Paul, 2
Nichols, Mike, 271
Night People, 301
Nitze, Paul, 209–10, 247, 275n29
Nixon, 300
Nixon, Richard, 2, 52, 64–65, 68, 105n3,
    68; "Checkers" speech, 25–26, 94;
    and Ford, Gerald, 11; Hiss, Alger,
    60, 90, 107n46; as interventionist,
    146–47; and polls, 48; as populist,
    16–17; presidential campaign, 143,
    145; and silent majority, 123,
    139n42; and South America, 127
    and Wayne, John, 162. *See also*
    Vietnamization
Nixon-Kennedy debates, 25–27, 50,
    93
non-interventionism. *See* isolationism
North Atlantic Treaty Organization,
    146, 179, 209
The North Star, 301
NSC 68. *See* National Security Council
    Document 68
Nuclear Nonproliferation Treaty
    (1969), 242, 252
nuclear war, accidental, 244–45, 271

Nugent, Frank, 30, 34
Nye, Joseph S., 210

Objective Burma, 106n33
O'Brien, Edmund, 123, 137
O'Brien, Pat, 17
O'Connor, Carroll, 3, 33
O'Connor, Edwin, 18–19, 31, 33–34, 38n25
Odets, Clifford, 87–88
Oedipus, 223–26
O'Hara, Maureen, 25
Old Man and the Sea, 31
Olds, William, 150
Oliver, Laurence, 166
Olson, James S., 161, 164, 167
On the Beach, 254, 301
O'Neill, Tip, 14, 38n47
O'Neill, William, 217
One Minute to Zero, 300
One of Our Aircraft Is Missing, 300
"Operation Paperclip," 263, 268
Operation Petticoat, 160
Ophuls, Max, 257
Oppenheimer, J. Robert, 244
Ornitz, Samuel, 86, 106n33
Oswald, Lee Harvey, 215
Our Daily Bread, 6, 11, 299, 293

pacifism, 146, 179, 199
Packard, David, 65
Page, Geraldine, 20
Paine, Thomas, 43
Pakula, Alan, 271
Paper Chase, 140n50
paramilitary organization, 81, 124
Paris peace talks, 146
Parker, Dorothy, 20, 87
Parks, Larry, 87
parody, 252, 259
Parrish, Leslie, 215
Pate, Lloyd, 213
Paths of Glory, 34, 276n67, 277n71
Patton, 300
Patton, George, 67, 197
Pauling, Linus, 244
Paullson, Albert, 219
Pavlov, Ivan Petrovich, 211, 219, 221

Pearl Harbor, 179, 182
Pegler, Westbrook, 89
Pendergast, Thomas J., 14–15
Penn, Artur, 271
Pentagon. *See* Defense, Department of
Pentagon Papers, 148
People's Party of America, 13, 52. *See* populism
Perón, Juan Domingo, 80; as antidemocratic, 118; and Evita, 84; and labor, 115; overthrow of, 129
Perry, Mort, 159
Persius (Aulus Persius Flaccus), 251
phallic symbols, 259–60, 278n109
The Phantom President, 100
philosopher kings. *See* Plato
Pichel, Irving, 87
Pickens, Slim, 165, 250, 272
Pickup on South St., 301
Pidgeon, Walter, 50
Pierce, Franklin, 126
Pierot Le Fou, 187
Pius XI (pope), 116–17
Pius XII (pope), 116
Plato, 42, 44
political equality. *See* democracy
political film genre, 6
political ideology definition, 6
political machine, 14, 27, 30, 83. *See also* Curley, James Michael; Pendergast, Thomas J.
political science fiction film genre, 57
politics and military, 125, 129
polling, 48
"Pony Boy," 34
popular front, 115. *See also* communism
popular sovereignty. *See* democracy
populism, 4, 44, 60–62, 69; and fascism, 96; history, 9–13; in nineteen-fifties and sixties, 14–17, 292;
populist meritocracy, 45
Powell, Colin, 68
Powell, Dick, 175n121
Powell, Enoch, 62
Powers, Richard Gid, 90, 256
Powers, Thomas, 262, 279n131

The Powers Girl, 238n103
Pratley, Gerald, 127, 139, 231, 233
Preminger, Otto, 4, 50–51, 87–88,
    66–73, 286, 291
Preminger, Erik Lee, 68
presidential job description, 47
The President's Lady, 299
The President Vanishes, 300
preventable war, 262
Pride of the Marines, 106n31, 106n33
Primary Colors, 299
The Prize, 301
Protocol, 299
Puff the Magic Dragon, 152, 157, 170,
    172n36
Purdy, Jim, 219
Putney Swope, 299
Pynchon, Thomas, 227

Quart, Leonard, 160
Quayle, Dan, 2
Quigley poll, 162
quiz show scandals, 108n76

Raintree County, 106n32
Rand, Ayn, 86
Rand Corporation, 252, 269
Rathbone, Basil, 17
Ray, Aldo, 149
Ray, Elizabeth, 65
Reagan, Ronald, 3, 68, 86, 167–68,
    283
Reap the Wild Wind, 167
The Red Danube, 301
Red Dawn, 301
The Red Menace, 301
The Red Nightmare, 301
Red River, 166
Reds, 301
Reeves, Rosser, 2, 50, 94
Remarque, Erich Maria, 177–78
Remick, Lee, 99, 103
Republicans, 53
resistance movements: Belgian, 114;
    French, 114; German, 114; Italian,
    114; Jewish, 117–18
Retreat, Hell!, 300
Return of the Jedi, 300

Rhee, Syngman, 181–83
Rhysdael, Basil, 25
Rice, Donna, 65
Ridgway, H. B., 186, 201n36
Ridgway, Matthew, 247–48
Riefenstahl, Leni, 106n24
Riesel, Victor, 189
Riessman, David, 121
Rill, Yvonne, 220
Rio Bravo, 301
Robbins, Tim, 196, 202n84
The Robe, 134
Roberts, Clete, 22, 24
Roberts, Randy, 161, 164, 167
Roberts, William L., 182
Robinson, Harlow, 264
Rockwerk, Louis N., 212
Rocky, 299
Roffman, Peter, 219
Rogers, Will, 54, 98–99; and Mussolini,
    Benito, 99
Roosevelt, Franklin Delano, 1–2, 5,
    47–48, 64, 66–67; and anti-
    communists, 206; and fascist coup,
    130; and McArthur, Douglas, 133;
    and oil embargo, 129; and
    populism, 11, 13–14; and relocation
    centers, 190–91; and Truman, Harry
    S, 62–63, 285
Roosevelt, Theodore, 13, 22, 126, 146
Roper, Elmo, 48
Rosenberg, Alfred, 79
Rosenberg, Julius and Ethel, 88, 120
Rosenthal, Benjamin, 156
Rosie the Riveter, 139n37
Rostow, Walt, 216. *See also* McNamara-
    Rusk-Rostow rationale
Rousseau, Jen-Jacques, 45, 179
Rule XXII. *See* filibuster
Rusk, Dean, 148, 200n13, 217. *See
    also* McNamara-Rusk-Rostow
    rationale
Russell, Richard, 61–62, 155
Russo, Vita, 71
Russo-Japanese War, 146

Sadler, Barry, 151–53
Sagon, Scott D., 245

Sahara, 106n31

Sahl, Mort, 254, 268

Salinger, Pierre, 136

Salt of the Earth, 106n32

Samuels, Stuart, 6, 289–90

Sanders, Joe, 227

Sands of Iwo Jima, 154, 159, 162, 167

Santayana, George, 295

Sarris, 57, 59, 68, 72, 199, 222, 252, 256, 289, 291–92

satire, 251–56, 258–59, 272–73, 291

"Saturday Night Live," 205, 254

Sayre, Nora, 194, 219, 293

Scarface, 300

Schelling, Thomas, 254

Schindler's List, 138n23, 300

Schlesinger, Arthur M., 209

Schulberg, Budd: as Mel, 100–110; as communist, 87, 109n105; wife of, 103–4

Scorsese, Martin, 271

Scott, Adrian, 86, 106n33

Scott, George C., 165, 250, 253

Scott, Ian, 284

Seabiscuit, 299

The Searchers, 12, 162, 169

The Seduction of Joe Tynan, 299

Seeger, Pete, 87

Segal, Clancy, 187–88

Segal, Eric, 266

Sellers, Peter, 7, 253, 255–58, 266–67, 277n84, 278n101, 280n153

Selznik, Daniel, 194

Selznik, David, 288

Senate, U.S., 4, 51–60; and *Advise and Consent*, 52, 54, 291; code of conduct, 55–60

The Senator Was Indiscreet, 300

September 11, 2001, 79, 295

Sergeant York, 300

Serling, Rod, 51, 134–35, 137

Server, Lee, 195

Seven Days in May, 5, 285, 288, 291–92, 300; audience response to, 136–38; and delay, 137; and enemies of fascism, 128–30; and military–industrial complex, 125; plot, 123–24; and preconditions for coup, 127–28; and television, 133–36; and title, 136

Seventeenth Amendment, 52

sex and death, 259

A Shade of Difference, 77n86

Shalikashvili, John, 162

Shampoo, 88

Shane, 301

Sharp, Henry, 98

Sheehan, Neil, 159

Shelley, Mary, 101

Shenandoah, 153

Sherry, Michael, 262

She Wore a Yellow Ribbon, 22

Shirer, William L., 88

Shivas, Mark, 55

Shurlock, Geoffrey, 71, 253, 260. See also Motion Picture Production Code

The Siege of Firebase Gloria, 300

silent majority, 123, 139n42, 170, 294

Silva, Henry, 218

Simmon, Scott, 11

Simon, Jeff, 251

Sinatra, Frank, 2, 6–7, 71, 265; and *Manchurian Candidate*, 214–15, 233, 236n43

Sinclair, Upton, 2

sixties America, 122

Slotkin, Richard, 161

Smalley, Gary, 289

Smith, Alfred E., 35, 99

Smith, Howard K., 2

Smith, Margaret Chase, 75n45

Smith, Martha, 243

Smith Act, 120, 105n3, 139n26

Song of Russia, 5, 301

Sonnenfeld, Barry, 251

So Proudly We Hail, 301

Southeast Asia Treaty Organization, 209

Southern, Terry, 6, 252, 255–59, 264, 266, 277n84

Spanish–American War, 146, 179

Spanish Civil War, 114, 179

Spartacus, 87

Speer, Albert, 268

Spellman (cardinal), 148

Spielberg, Steven, 201n42
Spock, Benjamin, 224–25
Sprague, Robert, 262
Sputnik, 1137, 242, 263, 279n137
The Spy Who Came in from the Cold, 301
Stalin, Joseph, 68, 115; and atrocities, 234n3, 265; and death, 245; and Nazi–Soviet Pact, 111; and Poland, 207
Star Wars, 300
State of the Union, 299
Steel Helmet, 5, 285, 289, 301; analysis of, 187–99; as antiwar film, 197–99; audience response to, 199–200; plot, 187; and spirituality, 198–99
Stennis, John C., 62
Stevenson, Adlai E., 15, 48, 94–95, 262
Stewart, Donald Ogden, 107n42
Stewart, Jimmy, 167–68
St. Jacques, Raymond, 150, 155
Storm Center, 300
The Story of G.I. Joe, 197
The Story of Mankind, 300
Strategic Air Command, 301
Strategic Arms Limitation Treaty (1972), 271
Stratton, Richard, 211
Strauss, Lewis, 52
Strauss, William, 295
Strecker, Edward, 225
Student Peace Union, 244
Stuhlinger, Ernst, 269
Subversive Activities Control Act, 89, 120
Suddenly, 215
Suid, Lawrence H., 128, 131, 258
The Sun Shines Bright, 13, 33
Superman IV: The Quest for Peace, 301
Swanson, Gloria, 76n64
Swift, Jonathan, 251, 273, 278n108
Swope, Herbert Bayard, 206
Symington, Stuart, 95

"Ta-Ra-Ra-Boom-Dee-Ay," 34
Taft, Robert A., 58
Taft Hartley Act, 58
Takai, George, 154
Taylor, Elizabeth, 165

Taylor, Maxwell, 136, 247
Taylor, Philip, 179, 288
Taylor, Robert, 86
Tea with Mussolini, 300
Teller, Edward, 254, 263, 266
television, 4, 14, 17; advertising, 93; *Advise and Consent*, 61; as entertainment, 93; image maker, 50, 100; *The Last Hurrah*, 24–27; *Manchurian Candidate*, 230–33; McCarthy, Joseph, 90–92; political influence of, 93–94, 104; radio and, 92; *Seven Days*, 134–36; as target of film, 7, 286–88; threat to film, 133
Tet Offensive, 143–46, 170, 171n7, 244
"That Was the Week That Was," 254
Thatcher, Molly Day. *See* Kazan, Elia
Them!, 301
They Were Expendable, 154
The Thief, 301
Thieu, Nguyen Von, 144–45, 244
The Thing, 300
Thirty Seconds over Tokyo, 106n31
This Day and Age, 300
Thomas, J. Parnell, 86, 106n30
Thompson, David, 163
Thompson, Turkey, 189
Three Faces West, 106n33
The Three Kings, 300
Thurmond, Strom, 149, 169
Tierney, Gene, 51, 65–66
The Tin Star, 301
Tito, Marshall, 265
To Be or Not To Be, 83
To Have and Have Not, 228
de Tocqueville, Alexis, 206, 295
Tojo, General Hideki, 84
Toland, John, 117, 181
Tone, Franchot, 50, 66–67
Tonkin Gulf Resolution, 148
Topaz, 301
Townsend, Leo, 87
Tracy, Spencer, 7, 17, 31
Trent, John, 289
Trial, 301
Trillin, Calvin, 253
Triumph of the Will, 106n24
True Believer, 299

True Grit, 168
Truffaut, Francois, 29, 102
Truman, Harry S, 151, 238n109; as anticommunist, 206–7; and bomb, 184, 242, 246; Executive Order 9835, 120; and integration of military, 139n37, 185, 191; as isolationist, 207; and Korea, 147, 180, 183; and McArthur, Douglas, 124–25, 133; as populist, 14–15; as vice president, 62–64, 67–68, 72, 285. *See also* Truman Doctrine
Truman Doctrine, 207–8
Trumbo, Dalton, 86–87, 106n33, 107n42
"Try a Little Tenderness," 255, 259
Tsu, Irene, 150
Tucker, 299
Turan, Kenneth, 164
Turnbull, Agnes Sligh, 29
Tuttle, Frank, 87
Twelve O'Clock, High, 275n39
"Twentieth Century," 190
Twilight's Last Gleaming, 301
"Twilight Zone." *See* Rod Serling
2001, 168, 289
tyranny, threat of, 46–47

Udall, Morris K., 165, 246
Uncle Don, 104
Underworld USA, 194
United Nations, 147, 180, 182, 200n7, 207, 265
Unruh, Jesse, 54
The Untouchables, 300
USA Patriot Act, 79, 80, 295
U.S. Army Special Forces, 151, 155, 173n44, 172n33
USS Kitty Hawk, 136

Valenti, Jack, 154–55
Vandiver, Ernest, 69
Velde, Harold, 87
Verniere, James, 272
Vidor, King, 6, 10–11
Vietnam, 4–5, 9, 17, 127, 146, 292, 294; history of, 147–49; Kennedy, John F., 217; rationale for war in, 145; as war of attrition, 149

Vietnamization, 145, 147, 172n16
Von Braun, Wernher, 6, 252, 266; biography, 266–71
Von Galen, Clemons, 114
Von Neumann, John, 280n157
Von Rath, Ernst, 112
voyeurism, 72

Wag the Dog, 301
Wainwright, Loudon, 272
Wake Island, 300
Walk a Crooked Mile, 301
Walk East on Beacon, 301
A Walk in the Sun, 197
Walk on the Wild Side, 106n32
Walker, Alexander, 251, 271
Walker, Edwin A., 131, 140n70
Walker, Michael, 149
Walker, Walton H., 183
Wallace, Henry A., 63
Wallach, Eli, 88
Wall Street, 299
Walsh, Raoul, 166
Wanger, Walter, 291
Waram, Percy, 98
War Games, 301
Warner, Jack, 86
War of the Worlds, 301
Warren, Vernon, 191–92
Washington, George, 5, 42–43, 126, 164; farewell address, 126, 178; first inaugural, 41
Washington Marry-Go-Round, 299
Washington, D.C., 1–3, 46
Watergate, 17
Waters, George, 90
Watkins, Arthur V., 91
Wayne, John, 5, 7, 11, 29, 149, 290, 174n84, 175n121, 188; *Big Red One*, 194–95; biography, 152–68
Wayne, Michael, 153, 159, 161
Wayne, Patrick, 167
Wayne, Pilar, 168
The Way We Were, 300
Webster, Daniel, 53
Wegner, Paul, 101
Welch, Bill, 156

Welch, Joseph, 69, 76n83, 91
"We'll Meet Again," 259, 27nn112–13.
  See also Lynn, Vera
Welles, Orson, 256, 281n187
Wellman, William, 197
Westmoreland, William, 144
What Price Glory, 300
"What's My Line?" 246, 256
"When Johnny Comes Marching
  Home," 258
Whitaker, Clem, 2
White, E. B., 9
White, Betty, 57
Whitehead, O. S., 32
Wilcox, Horace Henderson, 1
The Wild One, 301
Wild in the Streets, 300
Wilkie, Wendell, 146
Williams, William A., 206
Wills, Gary, 41, 153, 159–61, 163–64
Wilson, 299
Wilson, Charles E., 127
Wilson, Michael, 88
Winchell, Walter, 89
Winnington, Alan, 186
Wolff, Harold, 211–12
Wilson, Woodrow, 13, 60, 70, 179
Woman of the Year, 106n33

Wood, John S., 87
Wood, Natalie, 169
Woods, Michael, 179–80
Woolf, S. J., 82
World War I, 5, 146, 150, 177, 208;
  casualties, 179
World War II, 5, 146, 150, 159, 179, 208;
  casualties, 112; draft dodgers, 178;
  and Sam Fuller, 194; and TNT, 231
Wright, Orville and Wilbur, 236
Wyler, William, 86
Wylie, Philip, 225
Wynn, Keenan, 250

Yalta Conference, 181, 268
Year of the Tiger, 300
Yosarian, Chester, 168, 171
The Young Lions, 106n32
Young Mr. Lincoln, 33, 297
Young, Stephen, 73, 77n102
You've Got Mail, 299

Z, 135
Zack, Anthony D., 195
Zanuck, Darryl F., 101, 287
Zedong, Mao, 89, 115, 209, 264
Zinn, Howard, 126
Zumwalt, Elmo, 1651

About the Author

Beverly Merrill Kelley is a full professor and the founder of the communication department at California Lutheran University in Thousand Oaks, California. She holds bachelor's and master's degrees from San Diego State University and a Ph.D. in communications from the University of California at Los Angeles. A former radio and television talk-show host, she writes an opinion column for the *Ventura County Star* and has been a frequent contributor to the Ventura County Perspective pages of the *Los Angeles Times*. She managed a California State Assembly campaign in 1998 and is frequently called upon to speak on politics and media.